PAKISTAN

INVESTMENT AND BUSINESS GUIDE

VOLUME 1

STRATEGIC AND PRACTICAL INFORMATION

International Business Publications, USA
Washington DC, USA- Pakistan

PAKISTAN

INVESTMENT AND BUSINESS GUIDE

VOLUME 1 STRATEGIC AND PRACTICAL INFORMATION

UPDATED ANNUALLY

We express our sincere appreciation to all government agencies and international organizations which provided information and other materials for this guide

Cover Design: **International Business Publications, USA**

2014 Edition Updated Reprint International Business Publications, USA
ISBN 1-57751-874-8

For customer service and information, please contact:

in the USA: **International Business Publications, USA**
P.O.Box 15343, Washington, DC 20043
Phone: (202) 546-2103, Fax: (202) 546-3275.
E-mail: rusric@erols.com

Printed in the USA

PAKISTAN

INVESTMENT AND BUSINESS GUIDE

VOLUME 1 STRATEGIC AND PRACTICAL INFORMATION

TABLE OF CONTENTS

STRATEGIC AND DEVELOPMENT PROFILE **8**
BASIC FACTS 8
Geography *10*
People *12*
Government *12*
Economy *16*
Energy *21*
Communications *23*
Transportation *23*
Military *25*
Transnational Issues *25*
IMPORTANT INFORMATION FOR UNDERSTANDING PAKISTAN **27**
PROFILE 27
PEOPLE 28
GOVERNMENT 28
POLITICAL SYSTEM AND GOVERNMENT 28
FATHER OF THE NATION *28*
EXECUTIVE GOVERNMENT STRUCTURE *29*
Cabinet departments *30*
Military *31*
Air Force *31*
Army *32*
NATIONAL SECURITY 34
ECONOMY 34
Agriculture and Natural Resources *36*
Industry *37*
Foreign Trade and Aid *37*
FOREIGN RELATIONS 38
India *38*
Afghanistan *39*
Russian Federation *39*
People's Republic of China *39*
Iran and the Persian Gulf *40*
U.S.-PAKISTAN RELATIONS 40
Principal U.S. Embassy Officials *41*
TRAVEL AND BUSINESS INFORMATION 41
STRATEGIC INFORMATION FOR CONDUCTING BUSINESS **43**
POLITICAL ENVIRONMENT 43
Nature of Political Relationship with the United States *43*
Major Political Issues Affecting Business Climate *43*

Political System ... *44*
INTERNATIONAL ASSISTANCE TO PAKISTAN ... 46
TECHNOLOGY POLICY ... 47
PETROLEUM POLICY OF PAKISTAN ... 48
POWER POLICY ... 49
CORPORATE AGRICULTURE FARMING (CAF) ... 50
POLICY PACKAGE FOR DEVELOPING UP COUNTRY GRAINS STORAGE FACILITIES ... 54
TEXTILE VISION ... 55
NATURAL RESOURCE ASPECTS OF SUSTAINABLE DEVELOPMENT IN PAKISTAN ... 57
AGRICULTURE ... *57*
ATMOSPHERE ... *58*
BIODIVERSITY ... *59*
DESERTIFICATION AND DROUGHT ... *61*
FORESTS ... *62*
FRESHWATER ... *62*
LAND MANAGEMENT ... *63*
MOUNTAINS ... *63*
OCEANS AND COASTAL AREAS ... *64*
TOXIC CHEMICALS ... *64*
WASTE AND HAZARDOUS MATERIALS ... *65*
GOVERNMENT REGULATION OF ECONOMIC DEVELOPMENT & ENVIRONMENT ... 66
INTEGRATED DECISION-MAKING ... *66*
MAJOR GROUPS ... *67*
INTERNATIONAL COOPERATION AND TRADE ... 68
CHANGING CONSUMPTION PATTERNS ... 69
FINANCING ... 70
TECHNOLOGY ... 71
ECONOMIC DEVELOPMENT TRENDS ... 72
Major Trends and Outlook ... *73*
Growth Sectors ... *74*
Energy ... *81*
Environment ... *85*
GOVERNMENT ROLE IN THE ECONOMY ... 86
Monetary policy ... *86*
Fiscal Policy ... *86*
PRIVATIZATION ... 87
Balance of Payment Situation ... *87*
INDUSTRIAL POLICY ... 91
INVESTMENT POLICY ... *91*
Agriculture Sector ... *91*
Services Sectors ... *92*
Infrastructure Sector/ Hotels & Tourism ... *92*
PROTECTION MEASURES ... *93*
ASSITANCE TO FOREING INVESTORS ... *94*
Incentives ... *95*
EXISTING VISA POLICY ... *98*
FURTHER CONCESSIONS IN THE NEW POLICY ... *99*
EXPORT INCENTIVES ... *100*
INCENTIVES IN INDUSTRIAL ZONES ... *101*
INCENTIVES IN PRIORITY AREAS ... *102*

PRACTICAL INFORMATION FOR CONDUCTING BUSINESS ... 104

PAKISTAN'S BUSINESS STRENGTHS ... 104
FORMS OF BUSINESS ... 105

Required Documents ... 107
FOREIGN COMPANIES ... 107
LIAISON / BRANCH OFFICES ... 108
INVESTMENT OPPORTUNITIES ... 108
PERFORMANCE OF SELECTED INDUSTRIES ... 111
INDUSTRIAL ZONES ... 111
Industrial Zone Punjab ... 111
Industrial Zones Sindh ... 119
Industrial Zones NWFP ... 126
DOING BUSINESS IN PAKISTAN ... 130
Market Overview ... 130
Market Challenges ... 131
Market Opportunities ... 131
Market Entry Strategy ... 131
SELLING PRODUCTS AND SERVICES ... 132
Using an Agent or Distributor ... 132
Establishing an Office ... 132
Franchising ... 134
Direct Marketing ... 134
Joint Ventures/Licensing ... 135
Selling to the Government ... 135
DISTRIBUTION AND SALES CHANNELS ... 136
Selling Factors/Techniques ... 137
Electronic Commerce ... 137
Trade Promotion and Advertising ... 138
Pricing ... 139
Sales Service/Customer Support ... 140
Protecting Your Intellectual Property ... 140
Due Diligence ... 142
Local Professional Services ... 142
Web Resources ... 143
LEADING SECTORS FOR U.S. EXPORT AND INVESTMENT ... 143
Oil & Gas Field Equipment and Services ... 143
Telecommunication Equipment & Services ... 144
Sub-Sector Best Prospects ... 146
Electrical Power Systems ... 147
Renewable Energy ... 149
Construction Equipment & Services ... 151
BEST PROSPECTS/SERVICES ... 152
Computers & Peripherals ... 153
Best Prospects ... 154
Opportunities ... 155
Agricultural Machinery and Implants ... 155
Sub-Sector Best Prospects ... 155
Aviation - Airport and Ground Support Equipment ... 156
Sub-Sector Best Prospects ... 157
Franchising ... 158
Sub-Sector Best Prospects ... 158
Movie Theaters/Entertainment Complexes ... 158
AGRICULTURAL SECTORS OPPORTUNITIES ... 159
Agriculture in the Economy ... 159
Domestic Agricultural Policy ... 160
Agricultural Trade Environment ... 160
Agricultural Trade with the United States ... 161

Duties on Agricultural Products ... 162
Leading Sectors for U.S. Exports ... 162
TRADE REGULATIONS, CUSTOMS AND STANDARDS ... 164
Import Tariffs ... 164
Trade Barriers ... 164
Import Requirements and Documentation ... 164
U.S. Export Controls ... 164
Temporary Entry ... 165
Labeling and Marking Requirements ... 165
Prohibited and Restricted Imports ... 165
Customs Regulations and Contact Information ... 165
TRADE AND CUSTOMS STANDARDS ... 166
Standards Organizations ... 166
Conformity Assessment ... 166
Product Certification ... 167
Accreditation ... 167
Publication of Technical Regulations ... 167
Labeling and Marking ... 167
Contacts ... 167
TRADE AGREEMENTS ... 168
Web Resources ... 168
INVESTMENT AND BUSINE CLIMATE ... 169
1. Openness To, and Restrictions Upon, Foreign Investment ... 169
2. Conversion and Transfer Policies ... 173
3. Expropriation and Compensation ... 174
4. Dispute Settlement ... 174
5. Performance Requirements and Investment Incentives ... 175
6. Right to Private Ownership and Establishment ... 177
7. Protection of Property Rights ... 177
8. Transparency of the Regulatory System ... 181
9. Efficient Capital Markets and Portfolio Investment ... 181
10. Competition from State-Owned Enterprises ... 183
11. Corporate Social Responsibility ... 186
12. Political Violence ... 187
13. Corruption ... 187
14. Bilateral Investment Agreements ... 189
16. Labor ... 189
17. Foreign Trade Zones/Free Ports/Trade Facilitation ... 190
18. Foreign Direct Investment and Foreign Portfolio Investment Statistics ... 190
IMPORTANT CONTACTS ... 192
Attorneys ... 192
TRADE AND PROJECT FINANCING ... 194
Methods of Payment ... 194
Banking System ... 194
Foreign-Exchange Controls ... 194
U.S. Banks and Local Correspondent Banks ... 195
Project Financing ... 195
Web Resources ... 195
BUSINESS TRAVEL ... 196
Business Customs ... 196
Travel Advisory ... 196
Visa Requirements ... 196
Telecommunications ... 197
Transportation ... 197

Language ... *198*
Health ... *198*
Local Time, Business Hours, and Holidays ... *199*
TEMPORARY ENTRY OF MATERIALS AND PERSONAL BELONGINGS ... 200
Web Resources ... *200*
IMPORTANT GOVERNMENT AND BUSINESS CONTACTS ... 200
U.S. Government Trade Related Contacts in Pakistan ... *200*
Pakistan Mission in the United States ... *202*
SETTING UP A BUSINESS IN PAKISTAN ... 208
Incorporation of Companies ... *208*
COMPANY ... *209*
Industrial Sub-contracting ... *210*
FREE EXPORT ZONES ... 211
PROFILE OF EXPORT PROCESSING ZONES AUTHORITY ... *211*
CHARTER OF EXPORT PROCESSING ZONES AUTHORITY: ... *211*
MANAGEMENT: ... *211*
Incentives ... *213*

TRAVELING TO THE COUNTRY ... 226

US STATE DEPARTMENT SUGGESTIONS ... 226
GETTING THERE ... 230
GETTING AROUND ... 231
ACCOMMODATION ... 232
Hotels ... *232*
MONEY ... 233
Currency ... *233*
Costs ... *233*
Credit cards ... *233*
Travelers checks ... *233*
Exchange rate indicators ... *233*
Currency restrictions ... *234*
Baksheesh ... *234*

SUPPLEMENT ... 235

OVERSEAS PAKISTANIS ASSOCIATIONS ... 235
Pakistani Associations in USA ... *236*
FACILITIES FOR OVERSEAS PAKISTANIS ... 241
LIST OF POTENTIAL OVERSEAS PAKISTANIS IN U.S.A ... 243
IMPORTANT BUSINESS INFORMATION SOURCES ... 250
STRATEGIC GOVERNMENT AND BUSINESS CONTACTS ... 253
U.S. Embassy Trade Related Contacts ... *253*
Bilateral Business Councils ... *254*
Trade & Industry Associations ... *254*
Contacts in Pakistan ... *254*
Government of Pakistan Offices ... *255*
Commercial Banks ... *258*
PREFERENTIAL TRADE AGREEMENT ... 259
Consolidated National Schedule of Concessions ... *260*
TOP 300 COMPANIES IN PAKISTAN BY ALPHABETICAL ORDER ... 270
THE TOP 300 COMAPNIES (By Income) ... *279*
BASIC TITLE ON PAKISTAN ... 288

STRATEGIC AND DEVELOPMENT PROFILE

BASIC FACTS

Capital	Islamabad 33°40′N 73°10′E33.667°N 73.167°E
Largest city	Karachi
Official languages	• English • Urdu
Regional languages	Punjabi, Pashto, Sindhi, Saraiki, Balochi, Kashmiri, Brahui, Dogri, Hindko, Shina, Balti, Khowar, Burushaski Yidgha, Dameli, Kalasha, Gawar-Bati, Domaaki[4][5]
Demonym	Pakistani
Government	Federal parliamentary republic
- President	Mamnoon Hussain (PML-N)
- Prime Minister	Mian Nawaz Sharif (PML-N)
- Chief Justice	Nasir-ul-Mulk
- Chairman Senate	Nayyar Hussain Bukhari (PPP)
- Speaker National Assembly	Ayaz Sadiq (PML-N)
Legislature	Majlis-e-Shoora
- Upper house	Senate
- Lower house	National Assembly
	Formation
- Conception of Pakistan[6]	29 December 1930
- Pakistan Declaration	28 January 1933
- Pakistan Resolution	23 March 1940
- Independence and Dominion	14 August 1947
- Islamic Republic	23 March 1956
- Breakup of East and West Pakistan	16 December 1971
- Current constitution	14 August 1973
	Area
- Total	796,095 km^2 (36th) 307,374 sq mi
- Water (%)	3.1
	Population
- 2014 estimate	196,174,380 (6th)
- Density	234.4/km^2 (55th) 607.4/sq mi
GDP (PPP)	2014 estimate
- Total	$855 billion (25th)
- Per capita	$3,144 (139th)
GDP (nominal)	2014 estimate
- Total	$236.518 billion (45th)
- Per capita	$1,295 (147th)
Gini (2008)	30.0 medium
HDI (2014)	0.537

	medium · 146th
Currency	Pakistani rupee (PKR)
Time zone	PKT (UTC+5)
- Summer (DST)	(UTC+6)
Drives on the	left
Calling code	+92
ISO 3166 code	PK
Internet TLD	.pk

Republic of Pakistan is a sovereign country in South Asia. With a population exceeding 180 million people, it is the sixth most populous country and with an area covering 796,095 km^2 (307,374 sq mi), it is the 36th largest country in the world in terms of area. Pakistan has a 1,046-kilometre (650 mi) coastline along the Arabian Sea and the Gulf of Oman in the south and is bordered by India to the east, Afghanistan to the west, Iran to the southwest and China in the far northeast. It is separated from Tajikistan by Afghanistan's narrow Wakhan Corridor in the north, and also shares a marine border with Oman.

The territory that now constitutes Pakistan was previously home to several ancient cultures, including the Mehrgarh of the Neolithic and the Bronze Age Indus Valley Civilisation, and was later home to kingdoms ruled by people of different faiths and cultures, including Hindus, Indo-Greeks, Muslims, Turco-Mongols, Afghans and Sikhs. The area has been ruled by numerous empires and dynasties, including the Indian Mauryan Empire, the Persian Achaemenid Empire, Alexander of Macedonia, the Arab Umayyad Caliphate, the Mongol Empire, the Mughal Empire, the Durrani Empire, the Sikh Empire and the British Empire. As a result of the Pakistan Movement led by Muhammad Ali Jinnah and the subcontinent's struggle for independence, Pakistan was created in 1947 as an independent nation for Muslims from the regions in the east and west of Subcontinent where there was a Muslim majority. Initially a dominion, Pakistan adopted a new constitution in 1956, becoming an Islamic republic. A civil war in 1971 resulted in the secession of East Pakistan as the new country of Bangladesh.

Pakistan is a federal parliamentary republic consisting of four provinces and four federal territories. It is an ethnically and linguistically diverse country, with a similar variation in its geography and wildlife. A regional and middle power,[14][15] Pakistan has the seventh largest standing armed forces in the world and is also a nuclear power as well as a declared nuclear-weapons state, being the only nation in the Muslim world, and the second in South Asia, to have that status. It has a semi-industrialised economy with a well-integrated agriculture sector, its economy is the 26th largest in the world in terms of purchasing power and 45th largest in terms of nominal GDP and is also characterized among the emerging and growth-leading economies of the world.

The post-independence history of Pakistan has been characterised by periods of military rule, political instability and conflicts with neighbouring India. The country continues to face challenging problems, including overpopulation, terrorism, poverty, illiteracy, corruption and it ranks among the countries with the most income equality.[16] It ranked 16th on the 2012 Happy Planet Index.[17] It is a member of the United Nations, the Commonwealth of Nations, the Next Eleven Economies, SAARC, ECO, UfC, D8, Cairns Group, Kyoto Protocol, ICCPR, RCD, UNCHR, Group of Eleven, CPFTA, Group of 24, the G20 developing nations, ECOSOC, founding member of the Organization of the Islamic Conference (now the Organisation of Islamic Cooperation), and CERN

GEOGRAPHY

The separation in 1947 of British India into the Muslim state of Pakistan (with two sections West and East) and largely Hindu India was never satisfactorily resolved. A third war between these countries in 1971 resulted in East Pakistan seceding and becoming the separate nation of Bangladesh. A dispute over the state of Kashmir is ongoing. In response to Indian nuclear weapons testing, Pakistan conducted its own tests in 1998.

Location: Southern Asia, bordering the Arabian Sea, between India on the east and Iran and Afghanistan on the west and China in the north
Geographic coordinates: 30 00 N, 70 00 E
Map references: Asia
Area:
total: 803,940 sq km
land: 778,720 sq km
water: 25,220 sq km
Area - comparative: slightly less than twice the size of California
Land boundaries:
total: 6,774 km
border countries: Afghanistan 2,430 km, China 523 km, India 2,912 km, Iran 909 km
Coastline: 1,046 km

Maritime claims:
contiguous zone: 24 nm
continental shelf: 200 nm or to the edge of the continental margin
exclusive economic zone: 200 nm
territorial sea: 12 nm

Climate: mostly hot, dry desert; temperate in northwest; arctic in north
Terrain: flat Indus plain in east; mountains in north and northwest; Balochistan plateau in west

Elevation extremes:
lowest point: Indian Ocean 0 m *highest point:* K2 (Mt. Godwin-Austen) 8,611 m

Natural resources: land, extensive natural gas reserves, limited petroleum, poor quality coal, iron ore, copper, salt, limestone

Land use:
arable land: 27% *permanent crops:* 1% *permanent pastures:* 6% *forests and woodland:* 5% *other:* 61%
Irrigated land: 171,100 sq km
Natural hazards: frequent earthquakes, occasionally severe especially in north and west; flooding along the Indus after heavy rains (July and August)
Environment - current issues: water pollution from raw sewage, industrial wastes, and agricultural runoff; limited natural fresh water resources; a majority of the population does not have access to potable water; deforestation; soil erosion; desertification

Environment - international agreements:
party to: Biodiversity, Climate Change, Desertification, Endangered Species, Environmental Modification, Hazardous Wastes, Law of the Sea, Marine Dumping, Nuclear Test Ban, Ozone Layer Protection, Ship Pollution, Wetlands
signed, but not ratified: Marine Life Conservation

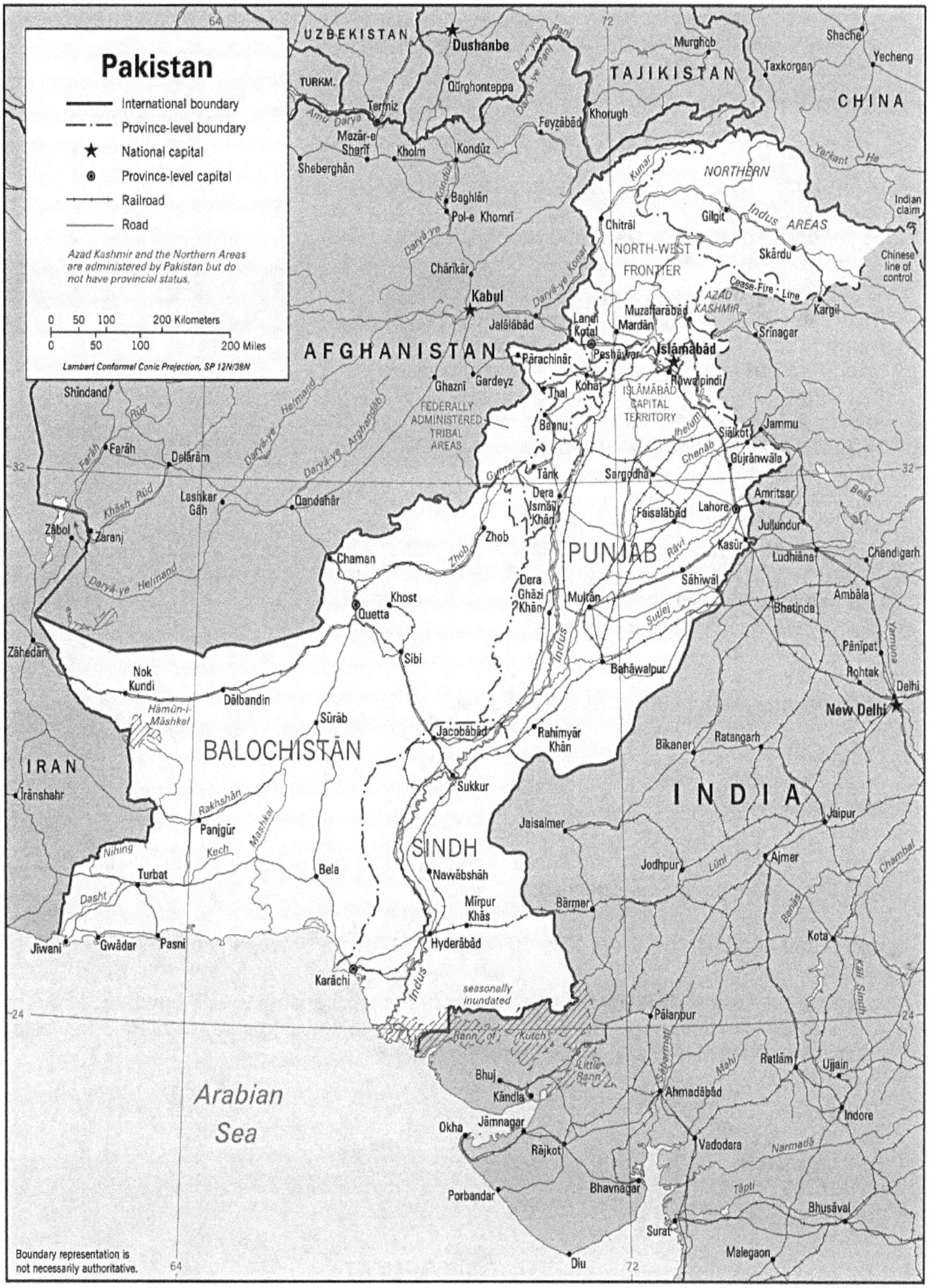

Base 802458 (R02122) 6-96

Geography - note: controls Khyber Pass and Bolan Pass, traditional invasion routes between Central Asia and the Indian Subcontinent

PEOPLE

Population: 141,553,775

Age structure:
0-14 years: 41% (male 29,880,574; female 28,145,247)
15-64 years: 55% (male 39,751,222; female 37,981,378)
65 years and over: 4% (male 2,856,305; female 2,939,049)

Population growth rate: 2.17%
Birth rate: 32.11 births/1,000 population
Death rate: 9.51 deaths/1,000 population
Net migration rate: -0.9 migrant(s)/1,000 population
Sex ratio:
at birth: 1.05 male(s)/female
under 15 years: 1.06 male(s)/female
15-64 years: 1.05 male(s)/female
65 years and over: 0.97 male(s)/female
total population: 1.05 male(s)/female
Infant mortality rate: 82.49 deaths/1,000 live births

Life expectancy at birth:
total population: 61.07 years
male: 60.27 years
female: 61.91 years
Total fertility rate: 4.56 children born/woman

Nationality:
noun: Pakistani(s)
adjective: Pakistani

Ethnic groups: Punjabi, Sindhi, Pashtun (Pathan), Baloch, Muhajir (immigrants from India at the time of partition and their descendants)

Religions: Muslim 97% (Sunni 77%, Shi'a 20%), Christian, Hindu, and other 3%

Languages: Punjabi 48%, Sindhi 12%, Siraiki (a Punjabi variant) 10%, Pashtu 8%, Urdu (official) 8%, Balochi 3%, Hindko 2%, Brahui 1%, English (official and lingua franca of Pakistani elite and most government ministries), Burushaski, and other 8%

Literacy:
definition: age 15 and over can read and write
total population: 37.8%
male: 50%
female: 24.4% (1995 est.)

GOVERNMENT

Country name:

conventional long form:
Islamic Republic of Pakistan
conventional short form:
Pakistan
local long form:
Jamhuryat Islami Pakistan
local short form:
Pakistan
former:
West Pakistan

Government type:
federal republic

Capital:
name:
Islamabad
geographic coordinates:
33 41 N, 73 03 E
time difference:
UTC+5 (10 hours ahead of Washington, DC, during Standard Time)

Administrative divisions:
4 provinces, 1 territory*, and 1 capital territory**; Balochistan, Federally Administered Tribal Areas*, Islamabad Capital Territory**, Khyber Pakhtunkhwa (formerly North-West Frontier Province), Punjab, Sindh
note:the Pakistani-administered portion of the disputed Jammu and Kashmir region consists of two administrative entities: Azad Kashmir and Gilgit-Baltistan

Independence:
14 August 1947 (from British India)

National holiday:
Pakistan Day (also referred to as Pakistan Resolution Day or Republic Day), 23 March (1940); note - commemorates both the adoption of the Lahore Resolution by the All-India Muslim League during its 22-24 March 1940 session, which called for the creation of independent Muslim states, and the adoption of the first constitution of Pakistan on 23 March 1956 during the transition to the Islamic Republic of Pakistan

Constitution:
several previous; latest endorsed 12 April 1973, passed 19 April 1973, entered into force 14 August 1973 (suspended and restored several times); amended many times, last in 2012 (2012)

Legal system:
common law system with Islamic law influence

International law organization participation:
accepts compulsory ICJ jurisdiction with reservations; non-party state to the ICCt

Suffrage:
18 years of age; universal; note - there are joint electorates and reserved parliamentary seats for women and non-Muslims

Executive branch:
chief of state:
President Mamnoon HUSSAIN (since 9 September 2014)
head of government:
Prime Minister Mohammad Nawaz SHARIF (since 5 June 2014)
cabinet:
Cabinet appointed by the president upon the advice of the prime minister
(For more information visit the World Leaders website **)**
elections:
president elected by secret ballot through an Electoral College comprising the members of the Senate, National Assembly, and provincial assemblies for a five-year term; election last held on 9 September 2014 (next to be held in 2018); prime minister selected by the National Assembly
election results:
Mamnoon HUSSAIN elected president; Mamnoon HUSSAIN 432 votes, Wajihuddin AHMED 77 votes

Legislative branch:
bicameral parliament or Majlis-e-Shoora consists of the Senate (104 seats; members indirectly elected by provincial assemblies and the territories' representatives in the National Assembly to serve six-year terms; one half are elected every three years) and the National Assembly (342 seats; 272 members elected by popular vote; 60 seats reserved for women; 10 seats reserved for non-Muslims; members serve five-year terms)
elections:
Senate - last held on 2 March 2012 (next to be held in March 2015); National Assembly - last held on 11 May 2014 (next to be held in 2018)
election results:
Senate - percent of vote by party - NA; seats by party - PPPP 41, PML-N 14, ANP 12, JUI-F 7, MQM 7, PML-Q 5, BNP-A 4, NPP 1, PML-F 1, independents 12; National Assembly - percent of votes by party - NA; seats by party as of June 2014) - PML-N 126, PPPP 31, PTI 28, MQM 18, JUI-F 10, PML-F 5, other 22, independents 25, unfilled seats 7; 60 seats reserved for women, 10 seats reserved for non-Muslims

Judicial branch:
highest court(s):
Supreme Court of Pakistan (consists of the chief justice and 16 judges)
judge selection and term of office:
justices nominated by an 8-member Majlis-e-Shoora (parliamentary) Committee upon the recommendation of the Judicial Commission (a 9-member body of several judges and other judicial professionals), and appointed by the president of Pakistan; justices can serve until age 65
subordinate courts:
High Courts; Federal Shariat Court; provincial and district civil and criminal courts; specialized courts for issues such as taxation, banking, customs, etc.

Political parties and leaders:
Awami National Party or ANP [Asfandyar Wali KHAN]
Balochistan National Party-Awami or BNP-A
Balochistan National Party-Hayee Group or BNP-H [Dr. Hayee BALOCH]
Balochistan National Party-Mengal or BNP-M

Jamaat-i Islami or JI [Syed Munawar HASAN]
Jamhoori Watan Party or JWP
Jamiat Ahle Hadith or JAH [Sajid MIR]
Jamiat-i Ulema-i Islam Fazl-ur Rehman or JUI-F [Fazl-ur REHMAN]
Jamiat-i Ulema-i Islam Sami-ul HAQ or JUI-S [Sami ul-HAQ]
Jamiat-i Ulema-i Pakistan or JUP [Abul Khair ZUBAIR]
Millat-e-Jafferia [Allama Sajid NAQVI]
Muttahida Qaumi Movement or MQM [Altaf HUSSAIN]
National Peoples Party or NPP
Pakhtun-khwa Milli Awami Party or PKMAP [Mahmood Khan ACHAKZAI]
Pakistan Awami Tehrik or PAT [Tahir ul QADRI]
Pakistan Muslim League-Quaid-i Azam or PML-Q [Chaudhry Shujaat HUSSAIN]
Pakistan Muslim League-Functional or PML-F [Pir PAGARO]
Pakistan Muslim League-Nawaz or PML-N [Nawaz SHARIF]
Pakistan Peoples Party Parliamentarians or PPPP [Bilawal Bhutto ZARDARI, chairman; Asif Ali ZARDARI, co-chairman]
Pakistan Peoples Party-S [Aftab Ahmad SHERPAO]
Quami Watan Party or QWP [Aftab Ahmed Khan SHERPAO]
Pakistan Tehrik-e Insaaf or PTI [Imran KHAN]
note:political alliances in Pakistan can shift frequently

Political pressure groups and leaders:
other:
military (most important political force); ulema (clergy); landowners; industrialists; small merchants

International organization participation:
ADB, ARF, ASEAN (dialogue partner), C, CICA, CP, D-8, ECO, FAO, G-11, G-24, G-77, IAEA, IBRD, ICAO, ICC (national committees), ICRM, IDA, IDB, IFAD, IFC, IFRCS, IHO, ILO, IMF, IMO, IMSO, Interpol, IOC, IOM, IPU, ISO, ITSO, ITU, ITUC (NGOs), LAIA (observer), MIGA, MINURSO, MONUSCO, NAM, OAS (observer), OIC, OPCW, PCA, SAARC, SACEP, SCO (observer), UN, UNAMID, UNCTAD, UNESCO, UNHCR, UNIDO, UNISFA, UNMIL, UNMIT, UNOCI, UNWTO, UPU, WCO, WFTU (NGOs), WHO, WIPO, WMO, WTO

Diplomatic representation in the US:
chief of mission:
Ambassador Jalil Abbas JILANI (since 10 March 2014)
chancery:
3517 International Court, Washington, DC 20008
telephone:
[1] (202) 243-6500
FAX:
[1] (202) 686-1534
consulate(s) general:
Chicago, Houston, Los Angeles, New York, Sunnyvale (CA)
consulate(s):
Chicago, Houston

Diplomatic representation from the US:
chief of mission:
Ambassador Richard OLSON (since 24 September 2012)

embassy:
Diplomatic Enclave, Ramna 5, Islamabad
mailing address:
8100 Islamabad Pl., Washington, DC 20521-8100
telephone:
[92] (51) 208-0000
FAX:
[92] (51) 227-6427
consulate(s) general:
Karachi
consulate(s):
Lahore, Peshawar

Flag description:
green with a vertical white band (symbolizing the role of religious minorities) on the hoist side; a large white crescent and star are centered in the green field; the crescent, star, and color green are traditional symbols of Islam

National symbol(s):
star and crescent

National anthem:
name:
"Qaumi Tarana" (National Anthem)

ECONOMY

Economy - overview:
Decades of internal political disputes and low levels of foreign investment have led to slow growth and underdevelopment in Pakistan. Agriculture accounts for more than one-fifth of output and two-fifths of employment. Textiles account for most of Pakistan's export earnings, and Pakistan's failure to expand a viable export base for other manufactures has left the country vulnerable to shifts in world demand. Official unemployment was 6.6% in 2014, but this fails to capture the true picture, because much of the economy is informal and underemployment remains high. Over the past few years, low growth and high inflation, led by a spurt in food prices, have increased the amount of poverty. As a result of political and economic instability, the Pakistani rupee has depreciated more than 40% since 2007. The government agreed to an International Monetary Fund Standby Arrangement in November 2008 in response to a balance of payments crisis. Although the economy has stabilized since the crisis, it has failed to recover. Foreign investment has not returned, due to investor concerns related to governance, energy, security, and a slow-down in the global economy. Remittances from overseas workers, averaging about $1 billion a month since March 2011, remain a bright spot for Pakistan. However, after a small current account surplus in fiscal year 2011 (July 2010/June 2011), Pakistan's current account turned to deficit in the following two years, spurred by higher prices for imported oil and lower prices for exported cotton. Pakistan remains stuck in a low-income, low-growth trap, with growth averaging about 3.5% per year from 2008 to 2014. Pakistan must address long standing issues related to government revenues and energy production in order to spur the amount of economic growth that will be necessary to employ its growing and rapidly urbanizing population, more than half of which is under 22. Other long term challenges include expanding investment in education and healthcare, adapting to the effects of climate change and natural disasters, and reducing dependence on foreign donors.

GDP (purchasing power parity):
$574.1 billion (2014 est.)
country comparison to the world: 27
$554.2 billion (2012 est.)
$531 billion (2011 est.)
note:data are in 2014 US dollars

GDP (official exchange rate):
$236.5 billion (2014 est.)

GDP - real growth rate:
3.6% (2014 est.)
country comparison to the world: 88
4.4% (2012 est.)
3.7% (2011 est.)

GDP - per capita (PPP):
$3,100 (2014 est.)
country comparison to the world: 177
$3,100 (2012 est.)
$3,000 (2011 est.)
note:data are in 2014 US dollars

Gross national saving:
12.7% of GDP (2014 est.)
country comparison to the world: 120
13.3% of GDP (2012 est.)
12.9% of GDP (2011 est.)

GDP - composition, by end use:
household consumption:
81%
government consumption:
10.8%
investment in fixed capital:
12.6%
investment in inventories:
1.6%
exports of goods and services:
12.7%
imports of goods and services:
-18.8%
(2014 est.)

GDP - composition, by sector of origin:
agriculture:
25.3%
industry:
21.6%
services:

53.1% (2014 est.)

Agriculture - products:
cotton, wheat, rice, sugarcane, fruits, vegetables; milk, beef, mutton, eggs

Industries:
textiles and apparel, food processing, pharmaceuticals, construction materials, paper products, fertilizer, shrimp

Industrial production growth rate:
3.5% (2014 est.)
country comparison to the world: 86

Labor force:
59.21 million
country comparison to the world: 10
note:extensive export of labor, mostly to the Middle East, and use of child labor (2012 est.)

Labor force - by occupation:
agriculture:
45.1%
industry:
20.7%
services:
34.2% (2010 est.)

Unemployment rate:
6.6% (2014 est.)
country comparison to the world: 68
6% (2012 est.)
note:substantial underemployment exists

Population below poverty line:
22.3% (FY05/06 est.)

Household income or consumption by percentage share:
lowest 10%:
3.9%
highest 10%:
39.3% (FY05/06)

Distribution of family income - Gini index:
30.6 (FY07/08)
country comparison to the world: 119
41 (FY98/99)

Budget:
revenues:
$29.71 billion
expenditures:

$47.97 billion (2014 est.)

Taxes and other revenues:
12.6% of GDP (2014 est.)
country comparison to the world: 202

Budget surplus (+) or deficit (-):
-7.7% of GDP (2014 est.)
country comparison to the world: 191

Public debt:
54.6% of GDP (2014 est.)
country comparison to the world: 57
52.1% of GDP (2012 est.)

Fiscal year:
1 July - 30 June

Inflation rate (consumer prices):
7.7% (2014 est.)
country comparison to the world: 194
9.7% (2012 est.)

Central bank discount rate:
12% (31 January 2012 est.)
country comparison to the world: 13
14% (31 December 2010 est.)

Commercial bank prime lending rate:
11.5% (31 December 2014 est.)
country comparison to the world: 60
12.41% (31 December 2012 est.)

Stock of narrow money:
$71.96 billion (31 December 2014 est.)
country comparison to the world: 42
$62.29 billion (31 December 2012 est.)

Stock of broad money:
$93.11 billion (31 December 2014 est.)
country comparison to the world: 55
$82.63 billion (31 December 2012 est.)

Stock of domestic credit:
$106.8 billion (31 December 2014 est.)
country comparison to the world: 50
$94.65 billion (31 December 2012 est.)

Market value of publicly traded shares:
$NA (31 December 2012 est.)

$NA (31 December 2011)
$38.17 billion (31 December 2010 est.)

Current account balance:
-$2.36 billion (2014 est.)
country comparison to the world: 147
-$2.072 billion (2012 est.)

Exports:
$25.05 billion (2014 est.)
country comparison to the world: 70
$24.71 billion (2012 est.)

Exports - commodities:
textiles (garments, bed linen, cotton cloth, yarn), rice, leather goods, sports goods, chemicals, manufactures, carpets and rugs

Exports - partners:
US 13.6%, China 11.1%, UAE 8.5%, Afghanistan 7.8% (2012)

Imports:
$39.27 billion (2014 est.)
country comparison to the world: 61
$40.07 billion (2012 est.)

Imports - commodities:
petroleum, petroleum products, machinery, plastics, transportation equipment, edible oils, paper and paperboard, iron and steel, tea

Imports - partners:
China 19.7%, Saudi Arabia 12.3%, UAE 12.1%, Kuwait 6.3% (2012)

Reserves of foreign exchange and gold:
$11.18 billion (31 December 2014 est.)
country comparison to the world: 73
$13.8 billion (31 December 2012 est.)

Debt - external:
$52.43 billion (31 December 2014 est.)
country comparison to the world: 61
$54.5 billion (31 December 2012 est.)

Stock of direct foreign investment - at home:
$24.33 billion (31 December 2014 est.)
country comparison to the world: 68
$22.73 billion (31 December 2012 est.)

Stock of direct foreign investment - abroad:
$1.569 billion (31 December 2014 est.)
country comparison to the world: 74

$1.519 billion (31 December 2012 est.)

Exchange rates:
Pakistani rupees (PKR) per US dollar -
100.4 (2014 est.)
93.3952 (2012 est.)
85.194 (2010 est.)
81.71 (2009)
70.64 (2008)

ENERGY

Electricity - production:
94.65 billion kWh (2011 est.)
country comparison to the world: 35

Electricity - consumption:
70.1 billion kWh (2011 est.)
country comparison to the world: 39

Electricity - exports:
0 kWh (2012 est.)
country comparison to the world: 182

Electricity - imports:
0 kWh (2012 est.)
country comparison to the world: 186

Electricity - installed generating capacity:
22.27 million kW (2010 est.)
country comparison to the world: 35

Electricity - from fossil fuels:
68.3% of total installed capacity (2010 est.)
country comparison to the world: 111

Electricity - from nuclear fuels:
2.1% of total installed capacity (2010 est.)
country comparison to the world: 27

Electricity - from hydroelectric plants:
29.6% of total installed capacity (2010 est.)
country comparison to the world: 80

Electricity - from other renewable sources:
0% of total installed capacity (2010 est.)
country comparison to the world: 112

Crude oil - production:
61,660 bbl/day (2012 est.)
country comparison to the world: 58

Crude oil - exports:
0 bbl/day (2010 est.)
country comparison to the world: 167

Crude oil - imports:
151,200 bbl/day (2010 est.)
country comparison to the world: 41

Crude oil - proved reserves:
247.5 million bbl (1 January 2014 est.)
country comparison to the world: 57

Refined petroleum products - production:
210,100 bbl/day (2010 est.)
country comparison to the world: 52

Refined petroleum products - consumption:
426,700 bbl/day (2011 est.)
country comparison to the world: 34

Refined petroleum products - exports:
34,660 bbl/day (2010 est.)
country comparison to the world: 67

Refined petroleum products - imports:
227,100 bbl/day (2010 est.)
country comparison to the world: 25

Natural gas - production:
39.15 billion cu m (2011 est.)
country comparison to the world: 23

Natural gas - consumption:
42.9 billion cu m (2011 est.)
country comparison to the world: 23

Natural gas - exports:
0 cu m (2011 est.)
country comparison to the world: 164

Natural gas - imports:
0 cu m (2011 est.)
country comparison to the world: 115

Natural gas - proved reserves:
679.6 billion cu m (1 January 2014 est.)
country comparison to the world: 31

Carbon dioxide emissions from consumption of energy:
139.7 million Mt (2011 est.)

COMMUNICATIONS

Telephones - main lines in use:
5.803 million (2012)
country comparison to the world: 29

Telephones - mobile cellular:
125 million (2014)
country comparison to the world: 9

Telephone system:
general assessment: the telecommunications infrastructure is improving dramatically with foreign and domestic investments in fixed-line and mobile-cellular networks; system consists of microwave radio relay, coaxial cable, fiber-optic cable, cellular, and satellite networks;
domestic: mobile-cellular subscribership has skyrocketed, exceeding 110 million by the end of 2011, up from only about 300,000 in 2000; more than 90 percent of Pakistanis live within areas that have cell phone coverage and more than half of all Pakistanis have access to a cell phone; fiber systems are being constructed throughout the country to aid in network growth; fixed line availability has risen only marginally over the same period and there are still difficulties getting fixed-line service to rural areas
international: country code - 92; landing point for the SEA-ME-WE-3 and SEA-ME-WE-4 submarine cable systems that provide links to Asia, the Middle East, and Europe; satellite earth stations - 3 Intelsat (1 Atlantic Ocean and 2 Indian Ocean); 3 operational international gateway exchanges (1 at Karachi and 2 at Islamabad); microwave radio relay to neighboring countries (2011)

Broadcast media:
media is government regulated; 1 dominant state-owned TV broadcaster, Pakistan Television Corporation (PTV), operates a network consisting of 5 channels; private TV broadcasters are permitted; to date 69 foreign satellite channels are operational; the state-owned radio network operates more than 40 stations; nearly 100 commercially licensed privately owned radio stations provide programming mostly limited to music and talk shows (2007)

Internet country code:
.pk

Internet hosts:
365,813 (2012)
country comparison to the world: 57

Internet users:
20.431 million (2009)
country comparison to the world: 20

TRANSPORTATION

Airports:

151 (2014)
country comparison to the world: 37

Airports - with paved runways:
total:
108
over 3,047 m:
15
2,438 to 3,047 m:
20
1,524 to 2,437 m:
43
914 to 1,523 m:
20
under 914 m:
10 (2014)

Airports - with unpaved runways:
total:
43
2,438 to 3,047 m:
1
1,524 to 2,437 m:
9
914 to 1,523 m:
9
under 914 m:
24 (2014)

Heliports:
23 (2014)

Pipelines:
gas 12,646 km; oil 2,576 km; refined products 1,087 km (2014)

Railways:
total:
7,791 km
country comparison to the world: 27
broad gauge:
7,479 km 1.676-m gauge (293 km electrified)
narrow gauge:
312 km 1.000-m gauge (2007)

Roadways:
total:
262,256 km
country comparison to the world: 20
paved:
189,218 km (includes 708 km of expressways)
unpaved:
73,038 km (2010)

Merchant marine:
total:
11
country comparison to the world: 110
by type:
bulk carrier 5, cargo 3, petroleum tanker 3
registered in other countries:
11 (Comoros 5, Marshall Islands 1, Moldova 1, Panama 3, Saint Kitts and Nevis 1) (2010)

Ports and terminals:
major seaport(s):
Karachi, Port Muhammad Bin Qasim
container port(s) (TEUs):
Karachi (1,545,434)

MILITARY

Military branches:
Pakistan Army (includes National Guard), Pakistan Navy (includes Marines and Maritime Security Agency), Pakistan Air Force (Pakistan Fiza'ya) (2014)

Military service age and obligation:
16-23 years of age for voluntary military service; soldiers cannot be deployed for combat until age 18; the Pakistani Air Force and Pakistani Navy have inducted their first female pilots and sailors; the Pakistan Air Force recruits aviation technicians at age 15; service obligation (Navy) 10-18 years; retirement required after 18-30 years service or age 40-52 (2012)

Manpower available for military service:
males age 16-49: 48,453,305
females age 16-49: 44,896,096 (2010 est.)

Manpower fit for military service:
males age 16-49: 37,945,440
females age 16-49: 37,381,549 (2010 est.)

Manpower reaching militarily significant age annually:
male: 2,237,723
female: 2,104,906 (2010 est.)

Military expenditures:
3.04% of GDP (2012)
country comparison to the world: 20
3.13% of GDP (2011)
3.04% of GDP (2010)

TRANSNATIONAL ISSUES

Disputes - international:

various talks and confidence-building measures cautiously have begun to defuse tensions over Kashmir, particularly since the October 2005 earthquake in the region; Kashmir nevertheless remains the site of the world's largest and most militarized territorial dispute with portions under the de facto administration of China (Aksai Chin), India (Jammu and Kashmir), and Pakistan (Azad Kashmir and Northern Areas); UN Military Observer Group in India and Pakistan has maintained a small group of peacekeepers since 1949; India does not recognize Pakistan's ceding historic Kashmir lands to China in 1964; India and Pakistan have maintained their 2004 cease-fire in Kashmir and initiated discussions on defusing the armed standoff in the Siachen glacier region; Pakistan protests India's fencing the highly militarized Line of Control and construction of the Baglihar Dam on the Chenab River in Jammu and Kashmir, which is part of the larger dispute on water sharing of the Indus River and its tributaries; to defuse tensions and prepare for discussions on a maritime boundary, India and Pakistan seek technical resolution of the disputed boundary in Sir Creek estuary at the mouth of the Rann of Kutch in the Arabian Sea; Pakistani maps continue to show the Junagadh claim in India's Gujarat State; since 2002, with UN assistance, Pakistan has repatriated 3.8 million Afghan refugees, leaving about 2.6 million; Pakistan has sent troops across and built fences along some remote tribal areas of its treaty-defined Durand Line border with Afghanistan, which serve as bases for foreign terrorists and other illegal activities; Afghan, Coalition, and Pakistan military meet periodically to clarify the alignment of the boundary on the ground and on maps

Refugees and internally displaced persons:
refugees (country of origin): 2.6 million (1.6 million registered, 1 million undocumented) (Afghanistan) (2014)
IDPs: 930,000 (primarily those who remain displaced by counter-terrorism and counter-insurgency operations and violent conflict between armed non-state groups in the Federally Administered Tribal Areas (FATA) and Khyber-Paktunkwa Province; individuals also have been displaced by repeated monsoon floods) (2014)

Illicit drugs:
significant transit area for Afghan drugs, including heroin, opium, morphine, and hashish, bound for Iran, Western markets, the Gulf States, Africa, and Asia; financial crimes related to drug trafficking, terrorism, corruption, and smuggling remain problems; opium poppy cultivation estimated to be 2,300 hectares in 2007 with 600 of those hectares eradicated; federal and provincial authorities continue to conduct anti-poppy campaigns that utilizes forced eradication, fines, and arrests

IMPORTANT INFORMATION FOR UNDERSTANDING PAKISTAN

PROFILE

OFFICIAL NAME: Islamic Republic of Pakistan

Geography

Area: 803,943 sq. km. (310,527 sq. mi.); about twice the size of California.
Cities: *Capital*--Islamabad and adjacent Rawalpindi comprise a national capital area with a combined population of 3.7 million. *Other cities*--Karachi (10 million), Lahore (5.7 million), Faisalabad (6.5 million).

People

Nationality: *Noun and adjective*--Pakistan(i).
Population: 135 million.
Annual growth rate : 2.6%.
Ethnic groups: Punjabi, Sindhi, Pathan (Pushtun), Baloch, Muhajir (i.e., Urdu-speaking immigrants from India and their descendants), Saraiki, Hazara.
Religions: Muslim 97%; small minorities of Christians, Hindus, and others.
Languages: Urdu (national and official), English, Punjabi, Sindhi, Pushtu, Baloch.
Education: Literacy 45%. Unofficial estimates are as low as 35%.
Health: *Infant mortality rate* (1997)--85/1,000. *Life expectancy* --men 63 yrs., women 63 yrs.
Work force : *Agriculture*--44%. *Services*--30%. *Industry*--26%.

Government

Type: Military. Parliamentary democracy suspended on October 12, 1999.
Independence: August 14, 1947.
Branches: *Executive*--The Chief of Army Staff serves as Chief Executive and is advised by a mixed civilian/military National Security Council and civilian Cabinet. Provinces are headed by a Governor and provincial cabinet, who are civilians appointed by the Chief Executive. *Judicial*--Supreme Court, provincial high courts, and Federal Islamic Court. On January 26, 2004, justices were required to take an oath of loyalty to the Chief Executive and the Provisional Constitutional Order that placed the constitution in abeyance.
Political parties: The Pakistan Muslim League (PML) and the Pakistan People's Party (PPP) are national political parties. Other parties with a strong regional, ethnic or religious base include the Awami National Party (ANP), the Muttahida Qaumi Movement (MQM), and the Jamaat-i-Islami (JI).
Suffrage: Universal at 21. Following the October 12, 1999, ouster of the government of Prime Minister Nawaz Sharif, the military-led government stated its intention to restructure the political and electoral systems. Elections for local government are anticipated in late 2004. No time frame has yet been provided for provincial and national elections.

Political subdivisions: Each of the four provinces--Punjab, Sindh, Northwest Frontier, and Balochistan--comes under the authority of the Governor and provincial cabinet, appointed by the Chief Executive. The Northern Areas and Federally Administered Tribal Areas (FATA) are administered by the federal government, but enjoy considerable autonomy.

Economy

GDP: $59 billion.
Real annual growth rate: 3.1%.
Per capita GDP: $441.
Natural resources: Arable land, natural gas, limited petroleum, substantial hydropower potential, coal, iron ore.
Agriculture: *Products*--wheat, cotton, rice, sugarcane, tobacco.
Industry: *Types*--textiles, fertilizer, steel products, chemicals, food processing, oil and gas products, cement.
Trade: *Exports*--$7.8 billion: raw cotton, rice, cotton yarn, textiles, fruits, vegetables. *Major partners*--U.S., Japan, U.K., Saudi Arabia, Germany. *Imports*--$9.4 billion: wheat, crude oil, cooking oil, fertilizers, machinery. *Major partners*--U.S., Japan, Saudi Arabia, Malaysia, U.K., Sri Lanka.

PEOPLE

The majority of Pakistan's population lives along the Indus River valley and along an arc formed by the cities of Faisalabad, Lahore, Rawalpindi/Islamabad, and Peshawar.
Although the official language of Pakistan is Urdu, it is spoken as a first language by only 9% of the population; 65% speak Punjabi, 11% Sindhi, and 24% speak other languages (Pushtu, Saraiki, Baloch, Brahui). Urdu, Punjabi, Pushtu, and Baloch are Indo-European languages; Brahui is believed to have Dravidian (pre-Indo-European) origins. English is widely used within the government, the officer ranks of the military, and in many institutions of higher learning.

GOVERNMENT

The Pakistan Constitution of 1973, amended substantially in 1985 under Zia, was suspended by the military government on October 12, 1999. Musharraf has committed to return Pakistan to democratic, civilian rule but the implications of his promised structural reforms on the country's previous parliamentary system are unknown.

Under the Provisional Constitutional Order and its amendments, all power flows from and to the Chief Executive, who also holds the posts of Chief of Army Staff and Chairman, Joint Chiefs of Staff. The Judiciary is proscribed from issuing any order contrary to the decisions of the Chief Executive, and the President, Cabinet, National Security Council, and Governors serve at his discretion. In practice, Musharraf consults extensively with his civilian appointees and Corps Commanders and in certain policy areas (e.g., economic reform) civilian appointees have exhibited wide policy latitude.
Although the Judiciary was compelled to take an oath to the PCO and the Chief Executive, courts continue to function and exercise that authority which does not conflict with the PCO. The Supreme Court is Pakistan's highest court. The President, in consultation with the Chief Executive, appoints the Chief Justice and they together determine the other judicial appointments. Each province has a high court, the justices of which are appointed by the President after conferring with the Chief Justice of the Supreme Court and the provincial chief justice.

POLITICAL SYSTEM AND GOVERNMENT

FATHER OF THE NATION

Father of the Nation Quaid-i-Azam Mohammad Ali Jinnah's achievement as the founder of Pakistan, dominates everything else he did in his long and crowded public life spanning some 42 years. Yet, by any standard, his was an eventful life, his personality multidimensional and his achievements in other fields were many, if not equally great. Indeed, several were the roles he had played with distinction: at one time or another, he was one of the greatest legal luminaries

India had produced during the first half of the century, an `ambassador of Hindu-Muslim unity, a great constitutionalist, a distinguished parliamentarian, a top-notch politician, an indefatigable freedom-fighter, a dynamic Muslim leader, a political strategist and, above all one of the great nation-builders of modern times. What, however, makes him so remarkable is the fact that while similar other leaders assumed the leadership of traditionally well-defined nations and espoused their cause, or led them to freedom, he created a nation out of an inchoate and down-trodeen minority and established a cultural and national home for it.

And all that within a decase. For over three decades before the successful culmination in 1947, of the Muslim struggle for freedom in the South-Asian subcontinent, Jinnah had provided political leadership to the Indian Muslims: initially as one of the leaders, but later, since 1947, as the only prominent leader- the Quaid-i-Azam. For over thirty years, he had guided their affairs; he had given expression, coherence and direction to their ligitimate aspirations and cherished dreams; he had formulated these into concerete demands; and, above all, he had striven all the while to get them conceded by both the ruling British and the numerous Hindus the dominant segment of India's population. And for over thirty years he had fought, relentlessly and inexorably, for the inherent rights of the Muslims for an honourable existence in the subcontinent. Indeed, his life story constitutes, as it were, the story of the rebirth of the Muslims of the subcontinent and their spectacular rise to nationhood, phoenixlike.

EXECUTIVE GOVERNMENT STRUCTURE

Minister - Term		
Prime Minister of Pakistan	Nawaz Sharif MP	June 2014-
Ministry of Textile Industry	Abbas Khan Afridi MP	June 2014-
Minister of Commerce	Khurram Dastgir Khan MP	January 2014-
Minister for Defence Production	Rana Tanveer Hussain MP	June 2014-
Minister of Finance, Revenue, Economic Affairs and Statistics	Ishaq Dar Senator	June 2014-
Minister of Housing and Works	Akram Khan Durrani MP	June 2014-
Ministry of Water and Power Minister of Defence	Khawaja Muhammad Asif MP	June 2014-
Minister of Information, Broadcasting and National Heritage Minister for Law, Justice and Human Rights	Pervez Rasheed Senator	June 2014-
Minister of Industries and Production	Ghulam Murtaza Khan Jatoi MP	June 2014-
Ministry of Inter Provincial Coordination	Riaz Hussain Pirzada MP	June 2014-
Minister of Interior and Narcotics Control	Nisar Ali Khan MP	June 2014-
Ministry of Kashmir Affairs & Gilgit Baltistan	Chaudhry Muhammad Barjees Tahir MP	June 2014-
Minister of National Food Security & Research	Sikandar Hayat Khan	June 2014-
Minister of Petroleum and Natural Resources	Shahid Khaqan Abbasi	June 2014-
Minister of Planning,Development and Reform(also the Chairman of National Development and Reform Commission	Ahsan Iqbal	June 2014-
Minister of Ports and Shipping	Kamran Michael	June 2014-
Minister of Railways	Khawaja Saad Rafique	June 2014-
Religious Affairs and Interfaith Harmony	Sardar Muhammad Yousuf	June 2014-
Minister of Science and Technology	Zahid Hamid	June 2014-

Minister for States and Frontier Regions	Abdul Qadir Baloch	June 2014-

CABINET DEPARTMENTS

Federal Departments, autonomous and independent institutions.	Executive designation(s)	Reporting name
Alternative Energy Development Board	Chairman	AEDB
Anti-Narcotics Force	Director-General	ANF
Auditor General of Pakistan	Auditor-General	AGP
Capital Development Authority	Chairman	CDA
Civil Aviation Authority	Chairman	CAA
Directorate-General of Intelligence and Investigation	Director-General	DGII
Election Commission of Pakistan	Chief Election Commissioner	ECP
Earthquake Reconstruction and Rehabilitation Authority	Chairman	ERRA
Federal Board of Revenue	Chairman	FBR
F.I.A	Director-General	FIA
Federal Public Service Commission	Chairman	FPSC
Financial Monitoring Unit	Director	FMU
The Gazette	Editor-General	
Geological Survey of Pakistan	Director-General	GSP
Higher Education Commission	Chairman	HEC
Marine Fisheries Department	Director-General	MFD
Environmental Protection Agency	Director-General	EPA
National Accountability Bureau	Chairman	NAB
National Commission for Human Development	Chairman	NCHD
National Database and Registration Authority	Chairman	NADRA
National Disaster Management Authority	Chairman	NDMA
National Electric Power Regulatory Authority	Chairman	NEPRA
National Highway Authority	Chairman	NHA
NH&MP	Inspector-General	NH&MP
National Institute of Health	Director-General	NIH
National Institute of Oceanography	Director-General	NIO
National Reconstruction Bureau	Chairman	NRB
National Telecommunication Corporation	Chairman	NTC
Pakistan Atomic Energy Commission	Chairman	PAEC
Pakistan Bureau of Statistics	Chairman	PBS
Pakistan Council for Architects and Town Planners	Chairman	PCATP
Pakistan Customs	Director-General	
Pakistan Electronic Media Regulatory Authority	Chairman	PEMRA
Pakistan Engineering Council	Chairman	PEC
Pakistan Human Development Fund	Chairman	PHDF
Pakistan Meteorological Department	Director-General	PMD
Pakistan Nuclear Regulatory Authority	Chairman	PNRA
Pakistan Public Works Department	Director-General	PPWD

Federal Departments, autonomous and independent institutions.	Executive designation(s)	Reporting name
Pakistan Software Export Board	Chairman	PSEB
Pakistan Telecommunication Authority	Chairman	PTA
Planning Commission of Pakistan	Deputy Chairman	PC
Protectorate of Emigrants Pakistan	Director	PEP
Securities and Exchange Commission	Chairman	SEC
Space and Upper Atmosphere Research Commission	Chairman	SUPARCO
Mathematics and Statistics Division	Director-general	Stats
Survey of Pakistan	Surveyor-General	SP
Trade Development Authority	Chairman	TDA
Trading Corporation of Pakistan	Chairman	TCP
Water and Power Development Authority	Chairman	WAPDA
Zakat Council	Chairman	
Zarai Taraqiati Bank Ltd.	CEO	ZTBL

MILITARY

Pakistan's Armed Forces came into being when the country gained independence from Britain in 1947.

Air Chief Marshal Farooq Feroze Khan is the present Chairman Joint Chiefs of Staff Committee.

The Pakistan armed forces have the mission of defending the country against external attack and assisting the civil authority, as directed, in maintaining internal security.

The maintenance of law and order in the country is basically a provincial function: that is, the primary police agencies are provincial rather than national forces. Certain agencies, however, exist at the national level under the direct supervision of the Ministry of Interior.

The legitimizing authority for the existence, control, and missions of the armed forces is contained in the 1973 Constitution. Regarding the armed forces, the president of the republic is empowered to "raise and maintain the Military, Naval, and Air Forces of Pakistan and the Reserves of such Forces; to grant commissions in such Forces; and to appoint the Chief of the Army Staff; the Chief of Navy Staff and the Chief of the Air Staff, and determine their salaries and allowances."

The army, navy, and the air force are subordinate to the minister of defense.

AIR FORCE

Personnel:

65,000 + 8000 reserves

Structure: Combat: 8 Interceptor Squadrons with 160 F-7Ps
10 Fighter/Ground Attack squadrons with 36 F-16s, 18 MIRAGE III, 58 MIRAGE Vs, 70 F-6s, 60 Q/A-5s. 1 Recce Squadron with 12 MIRAGE IIPRs

Transport: 2 squadrons with 16 C-130s
1 Lockheed L-100, 1 F-27, 1 FALCON2 + aircraft for VIP duties

Training: 4 squadrons80 MFI-17Bs, 25 FT-5s, T-37s, 11 F-16Bs, 15 FT-7Ps, 2 MIRAGE IIDPs, 20+ K-8

Helicopters: ALOUETTEs, PUMAs

Major Airbases:
Sargodha, Malir, Masrur, Gilgit, Mauripur, Peshawar, Quetta, Risalpur

The Air Force is charged with the missions of providing operational support to ground, naval, and paramilitary security forces and of defending the country against air attacks. Secondary missions include the provisions of air transport to ground troops when needed, the coordination of civil and military aviation activities, and the conduct of technical training for civil aviation specialists.

The chief of air staff commands the air force. He is Air Cheif Marshal Abbas Khattak. There are three defense districts; north, central and south.

The air force began acquiring modern jet aircraft in 1956. Most of these aircraft were supplied by the United States, but numbers have also been obtained from Great Britian, France, and PRC. Air force training was modeled after that of the British Royal Air Force until 1956, when many officers and airmen began to attend courses in the United States. Training installations in Pakistan provide courses for pilots and navigators, and technical trade schools are available for both officers and airmen.

Air force operates Air Force College at Risalpur, Peshawar; Air Force Staff College, Karachi; and the Air Force College of Aeronautical Engineering, Karachi for academic training. **ARMY**

Personnel:
562,000 + 500,000 reserves

Structure:
9 Corps HQs
2 Armoured Divisions
19 Infantry Divisions
1 Artillery Division
6 Independent Armoured Brigades
6 Independent Mechanized Infantry Brigades
8 Air Defence Brigades
9 Artillery Brigades
7 Engineer Brigades
3 Armoured Recce Regiments
1 Special Services Group (3 Battalions, 1 independent counter-terrorism company)

EQUIPMENT:

Main Battle Tanks:200 T-85II APs, 51 T-55s, 250 T-69s, 1200 T-59s, 100 T-60/63s, 450 M-47/48s (being withdrawn) Work continues on MBT-2004 Al-Khalid.
Anti-Tank AH-1 Cobras, 5500 TOWs & TOW-IIs

Armoured Personnel Carriers 800 M113s, 120 BTR 70s. M113s Manufactured at Heavy Industries Taxila.

Artillery: AMERICAN: 105/150/255 mm Self Propelled and Towed Howitzers. Also 85mm/122mm CHINESE guns. Old 25 pounders. Some Bofors. Additional M-198 Howitzers being delivered from the US under the **Brown Amendment**

Army Aviation:20 AH-1 COBRA Gunships, Mi-8s, French Alloute IIIs, PUMAs, Mi-17s, UH-1s, Bell-47, Cessna O-1Es

Army Air Defence: AA guns ZU-23/33 30, 36, 37mm. **SAMs** CROTALEs, 400 RBS-20, SAM-7, STINGERS, Anza mk II

Surface-to-Surface Missiles Work Stopped on indegenous HATF-I,II Reportedly CHINESE M-11s acquired clandestinely from China

Local Production of M113A2
source: Jane's Armour & Artillery 95-96, 16th Edition p. 393

The chief of the army staff supervises his service through the Army General Headquarters in Rawalpindi. The four principal staff officers under the chief in Army General Headquarters are the chief of the general staff, the adjutant general, the quartermaster general, and the master general of ordnance. These positions are usually filled by major generals. The operations and intelligence functions were the responsibility of the chief of the general staff.

The Chief of army staff is General Jehangir Karamat.

The army components are categorized as arms or services. The arms are infantry, artillery, armor, engineers, and communications. The services include various components, such as the ordnance corps; maintenance and repair corps; electrical and mechanical engineer corps; education corps; military police corps; and the remount, veterinary, and farm corps.

A corps usually consisted of two or more divisions and is commanded by a lieutenant general whose headquarters is a scaled-down version of the Army General Headquarters. An infantry division, the major ground force combat formation, usually consisted of infantry, artillery, engineers, and communications units in addition to the supply and service support required for sustained independent action. Three infantry brigades usually comprised the primary organic combat units of an infantry division; armored units would be attached depending on the mission of the division and the terrain in which it operated.

Auxiliary or paramilitary forces include the Pakistan Rangers, the Frontier Corps, and the Frontier Constabulary.

The 20 Infantry & 2 Armoured Divisions are grouped under 9 different Corpsheadquarters commanded by 3-star Lieutenant Generals. These are:

I Corps (Mangla)
II Corps (Multan)
IV Corps (Lahore)
V Corps (Karachi)
X Corps (Rawalpindi)

XI Corps (Peshawar)
XII Corps (Quetta)
XXX Corps (Gujranwala)
XXXI Corps (Bahawalpur)

Navy (No data available)

NATIONAL SECURITY

Pakistan's 610,000-member armed forces, the world's eighth largest, are well trained and disciplined. However, budget constraints and nation-building duties have reduced Pakistan's normal robust training tempo, which if not reversed, will eventually impact on the operational readiness of the Armed Forces. Likewise, Pakistan has had an increasingly difficult time maintaining their aging fleet of United States, Chinese, United Kingdom and French equipment. While the industrial base capabilities have expanded significantly, limited fiscal resources and various sanctions have significantly constrained the government's efforts to modernize the armed forces.

Until 1990, the United States provided military aid to Pakistan to modernize its conventional defensive capability. The United States allocated about 40% of its assistance package to non-reimbursable credits for military purchases, the third largest program behind Israel and Egypt. The remainder of the aid program was devoted to economic assistance. While sanctions have been in effect since 1990, various amendments have authorized return of spare parts and end items already paid for by Pakistan. In addition, the U.S. and Pakistan have come to a financial agreement on the non-delivery of F-16s. However, Pakistan's nuclear tests in response to India's May 1998 tests and the recent military coup have placed additional sanctions on Pakistan.

Principal Government Officials

President--Rafiq Tarar
Chief Executive--General Pervez Musharraf
Minister of Foreign Affairs--Abdul Sattar
Ambassador to the U.S.--Maleeha Lodhi
Ambassador to the UN--Shamshad Ahmed

Pakistan maintains an embassy in the United States at 2315 Massachusetts Avenue, N.W., Washington, DC 20048 (Tel. 202-939-6200).

ECONOMY

Rank	26th (PPP) 44th (Nominal)
Currency	1 Pakistani Rupee (PKR) Rs.1 = 100 Paisas
Fiscal year	1 July – 30 June
Trade organisations	ECO, SAFTA, ASEAN, WIPO and WTO
	Statistics
GDP	$245 billion (nominal) (2014) $576 billion (2014 est.)(PPP)
GDP growth	3.7% (2012) 3.3% (2014)
GDP per capita	$1,307 (nominal; 143rd; 2014) $3,149 (PPP; 140th; 2014)[4]
GDP by sector	agriculture: 21.2%, industry: 25.4%, services: 53.4% (2010 est.)
Inflation (CPI)	7.93% (March 2014)
Population below poverty line	21% (2014)

Labour force	59.74 million (2012-13)
Labour force by occupation	agriculture: 49.1%, Construction: 15.2%, Manufacturing: 13.3%, Wholesale and Retail: 9.2%, Transport and Communication: 7.3% (2012-13)
Unemployment	5.6%
Main industries	textiles and apparel, food processing, pharmaceuticals, construction materials, chemicals, cement, mining, machinery, steel, engineering, software and hardware, automobiles, motorcycle and auto parts, electronics, paper products, fertiliser, shrimp, defence products, shipbuilding
Ease-of-doing-business rank	107th
	External
Exports	$25.05 billion
Export goods	textiles (garments, bed linen, cotton cloth, yarn), rice, leather goods, sports goods, chemicals, manufactures, carpets, steel, foodstuffs, fertilizer, Cement, sugar, animals, electrical equipment, petroleum and rugs
Main export partners	United States 13.3% China 10.9% United Arab Emirates 8.6% Afghanistan 8.5%
Imports	$33 billion
Import goods	petroleum, petroleum products, machinery, plastics, transportation equipment, edible oils, paper and paperboard, iron and steel, tea
Main import partners	China 19.8% Saudi Arabia 12.0% United Arab Emirates 11.9% Kuwait 6.2%
	Public finances
Public debt	62% of GDP (2014 est.)[17]
Revenues	Rs 1939 billion ($19.39 billion) (2014)[18]
Expenses	$39.3billion (2014-15)
Credit rating	Standard & Poor's: B- (Domestic) B- (Foreign) B- (T&C Assessment) Outlook: Stable Moody's: Caa1 Outlook: Stable

The **economy of Pakistan** is the 26th largest in the world in terms of purchasing power parity (PPP), and 44th largest in terms of nominal GDP. However as Pakistan has a population of over 186 million (the world's 6th-largest), thus GDP per capita is $3,149 ranking 140th in the world. Pakistan is a rapidly developing country and is one of the Next Eleven, the eleven countries that, along with the BRICs, have a high potential to become the world's largest economies in the 21st century. However, after decades of war and social instability, as of 2014, serious deficiencies in basic services such as railway transportation and electric power generation had developed. The economy is semi-industrialized, with centres of growth along the Indus River. Major industries includes textiles (garments, bed linen, cotton cloth, yarn), chemicals, food processing (mainly sugar, salt, wheat, rice, fruit), agriculture, fertilizer, cement, dairy and rugs.

Growth poles of Pakistan's economy are situated along the Indus River; the diversified economies of Karachi and major urban centers in the Punjab, coexisting with lesser developed areas in other parts of the country. The economy has suffered in the past from internal political disputes, a fast-growing population, mixed levels of foreign investment. Foreign exchange reserves are bolstered by steady worker remittances, but a growing current account deficit – driven by a widening trade gap as import growth outstrips export expansion – could draw down reserves and dampen GDP growth in the medium term. Pakistan is currently undergoing process economic liberalization with includes privatization of all government corporations, aimed to attract foreign investment and decrease budget deficit.[33] In 2014, foreign currency reserves crossed $15 billion which has led to stable outlook on the long-term rating by *Standard & Poor's*

Extreme poverty and underdevelopment in Pakistan, as well as fiscal mismanagement that has produced a large foreign debt, obscure the potential of a country which has the resources and entrepreneurial skill to support rapid economic growth. In fact, the economy averaged an impressive growth rate of 6 percent per year during the 1980s and early 1990s. However, the economy is extremely vulnerable to Pakistan's external and internal shocks, such as in 1992-93, when devastating floods and political uncertainty combined to depress economic growth sharply and the financial crisis in Asia which hit major markets for Pakistani textile exports. Average real GDP growth from 1992 to 1998 dipped to 4.1 percent annually.

Since the early 1980s, the government has pursued market-based economic reform policies. Market-based reforms began to take hold in 1988, when the government launched an ambitious IMF-assisted structural adjustment program in response to chronic and unsustainable fiscal and external account deficits. Since that time the government has removed barriers to foreign trade and investment, begun to reform the financial system, eased foreign exchange controls, and privatized dozens of state-owned enterprises. Pakistan continues to struggle with these reforms, having mixed success, especially in reducing its budget and current account deficits. The budget deficit in FY 1996-97 was 6.4% of GDP. Initial data implied a reduction in 1997-98 to 5.4% and in 1998-99 to 4.3%, but revised data indicates that the deficit is probably still over 5.0%. In that same 2-year period, the rupee was devalued against the dollar 12% and 10.5% respectively.

Economic reform was further set back by Pakistan's nuclear tests in May 1998 and the subsequent economic sanctions imposed by the G-7. International default was narrowly averted by the partial waiver of sanctions and the subsequent reinstatement of Pakistan's IMF ESAF/EFF in early 1999, followed by Paris Club and London Club reschedulings. The Sharif government had difficulty meeting the conditionality of the IMF program, which was suspended in July 1999. The current government has announced a program of reforms and is in discussion with the IMF regarding a Poverty Reduction and Growth Facility to begin in July 2004.

With a per capita GDP of about USD 441, the World Bank considers Pakistan a low-income country. No more than 39 percent of adults are literate, and life expectancy is about 62 years or less. The population, currently about 130 million, is growing at about 2.6%, very close to the GDP growth rate. Relatively few resources have been devoted to socio-economic development on infrastructure projects. Inadequate provision of social services and high population growth have contributed to a persistence of poverty and unequal income distribution.

AGRICULTURE AND NATURAL RESOURCES

Pakistan's principal natural resources are arable land and water. About 25% of Pakistan's total land area is under cultivation and is watered by one of the largest irrigation systems in the world.

Agriculture accounts for about 24% of GDP and employs about 50% of the labor force. The most important crops are wheat, sugarcane, cotton, and rice, which together account for more than 75% of the value of total crop output. Despite intensive farming practices, Pakistan remains a net food importer. Pakistan exports rice, cotton, fish, fruits, and vegetables and imports vegetable oil, wheat, cotton, pulses and consumer foods.

The economic importance of agriculture has declined since independence, when its share of GDP was around 53%. Following the poor harvest of 1993, the government introduced agriculture assistance policies, including increased support prices for many agricultural commodities and expanded availability of agricultural credit. From 1993 to 1997, real growth in the agricultural sector averaged 5.7% but has since declined to less than 4%. Agricultural reforms, including increased wheat and oilseed production, play a central role in the new government's economic reform package.

Pakistan has extensive energy resources, including fairly sizable natural gas reserves, some proven oil reserves, coal, and large hydropower potential. However, the exploitation of energy resources has been slow due to a shortage of capital and domestic political constraints. For instance, domestic petroleum production totals only about half the country's oil needs. The need to import oil also contributes to Pakistan's persistent trade deficits and the shortage of foreign exchange. The current government has announced that privatization in the oil and gas sector is a priority, as is the substitution of indigenous gas for imported oil, especially in the production of power.

INDUSTRY

Pakistan's manufacturing sector accounts for about 26% of GDP. Cotton textile production and apparel manufacturing are Pakistan's largest industries, accounting for about 64% of total exports. Other major industries include cement, fertilizer, edible oil, sugar, steel, tobacco, chemicals, machinery, and food processing. Despite ongoing government efforts to privatize large-scale parastatal units, the public sector continues to account for a significant proportion of industry. In FY 1998-99, gross fixed capital formation in the public sector accounted for about 38% of the total. In the face of an increasing trade deficit, the government hopes to diversify the country's industrial base and bolster export industries.

FOREIGN TRADE AND AID

Weak world demand for its exports and domestic political uncertainty have contributed to Pakistan's high trade deficit. In FY 1998-99, Pakistan recorded a current account deficit of $1.7 billion, only a slight improvement over the FY 1997-98 current account deficit of $1.9 billion. Pakistan's exports continue to be dominated by cotton textiles and apparel, despite government diversification efforts. Major imports include petroleum and petroleum products, edible oil, wheat, chemicals, fertilizer, capital goods, industrial raw materials, and consumer products. External imbalance has left Pakistan with a growing foreign debt burden. Principal and interest payments in FY 1998-99 totaled $2.6 billion, more than double the amount paid in FY 1989-90. Annual debt service now exceeds 34% of export earnings.

Pakistan receives about $2.5 billion per year in loan/grant assistance from international financial institutions (e.g., the IMF, the World Bank, and the Asian Development Bank) and bilateral donors. Increasingly, the composition of assistance to Pakistan has shifted away from grants toward loans repayable in foreign exchange. All new U.S. economic assistance to Pakistan was suspended after October 1990, when then-President Bush could no longer certify under the Pressler Amendment to the Foreign Assistance Act (Section 620e[e]) "that Pakistan does not possess a nuclear explosive device and that the proposed assistance package reduces significantly the risk that Pakistan will acquire a nuclear explosive device."

FOREIGN RELATIONS

Pakistan is a prominent member of the Organization of the Islamic Conference (OIC) and an active member of the United Nations. Its foreign policy encompasses historically difficult relations with India, a desire for a stable Afghanistan, long-standing close relations with China, extensive security and economic interests in the Persian Gulf, and wide-ranging bilateral relations with the United States and other Western countries.

INDIA

Since partition, relations between Pakistan and India have been characterized by rivalry and suspicion. Although many issues divide the two countries, the most sensitive one since independence has been the status of Kashmir.

At the time of partition, the princely state of Kashmir, though ruled by a Hindu Maharajah, had an overwhelmingly Muslim population. When the Maharajah hesitated in acceding to either Pakistan or India in 1947, some of his Muslim subjects, aided by tribesmen from Pakistan, revolted in favor of joining Pakistan. In exchange for military assistance in containing the revolt, the Kashmiri ruler offered his allegiance to India. Indian troops occupied the eastern portion of Kashmir, including its capital, Srinagar, while the western part came under Pakistani control.

India addressed this dispute in the United Nations on January 1, 1948. One year later, the UN arranged a cease-fire along a line dividing Kashmir, but leaving the northern end of the line undemarcated and the vale of Kashmir (with the majority of the population) under Indian control. India and Pakistan agreed with Indian resolutions which called for a UN-supervised plebiscite to determine the state's future.

Full-scale hostilities erupted in September 1965, when India alleged that insurgents trained and supplied by Pakistan were operating in India-controlled Kashmir. Hostilities ceased three weeks later, following mediation efforts by the UN and interested countries. In January 1966, Indian and Pakistani representatives met in Tashkent, U.S.S.R., and agreed to attempt a peaceful settlement of Kashmir and their other differences.
Following the 1971 Indo-Pakistan conflict, President Zulfiqar Ali Bhutto and Indian Prime Minister Indira Gandhi met in the mountain town of Shimla, India, in July 1972. They agreed to a line of control in Kashmir resulting from the December 17, 1971 cease-fire, and endorsed the principle of settlement of bilateral disputes through peaceful means. In 1974, Pakistan and India agreed to resume postal and telecommunications linkages, and to enact measures to facilitate travel. Trade and diplomatic relations were restored in 1976 after a hiatus of five years.

India's nuclear test in 1974 generated great uncertainty in Pakistan and is generally acknowledged to have been the impetus for Pakistan's nuclear weapons development program. In 1983, the Pakistani and Indian governments accused each other of aiding separatists in their respective countries, i.e., Sikhs in India's Punjab state and Sindhis in Pakistan's Sindh province. In April 1984, tensions erupted after troops were deployed to the Siachen Glacier, a high-altitude desolate area close to the China border left undemarcated by the cease-fire agreement (Karachi Agreement) signed by Pakistan and India in 1949.

Tensions diminished after Rajiv Gandhi became Prime Minister in November 1984 and after a group of Sikh hijackers was brought to trial by Pakistan in March 1985. In December 1985, President Zia and Prime Minister Gandhi pledged not to attack each other's nuclear facilities. (A formal "no attack" agreement was signed in January 1991.) In early 1986, the Indian and Pakistani governments began high-level talks to resolve the Siachen Glacier border dispute and to improve trade.

Bilateral tensions increased in early 1990, when Kashmiri militants began a campaign of violence against Indian Government authority in Jammu and Kashmir. Subsequent high-level bilateral meetings relieved the tensions between India and Pakistan, but relations worsened again after the destruction of the Ayodhya Mosque by Hindu extremists in December 1992 and terrorist bombings in Bombay in March 1993. Talks between the Foreign Secretaries of both countries in January 1994 resulted in deadlock.
In the last several years, the Indo-Pakistani relationship has veered sharply between rapprochement and conflict. After taking office in February 1997, Prime Minister Nawaz Sharif moved to resume official dialog with India. A number of meetings at the foreign secretary and prime ministerial level took place, with positive atmospherics but little concrete progress. The relationship improved markedly when Indian Prime Minister Vajpayee traveled to Lahore for a summit with Sharif in February 1999. There was considerable hope that the meeting could lead to a breakthrough. Unfortunately, in spring 1999 infiltrators from Pakistan occupied positions on the Indian side of the Line of Control in the remote, mountainous area of Kashmir near Kargil, threatening the ability of India to supply its forces on Siachen Glacier. By early summer, serious fighting flared in the Kargil sector. The infiltrators withdrew following a meeting between Prime Minister Sharif and President Clinton in July. Relations between India and Pakistan have since been particularly strained, especially since the October 12, 1999 coup in Islamabad.

AFGHANISTAN

Following the 1979 Soviet invasion of Afghanistan, the Pakistani Government played a vital role in supporting the Afghan resistance movement and assisting Afghan refugees. After the Soviet withdrawal in February 1989, Pakistan, with cooperation from the world community, continued to provide extensive support for displaced Afghans. In 1999, the United States provided approximately $70 million in humanitarian assistance to Afghanistan and Afghan refugees in Pakistan, mainly through multilateral organizations and NGOs. As such, the United States in 1999 was the largest single donor. In 1999, more than 1.2 million registered Afghan refugees remained in Pakistan, as fighting between rival factions continued. Pakistan has recognized the Taliban as the government in Afghanistan and provides the Taliban assistance. Pakistan has periodically offered to try to help bring Afghanistan's warring factions to the negotiating table, thus far with negligible results.

RUSSIAN FEDERATION

Under military leader Ayub Khan, Pakistan sought to improve relations with the Soviet Union; trade and cultural exchanges between the two countries increased between 1966 and 1971. However, Soviet criticism of Pakistan's position in the 1971 war with India weakened bilateral relations, and many Pakistanis believed that the August 1971 Indo-Soviet Treaty of Friendship, Peace and Cooperation encouraged Indian belligerency. Subsequent Soviet arms sales to India, amounting to billions of dollars on concessional terms, reinforced this argument.

During the 1980s, tensions increased between the Soviet Union and Pakistan because of the latter's key role in helping to organize political and material support for the Afghan rebel forces. The withdrawal of Soviet forces from Afghanistan and the collapse of the former Soviet Union resulted in significantly improved bilateral relations, but Pakistan's support for and recognition of the Taliban regime in neighboring Afghanistan is an ongoing source of tension.

PEOPLE'S REPUBLIC OF CHINA

In 1950, Pakistan was among the first countries to recognize the People's Republic of China (P.R.C.). Following the Sino-Indian hostilities of 1962, Pakistan's relations with China became stronger; since then, the two countries have regularly exchanged high-level visits resulting in a variety of agreements. China has provided economic, military, and technical assistance to Pakistan.

Favorable relations with China have been a pillar of Pakistan's foreign policy. The P.R.C. strongly supported Pakistan's opposition to Soviet involvement in Afghanistan and is perceived by Pakistan as a regional counterweight to India and Russia.

IRAN AND THE PERSIAN GULF

Historically, Pakistan has had close geopolitical and cultural-religious linkages with Iran. However, strains in the relationship appeared in the last decade. Pakistan and Iran support opposing factions in the Afghan conflict. Also, some Pakistanis suspect Iranian support for the sectarian violence which has plagued Pakistan. Nevertheless, Pakistan pursues an active diplomatic relationship with Iran, including recent overtures to seek a negotiated settlement between Afghanistan's warring factions.
Despite popular support for Iraq in 1991, the Pakistani government supported the coalition against Iraq's invasion of Kuwait and sent 11,600 troops to defend Saudi Arabia. Pakistan provides military personnel to strengthen Gulf-state defenses and to reinforce its own security interests in the area.

U.S.-PAKISTAN RELATIONS

The United States and Pakistan established diplomatic relations in 1947. The U.S. agreement to provide economic and military assistance to Pakistan and the latter's partnership in the Baghdad Pact/CENTO and SEATO strengthened relations between the two nations. However, the U.S. suspension of military assistance during the 1965 Indo-Pakistan war generated a widespread feeling in Pakistan that the United States was not a reliable ally. Even though the United States suspended military assistance to both countries involved in the conflict, the suspension of aid affected Pakistan much more severely. Gradually, relations improved and arms sales were renewed in 1975. Then, in April 1979, the United States cut off economic assistance to Pakistan, except food assistance, as required under the Symington Amendment to the Foreign Assistance Act of 1961, due to concerns about Pakistan's nuclear program.

The Soviet invasion of Afghanistan in December 1979 highlighted the common interest of Pakistan and the United States in peace and stability in South Asia. In 1981, the United States and Pakistan agreed on a $3.2-billion military and economic assistance program aimed at helping Pakistan deal with the heightened threat to security in the region and its economic development needs.

Recognizing national security concerns and accepting Pakistan's assurances that it did not intend to construct a nuclear weapon, Congress waived restrictions (Symington Amendment) on military assistance to Pakistan. In March 1986, the two countries agreed on a second multi-year (FY 1988-93) $4-billion economic development and security assistance program. On October 1, 1990, however, the United States suspended all military assistance and new economic aid to Pakistan under the Pressler Amendment, which required that the President certify annually that Pakistan "does not possess a nuclear explosive device."

There have been several incidents of violence against American officials and U.S. mission employees in Pakistan. In November 1979, false rumors that the United States had participated in the seizure of the Grand Mosque in Mecca provoked a mob attack on the U.S. embassy in Islamabad. The government's delayed response enabled the mob to burn the embassy. Four people died, two of them U.S. nationals. The American Cultural Center in Lahore also was destroyed by fire. In 1989, there was an attack on the American Center in Islamabad, where six Pakistanis were killed in the crossfire with the police. In March of 1995, two American employees of the consulate in Karachi were killed and one wounded in an attack on the home-to-office shuttle. In November of 1997, four U.S. businessmen were brutally murdered while being driven to work in Karachi. In November 1999, the Embassy and the American Center were the targets of rocket attacks that wounded one local national security guard.

The decision by India to conduct nuclear tests in May 1998 and Pakistan's matching response set back U.S. relations in the region, which had seen renewed U.S. Government interest during the second Clinton Administration. A presidential visit scheduled for the first quarter of 1998 was postponed and, under the Glenn Amendment, sanctions restricted the provision of credits, military sales, economic assistance, and loans to the government. An intensive dialogue on nuclear nonproliferation and security issues between Deputy Secretary Talbott and Foreign Secretary Shamshad Ahmad was initiated, with discussions focusing on CTBT signature and ratification, FMCT negotiations, export controls, and a nuclear restraint regime. The October 1999 overthrow of the democratically elected Sharif government triggered an additional layer of sanctions under Section 508 of the Foreign Appropriations Act which include restrictions on foreign military financing and economic assistance. Presently, U.S. Government assistance to Pakistan is limited mainly to refugee and counter-narcotics assistance.

PRINCIPAL U.S. EMBASSY OFFICIALS

Ambassador-- Richard Olson

Richard Olson presented credentials as U.S. Ambassador to the Islamic Republic of Pakistan to President Asif Ali Zardari at the Governor's House in Karachi on October 31, 2012.

Deputy Chief of Mission--Peter Bodde
Counselor for Political Affairs--Cecile Shea, Acting
Counselor for Economic Affairs--Mary Townswick
Counselor for Public Affairs--James Williams
Consul General--Kay Anske
Defense Attaché--Col. Mark Boettcher
Consul General, Karachi--Mary H. Witt
Principal Officer, Lahore--Bryan Hunt
Principal Officer, Peshawar--Lynne Tracy

The U.S. Embassy is located at the Diplomatic Enclave, Ramna 5, Islamabad [Tel. (92)-(51)-2080-2004; telex 82-5-864].

TRAVEL AND BUSINESS INFORMATION

The U.S. Department of State's Consular Information Program provides Consular Information Sheets, Travel Warnings, and Public Announcements.

Consular Information Sheets exist for all countries and include information on entry requirements, currency regulations, health conditions, areas of instability, crime and security, political disturbances, and the addresses of the U.S. posts in the country.

Travel Warnings are issued when the State Department recommends that Americans avoid travel to a certain country.

Public Announcements are issued as a means to disseminate information quickly about terrorist threats and other relatively short-term conditions overseas which pose significant risks to the security of American travelers. Free copies of this information are available by calling the Bureau of Consular Affairs at 202-647-5225 or via the fax-on-demand system: 202-647-3000. Consular Information Sheets and Travel Warnings also are available on the Consular Affairs Internet home page: http://travel.state.gov. Consular Affairs Tips for Travelers publication series, which contain information on obtaining passports and planning a safe trip abroad are on the internet and hard copies can be purchased from the Superintendent of Documents, U.S. Government Printing Office, telephone: 202-512-1800; fax 202-512-2250.

Emergency information concerning Americans traveling abroad may be obtained from the Office of Overseas Citizens Services at (202) 647-5225. For after-hours emergencies, Sundays and holidays, call 202-647-4000.

Passport information can be obtained by calling the National Passport Information Center's automated system ($.35 per minute) or live operators 8 a.m. to 8 p.m. (EST) Monday-Friday ($1.05 per minute). The number is 1-900-225-5674 (TDD: 1-900-225-7778). Major credit card users (for a flat rate of $4.95) may call 1-888-362-8668 (TDD: 1-888-498-3648). It also is available on the internet.

Travelers can check the latest health information with the U.S. Centers for Disease Control and Prevention in Atlanta, Georgia. A hotline at 877-FYI-TRIP (877-394-8747) and a web site at http://www.cdc.gov/travel/index.htm give the most recent health advisories, immunization recommendations or requirements, and advice on food and drinking water safety for regions and countries. A booklet entitled Health Information for International Travel (HHS publication number CDC-95-8280) is available from the U.S. Government Printing Office, Washington, DC 20402, tel. (202) 512-1800.

Information on travel conditions, visa requirements, currency and customs regulations, legal holidays, and other items of interest to travelers also may be obtained before your departure from a country's embassy and/or consulates in the U.S. (for this country, see "Principal Government Officials" listing in this publication).

U.S. citizens who are long-term visitors or traveling in dangerous areas are encouraged to register at the U.S. embassy upon arrival in a country (see "Principal U.S. Embassy Officials" listing in this publication). This may help family members contact you in case of an emergency.

STRATEGIC INFORMATION FOR CONDUCTING BUSINESS

POLITICAL ENVIRONMENT

NATURE OF POLITICAL RELATIONSHIP WITH THE UNITED STATES

Pakistan and the United States have had bilateral diplomatic relations since Pakistan's creation in 1947. Pakistan is a member of the United Nations (UN), the Organization of the Islamic Conference (OIC), the Economic Cooperation Organization (ECO), and the South Asian Association for Regional Cooperation (SAARC). Pakistan has worked effectively to promote and support peacekeeping operations in Somalia, Bosnia, Haiti, East Timor, Sierra Leone and Congo. In 1990, U.S. economic and military assistance to Pakistan was suspended as required by U.S. legislation (the so-called Pressler Amendment to the Foreign Assistance Act) when the U.S. President could no longer certify to Congress that Pakistan did not possess a nuclear explosive device.

The Brown Amendment enacted in 1996 provided some relief from the Pressler sanctions. However, Pakistan's nuclear tests in May 1998 resulted in the imposition of U.S. economic sanctions which have recently been relaxed (primarily to enable multilateral support for basic human need applications). However, following the October 1999 military coup, additional sanctions were imposed on Pakistan under Section 508 of the Foreign Appropriations Act. The United States has traditionally been Pakistan's leading trading partner and largest source of private foreign capital, but tariff disputes relating to independent power projects may affect future inflows of U.S. investment into Pakistan.

President Clinton visited Pakistan briefly in March 2004 and addressed the nation in a live broadcast. Anti-American sentiment runs high in some quarters as the clergy and the media, particularly the Urdu press, thrive on anti-Americanism. Yet the lure of America is quite strong. The American Embassy in Islamabad attracts more visa applicants than any other diplomatic mission.

MAJOR POLITICAL ISSUES AFFECTING BUSINESS CLIMATE

In 1988 Pakistan began moving toward a two-party system, dominated by the Pakistan Muslim League (PML) and the Pakistan People's Party (PPP). Both parties favored a liberalizing, market-oriented economic policy. This consensus, together with the macroeconomic discipline of structural economic adjustment programs adopted with the full support of the International Monetary Fund (IMF) and the World Bank, had a positive impact on the business climate. Alternating administrations between the PML and the PPP during the decade following the restoration of democratic government was difficult, however, with a corrosive impact on political stability.

In 1997, Nawaz Sharif was elected Prime Minister for a second time with a substantial majority, but on October 12, 1999, his government was removed in a bloodless military coup. The Chief of Army Staff, General Pervez Musharraf, took over as "Chief Executive" and suspended the constitution. Tensions between General Musharraf and Prime Minister Sharif had grown following Pakistan's incursion across the Line of Control into Kargil in the Indian-administered Kashmir and Sharif's subsequent decision to withdraw in July 1999.

Upon assuming power, Musharraf announced an ambitious reform agenda which included fighting corruption, devolving power to the local level, and fighting sectarianism. He appointed civilian cabinets at the federal and provincial levels. The military has long remained the predominant force in Pakistani decision-making. Musharraf, however, has had only limited success in implementing his policies thus far. In May 2004, the Supreme Court validated the coup but gave General Musharraf three years from October 12, 1999, to return to an elected government. Musharraf has said that he would respect this timeframe. Tensions with India, corruption, religious sectarianism, and political uncertainty are among the many challenges that confront this government.

As in many developing countries, corruption is an unwelcome, but ubiquitous, part of the business climate in Pakistan. Recent anecdotal reports suggest that this problem may be having a sclerotic impact on the economy. Efforts to reduce opportunities for corruption by improving management systems, for example, in the customs and tax services are under way. The military government has vowed to eliminate the culture of corruption. Also, important business organizations, including the Federation of Pakistan Chambers of Commerce & Industry (FPCCI), have made curbing corruption a principal plank of their policy agendas.

POLITICAL SYSTEM

Democracy has not yet taken root in Pakistan. The military has intervened several times in Pakistan's history, and the military is an important political player even when it is not in power. The latest military intervention took place on October 12, 1999, and elected institutions were initially suspended and then dissolved.

Under the suspended constitution, the parliament consists of two houses, a National Assembly elected directly through universal suffrage, and a Senate elected largely by the provincial legislatures. (The senators from the federal area are elected by the National Assembly and the FATA senators are chosen by the MNAs from FATA.) The Prime Minister is the head of government and is elected by the National Assembly. The President is the head of state. An electoral college consisting of the National Assembly, the Senate, and the provincial assemblies chooses him. The constitution requires that the President be a Muslim and provides for a five-year term. For all practical purposes, the Prime Minister has to be a Muslim as well. The wording of the oath takes it for granted that the Prime Minister, too, will be a Muslim. Pakistan is divided into four provinces: Punjab, Sindh, Baluchistan, and the Northwest Frontier Province (NWFP). Each province has its own directly elected provincial assembly, a government headed by a Chief Minister, and a Governor appointed by the President upon recommendation by the Prime Minister. (Since October 12, 1999, provinces have only governors, no assemblies and chief ministers.)

The 217-member National Assembly is elected for a five-year term and the 87-member Senate for six-year term. The National Assembly seats are currently apportioned 8 to the Federally-Administered Tribal Areas (FATA) and one to the federal capital of Islamabad, with ten additional seats reserved for religious minorities. (Under a system of separate electorate, Muslims vote for Muslim candidates and non-Muslims vote for non-Muslim candidates. Most members of minorities don't like this system saying that it had cut them off from mainstream politics.) Each of the four provinces has 19 senators; there are eight senators from the FATA and three from the federal capital area. Indirect elections for half the members of the Senate are held at three-year intervals.

The constitution guarantees the independence of the judiciary but in reality it has never been completely independent. The Supreme Court is the highest court in the country; High Courts in the provincial capitals of Lahore, Karachi, Peshawar, and Quetta stand at the head of the provincial judicial systems. Pakistan's press publishes freely for the most part. However, self-censorship is widely practiced by journalists and advertising and other tactics are used by the government to influence content. Hardly 10% of the people regularly read newspapers and over 90% of them read Urdu papers which are not noted for their objectivity, fairness or accuracy. The electronic media are strictly controlled by the state and are notorious for their acerbic propaganda against India and the domestic political opposition.

Pakistan came into existence in August 1947 with the partition of British India. The creation of a separate Muslim nation was accomplished largely through the efforts of Mohammed Ali Jinnah, Pakistan's first Governor General. In 1947-48, Pakistan and India fought the first war over the Muslim-majority territory of Kashmir, claimed by both states. The conflict ended in stalemate and Kashmir remains disputed territory, divided by a heavily militarized Line of Control. Kashmir continues to be the biggest obsession of the Pakistani establishment and the media. It is often described as the jugular vein of Pakistan.

Pakistan initially consisted of two parts, East Pakistan and West Pakistan, separated by 1,000 miles of Indian territory. In 1970 the Awami League swept the elections in East Pakistan and gained a majority in the country as a whole. The Pakistan People's Party (PPP), founded and led by Zulfikar Ali Bhutto, won a majority of the seats in West Pakistan. The outcome was a country completely divided with neither major party having support in the other part. Negotiations to form a coalition government broke down and in March 1971 a brutal military action was unleashed on East Pakistan. Hundreds of thousands of people were killed and many more fled to India. In December 1971 India militarily intervened and the independent nation of Bangladesh came into being. The leadership of the western part of Pakistan was handed over to Z. A. Bhutto, who became President and first civilian chief martial law administrator.

A new constitution, Pakistan's third, came into effect in August 1973 and Bhutto became the Prime Minister. His government implemented portions of the PPP's socialist manifesto, restructuring the economy, increasing the prominence of the public sector, and nationalizing many industries. Bhutto's centralizing policies and autocratic ways galvanized the opposition, which challenged his sweeping victory in the March 1977 national elections. In July 1977, Bhutto was deposed by the Chief of Army Staff, General Ziaul Haq, who became President in 1978. Bhutto was hanged in April 1979. Under Zia, the Government of Pakistan became increasingly Islamised and benefited from supporting mujahideen efforts to counter the Soviet troops in Afghanistan. Non-party elections were held in 1985 to the National Assembly and the four provincial assemblies. In August 1988, General Zia, along with US Ambassador Arnold Raphel and many other senior officials, died in an air crash.

General elections were held in November 1988 and the PPP, headed by Benazir Bhutto, daughter of Z. A. Bhutto, won a plurality of seats and formed a coalition government. In August 1990, President Ghulam Ishaq Khan exercised his constitutional right to dissolve the National Assembly, dismiss the Prime Minister, and call new elections. In the general elections held in October 1990, the Islamic Democratic Alliance won the largest number of seats and Mian Nawaz Sharif, leader of its largest component party, the Pakistan Muslim League (PML), became Prime Minister. Nawaz Sharif, the first industrialist to lead Pakistan, continued the trend toward liberalization of the economy and promotion of private sector growth.

In April 1993, President Ghulain Ishaq Khan again dissolved the National Assembly and dismissed the Prime Minister, but a month later the Pakistan Supreme Court reinstated the National Assembly and the Nawaz Sharif government. Continued tensions between the reinstated Prime Minister and the President resulted in governmental gridlock; the Chief of Army staff brokered an arrangement under which both the President and Prime Minister resigned their offices in July 1993. Elections in October 1993 resulted in a plurality for the PPP and Benazir Bhutto secured sufficient additional support to become the Prime Minister. Bhutto's hold on power received a further boost in November 1993, when Farooq Leghari, a PPP stalwart, was elected

President.

In November 1996, however, President Leghari dismissed the Bhutto government, charging it with corruption, mismanagement of the economy, and implication in extra-judicial killings in Karachi. Elections in February 1997 resulted in an overwhelming victory for the PML-Nawaz and Nawaz Sharif was again called upon to form government. In April 1997, Sharif proposed and parliament passed a constitutional amendment removing the President's power to dissolve the National Assembly and making his power to appoint military services chiefs and provincial governors contingent to the "advice" of the prime minister. A constitutional confrontation between Sharif and the Chief Justice of the Supreme Court resulted in the resignation of Leghari and the subsequent election of the Prime Minister's own presidential candidate, Rafiq Tarar. This was followed by the removal of Chief Justice Sajjad Ali Shah, an act that damaged the prestige and independence of the judiciary.

Schedule for Elections: The most recent elections to the national and provincial assemblies took place in February 1997. The general election was scheduled to be held again in February 2002 and indirect elections for half of the members of the Senate in March 2004. The indirect election of the President was held in December 1997. As mentioned earlier, initially the assemblies and the senate were suspended, not dissolved. In June 2005, General Musharraf appointed himself the president and the assemblies and the senate were dissolved. Elections to the national and provincial elections are expected to take place by October 2002.

Major Political Parties: The two largest political parties are the Nawaz Sharif group of the Pakistan Muslim League (PML-N), led by former Prime Minister Nawaz Sharif, and the Pakistan People's Party (PPP), led by Benazir Bhutto. Both parties have a centrist orientation and support private enterprise and the free market. The PPP espouses a somewhat more activist view of government, especially in the social sector. The PML-N is slightly to the right of the PPP. Both parties stand discredited because their rule was marked by corruption, mismanagement and bad governance. (Some cynics say that the army is the biggest political party in Pakistan).

There are several other smaller, but significant, parties. The Muttahidda Qaumi Movement (United National Movement-MQM) is a party that claims to represent the interests of Pakistan's mohajirs (Urdu-speaking descendents of Muslims who migrated from India following the partition). The Awami National Party (ANP) is a Pushtun nationalist party in the NWFP. Both parties were allied with the PML-N for brief intervals. The Jamaat-i-Islami (JI) is the most organized Islamist political party. It has a formidable street power but very little electoral following. The Jamiat Ulema-i-Islam (JUI) of Maulana Fazlur Rahman has a significant following among the Pathans of the NWFP and Baluchistan.

INTERNATIONAL ASSISTANCE TO PAKISTAN

Pakistan's assets include a rich cultural heritage, abundant natural and human resources, a dynamic business community, a large and potentially more productive agriculture sector, and a strategic location for trade. Although Pakistan has been burdened by internal political instability and costly regional conflicts in its first 50 years of independence, it has still managed to achieve substantial economic growth.

While Pakistan's social welfare indicators have improved over the past two decades, progress remains slow and the challenges daunting. Only 40 percent of the population is literate (28 percent of women), compared to the average literacy rate of 49 percent in South Asia and 53 percent in low-income countries worldwide. Despite some improvements, gender disparities in education remain, with 62 percent of Pakistan's girls enrolling in school compared to 80 percent of its boys.

Pakistan has achieved some improvements in its health sector. The rates of immunization of most groups of children have more than doubled over the past decade and knowledge of family planning has increased remarkably and is almost universal.

Yet health indicators have been improving very slowly. One in every 38 women dies from pregnancy-related causes. And infant mortality remains high at about 90 per 1,000 live births, compared with an average of 73 per 1,000 in South Asian countries and 83 per 1,000 in low-income countries worldwide.

A significant share of Pakistan's population still suffers from acute poverty.

TECHNOLOGY POLICY

For further details please visit: http://most.gov.pk/

- The Government will play the role of a moderator, facilitator and an enabler, rather than a director, in the local IT industry's development.
- Computer Software and Information Technology (IT) have been declared as Industry and placed in Category 'B' of Industries. Annex XXIII
- Zero percent customs duty on import of IT related machinery and equipment as listed at Annex XXIV.
- Tax relief : Initial Depreciation Allowace (IDA) @50% of machinery & equipment cost.
- The rate of depreciation on computer equipment is 30%.
- Information Technology (IT) enjoys the status of "industry".
- The cost of Internet bandwidth has been drastically reduced by 65%.
- To facilitate the private sector IT telecom industry and to enhance the investor's confidence in the Government, processing period for license applications in the deregulated sector has been reduced to 7 days.
- In order to deliver efficient IT infrastructure, PTCL, would now provide international bandwidth and Internet connectivity to the ISPs and other corporate customers within 4 to 8 weeks.
- As a first step towards, Electronic Commerce, the State Bank of Pakistan (SBP) has allowed banks to open Internet Merchant Accounts within Pakistan.
- Internet delivery on Cable TV has been permitted which would result in substantial increase in the Internet usage.
- Universal Access to the Internet even to non connected areas at the cost of a local using the unique '131' Universal Internet Numbers of ISPs has been extended.
- Call Centers, which are important potential source of foreign exchange earnings and employment creation, have been allowed to establish in the private sector.
- Computer networking and majority of IT equipment has been exempted from custom duties.
- Income tax holiday for the IT Training Institutions has been extended by another five years.
- Income of computer training institutions set up to 30-06-2005 is exempt from Income Tax.
- Banks are allowed to invest in the form of equity in dedicated venture.
- Software companies are allowed to retain 35% of their export earning in foreign exchange to meet the expenditure on purchase of hardware/software, foreign travel, marketing and hiring of consultants.
- Tax exemption on export of software for 15 years.

PETROLEUM POLICY OF PAKISTAN

- It provides package for both the upstream as well as downstream activities.
- It covers mobilization of greater resources and promoters private sector investment for enhancing domestic oil and gas production.
- Improved incentives package, procedure, regulatory frame work and transparency are the key features of 1997 - Petroleum Policy.
- Initiative has been taken and further efforts are underway to attract private investment in improving oil & gas infrastructure as well as its distribution.
- No government permission required for setting up refineries.
- Import parity price formula based on Singapore mean.
- Import of crude oil from any source will be allowed.
- Export of surplus products will also be allowed.
- 3 MNCs (PSO, Shell, Caltex) are marketing petroleum products.
- 2 new companies (Attock Petroleum and PARCO - Total) have also be allowed for marketing pet. products.
- Investment Policy covers oil refining and manufacture of petroleum products under Hi-Tech category. This import of PME is allowed at zero-rated customs duty and Initial Depreciation Allowance (IDA) @50% of PME cost is available.
- A new Offshore Prospectivity Zone 'O' created to provide following incentives for offshore E&P :
- Agreement : Production Sharing Contract.
- Royalty : 0% for first 4 years of Commercial Production rising to 5% in year 5, 10% in year 6 and 12.5% thereafter.
- Cost Recovery : Limited to 85% including royalty of 12.5%.
- Corporate Tax : capped at 40% (compared to 50-55% for Onshore).
- Import duties and taxes to be zero for exploration and 3% after the first commercial discovery.
- Production Bonuses :
- US$ 1 million at start of Production (within 90 days).
- US$ 2 million upon reaching 200 MMcfd or equivalent.
- US$ 5 million upon reaching 600 MMcfd or equivalent.
- Oil & Gas Price : Same as Petroleum Policy 1994.
- A Green Area Map has been identified where no clearance would be required for concession blocks falling inside the green areas.
- All applications for exploration licences are decided within 60 days. Applications, which are contested, may take up to 120 days but no more.
- The Government of Pakistan would institute programs like basin studies, geological/ geo-chemical studies, seismic surveys etc., directly on a multi-client basis, through services contractors.

OIL & GAS 10 YEAR ROAD MAP FOR PRIVATE INVESTMENT

- Deregulated oil and gas sector completely. Government to be responsible only for policy formulation.
- Increase number of exploratory wells per year from current 15 to 100.
- Increase oil production from current 56,000 to 100,000 barrels per day
- Increase gas production from current 2.4 to 5.0 billion cubic feet per day.
- Reduce import of refined products to 90% of total consumption. This will require additional refining capacity of above 6 million tones per year. Eliminate imports of fuel oil.
- Construct cross-country oil pipelines to introduce efficiency and reduce burden on roads.

- Increase oil storage capacity from current 19 days cover to 45 days.
- Strengthen R&D support to the Government.
- Eliminate lead in gasoline. Reduce sulphur in diesel oil from current 1% to 0.05%. Promote CNG for diesel oil substitution.
- Encourage trans-boundary trade of clean energy (natural gas) and promote regional energy cooperation in South Asia.

POWER POLICY

POLICY FOR POWER PROJECTS

- The basis for selection of private power project will be the minimum levelized tariff either through International Competitive Bidding (ICB) for solicited proposals or through
- Without a proper feasibility study for a particular site-specific hydel or indigenous fuel based/ renewable resource based project, it will not be possible to invite competitive bids
- Hydel projects will be implemented on Build-Own-Operate-Transfer (BOOT) basis.
- Thermal projects would either be built on BOOT or Build-Own-Operate (BOO) basis.
- Private power companies will be allowed to import plant and equipment (for hydel & thermal projects), not manufactured locally completely exempted from the payment of taxes

Incentives

Wapda, priority dispatch with economic load dispatch criteria under hydel projects are the key features of the special incentives announced in the new policy.

- Under the pre-qualification criteria, main sponsors to have a 20 percent stake in equity and together with other partners will have direct and relevant experience in development or implementation or ownership or operation in similar projects; demonstrated capability for financing (equity & debt) and main sponsors not to own 25 per cent of total generation.

CORPORATE AGRICULTURE FARMING (CAF)

Pakistan's Agriculture Base:

Strengths	Abundant agricultural land
Total area	79.6 Mn Hectares (MH)
Cultivated area	22 MH
Irrigated	18 MH
Rainfed (Barani)	4 MH

Contribution to economy

<TD < TD>

- 26% to GDP
- Employs 44% of labour force (16.35 Mn)
- 70% of exports (Agri-produce & processed products)

Natural Merits

<TD < TD>

- 4 seasons, tropical weather
- Crop production throughout the year
- Largest canal irrigation network
- Vast tracts of land along Indus Basin - comprising 5 rivers
- Centuries old farming culture

Amongst the lowest cost producers

<TD < TD>

- Cost effective and hardworking agricultural manpower
- Low cost irrigation water
- Reasonable price of land
- Farm to market road network
- Competitive cost of inputs
- Crops production

Wheat	21 Mn tons

Cotton	11 Mn bales
Rice	5 Mn tons
Sugarcane	55 Mn tons
Fruits/Vegetables	10 Mn tons
Fisheries & Livestock production	
Fisheries potential (annual catch)	7.5 Mn Tons
Buffaloes (Number)	23 Mn Tons
Cattle (Number)	22 Mn Tons
Sheep & Goats (Number)	75 Mn Tons
Poultry (Number)	530 Mn Tons

Country side

- Traditional but simple culture
- Inspiring music
- Lively folk

- **Strategic location**
  - Located in food deficit region:

<TD < TD> <TD < TD>

- Central Asian Republic (North)
- Middle East (South)
- Iran & Afghanistan (West)
- Principal gateway to CARs

- **Strong historical & traditional links**

Strong Potential

- Comparative advantage in the region
- Vast areas of cultivable waste land available
- Strong potential for expansion of agriculture base
- Corporate Agriculture Farming (CAF):
- Objectives
- Large local market increasing at 29% per year
- Internationally competitive unit cost of production for all major crops, fruits & vegetables
- High quality agricultural products due to favourable resource base
- Low transportation cost, and developed routes to Middle East, Iran, Afghanistan and CARs
- International Quality inputs available in country
- Market driven polices. Least Government interventions

Investment Policy, Incentives & Opportunities:

Corporate Agriculture Farming (CAF)

Pakistan has an Agri-based economy with a very well developed agriculture sector and most of the labour is engaged in the Agriculture Sector. It has vast tracts of cultivable land offering the prospective investor lucrative returns and rich harvests on his investment. Corporate Agriculture

Farming (CAF) Package is beening developed..

Investment Policy for CAF

<TD < TD>

- 60% foreign equity allowed
- Minimum $ 0.3 foreign investment
- Remittance of capital, profits, dividends allowed

Fiscal Incentives for CAF

Projects/Investment Opportunities

- Agri-produce storage facilities
- Marketing/export of agri-produce
- Cool chains

National Housing Policy 2005

Key Features:

- The overall housing stock comprise of 39% kuchha houses, 40% semi-pukka houses and 21% pukka houses.
- The housing backlog, as estimated according to the 1998 census, was 4.30 million units.
- The annual additional requirement is estimated around 570,000 housing units whereas the annual production is estimated around 300,000 housing units
- To make up the backlog and to meet the shortfall in the next 20 years the overall housing production has to be raised to 500,000 housing units annually.
- A Housing Advisory Board of nearly 40 members, half of them from private sector was constituted in the Ministry of Housing and Works to formulate a workable National Housing Policy.
- The objective is to create affordability, specially, for the middle and low-income groups. One of the corner stones of the Policy is to ensure

Policy Measures:

- HBFC and other financial institutions shall formulate packages of preferential/ concessional rates with affordable system of installments for repayment to provide affordable credit to low income groups
- Foreclosure laws shall be introduced to ensure effective recovery of loans and advances from the defaulters
  Property tax on rented property shall be reduced from the current high rate of 25% to 5%
- Mark-up on Housing loan installment for individuals shall be treated as expense in tax return
- Banks and DFIs shall extend credit facilities for Balancing, Modernisation and Replacement (BMR) of machinery used for Housing and Construction Industry
- Import of plant and machinery and spares by the housing and construction companies, not manufactured locally, shall be exempt from custom and import duties in excess of 10%
- Stamp duties and registration fees shall be adequately reduced to an aggregate total value of 1%
- Initiation of low cost housing scheme and provision of cross subsidy to the poor through auction of commercial plots
- Subsidized micro loaning facilities shall be extended for rural housing construction and improvements through micro financing systems and institutions like Khushhali Bank, Zakat funds, etc.
- Provision of trunk infrastructure shall be the responsibility of utility agencies like WAPDA, PTCL, SNGPL, SSGCL, KESC, etc. The cost of trunk infrastructure shall not be an additional charge to the public or private housing development scheme within the planned area

POLICY PACKAGE FOR DEVELOPING UP COUNTRY GRAINS STORAGE FACILITIES

Objective:

- To maintain domestic strategic reserves and exports specially through land route.

Type of Storage:

- Concrete/metallic Silos for dedicated grains storage

Scope of Services/Specifications:

- Purchase of wheat from farms/markets

- Investors can agree with MINFAL/PASSCO all or part of the above services. Facilities for additional services can also be established by the investors. Rate negotiable accordingly. Existing cost of the Government will be the guiding principle
  Specifications of Wheat at the time of receipt and delivery will be provided by PASSCO.

Capacity Utilization Assurance:

- Minimum 5 years

INVESTMENT POLICY & INCENTIVES:

- Build- Operate-Own (BOO)
- Credit availability at Mark-up as for agriculture sector
- 100% foreign equity will be allowed
- Remittances of capital, profits etc. allowed

Customs duty on import of Plant, machinery & equipment (PME):

- 5% (SRO: 358(I)/2002)

Tax Relief:

- Initial Depreciation Allowance (IDA) @ 50% of PME cost

TEXTILE VISION

MEASURES FOR THE TEXTILE SECTOR

INSTITUTIONAL:

•The concerned Government agencies like EPB and BOI should make a concerted effort to uplift the country image.
•A Textile Board (TB) should be established to continuously monitor the policy implementation and coordinate all the Government-related affairs in textile sector.
•Constitute TB by nominating members from public and private sector and providing the legal framework to define its role.
•To improve the country image as a quality textile product supplier and to facilitate the international buyers in Pakistan, Textile cities should be established in Karachi and Lahore.
•Initiate a study for establishment of textile cities.
•Revive the already established Federal Export Board (FEB) and hold regular meetings every alternate month. Timely remedial action should be initiated by the concerned authorities in case the performance is below the set targets.
•Ministry of Commerce should develop its strength for dealing with the listed issues.
•Participants of any trade fair from Pakistan should be meeting certain minimum standards.
•Steps should be taken to ensure dissemination of information to the exporters.
•Set up help desks in concerned Government departments for the purpose.
•Augment existing crop estimation committee with satellite monitoring.

•TCP should act as price stabilizing third buyer for lint. It should purchase lint at export parity price and act as a market maker in case a situation arises. (Phutti price falls below the economic threshold for the growers).
•Committee should be formed to study the pros and cons of Cotton Hedge Markets.
•Phutti and lint grading standards of Pakistan Cotton Standards Institute (PCSI) should be implemented.
•Ginning research institute should be established to support the ginning industry.

TARIFF:

•Ensure free availability of inputs for exporters.
•Revamp temporary import schemes.
•Pass book system.
•Involvement of commercial banks in monitoring temporary imports.
•Cotton should be allowed to be trade freely.
•Remove excise duty on import of cotton lint greater than 28 mm staple length.
•Imports of saw gin blades should be exempt from customs duty till the time that it is manufactured locally.

FISCAL & MONETARY:

•The rate of export refinance should be reduced keeping in view the recent reduction in interest rates in the country.
•The hurdles towards those cash awards on better export performance should be removed and awards should be given to the deserving exporters.
•Initiate a scheme (Export Growth Project Finance (EGPF) for provision of long-term credit at lower rates to textile industry, in which the amount of credit is linked with the past year's performance of the exporter. Interest rates in this scheme will be cascaded according to the extent of value addition in the textile value chain, the highest value-added sector getting the lowest interest rate. In case of forward integration, interest rate will be lower than that in case of backward integration.
•Rebates and duty drawback rates should be calculated on the basis of input output coefficients.
•Timely revision in the rates should be made in case of increased input cost.
•A vendor whose 80% of production is consumed for producing export goods should be treated as an Indirect Exporter and be able to avail the benefits of a similar tax structure as for direct exporters.
•Sales tax on cotton lint and oil cake at the ginning stage should be abolished.
•Export refinance facility should be available only to 40 count and above.
•The mechanism of linkage of exchange rate with basket of currencies should be strengthened.

PRODUCT MIX:

•Exempt the duty on import of manmade fibers not produced in Pakistan.
•Phase out the import duty on manmade fibers produced in Pakistan.
•Product and market diversification should be promoted through quota incentives.

QUOTA:

•Quota to be allocated on the basis of value not on performance alone.

•Ensure consistency in the quota policy. Policy once formulated in the best interest of the country should not be altered before the completion of its designated period.
•Provision should be made in the quota policy to facilitate the new exporters.

TECHNOLOGY:

•Imports of textile machinery older than ten years should be banned.
•Provide subsidized credit to textile manufacturers to upgrade their technology through a 'Technology Upgradation fund'. (TUF).
•Import of textile machinery for these sectors be allowed duty free.
•Top priority should be given to stitching industry that leads to highest value addition and employment generation.
•Provision of funds should be made through TUF.
•Existing exporters of garments and made ups should be provided financing through EGPF.
•Import of hand-held ultra low volume spraying equipment should be exempted from import duty and sales tax.
•Promote air jet weaving technology for cotton and blended fabrics.
•Upgrade smaller units of power looms (up to 50 looms) to auto looms and power loom units larger than 50 looms to air jet looms.
•Promote water jet technology for weaving of synthetic fabric.
•Develop special incentive package for promoting growth of processing industry in Pakistan.
•Provision of long-term funds for project financing should be made available through EGPF scheme and TUF.

HUMAN RESOURCES:

•Establish a separate training wing within proposed Textile Board.
•Provide licensing authority to the board for all new VTIs.
•Standardize courses, faculty and facilities in each subsection of textile.
'Introduce training courses of shorter duration.
•Initiate national textile curriculum development task. The exercise shall cover all sub sectors of the textile value chain.
•Evaluate possibility of hiring foreign consultants for short fixed duration to train the trainers.
•Institute for training the trainers.
•Utilization of EDF for equipping Vocational Training Institutions.
•Put manufacturers and exporters on the board of all Vocational Training Institutions and Government should discontinue funding after a specific grace period.

CUSTOMS DUTY & TAXATION (Investment Policy):

•5% Customs duty on import of machinery which is not manufactured locally.
•Initial Depreciation Allowance @ 50% of machinery cost.

NATURAL RESOURCE ASPECTS OF SUSTAINABLE DEVELOPMENT IN PAKISTAN

AGRICULTURE

Legislation covering Agriculture and Rural development includes: **Insect Pest Control Act of 1959**; **The Pesticide ordinance of 1971**; the **Pakistan Pesticides Rules of 1973**; and the **Pakistan Agriculture Research Centre XXXVIII of 1981**.

Pakistan is an agricultural country, and more than 50% of its population is employed in the agricultural sector. Less than 20% of Pakistan's land can be intensively farmed, nearly all of which is cultivated. In 1990, 209,400 km2 were in use as farmland. In general, farmers lack knowledge of operating characteristics and full capabilities of technologies within the agricultural sector. Pakistan is faced with some common problems in both irrigated and rainfed areas used for agriculture. These problems can be summarized as erosion of soil, underuse of organic fertilizers and overuse of synthetic chemicals. In rainfed areas, overextensive cultivation is common.

The decision for intensification of farm lands in Pakistan stems from demographic reality. In rough terms, one hectare of cultivated land supported an average 5 people in 1993; by the year 2010, it is estimated that the same land must support nearly 10. Pakistan has developed strategies to ensure food security by 1998, which also includes the agricultural sector. The strategies to ensure food security by 1998 and to address rural welfare include women, indigenous people, local communities and NGOs. Local communities and NGOs are taken into consideration to review international trade relations and agricultural production. Women, youth, indigenous people, and local communities are also involved through workshops in developing and strengthening institutional capacity for plant genetic resources.

In 1981-82, a programme called "Matching Grants Programme" (MGP) was initiated. The MGP focuses on the development of infrastructure in rural areas, and is based on community participation. To date, about 22,000 schemes have been implemented in 26.500 villages. The MGP is financed as follows: half is funded through the Union Councils together with the communities, either in cash, or in kind; and the other half through the Directorate General of Local Government and Rural Development (DGLGRD). An evaluation of the MGP showed that the programme has had a noteworthy effect on the communities in terms of raising both socio-economic standards, and mass-awareness of hygiene and environmental conditions. Numerous meetings and working groups have been initiated to strengthen the knowledge and capacity within food production, improve access to agricultural markets, and manage land and fertilizer use.

A National Rural Support Programme was established to promote education and health, based on community participation. In 1993, this programme was supported by the Government with Rs.1,000,000. MGP is structured so that the local councillor is normally the leader of the Project Committee which approves the projects. The councillor is responsible for collecting community finance.

In 1994-95, all of the Public Sector Development programmes were assisted by international organizations or foreign governments. The assistance provided included both human and financial resources, by various organizations such as FAO, UNDP, and the World Bank.

ATMOSPHERE

The Montreal Protocol (1987) was ratified in December 1992, the **London Amendment** (1990) was ratified in December 1992, and the **Copenhagen Amendment** (1992) was ratified on May 18, 1995. The **United Nations Framework Convention on Climate Change** was ratified on 1

June 1994 and entered into force on 30 August, 1994.

The Pakistan Environment Protection Council (PEPC) has jurisdiction in this area, and it has established **National Environmental Quality Standards** (NEQS). Protection of the atmosphere is one of the fourteen core issues in the **National Conservation Strategy** of Pakistan. PEPC has established a Committee on Clean Fuels, which has the mandate to make recommendations for the alleviation of atmospheric pollution. An incentive reduction scheme has been recommended in relation to the emissions from Compressed Natural Gas and Liquid Petroleum Gas powered buses, trucks, and urban public services, and a mandatory introduction of catalytic converters in two-stroke engines by July 1997 has been suggested. Vehicle emission regulations, are also being set to include Nox, Sox, SPM and Lead by the expert committee of PEPC.

Pakistan's greenhouse gas emissions are nominal, of which energy generation, industry and households are major consumers. A Cabinet Committee on Climate Change met for the first time on March 27th 1995. Its purpose is to monitor, evaluate and prepare strategies to cope with adverse impacts of climate change by creating an appropriate institutional mechanism which would operate by taking into account all sectors. Pakistan has developed a system of inventory of all green gases not controlled by the Montreal Protocol, which is periodically updated.

The diesel and furnace oil being marketed in Pakistan have a high sulphur (SO2) content. Pakistan is also facing numerous problems from the lack of efficient fuel burning, abnormal exhaust emissions from automobiles, inadequate tuning of engines, and improper repairs and maintenance. These problems mainly affect the larger cities where breathing difficulties can occur during peak-hours. Air quality clashing with the WHO standards is costing Pakistan about Rs. 25 billion a year from adverse health and other effects. The number of vehicles in the country increased from 0.85 million in 1982 to 2.8 million in 1995, showing an overall increase of 229%. It is envisaged that, with the present rate of growth, the number of vehicles will increase to 4.5 million by the year 2004, thereby adding to quantum green house gases.

The Energy Conservation Centre (ENERCON) has put together some programmes to reduce the output of greenhouse gases. These programmes involve:

- setting up tuning demonstration centres in nine cities;
- training 1,000 mechanics and workshop owners;
- providing funding for 100 tuning centres;
- conducting surveys that will lead to new policies and projects.

It has also proposed setting up a computerized database on the quality of air for the six largest cities in Pakistan.

The Ministry of Environment has approved the project "Fuel Efficiency in Road Transport" at a cost of Rs. 230.58 million, including a Rs. 220.55 million grant under GEF. The project will be executed by ENERCON. The United Nations has extended major support to this project through UNDP. Support for phasing out Ozone Depletion Substances is provided through cooperation with UNDP, the World Bank and UNIDO.

BIODIVERSITY

Pakistan is a party to a number of nature conservation **Conventions** which include :

- The Convention on International Trade in Endangered Species of Wild Fauna and Flora (CITES)
- The Convention on Conservation of Migratory Species (CMS) - Bonn Convention
- The Convention on Wetlands of international Importance Especially as Waterfowl Habitat (Ramsar Convention)
- World Heritage Convention
- The Convention on Biological Diversity (CBD)
- The Framework Convention on Climate Change
- The Convention to Combat Desertification in Countries Experiencing Drought and/or Desertification, Particularly in Africa (CCD) (Pakistan is a signatory and its ratification is being processed).

The Ministry of Environment, Local Government and Rural Development is responsible for the implementation of this sector. The Ministry is involved in national decision-making. Local communities, including women, are involved in the conservation of biodiversity. Pakistan has initiated preparation of a **Biodiversity Action Plan** (BAP) which should be completed in its first phase by the time that CSD V is convened (April 1997). The second phase of preparation will begin as soon as further GEF funding has been made available.

There is a great need for capacity-building in all of the relevant institutions in Pakistan in all of the components of biodiversity. For example, the conservation of species and protected areas management requires the capacity of the provincial wildlife departments.

There is a great need to appoint Park Managers in the National Parks. Presently, Forest Officers are posted in the National Parks as Park Managers, but they can be transferred wherever needed to other forest areas without the consideration of the needs of the specific National Park or Protected Area. The reason for this is because of financial constraints, as the Provincial Forests Departments cannot afford to place separate Wildlife Managers.

The Provincial Wildlife Departments need to have permanent resource persons to make inventories in the protected areas, since the inventories that are made for PAs are not sufficient for policy formulation. The protected areas need well-equipped staff for checking the poaching of wildlife. Well-equipped Park Centres are required in order to raise awareness within local communities. A sum of Rs. 52.5 million has been allocated to halt the decline in the state of Pakistan's biological resources within its ecosystems.

Pakistan has been successful in implementing the above-mentioned Conventions and this has resulted in a new lease on life for wild animals and the conservation of protected areas, including wetlands, and coastal areas. There is a great need to develop a mechanism for the implementation of all the Conventions.

CITES, for example, can only be made effective if the Management and Scientific Authorities in the developing countries under CITES are made strong by increasing their capacity both in terms of finance, technology and staffing. Their research capabilities need to be extended. Rescue centres, which are required to be designated by the Parties, do not have the capacity to host confiscated species, and therefore specific funding for this is required, particularly for Authorities and Custom Officers. Training of Customs Officers as well as Enforcement Officers is needed and which also requires funding in developing countries.

Pakistan has many wetlands of international importance, but so far, few could be identified for listing in the Wetlands Conventions. This Convention also does not have an effective funding mechanism. The Monitoring procedure of the Wetlands Convention could not assist Pakistan in developing its Wetlands and Coastal Areas, and there is a great need for such a mechanism to be strengthened.

Only the Convention on Biological Diversity has a funding mechanism, while other Conventions do not. The governments, especially developing country parties, have to bear the costs of implementation of the obligations of the Conventions. Therefore, there is a great need for all of the Conventions to be technically and financially supported through the GEF mechanism and extended to all developing country parties. CSD should ensure that the funding of the developing country Parties is made obligatory, without which the world's heritage is not likely to be conserved on a sustainable basis.

Pakistan has many sites which could qualify for designation as sites for the World Heritage Convention. The search for an outstanding site which may qualify needs special attention. All previous efforts of Pakistan have not been agreed to by the World Heritage Committee, and due to a lack of funds, Pakistan could not explore such sites. There is, therefore, a need for UN Agencies and other international donors to come forward and assist Pakistan and other developing country parties in the identification of World Heritage Sites so as to save them from any further deterioration and take measures for their development.

Pakistan is a Party to the Convention on Biological Diversity and has taken up many measures before becoming a Party to this Convention. Pakistan has 15 National Parks, 86 Wildlife Sanctuaries and an equal number of Game Reserves. Management Plans have been prepared for 3 National Parks. The implementation of the management plans of these National Parks and preparation of the management plans for the remaining National Parks is required immediately. Similarly, many species are endangered and plans for their recovery are to be made immediately.

Through the funding of US$ 313,000 being provided through the Global Environment Fund, Pakistan initiated the preparation of a Biodiversity Action Plan (BAP), to be completed by the first quarter of 1997. However, this is a continuous activity and the BAP is likely to require further funding for its second phase. An investment proposal is also being prepared for the management and development of three selected Protected Areas of Pakistan through possible funding by the GEF. A project entitled "Maintaining Biodiversity in Pakistan with Rural Community Development" is being funded by the GEF through UNDP at a cost of US$2.5 million. Upon the successful completion of the project, it is likely that Pakistan may receive another 3.5 million US$ from GEF through UNDP.

DESERTIFICATION AND DROUGHT

The International Convention to Combat Desertification in Countries Experiencing Drought and/or Desertification, Particularly in Africa was signed 15 October 1994 and ratified 24 February 1997. A **National Plan for Combatting Desertification** has been developed and approved by the Interim Secretariat of the Convention. The United Nations Environment Programme is providing financial assistance of US$60,000 for the preparation of the National Plan for Combatting Desertification, a plan which will soon become operational.

The institutions responsible for this sector are the Pakistan Agricultural Research Council, the Arid Zone Research Council, Pakistan Forest Institute, the Pakistan Council of Research in Water Resources, the Pakistan Environmental Protection Agency, Water and the Power Authority, and the Ministry of Environment, Urban Affairs, Forestry and Wildlife and Energy Conservation. The legislation to combat desertification was revised in 1994. NGOs have independent programming which includes women's participation. Youths are not involved.

Current land use knowledge in Pakistan is based on Satellite Imagery Interpretation. Relevant NGOs have mass-awareness programmes. Land degradation and human impact assessment have not yet been covered, although some surveys were done dating back to 1988. There is a serious shortage of trained staff and management, in addition to the lack of financial resources.

The **National Conservation Strategy** on restoring rangelands and improving livestock quality investment programme 1992-2005, is estimated to cost US$ 82.63 million.

Experts from Pakistan have assisted Mongolia and Iran in the preparation of their National Action Programmes.

FORESTS

The forest inventory identified a forest area of 0.042 million km2 in 1991. Forests are divided on the basis of whether they are state-owned or private-owned forests. The state-owned forests are again divided into four categories: reserved, protected, unclassified and resumed lands. Two-thirds of the public forest are non-commercial. The remaining one-third, located mostly on steep and unstable slopes of the Himalayas, is harvested. Production of timber from commercial forests is about 0.5 million m3.

Pakistan has the objective of doubling its forest area, from the existing 5% to 10% of total land area. In order to meet this target, the Government has initiated various projects in an umbrella campaign of a **Massive Afforestation Programme** (MAP). This programme has five main components:

- 1. Mobilization of resources;
- 2. Nursery development;
- 3. Procurement of large forest lands;
- 4. Ensuring adequate technical capacity; and
- 5. Monitoring plantations.

Numerous Public and Private Sector Corporations, from the National Highway Authority to Sui Southern Gas Company, have been involved in planting a total of

FRESHWATER

In general, Pakistan needs to address a vast array of problems regarding water usage since, for example forty percent of urban deaths are caused by water-borne diseases. Special focus is also needed in terms of sodicity, water mining and the accumulation of salt in commercial crop roots. Surface water from rivers is the primary source of water in Pakistan. Infiltration from rivers, canals, watercourses, and fields is the main source of groundwater, which is a secondary resource. The limitation on some of the water available cannot be facilitated through storage dams. Pakistan is struggling with the fact that only 30% of the diverted water at canal heads reaches crop roots. In general, Pakistan needs much integrated water and soil improvement. A nationwide study is being carried out to strengthen the baseline data on the state of existing urban and industrial waste water treatment facilities. This information will become the background material for a **National Master Plan** for this area.

Pakistan also has an on-going research-project which aims at assessing the water requirements of different species. The idea is to use the information for various forest extension projects. A water survey and analysis was carried out in Quetta, Pakistan.

The Kabul and Ravi Rivers provide food, directly through fishing and indirectly through irrigation, as well as water for both drinking and industry. The Asian Development Bank has worked with the Ministry of Environment, Urban Affairs, Forestry and Wildlife, under an Umbrella Technical Assistance Agreement, to study Rivers Kabul and Ravi and their environmental state. The initial study on River Kabul was conducted with the assistance of the International Union for Conservation of Nature (IUCN).

The Rawal Lake has been selected for special attention concerning unsustainable activities, such as building latrines at specific locations and construction of septic tanks in the existing settlements. In addition, three projects have been recommended, concerning improvement of catchment areas and the provision of septic tanks and watershed management. In the specific case of pollution control in the Rawal Lake, a Committee under the chairman of the Chief Commissioner in Islamabad was constituted by the Pakistan Environmental Protection Council (PEPC). The Government of Punjab has been asked to provide funding of Rs. 57.75 million for the projects recommended for the Rawal Lake.

A pilot project in Karachi has been cleared for implementation. The concept of the project is to recycle waste water by sewage collection and by conveying the waste water to irrigate areas via underground pipes. The project also involves the use of a low capital and operating costs [Lagoon] system, and developing 500 hectares of land for irrigation. This project is a joint venture between the Karachi Water and Sewerage Board, and a private Austrian firm.

LAND MANAGEMENT

The institutions responsible for implementation in this sector are the Water and Power Development Authority (WAPDA); the Pakistan Agricultural Research Council, NGOs and Planning and Development Departments. These bodies are members of National Coordination Mechanisms for Sustainable Development.

Pakistan faces a general lack of capacity of institutions to promote an integrated approach to the planning and management of land resources. However, policies related to capacity building, management and technology are at the planning stage.

MOUNTAINS

The institutions responsible for mountain issues are the Governments of Azad Jammu & Kashmir; North West Frontier Province; Northern Area; Punjab and Sindh. Legislation regarding this sector includes: the Pakistan Forest Act of 1927, the Hazara Guzara 1936 Act, the Provincial Wildlife Legislation and the Provincial Fisheries Legislation.

Pakistan has five significant mountain systems: Western Himalayas, Karakoram, Hindukush, Suleman and Kirthar. Pakistan is troubled by the lack of land-use planning and land-use control, uncertain land tenure and an inadequate policy on sustainable development in mountain areas. The monitoring systems of the meteorological situation are poor, and have not improved since the 1980s.

The mountain areas which are cultivated suffer from soil and water erosion, as well as limited infrastructure and marketing facilities. These problems lead to a need for sustainable economic diversification, especially since, despite intensification of the use of farmlands in the mountain areas, these lands will never be able to accommodate the additional population growth expected and already apparent.

The Cabinet Committee on Climate Change has made recommendations to strengthen legislation in order to protect an area called Margallah Hills. The idea is to extend the existing area of Margallah Hills and then impose special regulations to preserve fauna, flora, bio-diversity and forests. Recommendations for the legislation are focused on prohibiting mining and quarrying, and preventing industry and manufacturing from getting established in these areas.

OCEANS AND COASTAL AREAS

The **UN Convention on the Law of the Sea** was signed December 1982 and ratified 26 February 1997.

The Ministry of Environment, Urban Affairs, Forestry and Wildlife is responsible for the overall implementation in this sector. Pakistan has access to and applies state-of-art technologies in the Marine Environmental Unit. The Pakistani coast is exposed to negative environmental impacts from thermal pollution, increased oil spills, tarballs, and plastic and toxic effluents, including heavy metal. The coastal strip of Pakistan is arid, with fewer than 20 centimeters precipitation a year. Pakistan has mangrove on approximately 800,000 acres of swamp.

The Karachi Port is mostly polluted by non-port-related activities. An estimated 90,000 tons of oil products from vessels and the port's terminals are dumped every year in the port's water. To address the problem, the Karachi Port Trust has signed MARPOL 1972-1979. A green belt around Karachi Port is being implemented. The project includes planting 150,000 mangroves and 350,000 various other plants.

The Port Quasim Authority initiated a number of activities which include mangrove plantations and locating industries in large industrial estates to clear the coastline.

An allocation of Rs. 350 million was distributed among three projects: a Marine Pollution Control Centre which handles emergency oil spills; a Marine Environmental Unit to monitor water, air, sediment and biota quality; and a Marine Pollution Board. The last has been established to handle matters which are related to marine life and environment, and resources at risk; to provide advisory services to relevant organizations; and to review monthly progress in combatting and controlling marine pollution.

TOXIC CHEMICALS

The environmentally sound management of toxic chemicals is a core issue of the **National Conservation Strategy**. A Committee has been appointed by the Pakistan Environmental Protection Council, to make surveys and recommendations concerning the alarming conditions of Hospital Waste. In Pakistan, around 250,000 tones of hazardous medical waste are produced annually. Management of this type of waste has not yet been achieved. This committee is collaborating with the Ministry of Environment, Urban Affairs, Forestry and Wildlife, and they have launched a joint action plan. The joint action plan to deal with medical wastes underlines the need for more training and education of relevant personnel, identification and strengthening of the proper institutions, and an initiative to raise awareness of problems.

Pakistan is suffering from the adverse soil, air and occupational effects caused by the use of chemicals in the textile and leather industries. These problems have led to various projects aimed at reducing pollution from the industries. The projects address toxic effluent reduction by using appropriate technology transfer, recycling chrome recovery, establishing institutions for in-house pollution control in the tanneries, and by establishing industrial complexes which provide the leather industry with the infrastructure and utilities required.

A Government project regarding the tanneries in Kasur City has an estimated cost of Rs. 264 million, which is being financed partly by a UNDP grant of 6.85 million US $, and a 30% contribution of the total cost by the Tanneries Association of Kasur.

WASTE AND HAZARDOUS MATERIALS

Solid Waste and Sanitation

The privatization of solid waste management was initiated by the Ministry of Environment, Urban Affairs, Forestry and Wildlife. The Ministry is also responsible for the proposals in connection with the recycling of paper in Federal Government Offices.

There is practically no solid waste management in Pakistan. Around 40% of the waste is discarded in the streets or at collection sites. Projects to enhance the capacity for solid waste at the municipal level have been established. Only half of the urban wastes is disposed in sewers, with most remaining untreated. Solid waste treatment has been privatized in order to keep up with the demand for solid waste treatment services. Only Karachi and Islamabad have sewage treatment plants. Communities are being encouraged to participate in enhancing solid waste treatment capacities.

The environmentally sound management of sewerage and solid waste is a core issue in the **National Conservation Strategy** of Pakistan. Consequently, **National Environment Quality Standards** have been implemented for issues related to this sector. This has led to some concrete measures; for example the waste problems of cement factories are being addressed by installing anti-pollution technology. The installation of anti-pollution measures in the Cement Industry is being assisted by UNIDO, Chinese experts, and M/S Environmental Resources Management, U.S.A.

The following recommendations have been made to counter the consumption of 20,000 tonnes of paper within the Federal Administration:

- an improvement in paper collection,
- an emphasis on the use of recycling; and
- the launching of mass awareness campaigns.

Hazardous Wastes

The **Basel Convention on the Control of Transboundary Movements of Hazardous Wastes and their Disposal** was ratified on 26 July, 1994.

The environmentally sound management of hazardous waste is one of the core issues in the **National Conservation Strategy** of Pakistan. The National Environment Quality Standard is being applied to the issue of waste management. In addition, Pakistan has prohibited the import of hazardous waste in accordance with the Basel Convention.

The industrialization of Pakistan has had an effect on the environment, especially since the discharging of waste is being done without consideration of the treatment facilities that are required to maintain sustainability. The private sector, namely industry, is the target for national policy.

Pakistan has implemented a Pollution Release Project to monitor select industries in the Province of Punjab. The project includes data collection and data comparison of the **National Environment Quality Standards**. The **proposed action plan** involves the collection of a pollution charge from defaulting industries under the National Environment Quality Standards.

GOVERNMENT REGULATION OF ECONOMIC DEVELOPMENT & ENVIRONMENT

INTEGRATED DECISION-MAKING

The Ministry of Environment, Urban Affairs, Forestry and Wildlife, and Energy Conservation is responsible for environmental issues. Pakistan has a fully developed **National Conservation Strategy** (NCS), which was approved by the Government on 1 March, 1992. In 1992, the Sustainable Development Policy Institute was created as an independent policy research institute in order to supervise and monitor the National Conservation Strategy. The NCS works on a ten-year planning and implementation cycle. The current cycle is 1992-2005. The NCS deals with 14 core issues, which are:

- 1. Maintaining soils in cropland;
- 2. Increasing irrigation efficiency;
- 3. Protecting watersheds;
- 4. Supporting forestry and plantations;
- 5. Restoring rangelands and improving livestock;
- 6. Protecting water bodies and sustaining fisheries;
- 7. Conserving biodiversity;
- 8. Increasing energy efficiency;
- 9. Developing and deploying material and energy renewables;
- 10. Preventing/abating pollution;
- 11. Managing urban wastes;
- 12. Supporting institutions for common resources;
- 13. Integrating population and environment programmes; and
- 14. Preserving the cultural heritage.

Based on the experience of the National Conservation Strategy, policies are being redirected at institutional strengthening and human resource development, especially at the local and provincial level.

Pakistan has prepared a draft **National Environmental Act**, which is to replace the **Pakistan Environmental Protection Ordinance** of 1983. This draft was prepared after consultations with more than 5000 individuals, organizations and groups including, trade and industry, environmental experts and NGOs. It has been submitted to the Cabinet for approval and is likely to be passed by the Parliament soon. The **Pakistan Environmental Protection Council** (PEPC) was set up in accordance with the legislation of 1983. The major functions of the Council include enforcement of the 1983 Ordinance and formulation of comprehensive national environmental policy. The PEPC has recommended creating a **Pakistan Environmental Fund** and an **Environmental Bank**. The PEPC is also responsible for setting up pressure groups and environmental clubs at workplaces and factories, in order to raise awareness and improve the environment.

Every proponent of a project, the construction or completion of which is likely to have an adverse affect on the environment, has to submit at the time of planning an **Environmental Impact Assessment** to the concerned Environmental Protection Agency in the Province, confirming that the project will comply with the National Environmental Quality Standards (NEQS).

The NEQS, which have received assistance from the Canadian International Development Agency (CIDA), are meant as a vehicle for protection of the environment. Such standards now exist for industrial and municipal effluents, and for motor exhaust and noise. Standards to establish a charge on polluters and to introduce self-monitoring systems were to be introduced by the 1st of July 1996. There is a Standing Expert Advisory Committee in charge of regularly up-dating the NESQ. A mass-awareness campaign about NEQS has been launched. In order to test the NEQS for effective implementation, the Government has set up a Central Laboratory for Environmental Analysis (CLEAN). Companies within the Pharmaceutical, Chemical, Tanner and Textile industries have been approached to assess the status of compliance to the NEQS.

MAJOR GROUPS

WOMEN

The **Convention on the Elimination of All Forms of Discrimination Against Women** was ratified on 12 March 1996. Pakistan has acknowledged that a higher level of development for and contribution from women is a precondition for achieving broad-based sustainable development. A permanent Ministry for Women's Development has been established and is responsible for training and education as well as the implementation of projects. There are hundreds of women's organizations in Pakistan. However, in the rural areas there is no network among NGOs focusing on women's issues. Family planning is receiving increased governmental attention because the population growth rate is considered both a hindrance to growth and a threat to sustainability. The active participation of women is being accentuated in this process.

NON-GOVERNMENTAL ORGANIZATIONS

In Pakistan, there are thousands of NGOs, hundreds of which are involved in environmental issues. The most prominent NGO in Pakistan is the IUCN of Pakistan which helped the Government finalize the draft **Pakistan Environmental Act** of 1996. Others are involved in the promotion of education, mass awareness and the empowerment of women. Unfortunately, the NGOs are poorly developed and relatively ineffective. However the assistance of the NGOs to the

Government is appreciated and considered productive. The **National Conservation Strategy** is based on the early warning and awareness-building facilities that the NGOs provide.

The Ministry of Environment, Urban Affairs, Forestry and Wildlife allocates around Rs. 30 million annually to NGOs for undertaking small-scale projects. In 1995-1996, some 147 projects carried out by 141 NGOs were financially assisted (Rs. 22.3 million) by the Government. This allocation is being handled by a Committee which also approves the NGOs and their projects and is receiving financial aid from the Global Environmental Facility (GEF).

LOCAL AUTHORITIES

The implementation of projects related to Agenda 21 issues is very much the responsibility of Provincial Governments. Therefore, it is fair to say that strengthening of authority at this level goes hand in hand with the promotion of sustainable development in Pakistan. Pakistan has initiated cross-sectoral projects which will enhance capacity regarding infrastructure, collecting and managing solid waste data, as well as other services for ten urban areas. The Provinces of Punjab and Sindh are planning projects which will contribute to increased public awareness and educational training. Some of them will be funded by the Asian Development Bank and the World Bank.

SCIENTIFIC AND TECHNOLOGICAL COMMUNITY

The National Scientific and Technological councils and associations are widening their membership. These organizations have launched various programmes for the benefit of the general public.

FARMERS

Pakistan, being an agriculture-based country, is fully aware of the significance of sustainable development practices. Various projects and programmes are in operation whereby farmers are being encouraged to apply sustainable farming practices.

SCIENCE

Science for sustainable development is at an early stage, which is reflected in its weak capacity features. For example, the science sector is not involved in decision-making at any level. It has not been given the attention that Agenda 21 calls for, in terms of increasing the number of scientists, nor the number of women being trained as scientists. In addition to the lack of promoting more scientific personnel, Pakistan has a serious problem with brain-drain to other countries.

INTERNATIONAL COOPERATION AND TRADE

The Ministry of Environment, Local Government and Rural Development is responsible for policy decisions on various issues concerning the environment. The **Pakistan Environment Protection Council** (PEPC) also exists in the Ministry under the Chairmanship of the Prime Minister. Some of the major functions of the PEPC include enforcement of the **Pakistan Environmental Protection Act**, 1996; and the formulation of National Environmental Policies. In order to promote environmental protection, the Government created the federal Ministry of Environment, Local Government and Rural Development and its technical branches Pak-EPA; four Provincial Departments of Environment, and EPAs. To cope with the environmental situation, EPAs need to be strengthened and well equipped. The International Union for Conservation of Nature (IUCN) Pakistan operations have focused on the development and the implementation of the **National**

Conservation Strategy (NCS). The World Wide Fund (WWF), Sustainable Development Policy Institute (SDPI) and the Rotary Club are other major groups.

To meet the challenges of environment and development in Pakistan, the Government has decided to support and establish a viable and working new global partnership in the social, economic and environmental dimensions. Pakistan began paying priority attention to the protection of the environment soon after the Conference on Human Environment in Stockholm in 1972. As Chair of G-77, Pakistan played a leading role at the UN Conference on Environment and Development (UNCED) in Rio in 1992. Pakistan is one of a handful of developing countries to prepare a comprehensive National Conservation Strategy (NCS) in 1992 in cooperation with national and international organizations. To achieve the goal of environmental protection, Pakistan has signed international agreements, i.e., the UN Framework Convention on Climate Change (UNFCCC), 1994; Montreal Protocol on Ozone Depleting Substances; Basel Convention on Biological Diversity, 1994; International Convention to Combat Desertification, 1994. Pakistan has been quite successful in cooperating with international agencies, e.g., UNIDO, EU, UNDP, UNEP, UNESCAP, ECO, SAARC. SACEP.

In the regional context, Pakistan is working in close cooperation with regional organizations such as the South Asia Association for Regional Cooperation (SAARC), South Asia Cooperative Environment Programmes (SACEP), Economic Cooperation Organization (ECC), United National Economic and Social Commission for Asia and the Pacific (UNESCAP) and the United Nations Environment Programme (UNEP). A number of joint activities have been initiated and are being implemented successfully. To protect the marine environment from land-based activities, a regional Seas Programme of UNEP/SACEP is underway. Pakistan participated in the environmental Management Seminar organized by SACEP in Sri Lanka.

In pursuance of the Uruguay Agreement, the World Trade Organization (WTO) has come into existence. The first Ministerial Conference of the WTP was held recently. Pakistan actively participated in the meeting.

In order to accelerate sustainable development, both local financing and foreign funding are arranged through the Ministry of Finance and Economic Affairs Division. In addition, bilateral and regional cooperation to finance environmental projects is also undertaken. However, the availability of foreign funding has been a problem in the past.

CHANGING CONSUMPTION PATTERNS

One of the fourteen core issues in the **National Conservation Strategy** (NCS) is Increasing Energy Efficiency. In 1987, the Ministry of Environment, Urban Affairs, Wildlife and Forestry set up the autonomous Energy Conservation Centre (ENERCON), responsible for energy conservation and energy efficiency.

ENERCON has been conducting data collection and field research. The knowledge which stems from this experience has served as the basis for training and public awareness programmes, including publications, seminars, workshops and advertisements in newspapers, radio and television. ENERCON has worked to identify opportunities which will yield over US$ 56 million in energy savings. Energy savings of US$ 18 million have already been realized. ENERCON has conducted 52 detailed energy audits and 85 preliminary audits.

In addition, the Ministry of Environment, Urban Affairs, Wildlife and Forestry and ENERCON have initiated programmes to promote efficient energy use. Pilot projects in Karachi and Faisalabad have been proposed. These projects will produce 500 to 1000 kilowatts. The Government has also implemented a programme to audit the energy efficiency of water pumps. The programme includes training of local workshop mechanics, testing facilities and pilot projects.

ENERCON has developed a Home Energy Conservation Seminar targeted at housewives and working women. To date, more than 12,000 women have benefitted from the seminar. ENERCON has trained trainers who respond to requests from the women's organizations and educational institutions in the four provinces.

Inefficient use currently results from essentially three sources:

- 1. overload demand of natural gas from both household and industrial consumers, causing a drop in pressure;
- 2. energy consumption of water pumps; and

  3. inefficient lighting, hardware and appliances.

Annual Energy Conservation Targets in Percentage (1996-2004):

Sector	1996-1997	1997-1998	1998-1999	1999-2004
Industry	1.6%	3.3%	4.6%	5.5%
Transport	t 1.5%	3.0%	5.5%	5.1%
Buildings	1.1%	2.3%	3.2%	3.8%
Agriculture	1.2%	2.5%	3.4%	4.2%

Domestic resources are being made available for a **Five-year Multisectoral Energy Efficiency Investment Programme 1996-2005** (Rs. 93.5 million); a proposed Natural Gas project (Rs. 97 million), intended to be a joint investment from both public and private sectors; a municipal water pump programme (Rs. 158 million); and agricultural tubewell programme (Rs. 250 million); and a Lighting Efficiency Programme (Rs. 80 million).

In 1995-1996, ENERCON conducted jointly with the Energy Conservation Centre (ECC) Japan, UNIDO and UNDP a series of 9 Preliminary Energy Audits in Glass, Plastic Forming and Food Processing Industries. ENERCON has developed a Rs. 92 million five-year energy plan for lighting efficiency in commercial buildings on a national scale. This five-year plan was made in collaboration with the joint UNDP/World Bank Energy Sector Management Assistance Program (ESMAP).

FINANCING

In 1994, Pakistan was constrained by a weak fiscal capacity due to a narrow revenue base. Therefore it is unrealistic for the Government to impose more taxation for the financing of the implementation of the **National Conservation Strategy** (NCS). Pakistan is faced with having to rely entirely on donor support for the first three to five of the ten years of the NCS. In general Pakistan has many, and is getting even more, aid-worthy projects which are relevant for the NCS.

Since most of the projects in NCS are labour intensive, it is estimated that Pakistan stands to gain 80,000 jobs a year during the ten years of NCS. Consideration is being given to the use of an effluent tax as a means of enforcing National **Environmental Quality Standards**. The precise modalities are under consideration.

The financial philosophy behind the National Conservation Strategy is that of financial sustainability, meaning that a welfare economic surplus is to be expected, since the cost of the environmentally sound projects will be outweighed by the benefits in the long run. Recommendations have been made to redirect existing high-cost development programmes to fund 40% of the total NCS budget. The additional Rs. 90 million was to have come from the private sector, but because of the economic constraints, it may be difficult to meet this recommendation. Recommendations for raising domestic funding include: introduction of the Polluter Pays Principle and other taxation measures in various sectors; adjustment of projects, for example on water; encouragement of private investment, for example in "Conservation pays" projects like recycling paper; supplement lotteries, and fund-raising schemes.

One of the recommendations made in relation to international funding is the implementation of the debt-for-nature swaps, which would allow Pakistan to reduce its foreign debt by using the money for environmental conservation.

A Development Bank in Pakistan was found commercially unviable; therefore an off-shore Fund was recommended since it would have the necessary financial advantages, i.e. zero taxation, for attracting international investors. The Environmental Fund would have an Investment Advisory Company (IAC). The IAC would be composed of shareholders who provide the initial money US$5.0 million or 10% of the estimated requirements. The 90% would be private investors - local and foreign, and multilateral and bilateral institutions such as IBRD, IFC and the Asian Development Bank.

TECHNOLOGY

Transfer of Environmentally Sound Technology

The Government has encouraged the industrial sector to utilize clean production processes. For this purpose, various incentives are available to industry which include preferential treatment in loan facilities by banks and DFIs, and lower import tariffs on anti-pollution equipment. There has not been much headway on the adoption of environmental management systems because of the lack of awareness and the higher cost of ISO certification. However, the government is giving due importance to the matter and the proposal is under consideration to devise a mechanism so that PSI may be accredited to do ISO 14000 certification locally.

The Federation of Chambers of Commerce and Industry (FPCCI) has launched a five-year Environment Technology Programme for Industry (ETPI) with the support and assistance of the Government of the Netherlands. The main goal of the programme is to help Pakistani industries identify and implement the most economical pollution prevention and abatement technologies.

Pakistan is involved in a project called "Transfer of Technology for Sustainable Industrial Development" with the Swiss Government. The project is administered by the Pakistani Ministry of Environment, Urban Affairs, Forestry and Wildlife and will be carried out by the Sustainable Development Policy Institute (SDPI). It involves two phases:

- the first one focuses on transferring Swiss technology and investments to Pakistani companies;
- the second one focuses on capacity building, such as necessary legislation, training and education.

The Swiss government has granted US$1 million for the implementation of the second phase of the Pak-Swiss cooperation programme. The SDPI was supported in enhancing capacity and expertise concerning technology transfer by the Norwegian Agency for International Cooperation (NORAD), the Canadian International Development Agency (CIDA) and the Swiss Development Corporation (SDC). The Environment and Urban Affairs Division and Pakistan Environmental Protection Agency have been supported in capacity building by a World Bank funded project on Environmental Protection and Resource Conservation.

Pakistan is a member of APO and also benefits from the facilities available through UNIDO, UNEP, and UNDP.

Biotechnology

A special institutional body, the National Institute for Biotechnology and Genetic Engineering, (NIBGE) is in charge of this sector. In 1994, the national budget allocated to NIBGE amounted to US$ 0.36 million and it had a professional staff of 68. NIBGE has received support from the International Atomic Energy Agency and the U.S.A. NIBGE tries to involve industry in its work by inviting management to discuss marketing possibilities for environmental protection. Workshops are being organized on a quarterly basis to enhance awareness and understanding of biotechnology issues. Traditional methods and knowledge of indigenous peoples are being accommodated in the policies of NIBGE.

NIBGE has an evaluation committee which yearly reviews programmes and makes suggestions for improvements. A **Biotechnology Code of Conduct for the Release of Organisms into the Environment** has been prepared for national adoption. The Code of Conduct has been modelled from the code of conduct prepared by UNIDO. The enforcement of the code of conduct will be in the hands of the Biosafety Committee which will check all handling of Genetically Modified Organisms (GMO). The procedure contains principles on biotechnology risk assessment and risk management.

ECONOMIC DEVELOPMENT TRENDS

Pakistan is at a turning point. The new government that took office in October 1999 has made the restructuring and documentation of the economy as the cornerstone of its economic revival plan. However, the revival plan broadly hinges on the implementation of badly needed reforms for uplift of the economy, including the rebuilding of investors' confidence, sweeping tax reforms by broadening the tax base, application of General Sales Tax (GST) at retail level, and agriculture tax reforms. If the government can consolidate the reforms, clamp down on corruption, and have the courage of its convictions, Pakistan still has a chance to succeed in the global economy.

Even though Pakistan's many investment obstacles will not be eradicated overnight, the country, with a population of approximately 140 million, will continue to offer a challenging market for U.S. exporters and investors. Although the economy grew by almost 5.0 percent in 1999, it has the potential to achieve higher growth levels if the government manages to reduce a cumbersome bureaucracy which continues to impede the privatization of public enterprises, and also impedes emergence of an entrepreneurial class capable of competing in the modern world.

The most promising sectors for U.S. exports include oil and gas (exploration and transportation), agro-industry, information technology, textile machinery, gem mining, precious and semi-precious stone cutting, franchising, consumer goods, and environmental technologies. A major privatization effort in the telecommunication and financial sectors should offer additional markets for U.S. services, products and investors. In addition, Pakistan International Airlines also plans to replace its aging fleet of wide-bodied aircraft. Sales to Pakistan's government organizations, however, will be limited due to shrinking foreign exchange reserves and government funds.

The United States remains the biggest trading partner of Pakistan. The U.S. is also the largest contributor of the foreign direct investment in Pakistan. In 1999, Pakistan imported more than $725 million worth of U.S. products, while Pakistan's exports to the U.S. amounted to $1.7 billion. Major imports from the U.S. were wheat, chemicals, fertilizers, machinery, and transport equipment.

Principal competitors of U.S. businesses in Pakistan are European, Japanese, and South Korean firms. Financing of goods and services is sometimes crucial for importers in Pakistan, and these countries often offer credit terms that could make it difficult for U.S. suppliers to compete. Pakistanis also note that U.S. goods are bit pricey compared with those of some competitors, and that U.S. firms generally do not move as quickly as some competitors to meet demand.

Potential investors in Pakistan face many of the same challenges that exist in other developing economies, such as inconsistent, sometimes contradictory policies and backtracking on promised privatization of public sector entities.

Pakistan is a diverse and challenging market, requiring adaptability and persistence. Careful planning and patience are the prerequisites for success in this emerging market. U.S. firms that are willing to invest time to develop market presence should expect to be rewarded in the long-term.

MAJOR TRENDS AND OUTLOOK

Since the late 1980s Pakistan has pursued a program of market-oriented economic adjustment, reform and development, including strong encouragement of foreign direct investment. Supported by the international financial institutions and bilateral donors, this program has aimed at enhancing macroeconomic stability, instituting structural reforms to promote private sector and export-led industrial development, and reversing past neglect of key social sectors such as health, education and population planning.

Pakistan has made considerable progress under this program, but the process has not been entirely even, and key challenges remain for its $60 billion economy. Specifically, the government has sought to reduce fiscal and external imbalances, reduce trade barriers, modernize the financial sector, privatize state-owned industries, reform the tax system, encourage private investment in the critical energy sector, and offer specific incentives to attract foreign investment, which is considered critical to the overall development effort. These efforts have enjoyed generous support from the IMF, in the form of an Enhanced Structural Adjustment Facility approved in January 1999, which was later stalled due to non-fulfillment of some its conditionalities, especially regarding imposition of the General Sales Tax (GST) at retail level.

The new Government has prioritized the oil and gas sector, small and medium sized enterprises, information technology and agriculture as major areas of focus and is negotiating for Poverty Reduction and Growth Facility with the IMF.

Various problems have kept Pakistan's progress below its potential. Floods, drought and pestilence hurt agricultural output in the early 1990s. Domestic political instability throughout the Bhutto administration and sporadic ethnic and sectarian violence under the caretakers and the government of Nawaz Sharif and the long-drawn dispute between the government and Independent Power Producers have stunted foreign investment. And, finally, policy inconsistency and weak implementation have, along with reports of improper official influence in business and economic decisions, dampened investor interest and economic growth in Pakistan.

Pakistan's mixed economic performance reflects the interplay of these positive and negative trends. Real economic growth has been positive, but below government targets. Real GDP grew 1.3 percent in 1996-97; 4.3 percent in 1997-98; and 3.1 percent in 1998-99. GDP growth is expected to improve to 4.5 percent against a target of 5.0 percent during 1999-2004, which is still inadequate to make a dent in reducing poverty and unemployment. Recent annual consumer inflation of 6-7 percent has been moderated to match historically modest single-digit rates. In 1999-2004, consumer inflation is projected at 3.4 percent. Fiscal slippages have led to difficulties and delays in IMF programs. New investment inflows, both portfolio and direct, at an all-time high in 1995-96, have continued to drop substantially.

While Pakistan's economic fortunes remain closely linked to cotton and the textile products, the government has made some progress in diversifying the economy, and is committed to improving the quality of life for poorer citizens through the poverty alleviation strategy. This plan comprises the initiation of small infrastructure projects in the poorest and low income urban and rural areas, a food stamp program and the establishment of micro credit bank.

There are significant possibilities for U.S. and other foreign suppliers and investors in Pakistan. However, realizing these opportunities will require sound economic policies by the government as well as actions to improve political stability and better develop human resources.

GROWTH SECTORS

After growing at an average rate of over 6 percent per year from 1980 to 1991, real GDP growth has slowed in the 1990's. Real GDP growth dropped to 1.3 percent in 1996-97 due to a poor cotton crop and related setbacks in the textile industry. In 1997-98 growth hit 4.3 percent against a target of 6.0 percent. Real GDP grew only by 3.1 percent in 1998-99 and is projected to grow by 4.5 percent during 1999-2004.

The Pakistani economy is almost evenly divided between the commodity sector (51 percent of GDP) and the services sector (49 percent), shares that have held constant for about a decade.

Sectoral shares in 1999-2004 were estimated by the Ministry of Finance as follows:

Commodity Sector	51.0 % of which:	
Agriculture	25.9	
Manufacturing	16.8	
Construction	3.5	
Electricity & Gas Distribution	4.3	
Mining	0.5	
Services sector		49.0 % of which:

Wholesale and Retail Trade	14.9
Transport, Storage & Communication	10.1
Public Administration & Defense	6.3
Ownership of Dwellings	6.0
Finance and Insurance	2.5
Other Services	9.3

AGRICULTURE

Agriculture is the dominant sector of Pakistan's economy and accounts for around 24 percent of GDP, half the employed labor force, and a large share of foreign exchange earnings. Agricultural production also provides basic inputs for key industries, including textiles and sugar. During FY 1999/2004, agriculture growth rebounded to 5.4 percent due to bumper cotton and wheat production.

Pakistan depends on one of the world's largest irrigation systems to support production. There are two principal seasons. Cotton, rice and sugarcane are produced during the "kharif" season, which lasts from May to November. Wheat is the major "rabi" crop, which extends from November to April. Minor crops include pulses, potatoes, onion, chilies, and garlic.

Pakistan is a net importer of agricultural commodities. Annual imports total about $2 billion and include wheat, edible oils, pulses and consumer foods.

Wheat - Pakistan's MY 2004/2005 wheat crop is forecast at a record 19.3 million metric tons (MMT), compared to 17.8 MMT produced during the previous year. This increase is due largely to favorable weather and a 25-percent increase in the procurement price to about $135 per ton. About 85 percent of the crop is irrigated. White wheat is the sole type of wheat produced and the main type imported..

Despite the record production, Pakistan will continue to be a major wheat importer. The government is the sole importer following the decision to ban private imports in June 1999 to conserve foreign exchange. The government has imported an average of 2 .4 million annually over the past five years to augment domestic supplies and regulate prices. The United States and Australia are the major suppliers. Demand for wheat is increasing from Pakistan's rapidly growing population as well as from cross-border trade with Afghanistan. Demand for hard wheat also is expected to increase as the milling and baking industries diversify their product lines.

Cotton - Pakistan is the world's fourth largest producer and consumer of cotton and the economy depends primarily on cotton and textile exports as a major source of foreign exchange and employment. Textile exports have rebounded following the end of the Asian financial crisis and the industry is considering increased investment in value-added production.

Pakistan's MY 1999/2004 cotton production increased to 1.78 MMT, following a disappointing harvest the previous year. The government recently actively intervened in the market to boost prices and encourage production. Pakistan may either import or exports relatively small quantities of cotton. Imported cotton consists largely of U.S. Pima as well as SJV-equivalent cotton, which is not produced locally. The United States, Central Asia, and Australia are major suppliers of cotton to the Pakistani market.

Rice - MY 1999/2004 rice production was a record 4.8 MMT. Pakistan is a major rice exporter and annually exports about 2 MMT or about 10 percent of world trade. About 75 percent of exports are IRRI rice and the remainder is Pakistan's famous fragrant Basmati rice. Rice is

Pakistan's second leading source of export earnings. Private traders handle all exports. Pakistan's main competitors are Thailand and Vietnam for IRRI-type rice and India in the Basmati rice trade.

Sugar - Pakistan is forecast to import as much as 500,000 MT of sugar during MY 1999/2004, following exports of about 500,000 MT the previous year. The reasons for the turn around is the sharp decline in sugar cane production, due both to declining returns and lower sugar recovery levels. MY 1999/2004 sugar production is forecast at 2.6 MMT. The duty on imported sugar is 45 percent. China and Thailand are expected to be the main suppliers. Production is forecast to recover and no imports are expected in MY 2004/2005, depending on the availability to adequate irrigation supplies and the monsoon.

Tobacco - MY2004 total tobacco production is forecast to decrease 2 percent to 101,600 metric tons (MT) due to decreases in both area and yield. Market observers expect farmers will reduce oriental production sharply and switch to other varieties, following problems disposing of last year's bumper oriental crop.

Tobacco is grown mainly in the North West Frontier Province (NWFP) and Punjab and is an important cash crop. Flue-cured and burley tobaccos are used primarily in higher-quality cigarettes. Oriental varieties (known locally as White Patta) are used in low-quality cigarettes and for chewing tobacco. Dark air-cured varieties are used mainly for filler, while light air-cured varieties are used primarily for traditional Pakistani tobacco products. Yields in Pakistan are about twice those for neighboring countries largely due to the extension services provided by the industry. Quality, however, is improving only slowly due to problems related to climate and soil. Farmers have started inter-cropping tobacco with vegetables and sugarcane to increase returns.

About half of the total production is used for cigarette manufacturing and the remainder used in traditional ways of smoking (in hand-rolled cigarettes called birris, in water pipes, and as snuff). The U.S. share of imported tobacco is increasing gradually in response to increased demand for high quality cigarettes.

Minor crops - Minor crops account for only 5 percent of total cultivated area; these include oilseeds (sunflower, soybean, and safflower) chilies, pulses, potatoes, and onions.

Oil Seeds - Domestic oilseed production accounts for about 25 percent of Pakistan total edible oil needs. As a result, Pakistan spends more than $1 billion annually in scarce foreign exchange to import edible oils, while its oilseed processing industry operates at less than 25% of capacity due to an inadequate supply of oilseeds. For MY 2005 total oilseed production is forecast to decrease 10 percent to 3.6 MMT, due largely to a forecast decreases in cotton and sunflower production.

The new military government has highlighted development of the oilseed sector as a priority. Oilseed imports, mainly canola, have surged in response to improved crushing margins following the government's decision to raise tariffs on meal and oil and lower tariffs on oilseeds. Decision-makers increasingly realize that a viable processing industry, using both imported and domestic oilseeds, is a necessary condition for expanding oilseed production. Continued large imports of palm oil not only drain scarce foreign exchange but reduce margins and constitute the major disincentive to local oilseed production. Soybean imports continue to suffer from anomalies in both the tariff and tax structure, which makes importation of soybeans relatively less attractive. Even so, market observers expect demand for soybean meal from the poultry industry eventually will lead to commercial imports while the government works to make its tariffs and taxes more uniform. Pakistan's poultry industry consumes about 200,000 tons of soybean meal annually.

Fisheries - Pakistan's fishing industry is relatively modest, but has shown strong growth in recent years. The domestic market is quite small, with per capita annual consumption of approximately 2 kilograms. About 80 percent of production comes from marine fisheries from two main areas, the Sindh coast east from Karachi to the Indian border, and the Makran coast of Baluchistan. Ninety percent of the total marine catch is fish; the shrimp which constitute the remainder are prized because of their greater relative value and demand in foreign markets.

During 1999/00, total fish production was 620,000 MT, of which 440,000 MT consisted of marine species and the remainder were fresh water species. About one-third of the edible catch is consumed fresh, nine percent is frozen, eight percent canned, and about 43 percent used as fish meal for animal food.

Livestock - Livestock accounts for 40 percent of the value added by the agricultural sector and 9 percent of the total GDP. Principal products are milk, beef, mutton, poultry, and wool. During 1999, the livestock population increased to 120 million heads. 1999 production was as follows: Beef - 970,000 MT, Mutton - 640,000 MT, and Poultry - 190,000 MT.

In an effort to enhance milk and meat production, the GOP recently launched a comprehensive livestock development project with Asian Development Bank assistance. In addition, the GOP has broadened extension and artificial breeding services, rationalized animal health services, improved slaughterhouses, and introduced high yielding fodder varieties.

Poultry - Poultry production provides an increasingly popular low-cost source of protein. Modern poultry production is constrained by high mortality, high incidence of disease, poor quality of chicks and poor quality feed, combined with an inadequate marketing system. Frozen poultry have only recently been introduced.

Forestry - Forests cover an area of 4.2 million hectares or about 5 percent of the total area of Pakistan. One-third of the forest area is productive and the remaining two-thirds is maintained for environmental stability. The principal forest products are timber, principally for house construction and furniture, and firewood. Pakistan imports an estimated $150 million of wood products annually to meet the requirements of a growing population and rising standards of living. The GOP has restricted cutting to protect remaining resources and has lowered duties to encourage imports.

Vegetable Ghee/Cooking Oil - Vegetable ghee, hydrogenated vegetable oil, is the principal cooking medium in Pakistan. After the market outstripped the supply of milk-produced ghee, the vegetable ghee industry has grown rapidly (from two units in 1947 to more than 40 in 1998). The principal raw material is edible oil, the majority of which is imported palm oil. Pakistan suffers from a large and chronic gap between demand and domestic production of edible oils.

Importing edible oil is an important task. It consumes a big portion of valuable foreign exchange. Pakistan remains a major importer of palm oil followed by soybean oil and sunflower oil. In FY 1998/99, Pakistan spent Pak Rupees 40.5 billion (US$800 million approximately) on import of edible oils.

INDUSTRY

Pakistan, which had almost no large industrial units at the time of Partition in 1947, now has a fairly broad industrial base, and manufacturing accounts for about 17.0 percent of GDP.

Cotton textile production is the single most important industry, accounting for about 19 percent of large-scale industrial employment. Cotton yarn, cotton cloth, made-up textiles, ready-made garments, and knitwear collectively accounted for nearly 60.0 percent of Pakistan's exports in 1999-00. Other important industries are cement, vegetable oil, fertilizer, sugar, steel, machinery, tobacco, paper and paperboard, chemicals, and food processing. The GOP is attempting to diversify the country's industrial base and to increase the emphasis on export industries. Small-scale and cottage industries are numerically significant but account for a relatively small proportion of the GDP, about 6.0 percent. (Small-scale industry includes facilities which employ fewer than 50 workers and cottage industries are industrial units in which the owner works and is aided by family members but employs no hired labor.)

Manufacturing's share of GDP in 1999-00 was 17.0 percent, about the same as last year.

Public Industrial Sector - The public industrial sector, under the Production Wing of the Ministry of Industries and Production, comprises eight holding corporations which controlled 74 industrial units. A majority of these units have been privatized under the GOP's privatization program and the rest are to be sold off. The eight holding corporations include: Pakistan Steel; the State Cement Corporation; the National Fertilizer Corporation; Pakistan Automobile Corporation (PACO); Federal Chemical and Ceramics Corporation (FCCC); State Petroleum Refining & Petrochemical Corporation (PERAC); State Engineering Corporation (SEC); and the Pakistan Industrial Development Corporation (PIDC). These public sector units will continue to play a key role in certain sectors, such as heavy engineering, steel, automobile, petroleum and defense production.

Textiles - – Textiles is Pakistan's primary industry, and in PFY-99 accounted for 8.5 percent of the Gross Domestic Product, 31 percent of total investment, 27 percent of industrial value addition, 38 percent of industrial employment, and 62 percent of total exports. Cotton is the basic raw material for Pakistan's textile industry, which today has an installed capacity of 8,358,000 spindles, 150,000 rotors, 17,000 air jet and shuttleless looms and approximately 200,000 to 250,000 auto and power looms. The knitwear industry is comprised of approximately 3,000 units, with a total of 7,800 knitting machines in the organized sector, and an estimated 17,000 to 22,000 knitting machines in the unorganized sector.

The garment industry is comprised of approximately 4,000 units in the organized and unorganized sectors, with an estimated 250,000 industrial and 650,000 domestic sewing machines. Knitwear has been Pakistan's largest single segment of garment exports. During PFY-99, this sector earned USD 746 million from exports, showing an increase of 7.18 percent over the previous year. Exports are expected to reach USD 850 million (or to increase by nearly 14 percent) during the current fiscal year.

About 80 percent of the country's textile industry's consumption is based on cotton and the remaining 20 percent on man-made fibers, particularly polyester, acrylic and viscose. The country produces approximately 7 million bales (each bale weighing 480 lbs.) of cotton annually, and this production satisfies over 95 percent of the textile industry's cotton requirements. Long staple and extra long staple cotton is imported to meet the demand for finer cottons. The demand for blended fabrics in increasing in the domestic market. Polyester staple fiber and polyester filament yarn are manufactured locally, but acrylic and viscose staple fibers are imported.

In PFY-99 Pakistan produced 1.54 billion kgs. of yarn, the organized sector 380.47 million square meters of cloth, and the unorganized sector, comprised of power, auto and shuttleless looms, 3,618.53 million square meters of cloth. The country has a capacity to also produce 750 million pieces of woven garments as well as knitwear, towels, tarpaulin and canvas. As a rule, large firms concentrate on spinning and weaving, leaving garment manufacturing to highly fragmented small to medium-scale producers.

The industry, particularly its spinning and weaving sectors, have been under pressure for the last 7-8 years owing to the lower production and higher prices for domestically-produced cotton, increased competition in the international market, financial mismanagement within the industry, rising global demand for value-added textiles as well as the increase in production capacity in some of the developing countries.

Pakistan's textile sector must move to higher value-added production to meet challenges and opportunities beyond 2005, when quotas are removed and tariff barriers lowered under the WTO. Various government incentives and an improved cotton crop have improved the outlook for the textile industry. Yarn exports have increased as domestic prices of cotton have become favorable and because the worldwide recession is ending. The GOP's new 5-year textile policy is expected to greatly encourage investment in value-added manufacturing. Investments of approximately Rs. 300 billion (USD 60 million) are expected in the textile industry, including major investments in the spinning, weaving, knitting, processing and synthetic fiber manufacturing sectors.

Pakistan's woolen industry has 118 units with 157,321 spindles and 764 looms. Only 94 mills with 99,413 spindles and 544 looms are operational. The spinning sector, which is considered saturated, uses imported synthetic fibers and raw wool to manufacture yarn. The weaving sector is comprised of a number of mills in the unorganized sector and five composite mills, and is not expected to grow over the next 2-3 years.

Pakistan also has 11 jute mills with an installed capacity of 38,151 spindles and 1,223 looms. The industry's main products are jute sacks and hessian cloth. The industry produced 85,200 metric tons of jute products in 1998-99. Its production from July 1, 1999 to April 30, 2004 was 66,252 metric tons.

Processed Foods – Food and its allied products industry is considered Pakistan's largest industry and is believed to account for approximately 27 percent of its value-added production and 16 percent of the total employment by the manufacturing sector. Major sub-sectors of Pakistan's food industry are cooking oils and hydrogenated vegetable oils, sugar, flour, tea, dairy products, beverages, biscuits, breads and confectionery, snack foods, processed chicken, and jams, jellies, squashes, sauces, pickles, spices and some cereals and canned foods.

The fish, meat and fruit and vegetable sectors remain underdeveloped, partly for lack of adequate infrastructure, including storage and transportation facilities. A small quantity of processed foods is imported to feed a few supermarkets catering to the country's elite. The vast agricultural resources and the country's geographic location make Pakistan an ideal country for investment in the food sector. Several foreign firms have entered the market and established their own presence as manufacturers, or established joint ventures with local partners. The fastest growing sectors are beverages, including carbonated soft drinks and juice and juice-flavored drinks, poultry and edible oils.

Food Processing and Consumer Products - Major segments include sugar, tea, aerated water, edible fats, dairy products, concentrates, juices, tobacco, detergents, and personal care products. Nearly all of these items are produced for domestic consumption.

Iron and Steel - Pakistan Steel, with an annual capacity of 1.1 million tons, is Pakistan's only integrated steel plant. It is located near Port Bin Qasim, 25 Kilometers East of Karachi. The Steel Mill was constructed with technical assistance from the former Soviet Union, and currently employs about 20,000 workers. Iron ore, manganese, and cocking coal for the plant are all imported. Pakistan Steel produces coke, pig iron, billets, hot and cold rolled coils and sheets, and galvanized sheets. Production in the last financial year was 76% of the capacity. For the current year –July 1999-June 2004 it was 83 percent, though in the second quarter the production October-December '99 went up to 91 percent of the capacity. Production in the third quarter reached record production of 100 percent capacity utilization during March 2004. The third quarter of the current financial year is the best ever quarter in the 18years of steel production at works.

The facility notched record production of over one million tons in 1993-94. That resulted in significant pre-tax profits for Pakistan Steel, which had been a chronic loss-maker for most of its operational history (in 1995-96, however, production of all major items declined by an average of 7.5%). Pakistan Steel had announced an expansion program to increase its production capacity to three million tons by mid-1999 but its privatization has now become the first priority of the government.

In June 1999, the first tin plate making plant of Pakistan, Siddqsons Tin Plate had started commercial production. This plant is a joint venture between a local company with French and Japanese firms. The plant cost US$32 million and has a production capacity of 120,000 tons of tin plate per annum.

Fertilizer - Pakistan has 10 fertilizer units, of which four are in the private sector. At the end of 1999, they had a total annual capacity of 4,651.6 thousand tons. In 1999-2004 the production of fertilizer has increased by 10.5% to 3,664 thousand tons compared to 3,046.6 thousand tons during 1998-99. There is no domestic production of potassic fertilizers.

Cement - Pakistan has 25 operating cement units, of which 21 units having capacity of 14,440 thousand tons are in the private sector and 4 units with capacity of 1,831 thousand tons are in public sector. The total annual capacity of the industry is 13,029 thousand tons. Cement production is recorded at 7.0 million tons during July-March 1999-2004 as compared to 6.9 million tons in 1998-99, a marginal increase of 1.3 percent. Pakistan has large quantities of both limestone and gypsum and a large domestic market. Cement was one of the few industries with an established base in Pakistan at the time of independence in 1947, when there were five cement factories. Pakistan currently produces five types of cement: Portland Grey, Portland slag, Sulphate resistant, Super Sulphate resistant, and White. In 1972, the Government of Pakistan nationalized cement factories and consolidated them under the State Cement Corporation of Pakistan. The current privatization process has reversed that initiative. In order to promote growth in the cement sector, the GOP has allowed duty-free import of plant and machinery not manufactured locally.

Chemicals - Pakistan produces some basic chemicals, such as soda ash, caustic soda, and sulfuric acid. Production of soda ash in 1999-2004 was 177,593 tons, and caustic soda 83,998 tons. Caustic soda is used in the textile, hydrocarbon refining, and soap industries; sulfuric acid is used in the textile, paper, fertilizer, and steel industries.

Leather Industry - Leather is one of the major foreign exchange earners for Pakistan, having an annual growth rate of 25 percent. The leather and leather products industry is labor-intensive (directly employing more than 200,000 workers) and there are over 500 tanneries in Pakistan. The recent growth of the industry is due in large part to its successful progression from the export of raw hides and skins and semi-processed leather towards high value-added finished leathers and leather products (including leather jackets, gloves, footwear, and sporting goods). The tanning sector is concentrated in the Punjab, where manufacturing units process primarily buffalo and cow hides; tanneries in the Sindh process primarily goat and sheep skins. The local market for leather is limited, and about 80 percent of production is exported. More sophisticated machinery and productivity increases can be expected to further boost exports. Pollution is a serious problem for this industry.

Pharmaceutical - There are around 25 multinational manufacturers of pharmaceutical products in Pakistan (of which twelve are U.S. firms) and they command over three-quarters of the domestic market. The number of multinationals has decreased in the past one year due to mergers of some multinationals in Pakistan.

Electronics and Electrical Goods Industry: The electronics and electrical goods industry is basically a consumer product industry, involved in the manufacturing of electric light bulbs, tubes, air conditioners, fans, refrigerators, freezers, television sets, radios, and other electrical appliances. Pakistan is currently facing the challenge to curtail the smuggling of electronic goods into the country via Afghanistan.

The northern areas (Punjab & NWFP) are especially affected by the influx of these smuggled products. Pakistan does not produce picture tubes, deflection yokes etc. which are some of the vital components for a number of electrical goods that are being assembled and manufactured locally. Hence there is a huge demand for spare parts and various accessories, which are presently being imported. According to available data, the market potential of TV (Color) is 500,000 per year. In 1999/2004 total TV manufactured were 288,834 sets thus generating a revenue of $ 9.6 million as compared to previous year 1998/99 when 224,286 sets were manufactured, thus generating revenue of $6.75 million.

Vegetable Ghee/Cooking Oil - Vegetable ghee, hydrogenated vegetable oil, is the principal cooking medium in Pakistan. After the market outstripped the supply of milk-produced ghee, the vegetable ghee industry has grown rapidly (from two units in 1947 to more than 40 in 1998). The principal raw material is edible oil, the majority of which is imported palm oil. Pakistan suffers from a large and chronic gap between demand and domestic production of edible oils.

Importing edible oil is an important task. It consumes a big portion of valuable foreign exchange. Pakistan remains a major importer of palm oil followed by soybean oil and sunflower oil.

ENERGY

ENERGY SECTOR OVERVIEW

Proven Oil Reserves (1/1/00E): 208 million barrels
Oil Production (1998E): 59,000 barrels per day (bbl/d), of which 55,000 bbl/d was crude oil
Oil Consumption (1998E): 350,000 bbl/d
Net Oil Imports (1998E): 290,000 bbl/d
Crude Oil Refining Capacity (1/1/00E): 143,350 bbl/d
Natural Gas Reserves (1/1/00E): 21.6 trillion cubic feet (Tcf)
Natural Gas Production (1998E): 0.7 Tcf
Natural Gas Consumption (1998E): 0.7 Tcf
Coal Production (1998E): 3.5 million short tons (Mmst)
Coal Consumption (1998E): 4.5 Mmst
Net Coal Imports (1998E): 1.1 Mmst
Recoverable Coal Reserves (12/31/96E): 3,228 Mmst
Electric Generation Capacity (1/1/98E): 13.0 gigawatts
Electricity Generation (1998E): 59 billion kilowatthours

Organization: Oil and Gas Development Corporation (OGDC), a state company, handles oil and gas exploration and development; Water and Power Development Authority (WAPDA) supplies electricity to most of the country; Karachi Electric Supply Corporation Limited (KESC) serves the greater Karachi metropolitan area; Pakistan Atomic Energy Commission (PAEC) operates one nuclear power plant
Major Foreign Energy Company Involvement: AES, Atlantic Richfield, British National Power, Coastal Power, Gaz de France, Total, General Electric, Lasmo Oil (U.K.), Marubeni (Japan), ExxonMobil, Monument Oil & Gas, Premier Oil, Royal Dutch Shell, Xenal (Saudi Arabia)
Major Ports: Gwadar, Karachi, Muhammed bin Qasim, Ormaro
Major Gas Fields: Bhit, Dhodak, Kadanwari, Mari, Prikoh, Qadipur, Sawan, Sui
Major Oil Fields: Dhurnal, Fimkasser, Liari, Mazari, Thora
Major Pipelines: Sui Northern Gas Pipeline; Sui Southern Gas Pipeline; Pak-Arab Refinery Company (PARCO) petroleum product pipeline
Major Refineries (Capacity): Attock Refinery in Rawalpindi (35,000 bbl/d), National Refinery in Korangi (62,050 bbl/d), Pakistan Refinery Ltd. in Karachi (46,300 bbl/d)

Pakistan's primary energy supply mix during the period July 1998 to June 1999 consisted of oil (42.8 percent), natural gas (38.6 percent), hydel 12.8 percent), coal (5.2 percent), liquid petroleum gas (0.4 percent) and nuclear (0.2 percent). The average crude oil production during this period was 54,755 bpd. The production of natural gas during the same period was 2,041 mmcfd. Development of the energy sector remains a high priority. Pakistan has faced chronic energy shortages and domestic energy demand has outstripped supply. From July 1998 to June 1999, the largest electricity consumption was by the industrial and transport sectors (34.4 percent each), followed by domestic (22.1 percent), commercial (3.2 percent), agriculture (3.0 percent) and other government (2.9 percent). Pakistan's commercial energy demand is estimated to double over the next 10 years and despite recent gas discoveries, the energy shortfall is expected to increase.

A series of new petroleum policies announced in late 1991, September 1993, February 1994 and again in May 1997, have helped boost investment in the oil and gas sector. Six gas discoveries have been made since the announcement of the newest policy. The energy shortfall has been particularly acute in electricity generation. This has resulted in regular rotating power outages (load shedding) and forced many industries to install their own alternative power sources. In early 1994, the electricity shortage was estimated at 2,000-MW during peak load hours. The Government of Pakistan (GOP) at that time announced a policy inviting the private sector to develop power generation projects. Subsequent tariff increases forced many industries to establish their own internal power plants. The installation of these plants whose combined capacity is estimated to be between 800 and 1,000 MW and the stagnation of industry resulted in a decrease in power demand.

Current Situation and Future Planning - Pakistan's electricity is supplied by two large state-owned utilities, the Water and Power Development Authority (WAPDA) and the Karachi Electric Supply Corporation (KESC). WAPDA, headquartered in Lahore, has an installed generation capacity of 9,945-MW consisting of 51.48 percent thermal, and 48.52 percent hydel. KESC, which generates and distributes electricity to Karachi and its suburbs as well as the adjacent parts of Baluchistan, has an installed generating capacity of 1,756-MW, all of it thermal.

KESC's present capability is limited to 1,400-MW, but it is required to meet a demand of 1,799-MW. It therefore purchases power from two IPPs, WAPDA, Pakistan Steel Mills and the Karachi Nuclear Power Plant. In addition, eleven private sector plants of a total installed generation capacity of 4,578 -MW supply power to WAPDA. The 137-MW Karachi Nuclear Power Plant, non-operational since January 1999, is reported to have recommenced operations around December 1999.

Future increases in power generation from thermal sources will be from two IPPs in CY-2004 which will have a total installed generation capacity of 821-MW; and from four IPPs in CY-2002 or CY 2003, which will have a total installed generation capacity of 146-MW. These plants will therefore increase the total installed generation capacity of IPPs to 5,790-MW. The increase in hydel power generation will be chiefly from the 1,450-MW Ghazi Barotha Hydel Power Project, whose first 290-MW unit is scheduled to come on line in 2002. The remaining 4 units will come on line the following year. The other increases in hydel power generation will be from the 184-MW Chashma Hydel Power Project, expected to be in commercial production by June 2005. Increases in nuclear power will be from the 325-MW Chashma Nuclear Power Plant, scheduled to commence generating power by mid-2004. There are no other new power projects scheduled for completion during Pakistan's 9th 5-year Plan (July 1, 1998 to June 30, 2003).

Hydroelectric Power - WAPDA, the sole operator of hydro projects, has three large hydroelectric projects: Tarbela, with a total generating capacity of 3,478-MWs; Mangla, with a total capacity of 1,000-MW, and Warsak with 240-MW. Together with 107-MW from scattered small hydro projects, the three major projects give WAPDA 4,825-MW of hydropower. Hydropower's drawback is its seasonal fluctuation. There is little rain from October to May when the demand for irrigation water is high, reducing the effective capability of hydroelectric units. Reservoirs can register up to a 45 percent difference between wet and dry season water levels. Nevertheless, Pakistan has vast untapped hydro potential suitable for development.

Plans for building the controversial 3,600-MW Kalabagh Hydropower Project on the River Indus downstream of the Tarbela Dam are held in abeyance. In 1998, the GOP announced a new Policy for Private Independent Power Projects, which encourages the use of indigenous resources for power generation. The policy is designed to bring on line private sector generation to meet the power deficit beyond PFY-2003. Five hydel projects of a combined power generation capacity of over 1,200-MW are scheduled to be on line to meet the power demand in PFY-2005 and beyond. Four of these projects are to be located in Pakistan's Northwest Frontier Province and the fifth in Azad Kashmir. Until then, the existing power generation facilities as well as those in the pipeline are expected to meet demand, which is estimated to have an annual growth rate of 2 to 3 percent.

Thermal Power - WAPDA has 5,120-MW of installed thermal generating capacity. Most of this capacity comes from two large complexes: Guddu (1,655-MW of steam and combined cycle units), and Jamshoro (880-MW of oil-fired units). Its third large thermal unit was Kot Addu (1,638-MW) has been partly privatized and its management handed over to the investor. KESC's installed generating capacity is concentrated in the six-unit Bin Qasim Power Station (1,260-MW).

Government management of the power sector has been considered very poor, line losses huge, and corruption and over employment rampant. In late 1998 the Pakistan Army was called in to improve WAPDA's financial status, control power theft and recover outstanding dues. Army's efforts have resulted in an overall reduction of 10 percent in systems losses. In late May 1999 the Pakistan Army was also handed control of KESC, ostensibly for a period of six months, in order to reduce power losses, ensure uninterrupted power supply and improve the recovery of dues. Despite these efforts, KESC's losses rose from 34.62 percent in PFY-98 to 38.64 percent in PFY-99. KESC has now targeted 30 percent losses for PFY-2004.

The GOP plans to restructure and privatize the thermal power generation, transmission and distribution functions of both WAPDA and KESC. As part of this initiative, WAPDA's eight electricity boards has been restructured into eight distinct corporate entities; its thermal power units converted into three separate power generation companies; its transmission and grid station network incorporated into a single entity; and a holding concern, the Pakistan Electric Power Company (PEPCO) created to coordinate their activities and to manage their transition from a bureaucratic structure to a corporate structure, and thus become commercially profitable entities. Licensing applications for each of the twelve entities have been filed with the National Electric Power Company (NEPRA).

NEPRA has already programmed three of these entities for public hearing in the near future. These entities will subsequently operate independently. WAPDA's shareholding is to be transferred to the Government of Pakistan, who will offer all but the National Transmission and Dispatch Company for privatization. PEPCO is currently in discussion with its lenders over the modalities, terms and commercial aspects of a USD 500 million World Bank Power Sector Adjustment Loan and a USD 750 million World Bank and Asian Development Bank jointly-financed Adaptive Power Loan. The latter loan is to be utilized to make investments to rehabilitate the existing system and make new investments in the distribution and transmission sectors.

The Faisalabad Electricity Supply Company and KESC are to be privatized within a year. The privatization of the remaining entities is to be completed a year later. Once the two utilities have been privatized, further investments in power generation facilities will become market driven and of no concern to the GOP.

Nuclear Power – In PFY-99 approximately 0.2 percent of Pakistan's total generation of electricity was nuclear. The Karachi Nuclear Power Plant (KANUPP), which has a gross generating capacity of 137-MW, was constructed in the early 1970s with Canadian technology. The plant, which has a life span of 30 years, recently underwent a major overhaul. Operations recommenced around December 1999, with the plant supplying 70-MW of electricity to KESC. A second nuclear plant of a gross generating capacity of 325-MW is under construction with Chinese technical assistance at Chashma, Punjab province. The plant is scheduled for commissioned by the end of CY-2004.

Demand for Electricity - WAPDA's customer base has expanded from 10.22 million in PFY98 to 10.8 million in PFY-99. By March 2004, the base had reached a figure of 11.4 million. The average annual compound growth rate over the previous year is therefore 5.68 percent. KESC presently has 1.59 million customers. Electricity is still, however, available to less than half of the population. By March 31, 2004 WAPDA had electrified a total of 68,046 villages. WAPDA's program for PFY-2004 envisaged the electrification of 4,097 villages, but only 863 have been completed and another 200 are likely to be completed owing to the non-availability of funding from the GOP. WAPDA's plans call for the electrification of a total of 15,500 villages during the next five years, that is, from July 1, 2004 to June 30, 2005. It will require Rs.26 billion for this purpose.

Minerals - Pakistan offers many opportunities for investors in the mining sector. GOP departments involved in mining development are trying to attract foreign investment through joint ventures for specific projects. Pakistan Mineral Development Corporation (PMDC) is seeking joint venture to develop deposits of Lead and Zinc, and rock salt purification. The Sindh Coal Authority is seeking joint venture for the development of its coal deposits in Lakhra. Several other mineral deposits have been discovered but mines are yet to be developed due to shortage of required funds.

The mining sector registered a negative growth rate of approximately 20% for the year 1999/2004. Saindak Metal Corporation that was responsible for commercial production of copper, gold and silver from the Saindak mines has ceased operation due to lack of funds. Various government departments such as Pakistan Mineral Development Corporation (PMDC), Saindak Metal Corporation, Sindh Coal Authority, Punjab Mineral Development Corporation, Sarhad Development Authority and Baluchistan Development Authority are responsible for mining development. Geological Survey of Pakistan (GSP) is responsible for the pre-investigation of soil and geological surveys while the Oil and Gas Development Company Ltd., (OGDCL) is involved in exploration of oil and natural gas.

Total value of estimated reserves of various minerals, other than oil and gas, is approximately US$1.7 billion. Industry specialists feel that initially US$ 300 million is required to develop the reserves that have already been identified. Major mineral deposits in Pakistan are: coal (185 billion tons), limestone (500 million tons) barite (200 million tons), chromite (50 million tons), iron ore (50 million tons), marble & onyx (50 million tons), gypsum (20 million tons), china clay (20 million tons), pink granite (20 million tons), feldspar (10 million tons), and fluorite and quartz (5 million tons each).

During 1998-99, mineral imports of Pakistan included iron ore, copper ore, zinc, lead and aluminum. Pakistan also exported chromite to Japan and China, rock salt to USA, Canada, Indonesia, India and Bangladesh, silica sand to United Arab Emirates.

Coal: Pakistan's coal reserves received a substantial boost from the discovery (with USAID assistance) of deposits estimated at 175 billion tons in the Thar Desert. The country's total coal reserves are now estimated at 185 billion metric tons. Presently, about 91% of total coal production is being utilized for brick burning and 9% for power generation. As an underground mineral resource, coal (and its extraction) falls within the jurisdiction of the provincial governments. The policy for development of Thar coal provides that its primary use will be to fuel large electric power plants built in tandem with the coal mines, and that development, ownership and operation of both mines and power plants will be in the private sector. The Thar coal field has enormous economic potential for Pakistan.

ENVIRONMENT

Pakistan's attempt to raise the living standards of its citizens has meant that economic development has largely taken precedence over environmental issues. Unchecked use of hazardous chemicals, vehicle emissions, and industrial activity has contributed to a number of environmental and health hazards, chief among them being water pollution. Much of the country suffers from a lack of potable water due to industrial waste and agricultural runoff that contaminates drinking water supplies. Poverty and high population growth have aggravated, and to a certain extent, caused, these environmental problems.

Although Pakistan is renowned for its mountain ranges and areas of untouched wilderness, the country passed legislation to protect its environment only in the past 10 years. Environmental groups have questioned the country's commitment to environmental protection, pointing to the decision in August 1999 to allow oil and gas exploration in Kirthar National Park, the country's oldest national wildlife park, by a multi-national company.

In the cities, widespread use of low-quality fuel, combined with a dramatic expansion in the number of vehicles on Pakistani roads, has led to significant air pollution problems. Although Pakistan's energy consumption is still low by world standards, lead and carbon emissions are major air pollutants in urban centers such as Karachi, Lahore, and Islamabad.

Theft or diversion of electricity in transmission, as well as a lack of energy efficiency standards, have contributed to Pakistan's high energy and carbon intensities. To increase energy efficiency, the country is stepping up its use of renewable energy sources to bring electricity to rural areas. As urbanization continues and the population grows at a rapid rate, in the 21st century Pakistan will need to confront its environmental problems in order to safeguard the health of it citizens.

GOVERNMENT ROLE IN THE ECONOMY

Since the late 1980s, the GOP has been pursuing a gradual strategy of deregulation, reduction of the public sector role in the economy, and opening the economy to international competition. The government has sought to reduce its direct productive or controlling role, and instead focus on creating the conditions to foster private sector investment and activity. While it has made much progress in this effort, the state remains an important player in the Pakistani economy, especially in the financial sector. Government-owned industrial enterprises employ almost 46,000 workers and remain important in such key sectors as steel, engineering and agro-processing.

MONETARY POLICY

The Government of Pakistan has followed a liberal monetary policy during 1999-2004 in order to provide cheap credit to the sagging industrial sector. In this regard, it has reduced the interest rates on treasury bills that act as a benchmark for the lending rates of banks. The demand for credit, however, has not come forth from the private sector. Although domestic credit expansion was higher this year due to large borrowing by the government sector, conversion of non-resident foreign currency accounts into rupees and an increase in liquid reserves, actual growth in money supply has remained stagnant due to low credit demand from the private sector.

Despite an aggressive loan recovery drive by the military government that has led to the recovery of $325.62 million, the major public sector banks and the development finance institutions continue to hold large number of defaulted loans. A Corporate and Industrial Restructuring Corporation has been established to take over the bad loans of the banking sector and to revive sick industries. It is expected that, with the taking over of bad loans by the Corporation, the banks' balance sheets will improve significantly and make them lucrative for privatization.

The GOP and State Bank of Pakistan (SBP, the central bank) are attempting structural reforms in an effort to move toward more indirect, market-based methods of monetary control along with greater autonomy for the SBP. Other GOP monetary reforms have included efforts to reduce concessional and government-directed credit schemes, enhance competition in the banking sector, and improve prudential regulation and supervision. Prudential regulations have occasionally been relaxed in ad hoc fashion to prop up loss-making public or private industries. The State Bank of Pakistan's autonomy was considerably strengthened with the passage of new banking laws in and the amendment of the State Bank Act in May 1997.

FISCAL POLICY

A central element of Pakistan's economic reforms has been the effort to reduce persistent government budget deficits. However, little overall progress has actually been made so far and the current financial position of the country remains fragile. The size of the fiscal deficit turned out to be higher than reported for 1998-99, primarily on the basis of higher expenditures. The reason for this appears to be a systemic failure that includes weak budgeting and poor reporting and accounting procedures. In light of these factors, the revised fiscal deficit target for 1999-2004 is 5.4 percent of GDP.

Deficit reduction is constrained by rigidities in spending patterns and a weak tax base. Defense spending and debt repayments absorb 67 percent of total federal spending, leaving little for other basic government functions and improving the long-neglected social sectors. Meanwhile, the country has a very narrow tax base; perhaps one in one hundred Pakistanis pays income tax. The country has had to rely on import and excise taxes for a very high share of revenues, thus protecting inefficient industries and encouraging smuggling, and on official transfers from external creditors, primarily the World Bank, the Asian Development Bank and the Government of Japan.

The present government appears serious about the documentation of the economy and consequent broadening of the tax base that is expected to generate additional tax revenue of $1.93 billion for the next fiscal year. According to World Bank survey, the undocumented economy in Pakistan is 71 percent of GDP. In order to document the economy the Government of Pakistan has started a tax survey of industrial, residential and commercial areas in thirteen major cities and plans to extend it to the whole country.

The GOP's medium-term adjustment program has aimed to broaden the tax base through extension to under-taxed sectors and reduction of exemptions; to shift from taxation of international trade to taxation of consumption; to move to market determination of administered prices; and to improve the productivity of public spending. Progress has been mixed. Agriculture remains very lightly taxed. A sales tax has been instituted. Maximum import tariffs were reduced from 70 percent in 1994-95 to 65 percent in 1995-96, to 45 percent in March 1997, and to 35 percent in March 1999. Increases in utility charges have attempted to keep pace with actual costs, but fee collection remains a serious problem.

PRIVATIZATION

Privatization of many state-owned enterprises is another key element of Pakistan's reform program. In 1991 the GOP identified a group of 118 state-owned industrial units for privatization. Of these, 97 units have been sold off. Industrial units, including factories producing cement, chemicals, automobiles, food products, etc., have mainly attracted domestic private investors.

The GOP plans to spend 90 percent of privatization proceeds for debt retirement and 10 percent for poverty alleviation. An upcoming privatization law is expected to introduce transparency and give legal protection to the contracts. A focused privatization policy has been developed by the present regime that is based on sector reforms and transaction restructuring prior to strategic sale, public offers and strategic sales, and an effective communication program. A Gas Regulatory Authority Ordinance has been promulgated and its chairman and members have been selected, and a communication strategy for privatization is being developed with World Bank assistance.

The government has laid out a timeframe for privatization of various organizations in the financial, oil and gas, power, industrial and telecommunication sectors and the privatization process is to be completed by June 30, 2002. In most cases, the GOP aims to find "strategic investors" to buy up to 26 percent of these firms and gain management control. The privatization process is a very complex undertaking, since new regimes for regulation of private sector entities in these sectors are still being established. The government is benefiting from World Bank technical assistance in this effort and has hired several foreign financial advisors to help with the preparation.

Foreign investors have shown interest in acquiring stakes in these firms but note that reliable independent audits would speed the bidding process.

The GOP and public-sector unions have agreed on a generous relief package for employees of divested state-owned enterprises. Labor opposition to the privatization program has held up some privatization initiatives through legal action.

BALANCE OF PAYMENT SITUATION

Foreign Exchange Policies and Reserves

The GOP has continued policies to liberalize and deregulate the exchange and payments regime. The Pakistani rupee has been on a managed floating exchange rate until July 21, 1998. Pakistan moved to a dual exchange rate system from July 22, 1998. Under this regime there existed two exchange rates, inter bank floating rate and composite rate, besides official exchange rate determined by the State Bank of Pakistan. While the inter-bank floating rate was determined by the market mechanisms, the composite rate was weighted average of official exchange rate and the inter bank floating rate. However in a major development the dual exchange rate was replaced with a market-based unitary exchange rate system from May 19, 1999. The rupee fell significantly against the dollar as the result of unification in May 1999; since then it has been stable. The stability of the exchange rate since its unification has resulted from low relative inflation rates, adequate levels of foreign exchange reserves, orderly payments of all foreign obligations, lower dollarization of domestic savings and depressed private demand.

The liquid reserves of Pakistan have remained stable above US$1.4 billion during 1999-2004. They are able to finance two months of imports for Pakistan. The accretion of liquid reserves has taken place due to outright purchases from the kerb market.

Foreign Trade

The country's trade performance showed some improvement during FY1999-2004 over FY 1998-1999. The trade deficit at the end of first nine months (July-March) of 1999-2004 stood at $1.471 billion, down by 3 percent over the same period of the previous year. Exports were up 9.8 percent while imports increased 10.9 percent.

In 1998-99, Pakistan's foreign trade decreased 8.5 percent over the previous year. However, a sharper fall in exports, increased the trade deficit to $2.085 billion. Exports for 1998-99 totaled $7.528 billion compared to $8.434 billion in 1997-98. Imports in 1998-1999 were $9.613 billion versus $10.3 billion in the previous year.

An export growth of 9.8 percent in 1999-2004 was mainly due to higher exports of textiles, rice, raw cotton, and fish and fish preparation. In 1998-99, the following countries were the largest recipients of Pakistani exports: the U.S. (21.8 percent); the UK (6.6 percent); Germany (6.6 percent); Japan (3.5 percent); Hong Kong (7.1 percent); United Arab Emirates (5.4 percent); France (3.2 percent); The Netherlands (3.1 percent).

Imports, at $8.33 billion during the first nine months (July-April) of 1999-2004, increased 10.9 percent over the previous year mainly due to higher imports of petroleum and petroleum products, chemicals and metal products. In 1998-99, the following countries were the major sources of Pakistan's imports: the U.S. (7.7 percent); Japan (8.3 percent); Malaysia (6.7 percent); Germany (4.1 percent); Kuwait (5.9 percent); UK (4.3 percent); Saudi Arabia (6.8 percent); China (4.2 percent).

Remittances from Overseas Workers

Remittances from overseas workers have been a major source of foreign exchange earnings for Pakistan. They peaked at $2.89 billion in 1982-83, then dropped to $1.5 billion in 1995-96. In FY 1997-98 workers' remittances further dropped to $1.4 billion. The relative importance of workers' remittances, however, continues to decline. In the past ten years they have fallen from 10 percent of GDP to about 5 percent.

The fall in workers' remittances has been a source of concern for policy makers. The sharp and unprecedented increase in the kerb premium in the first quarter of FY1999 forced official remitters to move to the "Hundi" system, an unofficial albeit reliable means of remittance. Despite normalization of the kerb premium following unification of the exchange rate in May 1999, official remittances have not returned to the pre-May 1998 levels.

The inflows under resident foreign currency accounts have also fallen drastically after the freezing of foreign currency accounts in May 1998. Although this fall has put an upward pressure on Pakistan's current account deficit, this is not the source of hard currency that the State Bank of Pakistan is trying to encourage. The State Bank prefers to purchase dollars from the kerb market in order to cushion the current account instead of relying on resident foreign currency accounts.

External Sector: No new inflows of foreign assistance have come forth from the international financial institutions during the financial year 1999-2004. In fact, Pakistan experienced net outflows to IFIs during this period, as these are preferred creditors. Negotiations with the International Monetary Fund are, however, expected for a new Poverty Reduction and Growth Facility in order to replace the suspended ESAF program.

INFRASTRUCTURE

Ports - Pakistan has two significant seaports – The Karachi Port (KPT) and Port Mohammed bin Qasim - and two proposed sites for future facilities - Gwadar and Pasni, both on Balochistan's Makran Coast. Karachi is the main port, handling the majority of all dry and liquid cargo. During FY1999-00, Karachi Port handled 18.004 million tons of cargo, an increase of 2.4 percent from the preceding year. In contrast, Port Qasim during the same period handled 9.5 million tons of cargo, showing an increase of 19 percent over the corresponding period last year.

To facilitate this expansion, the GOP has allowed two shipping companies to construct and operate specialized integrated container terminals at Port Qasim and on Karachi's West and East Wharves. The GOP also plans acquisition of a bucket dredging plant, development of a modern warehousing complex in Karachi, and construction of a liquid products marine terminal at Karachi. In addition, the GOP proposes private sector participation in contract dredging to deepen navigational channels.

Railroads - Pakistan Railways, an autonomous agency under the Ministry of Railways, operates the railroad system. The system is primarily broad-gauge, but there are also segments of meter-gauge and narrow-gauge track. Over the past fifteen years, there has been a marked shift in freight traffic from rail to highways, a trend that the GOP hopes to stabilize and reverse. Railways carry about 15 percent of freight traffic and road vehicles 85 percent. The rail system comprises 781 stations and 45 halts. Rolling stock includes about 550 locomotives, 4,250 passenger coaches, and 32,000 freight cars. Pakistan Railways plans to improve railroad's share of long-haul freight traffic, to upgrade track to permit trains to operate at higher speeds, and to rehabilitate infrastructure in order to improve capacity utilization. Specific priorities include double-tracking; rehabilitating about 380 traction motors; procurement of diesel-electric locomotive engines; and manufacturing air-conditioned cars and diesel-electric locomotives at a recently opened factory at Risalpur in the NWFP, as well as upgrading telecommunications and signaling systems.

Highways - The World Bank reports that Pakistan's road network is notable for its poor condition. About fifty percent of the road network is unpaved and over two-thirds of paved arterial roads do not have enough carriageway width for two lanes. The majority of paved and unpaved roads are in poor condition. According to the World Bank, on average, poorly maintained roads can cause

30-40 percent higher transportation costs. At both federal and provincial levels, Pakistan provides insufficient funding for road maintenance.

Over 90 percent of Pakistan's freight and passenger traffic travels by road. By March 2004 Pakistan had 249,959 kilometers of roads. The major north-south and east-west link is Lahore and Rawalpindi to Peshawar and carries over half of Pakistan's goods and passenger traffic.

The National Highway Authority (NHA), established in 1991, has the major responsibility to plan, promote, organize and implement programs for construction, development, operation, repairs and maintenance of national highways and strategic roads. The National Highway Council headed by the Prime Minister approves plans, policies and budget of the NHA. Presently, the NHA accounts for 4 percent of the road network and 63 percent of the road traffic in the country. The total length of roads under the NHA is 7,620 kilometers.

The GOP's key development priority in the highway sector is to upgrade and fill in gaps in the existing road network so the system can be more efficiently utilized. Proper maintenance of the network is a newly emphasized priority. Additional construction projects include completion of the Indus Highway, converting of the principal route (the N-5 National Highway) to double track, work on upgradation of critical reaches on N-35 and replacement of old steel bridges by permanent concrete bridges and construction of several inter-city expressways and by-passes. The Lahore-Islamabad motorway was opened for traffic in November 1997.

Air Transport - The GOP has opened the domestic aviation market to private sector competition. As of July 2004, four private carriers are operating on local and international routes. Three private airlines, namely Aero Asia, Shaheen Air International and Bhoja Air are operating on local and international routes, while the fourth private sector airline, Safe Air International is operating on domestic routes only. The national carrier, PIA, has a fleet of 48 planes (eleven Boeing 747s, ten Airbus 300s, six Airbus 310s, seven Boeing 737s, twelve Fokker-27s, two DeHavilland Twin Otters). PIA serves 35 domestic and 37 international destinations.

The GOP plans to continue modernizing and upgrading its civil aviation facilities. This includes construction of a new international airport at Lahore. New airports and improvements in runways are also planned for Islamabad, Peshawar, Karachi, Sialkot and other cities.

Utilities - Two public utilities, the Water and Power Development Administration (WAPDA) and the Karachi Electric Supply Corporation (KESC) are responsible for electric power generation and distribution. However, the GOP's policy to bring private firms into the generation of power has been inconsistent.

Telecommunications - In December 1990, Pakistan converted Pakistan Telephone and Telegraph (PTT) Department, which was directly controlled by the Ministry of Communications, into Pakistan Telecommunications Corporation, (PTC), and more recently into Pakistan Telecommunication Company Limited (PTCL), still the only provider of basic telephone services. The GOP plans to privatize PTC, by first selling 26 percent ownership to a "strategic investor", and then selling the rest after the firm is on a solid footing. The GOP has deregulated and privatized selected telecommunication services. At present there are three cellular mobile phone operators and a fourth one (owned by the PTCL) will commence operation by January 2005. In addition, there is one radio paging company; seven card-phone licensees; seventy telex, facsimile and PABX service providers; two manufacturers of large digital exchanges; 60 ISPs, and more than twenty data network operators in the private sector.

INDUSTRIAL POLICY

Foreign investors are allowed participation in industrial projects on 100 percent equity basis, without any permission of the Government.
No government sanction is required for setting up an industry in any field, place and size, except for the following four industries:

Arms and Ammunitions
High explosives
Radio-active substances
Security printing, currency and mint (establishment of new units for the manufacture of alcohol, except industrial alcohol, is banned).

There is no requirement for obtaining No Objection Certificate (NOC) from the provincial government for locating the project any where in the country except the areas which are notified as negative areas.

Hotels & Tourism have been declared as an Industry/ Industrial undertaking. Therefore, this sector is already open to foreign investment and is entitled to incentives and concessions as admissible under the Tourism Policy.

INVESTMENT POLICY

The Investment Policy has been formulated to provide an integrated strategy for creating an investor friendly environment with the focus on further opening up of the economy and marketing the potentials of all economic sectors for direct foreign investment. The essence of the policy is to keep Pakistan attractive in International Investment Market by improving the Policy Regime, offering fiscal and tariff relief and through providing additional procedural & social facilitation.

(a) Policies

Previously only manufacturing sector was open to foreign investment. Now, it has been decided to liberalize the Policy Regime, open up other economic sectors for FDI and mobilize the domestic financial resources towards long-term investment. Foreign investment on repatriable basis is now allowed in Agriculture, Service, Infrastructure and Social Sectors, thus opening up of all sectors of economy to foreign investment.
Foreign repatriable investment in above sectors will be subject to the following conditions:

AGRICULTURE SECTOR

Activities

Land Development/Reclamation of barren land, desert and hilly areas for Agriculture purpose and Crops Farming, Reclamation of Water Front areas/Creeks, crops, Fruits, Vegetable s, Flowers, Farming/Integrated Agriculture (Cultivation and Processing of Crops), Modernization & Development of irregation Facilities and Water Management, Plantation/ Forestry, Horticulture, Dairy, small ruminants (Sheep, Goat) & all other livestock farming & breeding.

Conditions:

The amount of foreign equity investment in the company/project shall be at least US$ 0.5 million.

A minimum of 40% of the equity shall be held by the Pakistani company or individuals in the company.

There is no upper ceiling of land holding for registered agricultural companies. However, the income of these companies
would be taxable.

The proposals related to foreign investment in the Agriculture Sector are processed by the BOI in consultation with the respective Provincial Governments for approval by the competent forum.

The land for agriculture purpose can be obtained on lease basis for long periods, i.e. initially upto 30 years, extendable for a further period of 20 years.

Foreign company, allowed for investment in agriculture sector is not allowed to transfer such land to any foreign company unless specifically permitted by the Federal & concerned Provincial Government.

Foreign Investment on repatriable basis is now allowed in under mentioned activities of Agriculture, Service, Infrastructure and Social sector subject to the conditions indicated below, provided these companies have been registered under the companies ordinance 1984 with securities and exchange Commission of Pakistan and the BOI.

SERVICES SECTORS

Activities

Wholesale Distribution and Retail trade, transportation, Storage and communications. Real Estate Development (Development of commercial Buildings, Apartment, Housing Projects, Super Markets/Shopping malls, Urban development, Development of New Communities), Technical Testing Facilities, Audio Visual Services, Sporting and other recreation services, Rental Services relating to Transport Equipment and Machinery, Equipment and Tools for Land development and Agricultural purposes, Environmental Services.

Conditions

- The amount of foreign equity investment in the company/project shall be at east US$ 0.5 million.
- Foreign investors are allowed to hold 100% foreign equity subject to condition that the repatriation of profits will be restricted to a maximum of 60% of total equity or profits and it will be mandatory to meet the condition that minimum 40% of the equity is held by Pakistani Investors (including sale of share in stock exchange within two years time.

INFRASTRUCTURE SECTOR/ HOTELS & TOURISM

Infrastructure Projects including development of Industrial Zones, Telecommunications
Hotels & Tourism or Tourism Related services

The amount of foreign equity investment in the company/project shall be at least US$ 0.5 Million. 100% foreign equity is allowed on repatriable basis.

Social sectors

Social Sector includes education, Technical/ Vocational Training, Human Resource Development (HRD) as well as hospitals, Medical and Diagnostic Services.

- The amount of foreign equity investment in the company project shall be at least US$ 0.5 Million.
- 100% foreign equity is allowed.

PROTECTION MEASURES

Protection to Domestic Manufacturing

The Concept to keep the domestic manufacturing competitive will continue to be followed in adjusting tariff structure. The duty on finished products will attract higher rate than the imported raw materials/inputs. Therefore, incidence of duties and taxes on locally produced goods would be less than the incidence of duties and taxes on finished imported goods. A reasonable tariff protection will be available to domestic manufacturing depending upon value addition.

Protection to Foreign Investment

The economic policies, and the existing legal cover for foreign and Pakistani investment will be extended to new areas/sectors. The benefits and incentives tor investment, provided by the Government shall continue in force and will not be reduced or altered to the disadvantage of investors. Accordingly Foreign Private Investment (Promotion and Protection) Act, 1976 and the Protection of Economic Reforms Act, 1992 shall be amended.

Guarantees

Government of Pakistan attaches great importance to the inflow of direct private foreign investment into the country as it brings in capital, advanced technology, managerial and technical skills and marketing expertise. In order to facilitate foreign investment, revolutionary measures have been taken to provide entreprenuers the maximum freedom for investment.

The Government of Pakistan is committed to providing full protection to foreign investment. For this purpose, adequate statuatory safe guards have been provided by the

Foreign Private Investment (Promotion and Protection), Act, 1976 and Economics Act no. XII of 1992. Both acts are placed as annexures I and II.

In addition, the Government has entered into bilateral investment treaties with:
Sweden, Germany, Romania, United Kingdom, Spain, France, The Netherlands, Portugal, Turkmenistan, Tajikstan, Kirgystan, Kazakhstan, Turkey, Kuwait, Malaysia, Singapore, China and South Korea.
Pakistan is also a signatory to the convention establishing the Multilateral Investment Guarantee Agency (MIGA).

REGISTRATION WITH BOI

FOREIGN COMPANIES REGISTRATION FORM
Note: Type or print in capital letters
1. NAME OF THE COMPANY
A) NAME OF THE CHIEF EXECUTIVE:
B) NATURE OF BUSINESS:
C) ADDRESS (OUTSIDE PAKISTAN): ______________________________

_________________________TELEPHONE: __________________________ FAX NO.
_______________E-MAIL:

____

D) ADDRESS (IN PAKISTAN): ____

____

TELEPHONE: ______________ FAX NO. _____________ E-MAIL: __________
2. COUNTRY OF ORIGIN:
(Attach Certificate of Incorporation along with list of Directors)
3. NAME & ADDRESS OF PERSON AUTHORIZED TO ACT ON BEHALF OF COMPANY:
A) IN PAKISTAN:

B) OUTSIDE PAKISTAN:
4. NAME OF COUNTRIES WHERE INVESTMENT HAS ALREADY BEEN MADE:
5. NAME OF THE PROPOSED COMPANY FOR WHICH REGISTRATION IS REQUIRED IN PAKISTAN:
6. REGISTERED OFFICE IN PAKISTAN
7. INTENDED FIELD OF BUSINESS/ACTIVITIES IN PAKISTAN:
(MAY PROVIDE DETAILS SEPARATELY)
8. DATE OF REGISTRATION OF COMPANY UNDER THE COMPANY ORDINANCE 1984:
(Attach the Certificate of Incorporation of Company in Pakistan if available)
9. WHETHER REPATRIATION FACILITIES ARE REQUIRED BY FOREIGN FIRM FOR CAPITAL AND PROFITS:
10. NAME & ADDRESS OF PAKISTANI PARTNER/COMPANY/DIRECTOR WITH DETAILS OF INVESTMENT:
11. WHETHER PROPOSED COMPANY IS SUBSIDIARY OF
ANY OTHER PRINCIPAL/ORGANIZATION:
12. NUMBER OF PERSONNEL TO BE EMPLOYED:

	EXECUTIVES/ MANAGERS	TECHNICAL/ PROFESSIONALS	WORKERS	TOTAL
LOCAL::				
FOREIGN:				
G. TOTAL:				

13. PROPOSED INVESTMENT WITH DETAILS, AS UNDER:

	FOREIGN	LOCAL	TOTAL
A) EQUITY:			
B) LOAN:			
G. TOTAL (A+B):			

14. NAME & ADDRESS OF BANK IN PAKISTAN:
15. ANY OTHER INFORMATION WHICH IS DEEMED APPROPRIATE FOR CONSIDERATION:
16. LIST OF PAPERS ATTACHED/ENCLOSURES:
SIGNATURE:
NAME:
DESIGANTION:
ADDRESS

ASSITANCE TO FOREING INVESTORS

To improve working relations among the employers & employees and to increase the productivity, Labour Laws will be revised:-

1. Manpower
i) Contract Labour

In order to improve the productivity and efficiency in the country the contract labour system will be encouraged for the industries to improve our work force and to be competitive in the world market.

ii) Right to Replace Unwilling Workers
The right to replace unwilling workers by willing workers will be exercised under the provisions of relevant Law for violence, indiscipline, and loss of productivity.

iii) Consolidation of Labour Laws

The difficulties are being faced by the employers in the country due to numerous laws which are at present in vogue in matters covering the labour field. The existing labour laws will, therefore, be reduced to a few essential laws covering terms and working conditions of employment,, wages and other benefits, safety and labour welfare. A commission will be constituted for the purpose of consolidation, simplification and rationalization of labour laws.

iv) Outsiders and Trade Union Activity
Outside trade union activity under ILO - Agreement will be trade based but not factory based. However, no steps will be taken contrary to ILO Convention which have been ratified by Pakistan.

v) Trade Unionism

The mushroom growth of trade unions at the plant level has been a source of constant disruption in the pace of industrial relations foiling genuine efforts by the parties to promote mutual confidence. In order to check mushroom growth of trade unions, the unions receiving less than a minimum level of support (20% of the votes) in referendum will stand dissolved automatically and their registration be canceled.

vi) National Productivity Council
National Productivity Council will be set up to suggest measures to increase productivity and to also link wages with productivity.

vii) Minimum Wage Council

A Tripartite National Wage Council will be set up to systematically determine the minimum wage for different business activities, industries and occupations in different provinces by taking into account the typical realities and state of economic growth of the province.

viii) Workers Profit Sharing
In view of rise in cost of living, the law of Worker's Profit Participation Fund will be amended so as to enhance the wage limit to a reasonable extent and to give benefit of profit share to a maximum number of workers. A committee consisting of representatives from Ministry of Labour, FPCCI and National Trade Unions shall decide the limit for this purpose.

INCENTIVES

Exchange Control

i) Full repatriation of capital, capital gains, dividend, profits is allowed.

ii) There are no restrictions for contracting foreign private loans (which do not involve any guarantee by the Government of Pakistan). Also, there is no restriction on source of foreign

currency loan. Long term loans can be arranged from a bank, financial institution, parent companies of multinationals or under suppliers credit.
Transfer of Technology

There are no ceilings on payment of royalties and technical service fee.

iv. UNILATERAL RELIEF

A person resident in Pakistan is entitled to a relief in tax on any income earned abroad, if such income has already been subjected to tax outside Pakistan. Proportionate relief is allowed on such income at an average rate of tax in Pakistan or abroad, whichever is lower.

v. AGREEMENTS FOR AVOIDANCE OF DOUBLE TAXATION

The Government of Pakistan has so far signed agreements to avoid double taxation with 37 countries including almost all the developed countries of the world. These agreements lay down the ceilings on tax rates applicable to different types of income arising in Pakistan. They also lay down some basic principles of taxation which cannot be modified unilaterally. The list of countries with which Pakistan has concluded tax treaties is given below:

1 LIST OF THE COUNTRIES

Austria
Belgium
Bangladesh
Canada
China
Denmark
Egypt
France
Finland
Germany
Greece
India
Indonesia
Iran
Ireland
Italy
Japan
South Korea
Lebanon
Libya
Malta
Mauritius
Saudi Arabia
Singapore
Poland
Romania
Sri Lanka
Switzerland
Sweden
Thailand
Turkmenistan
Tunisia

Turkey
Kazakistan
U.K.
U.S.A.
U.A.E.

In addition to the above, following new incentives have been granted by the Prime Minister while announcing the new investment policy in November 1997.

Notification

Force Commander,
Hqs ASF,
Karachi

MOST IMMEDIATE
NO. 11-30/96-SEC
Government of Pakistan Ministry of Defence
(Defence Division)
Rawalpindi, 11th Feb. ' 98

AIRRPORT ENTRY PASSES

Dear Sir,
I am directed to refer to his Ministery's letter No. 11-30/96-SEC dated, 5th January, 1998, on the above subject and to state that the Federal Cabinet in its special meeting held on 21-11-1997, in case No. 389/39/97 has decided that one Airport Entry Pass for protocol purpose will be issued to designated persons of foreign and local investor/companies, provided volume of equity investment is US $10 Million.
In view of the above the following new sub para (vii) may be added under para 9a) of this Ministry's above cited letter:-
These will also be issued valid for all lounges (less Exective Lounges) at all Airports to the designated persons of foreign and local investors/companies provided volume of equity investment is US $10 million.

Yours faithfully,
Sd
(GHULAM MOHIUDDIN)
SECTION OFFICER
TELE: 564617
DUTY FREE IMPORT OF FOOD STUFF
GOVERNMENT OFF PAKISTAN
CENTRAL BOARD OF REVENUE
C. NO. 10 (15)/73.CUS.FXM Islamabad, the 18th February, 1998.

CUSTOMS GENERAL ORDER NO.5
Subject:- DUTY FREE IMPORT OF FOOD STUFF BY FOREIGN INVESTORS, EXCUTIVES AND EXPATRIATES EMPLOYEES.

In super session of C.G.O 4/98 dated 9th January: 1998 and in partial modification of Customs \general Order in 15/96 dated 15th June, 1996, the central board of Revnue in federal to substitute sub para (n) there of as follows:-

"food shuff worth US $1000/- par annum per person mould be allowed to be imported/purchased from duty free shops and diplomatic banded warhousea without payment of customs duty and taxas by the foreign investors, executives and expatriate employees working in Pakisttan. However, this concession will not extand to any alcohol in bevarages."

(H.A. SHIRAYT)
Chief(CustomsProduct)
IMMIGRATION PROCEDURE

EXISTING VISA POLICY

To facilitate travel and stay in Pakistan of foreign businessmen and investors, the visa policy has been considerably relaxed.
* Businessmen and investors, from the 43 countries listed below, with substantial investment in Pakistan would be granted multiple entry visas valid for three years:

Australia
Austria
Bahrain
Belgium
Brunei
Canada
China
Czech Republic
Denmark
Finland
France
Germany
Greece
Hong Kong
Iceland
Indonesia
Iran
Ireland
Italy
Japan
Kenya
Kuwait
Luxembourg
Malaysia
Netherlands
New Zealand
Norway
Hungry
Oman
Poland
Portugal
Qatar
Saudi Arabia
Singapore
South Korea
Spain

Sweden
Switzerland
Thailand
Turkey
U.A.E.
U.K.
USA
.

* Businessmen from the listed countries who want to establish business offices in Pakistan would be issued multiple entry visa for one year on recommendations of their embassies/missions in Pakistan;

* Businessmen/investors from any of the listed countries where there is no Pakistani Embassy will also be allowed thirty days landing permit on arrival at the airport in Pakistan;

* Pakistani industrialists/businessmen interested to invite foreign entrepreneurs from countries, other than the listed, for promotion of trade and industrial cooperation would be allowed to sponsor, on their guarantee, the grant of visa for one month through Chambers of Commerce and Industry at Lahore, Karachi, Peshawar, Quetta, Islamabad and the Federation of Pakistan Chambers of Commerce and Industry.

FURTHER CONCESSIONS IN THE NEW POLICY

a. Work Permit

(i) The expatriate technical and managerial personnel working in manufacturing/industrial sector are exempt from obtaining work permits.

(ii) In other cases the work permits will be issued by the Board of Investment within a period of 4 to 6 weeks.

(iii) Work permits will be issued for a period of 3 to 5 years - or validity of the passports.

b. Opening of Project/ Branch/Liaison Office

(i) In case of requests for opening branch, liaison or representative office by a foreign company, and registration of foreign investing companies in service, social and agricultural sectors, time limit for processing and final response by the BOI will be 6-8 weeks.

(ii) The details pertaining to required documentation, etc., are available at all offices of BOI.

(iii) The permission for opening of branch/liaison office will be granted by BOI for a period of 3 to 5 years. Further extension will be granted by BOI after reviewing/examining the performance of foreign company during previous permitted period. The request for renewal/extension will be processed and disposed off by BOI within 2 weeks time provided such requests are supported with complete documentation.

c. Issuance of Work Visas

(i) Work visa will be issued within a maximum time of one (1) month after the receipt of request along with the required documentation.

(ii) Multiple entry visa for 3 years will be issued to foreign investors and expatriate employees subject to submission of complete documentation by their employer company and they hold work permit/passports valid for 3 years. In case multiple entry visa is granted, the number of entries will not be restricted to any specified limit.

(iii) The concerned Pakistani Mission abroad will grant work visa till the validity of work permit or passport which ever is earlier, within a week after the receipt of request provided BOI issues work permits on the basis of NOC of Ministry of Interior. In emergent cases, Ministry of Interior will issue work visas up to 3 months to a foreigner on the recommendation of BOI or on the request of the employer (as the case may be) without any clearance. However, further extension will be allowed after completing necessary formalities, i.e., production of work permit (in case it is required) and obtaining security clearance.

(iv) Business visa will be issued on the same day basis.

(v) In case of the projects in power, petroleum exploration, communication etc., concerned agency or the management of such projects will identify the requirement of expatriate personnel. Accordingly, Ministry of Interior would issue visas subject to condition that particulars along with supporting documents of the expatriate personnel are furnished to the Ministry.

(vi) For the purpose of changing the category of visa of foreign national employees/investors, from business visa to work visa, the condition to go out of Pakistan to any third country and get it converted from Pakistani Mission in that country, has been withdrawn. In future, Ministry of Interior will process such requests on getting verification from BOI. Further details may be obtained from BOI or from Ministry of Interior.

3. Grant of Pakistan's Citizenship to Foreign Nationals (Investors)
By allowing the Pakistani Citizenship to foreign investors, potential foreign businessmen could provide an additional source of foreign investment for Pakistan. Any person of a country recognized by Pakistan, may get Pakistani Citizenship by investing a minimum of US$ 0.75 million in tangible assets and $ 0.25 million (or equivalent in major foreign currency) in cash, both on non- repatriable basis and subject to fulfillment of the conditions of Pakistan Citizenship Law. It is clarified that transfer on non-repatriable means thatthe amount will be brought to Pakistan through normal banking channels, converted into rupee and never remitted back through the free market.

EXPORT INCENTIVES

VALUE ADDED OR EXPORT INDUSTRIES

The units which export minimum 50% (average) of their annual prduction for ten years or have minimum value-addition of 40% of production value (which may be specified from time to time), will be treated as Value-Added or Export Industry respectively. The indicative list for such industries is shown in Category (A). Any industry other than indicated in the list for Category (A) shall also be entitled for the same incentives provided it fulfills the criteria laid down for this category. A technical Sub-committee has been set up to determine the level of value addition in an Industry.

TARIFF

i) Zero rated tariff is applicable on imporrt of plant, machinery & equipment (which is not manufactured locally) for the industries falling under (A) & (B) i.e., Value Added Export and Hi-tech Industies.
Fiscal (Tax Relief)

(i) First Year Allowance (FYA)
For new investments, First Year Allowance (FYA) on capital expenditure/investment, will be granted. The capital expenditure/investment includes the cost of Plant, Machinery & Equipment (PME). However, FYA is allowed in case tax exemption/holiday is not available. FYA can be

utilized to set-off against the statutory income in the year of assessment. Any un-utilized allowance can be carried forward to subsequent years until the whole amount is used up.

INCENTIVES IN INDUSTRIAL ZONES

The present Government assigns high priority for revitalization of the economy and create more conducive and liberal environment for foreign and local investment in the country. The announcement of economic reform package and budgetary measures for rationalization of taxes and tariff are manifestation of Government support to provide concessions and facilities for activating private sector as engine of economic growth in the country.

Translating these objectives into practical realities, calls for adoption of pragmatic policy package for development of industrial zones that could effectively energize the process of efficient industrialization and development with adequate attraction for local and foreign investment.

INSTITUTIONAL FRAMEWORK

A scheme of National Industrial Zones (NIZs) engulfing industrial estates, free industrial zone and Free trade zone and Export Oriented Units and Estates for Small and Medium Industries within the areas of its boundary will be launched at a few selected prime sites. Export-Oriented Units will however be allowed to be set up all over the country.

The basic criteria of selection of the site will be availability of "access-net" infrastructure and utilities to the door steps of the zone involving minimal expenditure of the Government and participation of foreign and local investors in development of infrastructure within the zone, its marketing, management and establishment of industries.

Free Industrial Zone will be multi-product zone where a variety of export products can be manufactured, traded, exported or re-exported. The zone will offer incentives package on the pattern of EPZ, allowing trading activity/acting as a hub of warehousing of imported produce and their re-export in freely convertible foreign exchange.

Free Trade Zone will serve as an effective instrument to boost up Export trading. The zone set up as an enclave separated from Domestic Tariff Area by physical barriers are intended to provide an internationally competitive duty-free environment for trading of exportable production at low costs. Trading activities, namely, imports for re-export in freely convertible foreign exchange for activities such as repacking and labelling will be permitted. Import for reconditioning, repair and re-engineering will also be permissible for export in freely convertible foreign exchange. Private bonded warehouses will be permitted to be set up in the Zone to meet the requirements of industrial units in the Free Industrial Zones or other EOUs in the country. The Free Trade Zone will be allowed similar concessions and facilities as are admissible to the free industrial zones and Export Oriented Units for value addition and export.

An Export Oriented Unit (EOU) is an industrial unit which exports its entire production excluding permitted level of Domestic Tariff Area (DTA) sales and reject.

Infrastructure within the Zone will be developed by the Private Sector Investors. Development, management and marketing of Industrial, Estate/Free Industrial Zone and Free Trade Zone will be offered to local and foreign investors under the Investor, Developer and Promoter (IDP) Scheme. Provision of infrastructure and utility facilities upto the Zones will be the responsibility either of relevant agencies of the Government or the Developer/Investor. As added incentive to Developer/Investor, area surrounding the zone may be offered to them for development of township including commercial and residential facilities.

Country specific zones will be allowed to be established by Developer/Investor to attract setting up of industrial units preferably export-oriented industries. The developer of zone and the project investors may be allowed "bond facilities" for their community and cultural activities within the area of the zone. They may also be allowed to develop residential facilities for the personnel working in the zone.

A single National Industrial Zone Authority (NIZA) will be set-up with statutory powers to carry out the responsibility of management of the National Industrial Zone. However, the existing Export Processing Zone Authority Ordinance 1980 may continue to apply to the Free Industrial Zone (Export Processing Zone) and Free Trade Zones. The National Industrial Zone Authority (NIZA) will be established through an enactment to provide a legal framework for management and providing necessary facilities and services to the Zones.

The development, marketing and maintenance of the Estate, infrastructure facilities within the Zone will be responsibility of the Developer/Managing Company. Provision of utilities will be the responsibility of the developer of the estate/zone or the concerned departments depending on the agreement to be reached with the developer. The NIZA will deal with the regulation of public services, revenue collection and management of the affairs of the Zone for implementation of the NIZs Act and other enactments, and issuing of permission for projects under "One Window Facility".

The National Industrial Zone Authority (NIZA) will extend one window facility to give permissions incorporating all required clearance of various departments and arrange utility facility and other related services for the investors to undertake industrial project within the zone.
The policy matters and issues will be dealt by the Board of Investment. The implementation of the Policy of the National Industrial Zones (NIZs) will rest in the National Industrial Zone Authority (NIZA) Management Committee for the zone will run the administrative and management affairs of the Zone which will have representation of the developers, and the sponsors/investors of the projects in the Zones. The functionaries of various departments of the government working in the zone shall be under the administrative control of the Management Committee of the zone.

INCENTIVES IN PRIORITY AREAS

ENERGY

* Oil and Gas drilling and refining
* Power generation, particularly coal fired units using the high quality coal resources in the country

Communications

* Development of Ports
* Ship building
* Highway construction
* Expansion of the telecommunications network, based on fibre optic technology
* Rail and road construction linking Pakistan with Turkmenistan

Agribusiness

* Processing, including dehydration, packaging and preservation, of fruits and vegetables

SERVICES

* Hotels, Tourist resorts including ski resorts
* Hospitals

MANUFACTURING

* Precision technology and heavy industry
* Cement
* Chemicals including fertilizers
* Plastic based products including PVC items
* Electronics
* Software developments

TAX INCENTIVES

Major existing tariff and fiscal incentives for manufacturing sector are as follows:

a) TARIFF
Maximum Tariff Rate45%
Number of Slabs 5
with Rates of 10%,15%, 25%, 35% & 45

Imported Plant & Machinery (Not Manufactured locally)
10%
Machinery (not manufactured locally) imported by engineering units for export related production

Zero rate upto 200 % of the export value during the preceding financial year.
Import of certain machines and tools for gems & jewellery manufacturers/exporters:

Duty Free
Raw Materials Used in Producing for Export
Zero Rated
CASCADED TARIFF WITH FOLLOWING TARGET RATES:
Primary Raw Materials 10% - 15%
Secondary Raw Materials 15% - 25%
Intermediate Goods 35%
Finished Goods 45%
Assembly Kits

Duty Free (Corresponding to the number of exported units Import of raw materials and components for manufacture of engineering goods meant for exports

Duty Free (Against Bank Guarantee)
b) GENERAL SALES TAX (GST)
GST On Imported and Domestically
Manufactured Plant & Machinery
"NIL"
Standard GST Rate
12.5%

c) FISCAL
Corporate Tax Rates
Assessment Year 1998-99
Public Companies
30%
Other Companies
35%
Banking companies
55% (50 % for Assessment Year 1999-2004)

PRACTICAL INFORMATION FOR CONDUCTING BUSINESS[1]

PAKISTAN'S BUSINESS STRENGTHS

Abundant Land and Natural Resources

- Extensive agricultural land
- Crop production (wheat, cotton, rice, fruits and vegetables)
- Mineral reserves (coal, crude oil, natural gas, copper, iron ore, gypsum, etc.)
- Fisheries and livestock production

Strong Human Resources

- Educated and skilled work force
- Cost-effective Human Resource
- English is read & spoken throughout Pakistan

Large & Growing Domestic Market

- 140 million consumers with growing incomes
- A growing middle-class moving to sophisticated consumption habits

Well-Established Infrastructure and Legal Systems

- Comprehensive road, rail and sea links
- Good quality telecommunications and IT services
- Modern company law

Strategic Location as a Regional hub

- Principal gateway to the Central Asian Republics
- Strong and long-standing links with the Middle East and South Asia
- Comprehensive duty-free facilities for investors

Continuing trends to liberalization, deregulation and privatization - a truly market-oriented and business-friendly approach.

[1] US Department of Commerce, Government of Pakisan materials

FORMS OF BUSINESS

There are three main forms of business:
(a) Sole Proprietorship
(b) Partnership
(c) Company

Sole Proprietorship

In a sole proprietorship, an individual on his/her own account carries out the business or profession. No formal procedure or formality is required for setting up a sole proprietary concern.

Partnership

A partnership is a business relationship entered into by a formal agreement between two or more persons or corporations carrying on a business in common. The capital for a partnership is provided by the partners who are liable for the total debts of the firms and who share the profits and losses of the business concern according to the terms of the partnership agreement.

Partnerships (other than banking companies) are generally limited in size to twenty partners. The interest of a partner is transferable only with the prior consent of the other partner(s). However, a partner's right to a share of the partnership income may be received in trust for another person.

For taxation purposes, partnerships are classified into:

(i) Registered Firms
(ii) Unregistered Firms

The income of the registered firm is subject to Super Tax before distribution to the partners. Also the individual income of the partners is subject to income tax at the usual rates.

For unregistered firms, income tax is levied on the firm's income and the partners are not liable to pay tax on the shares of profit received from the unregistered firm(s).

Company

A company is a legal entity formed under the Companies Ordinance, 1984. It can have share capital or can be formed without share capital.

A company having share capital may be formed as:
(i) A company limited by shares.
(ii) A company limited by guarantee.
(iii) An unlimited company.

Company Limited by Shares

The liability of its members is limited to the extent of their shares in the paid-up capital of the company. These companies may further be classified as public limited and private limited companies.

Public Limited Companies can be formed by at least seven persons by subscribing their names to the 'Memorandum and Articles of Association' of the company. The word 'Limited' is used as the last word of its name.

Private Limited Companies may be formed by at least two persons by subscribing their names to the 'Memorandum and Articles of Association' of the company. A private limited company, by its Articles of Association:

(i) Restricts the right to transfer its shares;
(ii) Limits the number of its members to fifty; and;
(iii) Prohibits any invitation to the public to subscribe for shares or debentures of the company.

A private limited company is required to use the words "(Private) Limited" as the last words of its name.

Company Limited By Guarantee
Means a company having the liability of its members limited by memorandum to such amounts as the members may respectively undertake to contribute to the capital of the company in the event of its winding up. A company limited by guarantee is usually formed on a 'non profit basis'. Companies limited by guarantee use the words (Guarantee) Limited" as the last words of their name.
Unlimited Company
Means a company having unlimited liability of its members.

Company Registration

Mode of Forming Companies
Any seven or more persons associated for any lawful purpose may, by subscribing their names to the Memorandum of Association and complying with the requirements of the Companies Ordinance, in respect of the registration, form a public company, and any two or more persons, so associated may, in like manner, form a private company.

Prior approval of the ministries (which regulate their respective functions) noted against each category of the following specified nature of companies is required before incorporation of such companies.

(1) Banking Company	Ministry of Finance/State Bank of
(2) Insurance Company	Ministry of Commerce.
(3) Investment Finance Company	(i) Ministry of Finance.
(4) Leasing Company	Securities and Exchange Commission of
(5) Venture Capital Company	Securities and Exchange Commission of
(6) Asset Management Company	Securities and Exchange Commission of
A company which invests in any of the following industries	
(i) Arms and Ammunition	Ministry of Industries/Board of
(ii) Security Printing, Currency and	Ministry of Industries/Board of

Mint.	Investment.
(iii) High Explosives.	Ministry of Industries/Board of Investment.
iv) Radio Active Substances	Ministry of Industries/Board of Investment.

b) Availability of Name of the Company

The first step with regard to incorporation of a company is to confirm the availability of the name of the proposed company from the concerned registrar on payment of a fee of Rs.100, The name should not be inappropriate, deceptive or designed to offend the religious sensibilities of the people, and it should neither be identical nor have a close resemblance to the name of any existing company.

REQUIRED DOCUMENTS

A foreign company incorporated outside Pakistan, is required to submit the following documents to the concerned agencies within 30 days of establishing presence in Pakistan:

1. A certified copy of the charter, statute or Memorandum and Articles of the company, in English or Urdu, accompanied by prescribed Form 38;
2. Address of the registered or principal office of the company on Form 39;
3. A list of Directors, the Chief Executive and Secretaries (if any) of the company on Form 40;
4. Particulars of the principal officer of the company in Pakistan on Form 41;
5. Particulars of person (s) resident in Pakistan authorized to accept services on behalf of the foreign company on Form 42;
6. Address of the principal place of business in Pakistan of the foreign company on Form 43 (Section 451)

Any change or alteration in particulars stated at serial No. 1 to 6 above is required to be filed on Form 44 with the registrar concerned within 30 days of such change or alteration (section 452); and

Foreign company is required to file annually with the registrar concerned annual accounts in respect of its operations within Pakistan as well as its global accounts together with the list of Pakistani members and debenture holders and particulars of places of business of the company in Pakistan within the prescribed period (Section 453).

Foreign company is required to give notice on Form 46 to the registrar concerned at least 30 days before it intends to cease to have a place of business in Pakistan and to publish a notice of such intention at least in two daily newspapers circulating in the province or provinces in which such place or places of business are situate.;

FOREIGN COMPANIES

Foreign Company

A Foreign company, i.e. a company incorporated outside Pakistan, is required to deliver the following documents to the concerned Registrar within 30 days of the establishment of its place of business in Pakistan:

(i) A certified copy of the charter, statute or Memorandum and Articles of the company in the English or Urdu languages accompanied by prescribed

(ii) Address of the registered or principal office of the company on Form 39;

iii) A list of Directors, the Chief Executive and Secretaries (if any) of the company on Form 40;

iii) A list of Directors, the Chief Executive and Secretaries (if any) of the company on Form 40;

(iv) Particulars of the principal officer of the company in Pakistan on Form 41;

(v) Particulars of person(s) resident in Pakistan authorised to accept services on behalf of the foreign company on Form 42;

(vi) Address of the principal place of business in Pakistan of the foreign company on Form 43 (Section 451

LIAISON / BRANCH OFFICES

OPENING OF LIAISON / BRANCH OFFICES OF FOREIGN FIRM

(I) Foreign companies that intend to undertake export activities in Pakistan will be registered without any formality.

(II) Permission to companies engaged in contractual obligations of contracts with public sector entities will be granted on production of valid documents without circulating to government departments,

(III) For companies that wish to open their branch/ liaison or representative offices in Pakistan may apply to BOI for permission on prescribed form. The BOI will process and decide such cases within a period of 6 to 8 weeks

(IV) Details on the required documentation, etc, are available at all offices of BOI. a specimen of the application for permission to establish branch/ liaison office by foreign companies is presented in Annex-XXI

(V) Permission for opening of branch/ liaison office may be granted by the BOI for a period of 3 to 5 years. Further extension will be granted by the BOI after reviewing and examining the past performance of foreign companies. Request for renewal or extension will be processed by the BOI with two weeks provided the requests are supported with complete documentation.

INVESTMENT OPPORTUNITIES

Oil & Gas

- Onshore and offshore activities
- Exploration
- Production of explored wells
- Pipelines

Energy and Power

- Hydel
- Coal Based

IT Projects

- Software
- Cell Phone
- E-Commerce

Agri & Agro-based Projects

- Corporate & Integrated Agriculture - Earth Moving & Leveling Equipment
- Water Conservation & Irrigation Equipment - Pesticides Manufacturing
- Livestock Farming - Cattle Feed
- Dairy Farming - Leather Products
- Sea Food Processing - Byproducts of Sugar Industry
- Cool Chains & Refrigerated Transportation - Frozen Concentrated Citrus Juice
- Agricultural Machinery - Mango & Guava Pulps and Juice
- Tomato Juice

Textile Sector

- Garments Industry
- Knitwear Industry
- Relocation of Industry
- Fire proof tents, carpets
- Value Addition & Quality Control

Infrastructure

- Urban Mass transit Projects
- Airports
- Port Facility
- Motor way
- Waste Management & Recycling
- Water Supply
- Construction Projects

Industrial Infrastructure

- Development of Industrial Zones in Private Sector
- Industrial Development Centers for Capacity Building of SMEs

Health Projects

- Hospitals
- Diagnostic Centers

Mining & Minerals

- Thar Coalfield development
- Mining & Mineral Processing
  (Iron Ore, Coal, Lead, Zinc, Chromite, Dolomite, Natural Gas, Lime Stone Magnesite, Silica Sand, Gypsum Anhydrite, Bauxite, Gems)
- Steel Mill based on local Iron Ore

Privatization

- Oil and gas
- Information Technology (IT)
- Telecommunications
- Banking, Finance, Insurance
- Aviation
- Industries
- Power

Service Sector

- Departmental Stores (Chain)
- Insurance: Health, Crop; Cattle;
- Floods/Natural Hazards
- Flight Kitchens - Air Aviation

Tourism Projects

- Disneylands
- Beach Resorts (Karachi-Makran Coastal Highway)
- Hill Resorts
- Tourist Hostels/Complexes

Other Focused Industry

- Tele Communication
- SMEs
- Automotive Parts
- Relocation of Electronic Industry (Home Appliance)
- Edible Oil

Afghanistan – Related Projects

- Rail link with Afghanistan and Cars
- Gas Pipeline from Turkmenistan through Afghanistan
- Industrial/Export Processing Zones (close to Afghan Border)
- Power export.

PERFORMANCE OF SELECTED INDUSTRIES

INDUSTRY		No of Units	Installed capacity (Nos/MTons)	Production (Million Tons)		
				1999-00	2004-01	2005-02
Textile	Cotton yarn	443	8442 Mln. Spindles	1.7	2.1	1.79
	Cotton cloth		145796 Rotors	438 Mn.Sq.Mtr	490.0 Mn.Sq.Mtr	555.6 Mn.Sq.Mtr.
Sugar		78	5.0	2.43	2.7	3.27
Fertilizer		11	2.0	1.93	5.14	5.08
Cement		25	16.3	10	7.43	9.89
Vegetable Ghee/Oil		166	2.7	0.92	0.835	0.770
Polyester		6	0.546	0.368	0.496	0.580
PVC		1	0.1	0.075	0.065	0.069
Refineries		5	11.2	8.7	8.704	9.389
Steel		500+	2.53	2.30	2.13	2.7
Automotive Industry			Number			
Cars/ Light Vehicles		8 + 2	130,000	39,497	46658	49,656
Trucks/ Buses		6	5,000	2,485	2289	2,220
Tractors		3	40,000	34,909	32,413	23,801
Motor Cycles		7	120,000	94,881	1,17,858	1,20,627

INDUSTRIAL ZONES

INDUSTRIAL ZONE PUNJAB

Industrial Estate Musaverk Mian Chunnu

Location	G.T. Road, 8 KM fromMianChunnuCity
Year of Establishment	1989
Total Area	55.5 acres
Total Number of Plots	158 plots
Size of Plots	10 Marlas - 2 Kanals
Uptake/No of Plots Allotted	144 plots
Industrial Plots Availability	Available; Occupancy - 10%
Infrastructure	Road, Water, Power, Telephone
Type of Industry	Textiles Food, Chemicals
Nearest City	Lahore

Industrial Estate Khanewal

Location	Lodhran National Highway
Year of Establishment	1993
Total Area	64 acres
Total Number of Plots	313
Size of Plots	10 Marlas - 2 Kanals
Uptake/No of Plots Allotted	200 plots
Industrial Plots Availability	Available; Electrification to start
Infrastructure	Roads, Water Supply, Sewerage, Telephone

Type of Industry — Food, Cottage and handicrafts, Textiles
Nearest City — Lahore

Industrial Estate - I Sialkot
Location — Wazirabad Road
Year of Establishment — 1961
Total Area — 98.5 acres
Total Number of Plots — 330
Size of Plots — 1 - 4 Kanals
Uptake/No of Plots Allotted — 330 plots
Industrial Plots Availability — Nil; Occupancy - 70%
Infrastructure — Roads, Electricity, Water Supply, Sewerage, Telephone
Type of Industry — Sports goods, Kitchen utensils, Cutlery, Surgical
Instruments
Nearest City — Lahore

Industrial Estate Daska Road Sialkot
Location — Gujranwala Road Daska
Year of Establishment — 1984
Total Area — 52 acres
Total Number of Plots — 148
Size of Plots — 1 - 4 Kanals
Uptake/No of Plots Allotted — 111 plots
Industrial Plots Availability — Available; Occupancy - 10%
Infrastructure — Roads, Electricity, Water Supply, Sewerage, Telephone
Type of Industry — Sports goods, Kitchen utensils, Cutlery, Surgical
Instruments
Nearest City — Lahore

Industrial Estate - 1 Lahore
Location — Kot Lakhpat,Lahore Kasur Road
Year of Establishment — 1963
Total Area — 9.75 acres
Total Number of Plots — 40
Size of Plots — 0.5 - 2 Kanals
Uptake/No of Plots Allotted — 40 plots
Industrial Plots Availability — Not Available
Infrastructure — Roads, Electricity, Water Supply, Sewerage, Telephone
Type of Industry — Engineering, Electrical Fittings, Chemicals, Consumer
Goods, Steel Products
Nearest City — Lahore

Industrial Estate Raiwind Road, Lahore
Location — 40 km fromLahore
Year of Establishment
Total Area — 112 acres
Total Number of Plots — 800
Size of Plots — 2â€"32 Kanals
Uptake/No of Plots Allotted — 100%
Industrial Plots Availability — Nil
Infrastructure — Roads, Electricity, Water Supply, Sewerage, Telephone
Type of Industry — Textiles, Sugar, Power Generation, Garments,
Chemicals, Engineering, Food
Nearest City — Lahore

Kot Lakhpat Industrial Estate Lahore

Location	Kot Lakhpat,ModelTownLahore
Year of Establishment	1960
Total Area	875 acres
Total Number of Plots	193
Size of Plots	1 acre and above
Uptake/No of Plots Allotted	193 plots
Industrial Plots Availability	Not Available
Infrastructure	Roads, Electricity, Water Supply, Sewerage, Telephone
Type of Industry	Engineering, Electrical Fittings, Chemicals, Consumer Goods, Steel Products
Nearest City	Lahore Goto Map

Lahore Kasur Road Industrial Estate Lahore

Location	Kasur Road,Lahore Kasur Road
Year of Establishment	1994
Total Area	80 Acres
Total Number of Plots	304
Size of Plots	1-2 Kanals
Uptake/No of Plots Allotted	302 plots
Industrial Plots Availability	Not Available
Infrastructure	Roads, Electricity, Water Supply, Sewerage, Telephone
Type of Industry	Pharmaceuticals, Soft drinks, Leather Processing, Consumer Goods
Nearest City	Lahore

Industrial Estate Burewala

Location	15 kmChichawatani-Burewala Road
Year of Establishment	1992
Total Area	48 acres
Total Number of Plots	199
Size of Plots	Not specified
Uptake/No of Plots Allotted	18 plots
Industrial Plots Availability	Available; Work yet to start
Infrastructure	Road, Electricity Telephone
Type of Industry	Food, Textiles
Nearest City	Lahore

Industrial Estate Gujrat

Location	Main GT Road 6Km From City
Year of Establishment	1961-62
Total Area	126.32 acres
Total Number of Plots	457
Size of Plots	10 Marlas - 4 Kanals
Uptake/No of Plots Allotted	457
Industrial Plots Availability	No Plots Available
Infrastructure	Roads, Electricity, Water Supply, Sewerage, Telephone
Type of Industry	Electrical Items, Furniture
Nearest City	Lahore

Industrial Estate Shorekot

Location	Rakh Matla Jhang Road, Shorekot
Year of Establishment	
Total Area	100acrs

Total Number of Plots	800
Size of Plots	Variable
Uptake/No of Plots Allotted	Nil
Industrial Plots Availability	Available
Infrastructure	Roads, Electricity, Water Supply, Sewerage, Telephone
Type of Industry	Not specified
Nearest City	Lahore

Industrial Estate-I, Gujranwala

Location	Khiali By-Pass, 8 km from main city
Year of Establishment	1978
Total Area	106.15 acres
Total Number of Plots	551
Size of Plots	7 Marlas - 4 Kanals
Uptake/No of Plots Allotted	100%
Industrial Plots Availability	Nil; Occupancy â€" 30%
Infrastructure	Roads, Electricity, Water Supply, Sewerage, Telephone
Type of Industry	Engineering, Chemicals, Textiles, Ceramics, Leather
Nearest City	Lahore

Industrial Estate-II, Gujranwala

Location	G.T. Road,Gujranwala
Year of Establishment	1960-61
Total Area	103.5 Acres
Total Number of Plots	306
Size of Plots	1 - 48 Kanals
Uptake/No of Plots Allotted	306
Industrial Plots Availability	Nil; Occupancy â€" 100%
Infrastructure	Roads, Water, Power, Gas, Telephone
Type of Industry	Ceramics, Electrical Machines, Domestic Machines,
Fabrication, Consumers Goods	
Nearest City	Lahore

Industrial Estate Jhelum

Location	6 km from main city onGT Road
Year of Establishment	1978
Total Area	52.06 acres
Total Number of Plots	288
Size of Plots	5 Marlas - 2 Kanals
Uptake/No of Plots Allotted	276 plots
Industrial Plots Availability	Some available; Occupancy â€" 20%
Infrastructure	Roads, Electricity, Water Supply, Sewerage, Telephone
Type of Industry	Engineering, Furniture, Food
Nearest City	Lahore

Industrial Estate Sahiwal

Location	Kutcha Harapa Road, Sahiwal, 6 km from main city
Year of Establishment	1983
Total Area	51.99 acres
Total Number of Plots	187
Size of Plots	10 Marlas - 4 Kanals
Uptake/No of Plots Allotted	100%
Industrial Plots Availability	Nil; Occupancy <50%
Infrastructure	Roads, Electricity, Water Supply, Sewerage, Telephone

Type of Industry	Food, Textiles
Nearest City	Lahore

Industrial Estate Faisalabad	
Location	Nalka Kohala Road, 15 km from main city
Year of Establishment	1975
Total Area	258.03 acres
Total Number of Plots	1,019 plots
Size of Plots	7 Marlas - 4 Kanals
Uptake/No of Plots Allotted	953 plots
Industrial Plots Availability	Available; Occupancy - 75%
Infrastructure	Roads, Electricity, Water Supply, Sewerage, Telephone
Type of Industry	Textiles
Nearest City	Lahore

Industrial Estate Sargodha	
Location	Talibwala Road, 8 Km From main city
Year of Establishment	1976
Total Area	51.15 acres
Total Number of Plots	253
Size of Plots	3.5 Marlas - 4 Kanals
Uptake/No of Plots Allotted	122 plot
Industrial Plots Availability	Available; Occupancy - 10%
Infrastructure	Roads, Electricity, Water Supply, Sewerage, Telephone
Type of Industry	Textiles
Nearest City	Lahore

Industrial Area Jauharabad	
Location	20 KM from District Court, Jauharabad
Year of Establishment	1981
Nearest City	Peshawar

Industrial Area Bhakkar	
Location	20 KM from District Court, Bhakkar
Year of Establishment	1985
Nearest City	Peshawar

Industrial Estate, Mandi Town, Layyah	
Location	Adjacent to Layyah Sugar Mills, Layyah
Year of Establishment	1954
Nearest City	Peshawar

Industries Estate, Bahawalpur	
Location	Multan Road, Bahawalpur
Year of Establishment	1961-62
Total Area	51.8 acres
Total Number of Plots	203
Size of Plots	4â€"8 Kanals
Uptake/No of Plots Allotted	198
Industrial Plots Availability	Nil
Infrastructure	Road, water, electricity
Type of Industry	Not specified
Nearest City	Lahore

Industrial Zones Balchuistan

Industrial Estate, Chakwal

Location	Rawalpindi Road, Chakwal
Year of Establishment	1979
Total Area	16.86 acres
Total Number of Plots	119
Size of Plots	0.5 - 2 Kanals
Uptake/No of Plots Allotted	108
Industrial Plots Availability	Available; Occupancy - 20%
Infrastructure	Roads, Water, Power
Type of Industry	Poultry Feed, Food
Nearest City	Peshawar

Industrial Estate, Gujar Khan

Location	G.T. Road, Gujjar Khan
Year of Establishment	1979
Total Area	17.44 acres
Total Number of Plots	183
Size of Plots	1,200 - 4,000 sq ft
Uptake/No of Plots Allotted	161
Industrial Plots Availability	Available; Occupancy - 10%
Infrastructure	Roads, Water, Power, Telephone
Type of Industry	Approved for Food, Beverages, Handicrafts, Light engineering. No restriction except for manufacturing of defence parts and armaments and all kind of liquors and alcohols
Nearest City	Peshawar

Industrial Estate Sheikhupura

Location	30 Km from Lahore on Motorway
Year of Establishment	1950
Total Area	20 sq Km
Total Number of Plots	
Size of Plots	All size of Plots can be purchased
Uptake/No of Plots Allotted	All Allotted
Industrial Plots Availability	Free Hold land is available
Infrastructure	Roads, Electricity, Water Supply, Sewerage, Telephone
Type of Industry	Road,Gas,Electricity
Nearest City	Lahore

National Industrial Zone (RCCI Industrial Estate) Rawat Link Road Rawalpindi

Location	G.T. Road, Rawat
Year of Establishment	1985
Total Area	1,250 acres
Total Number of Plots	1,500
Size of Plots	4 Kanals and above
Uptake/No of Plots Allotted	1,344
Industrial Plots Availability	Available; Occupancy - 10%
Infrastructure	Roads, Water, Power,
Type of Industry	Chemicals, Engineering, Food
Nearest City	Peshawar

Industrial Estate Bahatar Road Taxila

Location	7 KM Taxila Bahatar Road
Year of Establishment	1993
Total Area	104.75 acres
Total Number of Plots	382
Size of Plots	10 Marlas - 4 Kanals
Uptake/No of Plots Allotted	354
Industrial Plots Availability	Some Available; Under development
Infrastructure	Roads, Electricity, Water Supply, Sewerage, Telephone
Type of Industry	Approved for Food, Beverages, Handicrafts, Light engineering. No restriction except for manufacturing of defence parts and armaments and all kind of liquors and alcohols
Nearest City	Peshawar

Industrial Estate Multan

Location	Multan
Year of Establishment	1983
Total Area	743 Acres
Total Number of Plots	246
Size of Plots	Variable
Uptake/No of Plots Allotted	All Allotted
Industrial Plots Availability	Not Available
Infrastructure	Roads, Electricity, Water Supply, Sewerage, Telephone

Hub Industrial & Trading Estate (HITE)

Location	Hub, District Lasbela
Year of Establishment	1982
Total Area	
Total Number of Plots	1,440 plots
Size of Plots	Variable
Uptake/No of Plots Allotted	150 plots but 76 closed down

Industrial Plots Availability Available; Occupancy – 5%
Infrastructure Road, Water, Gas, Power, Telephone
Type of Industry Power Generation, Plastic Industries
Nearest City Karachi

Uthal Industrial Estate
Location Along main RCD Highway at Uthal District, Lasbela
Year of Establishment 1976
Total Area
Total Number of Plots 152 plots
Size of Plots Variable
Uptake/No of Plots Allotted 5 plots but 4 closed down
Industrial Plots Availability Availabl
Infrastructure Road, Water, Gas, Power, Telephone
Type of Industry Approved for Food, Beverages, Handicrafts, Light engineering. No restriction except for manufacturing of defence parts and armaments and all kind of liquors and alcohols
Nearest City Karachi

Windher Industrial & Trading Estate
Location 80 km from SITE, Karachi, Lasbela
Year of Establishment 1989
Total Area
Total Number of Plots 240 plots
Size of Plots Variable
Uptake/No of Plots Allotted 7 plots but none in operation
Industrial Plots Availability Available
Infrastructure Road, Water, Power
Type of Industry Not specified
Nearest City Karachi

Industrial Estate Dara Murad Jamali
Location Dara Murad Jamali
Year of Establishment 1987-88
Total Area 40 Acres
Total Number of Plots 350
Size of Plots 2—4 Kanals
Uptake/No of Plots Allotted Nil
Industrial Plots Availability Available
Infrastructure Road
Type of Industry Approved for Food, Beverages, Handicrafts, Light engineering. No restriction except for manufacturing of defence parts and armaments and all kind of liquors and alcohols
Nearest City Quetta

Quetta Industrial & Trading Estate
Location Sariab By Pass 13 kms from QuettaCity
Year of Establishment 1986-87
Total Area
Total Number of Plots 160 plots
Size of Plots Variable
Uptake/No of Plots Allotted 6 plots but one has closed down
Industrial Plots Availability Available
Infrastructure Road, Water, Power, Gas

Type of Industry Approved for Food, Beverages, Handicrafts, Light engineering. No restriction except for manufacturing of defence parts and armaments and all kind of liquors and alcohols
Nearest City Quetta

Small Industrial Zone Quetta

Location	Girki Road, Quetta
Year of Establishment	1960
Total Area	50 Acres
Total Number of Plots	450
Size of Plots	2—4 Kanals
Uptake/No of Plots Allotted	Nil
Industrial Plots Availability	Available
Infrastructure	Roads, Water, Power, Gas, Telephone
Nearest City	Quetta

Gadani Industrial Estate

Location	Gadani, Lasbela District
Year of Establishment	1974
Total Area	50 Acres
Total Number of Plots	250
Size of Plots	2—20 Kanals
Uptake/No of Plots Allotted	2 plots
Industrial Plots Availability	Available
Infrastructure	Roads and electricity
Type of Industry	Ship breaking
Nearest City	Karachi

INDUSTRIAL ZONES SINDH

SITE KARACHI

Location	Mango Pir Road Karachi District West
Year of Establishment	1947
Total Area	4,460 acres
Total Number of Plots	1,956
Size of Plots	0.5--1.0 acres
Uptake	100%; Occupancy - full
Industrial Plots Availability	Nil
Infrastructure	Roads, Sewerage, Electricity, Water Supply, Telephone, Road Link to National Highway
Type of Industry	Engineering, Textiles, Consumer Goods, Defence vendors, Autoparts, etc
Nearest City	Karachi

SITE NORTH KARACHI

Location	Scheme No 33 North Karachi
Year of Establishment	1983
Total Area	1,029 acres
Total Number of Plots	280
Size of Plots	0.5 acres and to industry requirements
Uptake/No of Plots Allotted	98 plots; Occupancy - full
Industrial Plots Availability	Plots are available but the allotment has been frozen
Infrastructure	Power, Water, Gas, Telephone, Internet, Roads, Sewerage

Type of Industry Textile & Garments, Hosiery, Light Engineering, Soap, Poultry,Electronics, Cotton, Dyeing, Bleaching, Printing, Packing
Nearest City Karachi

KORANGI INDUSTRIAL AREA
Location South East of Karachi about 20 km from the city centre
Year of Establishment 1961-69
Total Area 3,500 acres
Total Number of Plots 2,700 plots
Size of Plots 160 sq yards - 5,000 sq yards
Uptake/No of Plots Allotted
2,571 operating units
Industrial Plots Availability
Available; Occupancy - 60%
Infrastructure Roads, Electricity, Water Supply, Sewerage, Telephone
Railway siding available
Type of industry Cotton Yarn, Textile & Garments, Hosiery, Leather products
Jute Thread, Pharmaceutical products, Cosmetics, Soap,
Sanitary Items, Basic Chemicals, paints, LPG Plants
Nearest City Karachi

NOORIABAD INDUSTRIAL ESTATE DADU
Location District Dadu on Super Highway 90 km From Karachi
Year of Establishment 1983
Total Area 3,342 acres
Total Number of Plots 1,150 plots
Size of Plots 0.5-1.0 acres
Uptake/No of Plots Allotted
522 plots; Occupancy - 30%
Industrial Plots Availability
Plots are available
Infrastructure Roads, Sewerage, Electricity, Water Supply, Telephone
Nearest City Karachi
Type of Industry Textile, Light Engineering, Food Processing, Chemical Plants

SMALL INDUSTRIAL ESTATE DADU
Location DaduJohiHaka, Dadu
Year of Establishment 1982-83
Total Area 10.7 acres
Total Number of Plots 45
Size of Plots 2-8 Kanals
Uptake/No of Plots Allotted 22
Industrial Plots AvailabilityAvailable; Occupancy - 30%
Infrastructure Roads, Water Supply, Sewerage, Telephone
Type of Industry Approved for Food, Beverages, Handicrafts, Light engineering. No restriction except for manufacturing of defence parts, armaments and all kind of liquors and alcohols
Nearest City Karachi

INDUSTRIAL ESTATE HYDERABAD
Location Tando Mohammad Khan RoadHyderabad
Year of Establishment 1950
Total Area 1,264 acres
Total Number of Plots 389

Size of Plots 0.5--5 acres
Uptake/No of Plots Allotted
389; Occupancy - 30% - 40%
Industrial Plots Availability Nil
Infrastructure Roads, Electricity, Water Supply, Telephone, Gas
Road Link to National Highway
Type of Industry Textiles, Heavy Engineering, Light Engineering, Beverages
Pharmaceuticals, Carpets, Garments, Glass Bangles,
Nearest City Karachi

INDUSTRIAL ESTATE HYDERABAD
Location Hyderabad Super Highway
Year of Establishment 1985-86
Total Area 50.1 acres
Total Number of Plots 96
Size of Plots 2-4 Kanals
Uptake/No of Plots Allotted 46
Industrial Plots Availability Available; Occupancy - 40%
Infrastructure Roads, Water Supply, Sewerage, Telephone
Type of Industry Food, Garments, Handicrafts
Nearest City Karachi
Goto Map

INDUSTRIAL ESTATE TANDO ADAM
Location Tando Adam
Year of Establishment 1952
Total Area 150 acres
Total Number of Plots 48
Size of Plots 0.5 acres
Uptake/No of Plots Allotted
48; Occupancy - 20%
Industrial Plots Availability Nil
Infrastructure Roads, Electricity, Water Supply, Telephone
Road Link to National Highway
Type of Industry Textile, Cigarettes, Cooking oil, Ice and Engineering
Nearest City Karachi
Goto Map

INDUSTRIAL ESTATE TANDO ADAM
Location Hyderabad Road, Tando Adam
Year of Establishment 1992-93
Total Area 13.5 acres
Total Number of Plots 75
Size of Plots 1-2 Kanals
Uptake/No of Plots Allotted 44
Industrial Plots Availability
Available; Occupancy - 20%
Infrastructure Roads, Electricity, Water Supply, Telephone, Road Link to National Highway
Type of Industry Power Looms Industry
Nearest City Karachi

INDUSTRIAL ESTATE KOTRI
Location Kotri District Dadu
Year of Establishment 1962
Total Area 1,875 acres
Total Number of Plots 179

Size of Plots 1.00--5.5 acres
Uptake/No of Plots Allotted
Industrial Plots Availability Nil
Infrastructure Roads, Electricity, Water Supply, Telephone, Gas, Road Link to NH
Type of Industry Textiles, Light Engineering, Flour Mills, Copper Wire, Beverages
Nearest City Karachi

INDUSTRIAL ESTATE SUKKUR
Location Shikarpur Road, Sukkur
Year of Establishment 1963
Total Area 1,060 Acres
Total Number of Plots 223
Size of Plots Wide range of selection available
Uptake/No of Plots Allotted
223; Occupancy - 40%
Industrial Plots Availability Nil
Infrastructure Roads, Electricity, Water Supply, Telephone, Gas
Road Link to National Highway
Type of Industry Light Engineering, Poultry Farm, Soap factory, Flour Mills
Food Industry
Nearest City Quetta

INDUSTRIAL ESTATE NAWABSHAH
Location Qazi Ahmad RoadNawabshah
Year of Establishment 1985-86
Total Area 239 acres
Total Number of Plots 12
Size of Plots Various sizes
Uptake/No of Plots Allotted
12; Occupancy - 10
Industrial Plots Availability Nil
Infrastructure Roads, Electricity, Water Supply, Sewerage, Telephone
Nawabshah Main Road linked to National Highway
Type of Industry Viscose Plant, Sugar Mill
Nearest City Karachi

INDUSTRIAL ESTATE NAWABSHAH
Location Nawabshah main road
Year of Establishment 1985-86
Total Area 50 acres
Total Number of Plots 98
Size of Plots Various sizes
Uptake/No of Plots Allotted 21
Industrial Plots Availability Available; Occupancy - 40%
Infrastructure Roads, Electricity, Water Supply, Sewerage, Telephone
Type of Industry Food, Auto Workshops, Handicrafts
Nearest City Karachi

INDUSTRIAL ESTATE SUKKUR
Location Sukkur
Year of Establishment 1963-64
Total Area 110 acres
Total Number of Plots 297 plots
Size of Plots 2 Kanals

Uptake/No of Plots Allotted
282 plots
Industrial Plots Availability Nil; Occupancy - 40%
Infrastructure Roads, Water Supply, Sewerage, Telephone
Type of Industry Food, Bangles, Garments and Small Vendors of auto parts
Nearest City Quetta

INDUSTRIAL ESTATE LARKANA
Location LarkanaCity
Year of Establishment 1964-65
Total Area 59 acres
Total Number of Plots 313
Size of Plots 1 - 2 Kanals
Uptake/No of Plots Allotted
201
Industrial Plots Availability Available; Occupancy - 20%
Infrastructure Roads, Water Supply, Sewerage, Telephone
Type of Industry Food, Garments
Nearest City Quetta

INDUSTRIAL ESTATE MIRPUR KHAS
Location MirpurKhasCity
Year of Establishment 1974
Total Area 5 acres
Total Number of Plots 32
Size of Plots 1 - 2 Kanals
Uptake/No of Plots Allotted 22
Industrial Plots Availability Available; Occupancy - 20%
Infrastructure Roads, Water Supply, Sewerage, Telephone
Type of Industry Food, Garments, Handicrafts
Nearest City Karachi

MALL INDUSTRIAL ESTATE MIRPURKHAS
Location Mirwah Road, Mirpurkhas
Year of Establishment 1985-86
Total Area 51.2 acres
Total Number of Plots 177
Size of Plots 2- 8 Kanals
Uptake/No of Plots Allotted
150
Industrial Plots Availability Some plots available; Occupancy - 30%
Infrastructure Roads, Water Supply, Sewerage, Telephone
Type of Industry Approved for Food, Beverages, Handicrafts, Light engineering. No restriction except for manufacturing of defence parts and armaments and all kind of liquors and alcohols
Nearest City Karachi

INDUSTRIAL PARK (IP) MIRPURKHAS
Location Mirwah Road, Mirpurkhas
Year of Establishment 1974
Total Area
Total Number of Plots
Size of Plots
Uptake/No of Plots Allotted

Industrial Plots Availability
Infrastructure Roads, Water, Power, Telephone
Type of Industry Approved for Food, Beverages, Handicrafts, Light engineering. No restriction except for manufacturing of defence parts and armaments and all kind of liquors and alcohols
Nearest City Karachi

INDUSTRIAL ESTATE SEHWAN
Location Indus Highway, Sehwan
Year of Establishment 1974
Total Area 5 acres
Total Number of Plots 36
Size of Plots 1-8 Kanals
Uptake/No of Plots Allotted 33
Industrial Plots Availability Nil; Occupancy - 20%
Infrastructure Roads, Water Supply, Sewerage, Telephone
Type of Industry Approved for Food, Beverages, Handicrafts, Light engineering. No restriction except for manufacturing of defence parts, armaments and all kind of liquors and alcohols
Nearest City Karachi

INDUSTRIAL ESTATE SHIRKARPUR
Location ShirkarpurCity
Year of Establishment 1984-85
Total Area 36 acres
Total Number of Plots 96
Size of Plots 2- 4 Kanals
Uptake/No of Plots Allotted 46
Industrial Plots Availability Available; Occupancy - 10%
Infrastructure Roads, Water Supply, Sewerage, Telephone
Type of Industry Approved for Food, Beverages, Handicrafts, Light engineering. No restriction except for manufacturing of defence parts and armaments and all kind of liquors and alcohols
Nearest City Quetta

INDUSTRIAL ESTATE KANDH KOT
Location Thull Road, Kandhkot
Year of Establishment 1984-85
Total Area 14.4 acres
Total Number of Plots 47
Size of Plots 2-4 Kanals
Uptake/No of Plots Allotted 11
Industrial Plots Availability Available; Occupancy 10%
Infrastructure Roads, Water Supply, Sewerage, Telephone
Type of Industry Approved for Food, Beverages, Handicrafts, Light engineering. No restriction except for manufacturing of defence parts and armaments and all kind of liquors and alcohols
Nearest City Quetta

INDUSTRIAL ESTATE BADIN
Location Kadan Road
Year of Establishment 1985-86
Total Area 30.2 acres
Total Number of Plots 107

Size of Plots 2-4 Kanals
Uptake/No of Plots Allotted 17
Industrial Plots Availability Available; Occupancy - 10
Infrastructure Roads, Water Supply, Sewerage, Telephone
Type of Industry Approved for Food, Beverages, Handicrafts, Light engineering. No restriction except for manufacturing of defence parts and armaments and all kind of liquors and alcohols
Nearest City Karachi

INDUSTRIAL ESTATE SANGHAR
Location Sanjbore Road, Sanghar
Year of Establishment 1985-86
Total Area 45 acres
Total Number of Plots 98
Size of Plots 2-4 Kanals
Uptake/No of Plots Allotted 52
Industrial Plots Availability Available; Occupancy - 20%
Infrastructure Roads, Water Supply, Sewerage, Telephone
Type of Industry Approved for Food, Beverages, Handicrafts, Light engineering. No restriction except for manufacturing of defence parts and armaments and all kind of liquors and alcohols
Nearest City Karachi

INDUSTRIAL ESTATE THATTA
Location Ghulamullah Road, Makli, Thatta
Year of Establishment 1986-87
Total Area 50 Acres
Total Number of Plots 98
Size of Plots 2-4 Kanals
Uptake/No of Plots Allotted 21
Industrial Plots Availability Available; Occupancy - 20%
Infrastructure Roads, Water, Power
Type of Industry Food and Handicrafts
Nearest City Karachi

INDUSTRIES ESTATE GAMBAT
Location Gambat
Year of Establishment 1991-92
Total Area 15 acres
Total Number of Plots 52
Size of Plots 2-4 Kanals
Uptake/No of Plots Allotted 2
Industrial Plots Availability
Available; Occupancy - nil
Infrastructure Roads, Water, Power, Telephone
Type of Industry Power Looms

INDUSTRIES ESTATE ROHRI
Location National Highway Ali-Wahan, Rohri
Year of Establishment 1992-93
Total Area 46.4 acres
Total Number of Plots 142
Size of Plots 2-4 Kanals
Uptake/No of Plots Allotted Nil

Industrial Plots Availability All available
Infrastructure Roads, Water, Power
Type of Industry Approved for Food, Beverages, Handicrafts, Light engineering. No restriction except for manufacturing of defence parts and armaments and all kind of liquors and alcohols

Karachi Export Processing Zone
Location Landhi Industrial Area, off Mehran Highway, Landhi
Year of Establishment 1989
Total Area 500 acres
Total Number of Plots
Size of Plots Variable
Uptake/No of Plots Allotted 103 plots
Industrial Plots Availability Available
Infrastructure Roads, Water, Power
Type of Industry Garments, Electrical/electronics, Precision Machining, Light Chemicals, Leather, Food Processing, Warehousing
Nearest City Karachi
Goto Map

Port Qasim Industrial Zones North Western Industrial Zone, Eastern Industrial Zone, South Western Industrial Zone
Location Port Qasim
Year of Establishment 1980
Total Area 2700 acres + 8300 acres + 1000 acres
Total Number of Plots Not fixed
Size of Plots Variable
Uptake/No of Plots Allotted Large tracts available
Industrial Plots Availability Available
Infrastructure Roads, Water, Power, Port
Type of Industry Port-related activities
Nearest City Karachi

INDUSTRIAL ZONES NWFP

Industrial Zone Profiles – NWFP Province

Location Industrial Estate Peshawar Jamrud Road, Peshawar
Year of Establishment 1965-66
Total Area 868 acres
Total Number of Plots 434
Size of Plots 8 –34 Kanals
Uptake/No of Plots Allotted All Allotted
Industrial Plots Availability Nil; Occupancy – 80% but 50% closed
Infrastructure Road, Water, Gas, Power, Telephone
Type of Industry Furniture, Food, Engineering, Marble
Nearest City Peshawar

Small Industrial Estate, Phase-I, Mardan
Location Nowshera Road, Near Rashaki
Year of Establishment 1974-75
Total Area 50 Acres
Total Number of Plots 450
Size of Plots 2—4 Kanals

Uptake/No of Plots Allotted 350
Industrial Plots Availability
Infrastructure Roads, Water, Power, Gas, Telephone
Type of Industry Approved for Food, Beverages, Handicrafts, Light engineering. No restriction except for manufacturing of defence parts and armaments and all kind of liquors and alcohols
Nearest City Peshawar

Small Industrial Estate, Phase-II, Mardan
Location Nowshera Road, Near Rashaki
Year of Establishment 1981-82
Total Area 40 Acres
Total Number of Plots 350
Size of Plots 4—8 Kanals
Uptake/No of Plots Allotted 200
Industrial Plots Availability
Infrastructure Roads, Water, Power, Telephone
Type of Industry Approved for Food, Beverages, Handicrafts, Light engineering. No restriction except for manufacturing of defence parts and armaments and all kind of liquors and alcohols
Nearest City Peshawar

Small Industrial Estate Abbottabad
Location Mansehra Road
Year of Establishment 1973-74
Total Area 50 acres
Total Number of Plots 300
Size of Plots 2—8 Kanals
Uptake/No of Plots Allotted No Information
Industrial Plots Availability Available; 70% occupancy
Infrastructure Roads, Water, Power, Gas, Telephone
Type of Industry Food, furniture
Nearest City Peshawar
]
Small Industrial Estate Kohat
Location Dhoda Road
Year of Establishment 1984-85
Total Area 40 Acres
Total Number of Plots 350
Size of Plots 1—4 kanals
Uptake/No of Plots Allotted150
Industrial Plots Availability Available
Infrastructure Roads, Electricity, Sewerage
Type of Industry Approved for Food, Beverages, Handicrafts, Light engineering. No restriction except for manufacturing of defence parts and armaments and all kind of liquors and alcohols
Nearest City Peshawar

Industrial Estate Hattar
Location Kot Najibullah, Haripur
Year of Establishment 1984-85
Total Area 1,063 acres
Total Allottable Area 920 acres
Size of Plots 8 Kanals minimum
Uptake/No of Plots Allotted 905 acres/ 347 plots
Industrial Plots Availability Available; Occupancy – 80%

Infrastructure Roads, Water, Gas, Power, Telephone, Electricity, Community facilities
Type of Industry Large Chemical Plants, Heavy Electrical Engineering, Textiles, Food, Steel, Vegetable Oil
Nearest City Peshawar

Industrial Estate Gadoon Amazai
Location Near Tarbela, Topi, District Swabi
Year of Establishment 1986-87
Total Area 1,116 acres
Total Allottable Area 992 acres
Size of Plots Minimum 8 Kanals
Uptake/No of Plots Allotted 672 acres/359 plots
Industrial Plots Availability Available; Occupancy – 70%
Infrastructure Roads, Water, Power, Telephone
Type of Industry Engineering, Chemicals, Textiles, Consumer Products, Plastic, Auto Parts, Cement Bags, Steel, Paper Products, Pharmaceuticals
Nearest City Peshawar

Industrial Estate D.I. Khan
Location D.I. Khan – Multan Road, 19 km From D.I. Khan City
Year of Establishment 1990-91
Total Area 189 acres
Total Allottable Area 160 acres
Size of Plots Minimum 8 Kanals
Uptake/No of Plots Allotted 4
Industrial Plots Availability Available; Occupancy – empty
Infrastructure Roads, Water, Power
Type of Industry No industry established yet
Nearest City Peshawar

Industrial Estate Nowshera
Location Nowshera – Mardan Road, Risalpur
Year of Establishment 1993-94
Total Area 108 acres
Total Allottable Area 76 acres
Size of Plots Minimum 8 Kanals
Uptake/No of Plots Allotted 67 plots
Industrial Plots Availability Available
Infrastructure Roads, Water, Power, Gas, Telecommunications
Type of Industry Special furniture, Electrical bulbs

Nearest City Peshawar

Risalpur Export Processing Zone
Location 50 kms from Peshawar, near Mardan Interchange
Year of Establishment 1996
Total Area 92 acres
Total Allottable Area 79 acres
Size of Plots Variable
Uptake/No of Plots Allotted 30% of Phase 1; Zone under construction
Industrial Plots Availability 70% of Phase 1
Infrastructure Water, Electricity, Telecommunications
Type of Industry Trading and Warehousing, minerals, fruits and vegetable processing, carpets, furniture

Nearest City Peshawar

Industrial Estate Ghazi
Location 23 km from Lawrancepur Junction on Peshawar – Islamabad Highway
Year of Establishment 1994
Total Area 90 acres
Total Allottable Area 76.72 acres
Minimum 8 Kanals
Size of Plots
Uptake/No of Plots Allotted Nil
Industrial Plots Availability Available
Infrastructure Planning stage
Type of Industry Not specified
Nearest City Peshawar

Industrial Estate Mattani
Location Mattani Village, Indus Highway
Year of Establishment 1994
Total Area 30 Acres
Total Number of Plots 450
Size of Plots 2—4 kanals
Uptake/No of Plots Allotted Nil
Industrial Plots Availability
Infrastructure Nil
Type of Industry No Industry established

Nearest City Peshawar

DOING BUSINESS IN PAKISTAN

MARKET OVERVIEW

The United States and Pakistan have a strong economic and commercial relationship, conducting two-way trade of approximately $5.3 billion in 2014. The U.S. is Pakistan's largest trading partner and its leading source of foreign direct investment. For the U.S., Pakistan represents a modest market with suppliers exporting goods and services worth $1.65 billion to Pakistan in 2014. This figure represents a 7% increase over the 2012 figure of $1.53 billion. The U.S was Pakistan's largest export market in 2014, accounting for almost 15% of total exports. Valued at $3.68 billion, Pakistan's exports to the U.S. in 2014 were1.6% greater than the previous year.

Overall, Pakistan's economic growth has been sluggish for the past four years, however it accelerated moderately in fiscal year 2012-13, growing by 4.1%. Severe energy shortfalls, domestic security issues, burgeoning public debt, and the slow pace of economic and tax reform implementation are major factors that continue to pose a challenge to the economy of Pakistan. On October 15, 2009, President Obama signed the Enhanced Partnership with Pakistan Act of 2009 (commonly known as the Kerry-Lugar-Berman bill). This act authorizes the United States to provide Pakistan with economic assistance worth $7.5 billion over a five-year period. This assistance, together with other bilateral and multilateral commitments, continues to provide funding for a wide array of soft and hard infrastructure development of potential interest to U.S. firms. Pakistan entered into a three-year, $6.7 billion International Monetary Fund program in September 2014, which will provide an infusion of foreign exchange and framework for structural reforms.

With a population of approximately 190 million and an overall GDP exceeding $245 billion, Pakistan is the fifth-largest market in the entire Middle East, Africa, and South Asia regions (after India, South Africa, Saudi Arabia and Egypt). Pakistan has a young population and a growing middle class, with English as the lingua franca of the business community, and a highly evolved services sector that contributes 58% of GDP. Pakistan has a number of attributes that make it an attractive market for multinational firms, particularly those in the fast moving consumer-goods sector. The World Bank's 2014 Doing Business Report, which surveys the ease of doing business in international markets, ranked Pakistan 110th among the 189 economies surveyed. By comparison, regional competitors Bangladesh and India ranked 130 and 134, respectively.

American firms have a fairly strong presence in Pakistan. Currently, there are more than 65 wholly- or majority-owned U.S. subsidiary firms registered with the American Business Council (ABC) of Pakistan and the Lahore-based American Business Forum

(ABF). The U.S.-Pakistan Business Council, an affiliate of the U.S. Chamber of Commerce and based in Washington, is another forum for U.S. companies with business and investment interests in Pakistan. There are also hundreds of local firms representing U.S. companies in the market. Some leading U.S. companies doing business in Pakistan include Pepsi-Cola, Coca-Cola, Procter & Gamble, NCR, Teradata, Pfizer, Abbott Laboratories, DuPont, Oracle, Microsoft, Dell, 3M, IBM, Monsanto, McDonald's, KFC, Pizza Hut, Domino's Pizza, and Caterpillar. Pakistan and the United States signed a Trade and Investment Framework Agreement in 2003, which provides a forum for discussion of bilateral trade issues. The most recent annual TIFA council meeting was held in May 2014.

The U.S. corporate members of the ABC and ABF play an influential role in Pakistan's economy by demonstrating global standards of corporate governance. According to the ABC, these companies have collectively invested over $1.5 billion in Pakistan and their cumulative annual revenue is approximately $3 billion. ABC/ABF members contribute a sizable sum to the national treasury every year in the form of direct and indirect taxes.

In spite of security threats and familiar emerging market concerns over intellectual property rights, contract enforcement, and governance issues, the Pakistan market offers many attractive trade and investment opportunities. With regard to investment, the market has few restrictions on the movement of capital for foreign companies, no shareholding restrictions (beyond a few sensitive industry sectors), simple work-permit rules, no technology transfer requirements and a large and sophisticated entrepreneurial class.

MARKET CHALLENGES

Principal competitors of U.S. businesses in Pakistan are Chinese, European, Japanese, and South Korean suppliers. They at times offer credit terms that can make it difficult for U.S. suppliers to compete on major projects or government tenders. In particular, state-owned Chinese firms are increasingly expanding into market segments traditionally dominated by Western firms.

Pakistanis generally consider U.S. goods more expensive compared to those of competitors, and that U.S. firms often do not move as quickly to meet demand. American products, however are well regarded for their perceived quality, and some U.S. firms meet these challenges by shipping goods to Pakistan from regional operations.

Potential investors in Pakistan face many of the same challenges that exist in other developing economies such as regulatory risk and a lack of transparency in public-sector decision-making. Pakistan is a diverse and challenging market, requiring adaptability and persistence. It is often difficult to sell in this market without a reliable local partner, thus choosing the right local partners and careful planning are critical to success. U.S. firms willing to invest time to develop market presence should expect to be rewarded in the long-term.

MARKET OPPORTUNITIES

With a population of approximately 190 million and a GDP exceeding $245 billion, Pakistan continues to offer significant trade opportunities for U.S. businesses.

The following areas have been identified as best industry prospects for the next several years: consumer goods, power generation, renewable energy, oil and gas exploration, telecommunication equipment and services, airport and ancillary facilities, construction, trucking/transportation, agricultural machinery and equipment, franchising and health care.

MARKET ENTRY STRATEGY

One strategy for U.S. manufacturers and suppliers to penetrate the Pakistan market is to utilize the benefits of the network services and programs of the U.S. Department of Commerce's Export Assistance Centers (USEAC), in association with the U.S. Commercial Service at the U.S. Embassy in Islamabad, Pakistan, and the U.S. Consulates in Karachi and Lahore.

Seeking the assistance of USEACs before exploring opportunities in this market is highly encouraged. It is recommended that U.S. firms from the very outset work with locally-registered firms to help navigate a complex business culture. U.S. firms are encouraged to review the following website www.Buyusa.gov/pakistan

Many foreign manufacturers and suppliers appoint one or more agents/distributors to cover the entire country. At times, foreign principals work through a regional office to cover this market such as Dubai, Singapore, or London. It is comparatively easy to switch agents and distributors in Pakistan without being exposed to legal liability.

U.S. firms are also encouraged to consider the International Company Profile (ICP) service offered by the U.S. Commercial Service. Through this service, the U.S. Commercial Service office in Pakistan can provide a comprehensive background check on any local firm operating in Karachi, Lahore, Islamabad and Rawalpindi, Peshawar, and beyond. U.S. firms can apply for this service through any of the U.S Export Assistance Centers located in their region. A complete list of USEACs is available on the following website: http://www.buyusa.gov/home/us.html

SELLING PRODUCTS AND SERVICES

USING AN AGENT OR DISTRIBUTOR

Many foreign firms in Pakistan appoint local agents to provide market intelligence and to facilitate distribution. These agents typically work on a fixed commission, which can range from two to 10 percent for plant and equipment purchases and from 15 to 20 percent for spare parts. Commissions may be computed on FOB, ex-factory, or CIF basis, as mutually agreed. Some agents prefer to have suppliers quote net prices to them and they, in turn, add the commission to arrive at their selling price. Other agents operate as consultants on a retainer basis, receiving their fee regardless of the volume of total sales.

Probably the most common arrangement is the exclusive agency agreement, under which the supplier agrees to neither appoint another dealer/distributor, nor to negotiate sales through any other party. In return, the agent is barred from handling similar items produced by other companies. Under this arrangement, the agent receives commissions on all sales of the product regardless of the channels through which the order is placed. The agent often imports and stocks the spares most frequently required by the end-users. Agency agreements typically extend for a term of one to three years and generally require 30 to 90 days' notice by either party for termination.

Overseas suppliers may look after the interests of their local agents in various ways. For example, the principal may arrange separate payments to the local agent in order to provide after-sales service during and beyond the warranty period. The principal often compensates the local agent for providing technical and administrative support services not directly related to any specific sales transaction.

The Commercial Service of the U.S. Department of Commerce (USDOC) can provide assistance in locating potential agents and representatives abroad through its "International Partner Search (IPS)" and "Gold Key" services available through U.S. Export Assistance Centers in the United States. The "International Company Profile" (ICP) can provide background information on individual agents.

ESTABLISHING AN OFFICE

A business in Pakistan may be organized as a sole proprietorship, a partnership, or as a public or private limited company. Foreign investors generally establish limited companies as required under the Companies Ordinance, 1984. They must register with the Securities & Exchange Commission of Pakistan (SECP). Company registration offices are located in each of the provincial capitals and also in Islamabad and Multan. The promoters of any proposed company must also obtain confirmation from the SECP that the proposed name of their company is not deceptive, inappropriate, nor identical to the name of an already existing company.

A company making any public offer of securities for sale or intending to issue capital is required to obtain approval from the Controller of Capital Issues (CCI). After completion of the required formalities, firms should apply for necessary utilities to the authorities below:

Electric Power: Karachi Electric Supply Corporation (KESC), recently renamed K-Electric, is a private power distribution company that provides electric power to the Karachi area. State-owned distribution companies provide power to Islamabad, Rawalpindi and other regions in Pakistan.

Natural Gas: The following two state-owned utility firms, Sui Northern Gas Pipelines (for Punjab and Khyber Pakhtunkhwa) and Sui Southern Gas Company (for Sindh and Balochistan) provide gas distribution service.

Fixed line telephone and Fax services is provided by the Pakistan Telecommunications Company Limited (PTCL).

Cellular telephone services are provided by the following companies: Mobilink, Telenor, Ufone, Warid, and Zong (China Mobile Company).

Internet & Broadband: Following are some of the leading service providers: PTCL, Nayatel, WorldCall, Quebee, Wateen, WiTribe and Comsats. In early 2014, the Government of Pakistan auctioned 3G network licenses to Mobilink, Ufone, and Telenor and a 3G/4G license to Zong. Blackberry services are available in Pakistan through Mobilink and Ufone.

Water: Local governmental authorities.

All manufacturing concerns employing more than 10 persons are required to register with the appropriate provincial Chief Inspector of Industries under the Factories Ordinance, 1984.

Companies are also required to register with the Income Tax Department of the Federal

Board of Revenue (FBR) and obtain a National Tax Number (NTN).

Within 30 days of establishment, foreign companies must file the following documents with the Registrar of Joint Stock Companies, Ministry of Finance:

– a certified copy of the charter, statutes, or memorandum, and articles of association of the company;

– the full address of the registered or principal overseas office of the company;

– the names of the chief executive and directors of the company;

– the names and addresses of persons resident in Pakistan who are authorized to accept any legal notice served on the company.

U.S. firms may find it advantageous to use the services of a local attorney in complying with these formalities.

Contact details and information regarding forming a company in Pakistan may be obtained from the following websites:

Securities & Exchange Commission of Pakistan - http://secp.gov.pk/

Pakistan Board of Investment - http://pakboi.gov.pk/

FRANCHISING

The concept of franchising is quickly gaining acceptance in Pakistan, especially in the hospitality and food service sectors. Several major U.S. hotel chains, along with a rapidly growing number of major U.S. restaurants and U.S. car rental companies are currently represented in Pakistan through franchisees.

Franchising provides U.S. companies with a quick way to enter the market without major capital commitment. By operating through local franchisees, U.S. firms can gain access to local expertise and significantly reduce the problems of adjusting to an unfamiliar business environment.

However, franchising in Pakistan is not without drawbacks. Potential areas of tension between franchisor and franchisee include quality control, intensity of marketing efforts by the local franchisee, and possible conflict of interest on part of the franchisee. The local affiliate may end up as a competitor once the franchise agreement expires or is terminated.

A key consideration in establishing a franchise operation in Pakistan is quality control, particularly if the enterprise proposes to use locally produced items. In Pakistan, all imported food items; particularly meat items must be certifiably "Halal" (slaughtered in accordance with Islamic law).

Selection of a franchisee is critical because usually it involves a long-term relationship. Prior to entering into an agreement with a local company, U.S. firms may commission an ICP on the local company, by paying the appropriate fee to their nearest U.S. Export Assistance Center (USEAC). U.S. firms are, of course, advised to identify a number of candidates and evaluate each carefully.

The franchise agreement must be carefully drafted to protect the interests of the parties. The franchisor must be able to retain some direct control over operations, even after transfer of business and technical know-how. Crucial elements of the franchise agreement include territorial coverage, duration, franchise rate, and protection of trade secrets, quality control and minimum performance clauses. The U.S. firm should ensure that its patents and trademarks will be registered in its own name rather than that of the franchisee.

Major U.S. companies with franchise operations in Pakistan include Marriott, Day's Inn, Best Western, Ramada, Pizza Hut, KFC, Subway, McDonald's, Dunkin Donuts, Domino's Pizza, Papa John's Pizza, Hardees, Fat Burger, Nike Retail, UPS, FedEx, Princeton Review, Berlitz, Gymboree, Gloria Jean's Coffee, TCBY, Hertz and Avis. Most of the franchise operations have concentrated their activities around Karachi and Lahore; however some of the food outlets have opened branches in Hyderabad, Faisalabad, Islamabad and Rawalpindi.

DIRECT MARKETING

Until recently, direct marketing in Pakistan was limited to direct mail advertising, with leading pharmaceutical firms and large publishing groups as major users. The pharmaceutical companies employed direct mail to reach out to doctors, hospitals, and other medical professionals, and the publishers used direct mail to reach out to their existing subscribers of magazines and publications for repeat business. However, the inception of telemarketing and the increased usage of courier services along with internet and mobile phones have recently broadened the scope of direct marketing.

The concept of direct marketing is gradually gaining acceptance in the Pakistan marketplace, driven by the efforts of several multinational companies. The low cost of domestic mail and local telephone calls makes this a potentially cost-effective sales medium. The major drawbacks to direct marketing in Pakistan are the lack of readily available mailing lists with up-to-date contact information, and the paucity of reports on consumer preferences. These limitations make it difficult to target and reach the intended audience. Efficient mail and courier services are now available in all major urban and semi-urban areas of the country.

U.S. companies considering direct marketing in Pakistan should take local customs and cultural values into consideration before launching a campaign. The use of a local advertising agency is advisable in implementing the direct marketing option. A few advertising agencies have separate direct marketing departments.

JOINT VENTURES/LICENSING

The three principal routes to entering the Pakistan market are: (1) formation of a wholly-owned private company; (2) formation of a public limited company (foreign firm retains majority control, but seeks public participation through stock flotation); and (3) establishment of a company in cooperation with joint venture partners who supply local expertise, management and capital.

The joint venture may be either a private or a public company. Joint ventures can be an attractive option in Pakistan today because there are many local entrepreneurs who have built a substantial base in their industrial enterprises and are seeking to combine their knowledge of local markets with foreign capital and technological know-how. The foreign joint venture partner limits its initial country exposure while enjoying the support of a local partner in a new market. Prominent joint ventures have been established in the automobile, fertilizer, electronics and home appliances, financial services, food and consumer product and energy sectors.

Firms wanting to delay direct entry into the Pakistan market should consider licensing arrangements with Pakistani firms, an option that permits them to enter the market in stages if the initial response is promising.

SELLING TO THE GOVERNMENT

Pakistani law requires that all government tenders be advertised in national newspapers and the Pakistan Procurement Regulatory Authority website for a minimum of 15 days, with the exception of government-to-government contracts. Pakistani government agencies and public sector companies allow only exclusive agents to submit bids for tenders to ensure that they receive only one quotation from each supplier. Many firms (especially Japanese) add a clause on direct negotiation that allows them to deal directly with the end-user, should the firm believe that the agent might have difficulty in concluding a sale. On such sales, the commission payable to the agent, if any, is determined by the principals and is based on the proportion of services rendered by the agent.

Pakistani law does not prohibit payment of commissions on commercial procurement of large amounts of military equipment. However, the Directorate General Defense Purchase (DGDP) requires that the foreign principal provide the following: ex-factory value of items supplied, FOB value of these items, and percentage or amount of commission/or any other fee for services provided by the local agent. Commercial procurement of small to medium amounts of military equipment is generally made through local agents of overseas manufacturers and suppliers. For government contracts, bidders are very often asked to submit refundable "earnest money",

"bid bonds" or bank guarantees along with their bids in order to demonstrate their seriousness in bidding for a contract. Some government agencies, such as the Directorate General of Defense Purchase (DGDP) require that all local agents registered with them submit a certification from their foreign principals' Embassy certifying the legitimacy of their foreign principal. The U.S. Commercial Service, Pakistan offers this service for a $50 charge to both U.S. and Pakistani firms that wish to have their agency agreements certified by the U.S. Embassy. Further details about government tenders may be obtained from the following website:

http://www.ppra.org.pk/

DISTRIBUTION AND SALES CHANNELS

Pakistan's retail industry is still developing with most of this segment fragmented and underdeveloped. There are in excess of 2.5 million shops in Pakistan, most of which offer only basic necessities. Consequently, food, beverages and tobacco account for as much as 75 percent of retail sales. There are less than one dozen shopping malls in operation and they are generally limited to the larger cities of Karachi and Lahore. Islamabad's first shopping mall opened in February 2014.

Large supermarkets or chain stores for general consumer items are not widely available in Pakistan, though a few multinational chains have started operations. European cash and carry retailers Makro and Metro, in joint collaboration with Pakistan's Habib Group, have opened several self-service wholesale outlets in Karachi, Lahore, and Islamabad. Carrefour Hypermarkets (Pakistan) with outlets in Karachi and Lahore is the latest entrant in the hyper-market segment, along with the UK's Greenvalley. The concept of chain stores for fashion apparel has also lately begun to emerge in the larger cities, where several such chains, stocking predominantly locally manufactured merchandise, are currently operating. In addition, hundreds of government-owned Utility Stores sell food and household items and serve as a mechanism for restraining inflationary price increases by following the government line on pricing. The military-owned Canteen Stores Department (CSD), a discount retail network, has also expanded to all major cities of the country.

The general perception among Pakistani consumers is that the prices in the larger and more upscale stores must be higher due to higher overhead and investment costs.

Many consumer retail stores stock general merchandise for everyday use. There are also large numbers of stores that sell a single commodity, for example, tires, cooking utensils, textiles or jewelry. Such stores are generally located in bazaar areas and tend to be situated near other shops carrying similar goods.

Foreign companies considering marketing their products in Pakistan may choose to use the services of local distributors or may develop their own distribution chain. Distributors in the urban areas generally deal on an exclusive basis. Some market consultants estimate that the services of 100-300 distributors would be required for nationwide coverage. One very large multinational company selling consumer products employs 500 distributors to reach a significant portion of Pakistan's small towns and villages.

As a matter of policy, most companies do not provide credit to distributors, and distributors in turn generally sell on cash basis to small retailers, but do supply on a short-term credit to large retailers that offer a heavy turnover.

Pakistan's wholesale market is fairly well developed, with about 1,000 - 1,500 wholesalers constituting this segment of the distribution network. Karachi is the major distribution center for wholesale goods. Approximately one-fifth of the wholesalers in Karachi sell on a consignment basis. Less than one-third of the wholesalers allow discounts to their customers, but the granting of 30- to 90-day credit is common. Because of limited financial resources, retailers generally sell on a cash-only basis. Consumer credit in Pakistan remains an insignificant portion of the total commercial credit. Foreign companies selling industrial or capital goods often sell directly to the end-user or, if the market is fairly large, they appoint one major distributor who then sells either to sub-distributors or directly to end-users.

SELLING FACTORS/TECHNIQUES

The traditional approach to selling in Pakistan has been through personal contact with a major wholesaler which serves a network of retailers throughout the country. However, this trend is changing. Advertising is now a growing industry and some of the large consumer manufacturers extensively promote their products through print and electronic media as well as the internet. Some of the banks regularly contact their potential customers through direct marketing. Nonetheless, personal relationships are very important, especially when selling non-consumer items to the government or large corporations. Since personal relationships take time to nurture, U.S. firms are advised to invest time in the market with preferably a local presence or at least very frequent trips to the area. This is not an activity that can be done arms-length. Face-to-face contact is the business norm, however under the current environment, this poses a significant challenge. U.S. business travelers may face delays in acquiring a Pakistani visa. Some U.S. corporations strictly adhere to the State Department Travel Advisory and this may also pose a challenge for U.S. business visitors to Pakistan. To overcome this challenge, at times U.S. firms meet with their Pakistani counterparts in a nearby third country, such as the United Arab Emirates.

In addition to personal relationships, price generally remains the dominant buying factor. Government procurement also places heavy emphasis on selection of the lowest bidder, provided the bidder meets the technical specifications and has relevant industry experience. Some foreign companies have mastered the art of providing initial lower bids and revising them later to a more realistic level, usually in connivance with "consenting" officials. Some U.S. firms have expressed their frustration in dealing with government contracts, especially in situations when they were technically qualified and submitted the lowest bids, yet were not awarded the contract or were asked to re-bid for a re-advertised contract.

U.S. products and services enjoy an excellent reputation in the local market, especially for their quality and durability. However, U.S. companies face tough competition from Chinese, Japanese and Korean companies, which generally have a larger presence in the country and are able to offer their products and services at competitive prices. Providing after-sales services is also essential and U.S. firms are advised to establish this service either through a local/agent distributor or through their own presence in the local market.

ELECTRONIC COMMERCE

Pakistan is still largely a cash-based, informal economy. The majority of transactions are conducted in cash, except for those that are very large and require a bank draft or pay order. Up to 60% of the economy is informal, according to some estimates, with the majority of local companies, particularly SMEs, undocumented and outside the tax net.

A number of government departments have started to offer services via the Internet. In the private sector, three Pakistani airlines now offer e-ticketing and almost all local banks offer online banking services. This segment of the economy is expected to grow steadily as there are approximately 30 million Internet subscribers in Pakistan and this figure is expected double during the next five years. There are also more than 10 million

Facebook subscribers in Pakistan and several local companies now use social media to promote their products and services. Pakistan has one of the highest rates of mobile penetration in South Asia at nearly 70%, and mobile banking is an area with some promise.

TRADE PROMOTION AND ADVERTISING

Over a dozen major advertising agencies operate in Pakistan, some with foreign affiliation. Advertising agency commissions are usually 15 percent of the cost of the advertisement. By US standards these agencies are fairly small concerns, with an annual billing of less than US$ 20 million each.

Television and newspapers are the most widely used mode of advertising. Others include radio, billboards, periodicals and trade journals, direct response advertising, slides and commercial film shorts in movie theaters, short messages (SMS) through cellular phones, as well as the Internet-based social media.

Pakistan has over 120 daily newspapers. The daily Jang, published in Urdu, is the single largest newspaper, with a claimed national circulation of almost 800,000 (estimated: 450,000). Combined circulation for the roughly 11 English-language newspapers is approximately 300,000. The principal English-language daily newspapers are the Dawn (published in Karachi, Lahore and Islamabad), The News (Islamabad, Lahore and Karachi), The Nation (Lahore and Islamabad), Daily Times, Express Tribune and The Business Recorder (Karachi). Although the English-language press reaches only a small fraction of the population, it is influential in political, business, academic and professional circles.

The two major English-language current affairs magazines are monthlies - the Herald and Newsline. The principal English-language weekly economic magazine is the Pakistan & Gulf Economist, published in Karachi, and there is also a widely read English weekly, The Friday Times, published from Lahore. Several special interest magazines such as Spider (Internet), Computerworld (Computer and IT) and Mobile Communications and Flare are steadily gaining prominence. Almost all the newspapers in Pakistan are now available on the Internet.

Television is broadcast on state-owned Pakistan Television and several other local channels, using the PAL system. English language programs, including news, are available on several satellite channels.

Cable and Satellite Television: Cable television has been available in Pakistan for more than ten years now and with the passage of time the channels are getting more professional and organized. The broadcast media is regulated by the Pakistan Electronic Media Regulatory Authority (PEMRA), which has issued more than 800 licenses to prospective operators. It is estimated that cable television reaches approximately 30 percent of households in Pakistan. Regulatory details about broadcast media are available on the PEMRA website www.pemra.gov.pk

Satellite television broadcasts have made rapid inroads in Pakistan and it is estimated that more than 200,000 dish antennas are presently installed in the country, although, with the advent of cable TV, the popularity of direct satellite television is gradually

diminishing. More than 100 channels are received via satellite. The most popular transponder received in Pakistan is "Asiasat,"" which carries most of the Indian TV channels.

Radio Pakistan reaches out to audiences within the country and abroad in 36 languages (19 regional and 17 foreign) from 24 medium and short wave stations and 6 FM stations, transmitting more than 600 hours of programs. The FM license granted by the government does not permit them to broadcast exclusive news and current affairs programs.

Pakistan currently allows trade-advertising material other than commercial catalogs to enter duty-free, but levies a 15.0 percent sales tax on those items. Samples may be admitted duty free only if they are representative parts of a complete shipment or are unsuitable for sale. The duties applicable to commercial shipments apply to samples having a commercial value.

Trade Shows - The textile and apparel, along with the leather and gemstones industries hold regular trade shows. Lately, the telecommunications, safety & security, higher education, information technology and oil and gas industries have become active in this area. Trade and seminar missions can also provide valuable first-hand insights into the Pakistani market, as well as serving to introduce U.S. equipment and technology. Trade missions can educate government and other end-users about product availability, technical characteristics, quality, and price, and can establish contacts with key organizations to promote product awareness. Presently, trade show business in Pakistan is suffering tremendously from the prevailing security situation.

U.S. firms should also consider participation in regional events (focusing on either South Asia or the Middle-East) in order to reach potential Pakistani purchasers, agents, and distributors.

PRICING

Product pricing is often difficult for new entrants to the Pakistan market, principally due to the country's complex tax structure. Foreign companies represented by a local agent, distributor, licensee, or other intermediary generally work closely with their local affiliates in determining prices.

Relatively high shelf prices frequently include a substantial tax component, which can add nearly 40 percent to the retailer's purchase price. High prices and taxes for imported consumer items have created a large market for goods coming into Pakistan through "informal channels." Expatriate Pakistanis and professional couriers bring in large quantities of goods from the Middle East Gulf region in their personal baggage. Goods are also frequently smuggled from Dubai via sea, misrepresented as destined for the Afghan market to avoid import tariffs, or undervalued on bills of lading to evade taxes. In some segments of the market, goods brought through these channels have market shares ranging from 50 to 95 percent

As an illustration of the scale and complexity of various taxes and duties imposed on imported consumer items, marketers of products build into their final sales price the following factors: landing charges (approximately 1.0 percent of initial price); customs duty; sales tax; bank charges; insurance, and the general sales tax.

Pricing of non-consumer items is based on different parameters. Most foreign companies in this market segment are also represented by agent/distributors and give their local affiliates significant latitude in pricing decisions. Agents often opt for higher sales turnover by reducing their margins, allowing them to generate more revenue through a higher volume of sales. In other cases, local agent/distributors may add up to 30 percent to the list price as their commission, depending on the nature of the product. For duty and tariff purposes, they quote the principal's list prices only. On average, retailers markup imported machinery and equipment by 10 to 15 percent and imported general merchandise 20 to 30 percent.

SALES SERVICE/CUSTOMER SUPPORT

In Pakistan, the end-user generally requires comprehensive and reliable after-sales support on all durable and non-consumer items, accompanied by good documentation and instructions for product installation, operation, and repair. Many purchasers choose a complete turnkey package, which often includes employee training.

Foreign sellers generally require local agent/distributors to maintain a certain minimum inventory of spare parts. Most agents provide a warranty and "free maintenance" for one year, building the cost of maintenance into their overall price.

It is a common practice for end-users to demand a guarantee that the supplier will respond to questions or rectify faults in the equipment within a specified period of time. The time period may vary from a few hours to several days, depending on the nature of the product and the fault in the equipment.

PROTECTING YOUR INTELLECTUAL PROPERTY

Several general principles are important for effective management of intellectual property (IP) rights in Pakistan. First, it is important to have an overall strategy to protect your IP. Second, IP is protected differently in Pakistan than in the U.S. Third, rights must be registered and enforced in Pakistan, under local laws. Your U.S. trademark and patent registrations will not protect you in Pakistan. There is no such thing as an “international copyright” that will automatically protect an author’s writings throughout the entire world. Protection against unauthorized use in a particular country depends, basically, on the national laws of that country. However, most countries do offer copyright protection to foreign works under certain conditions, and these conditions have been greatly simplified by international copyright treaties and conventions.

Registration of patents and trademarks is on a first-in-time, first-in-right basis, so you should consider applying for trademark and patent protection even before selling your products or services in the Pakistan market. It is vital that companies understand that intellectual property is primarily a private right and that the U.S. government generally cannot enforce rights for private individuals in Pakistan. It is the responsibility of the rights' holders to register, protect, and enforce their rights where relevant, retaining their own counsel and advisors. Companies may wish to seek advice from local attorneys or IP consultants who are experts in Pakistan law. The U.S. Commercial Service can provide a list of local lawyers upon request.

While the U.S. government stands ready to assist, there is little we can do if the rights holders have not taken these fundamental steps necessary to securing and enforcing their IP in a timely fashion. Moreover, in many countries, rights holders who delay enforcing their rights on a mistaken belief that the USG can provide a political resolution to a legal problem may find that their rights have been eroded or abrogated due to legal doctrines such as statutes of limitations, laches, estoppel, or unreasonable delay in prosecuting a law suit. In no instance should U.S. government advice be seen as a substitute for the obligation of a rights holder to promptly pursue its case.

It is always advisable to conduct due diligence on potential partners. Negotiate from the position of your partner and give your partner clear incentives to honor the contract. A good partner is an important ally in protecting IP rights. Consider carefully, however, whether to permit your partner to register your IP rights on your behalf. Doing so may create a risk that your partner will list itself as the IP owner and fail to transfer the rights should the partnership end. Keep an eye on your cost structure and reduce the margins (and the incentive) of would-be bad actors. Projects and sales in Pakistan require constant attention. Work with legal counsel familiar with Pakistan laws to create a solid contract that includes non-compete clauses, and confidentiality/non-disclosure provisions. The Intellectual Property Organization of Pakistan (www.ipo.gov.pk) is the government of Pakistan's focal point for IP issues.

It is also recommended that small and medium-sized companies understand the importance of working together with trade associations and organizations to support efforts to protect IP and stop counterfeiting. There are a number of these organizations in the U.S. These include:

- The U.S. Chamber and local American Chambers of Commerce
- National Association of Manufacturers (NAM)
- International Intellectual Property Alliance (IIPA)
- International Trademark Association (INTA)
- The Coalition Against Counterfeiting and Piracy
- International Anti-Counterfeiting Coalition (IACC)
- Pharmaceutical Research and Manufacturers of America (PhRMA)
- Biotechnology Industry Organization (BIO)

IP Resources

A wealth of information on protecting IP is freely available to U.S. rights holders. Some excellent resources for companies regarding intellectual property include the following:

- For information about patent, trademark, or copyright issues -- including enforcement issues in the US and other countries -- call the STOP! Hotline: 1-866-999-HALT or register at www.StopFakes.gov .
- For more information about registering trademarks and patents (both in the U.S. as well as in foreign countries), contact the US Patent and Trademark Office (USPTO) at: 1-800-786-9199.
- For more information about registering for copyright protection in the US, contact the US Copyright Office at: 1-202-707-5959.
- For more information about how to evaluate, protect, and enforce intellectual property rights and how these rights may be important for businesses, a free online training program is available at www.stopfakes.gov .

• For US small and medium-size companies, the Department of Commerce offers a "SME IP Advisory Program" available through the American Bar Association that provides one hour of free IP legal advice for companies with concerns in Brazil, China, Egypt, India, Russia, and . For details and to register, visit: http://www.abanet.org/intlaw/intlproj/iprprogram_consultation.html

• For information on obtaining and enforcing intellectual property rights and market-specific IP Toolkits visit: www.StopFakes.gov This site is linked to the USPTO website for registering trademarks and patents (both in the U.S. as well as in foreign countries), the U.S. Customs & Border Protection website to record registered trademarks and copyrighted works (to assist customs in blocking imports of IP-infringing products) and allows you to register for Webinars on protecting IP.

The U.S. Commerce Department has positioned IP attachés in key markets around the world. You can get contact information for the IP attaché in India, who also covers Pakistan at:

U.S. Patent & Trade Mark Office

Embassy of the United States of America

American Center, 24, K.G. Marg

New Delhi 110 001, India

Tel: +91 11 2347 2000 ext. 2101

Direct Dial: +91 11 2347 2101

Fax: +91 11 2331 4564

Website: www.uspto.gov

DUE DILIGENCE

U.S. companies seeking to do business in Pakistan are strongly advised to conduct a background check on the local company. It is always advisable to check the ownership of the company and its business track record.

It is recommended that U.S. companies carry out their due diligence on prospective partners or opportunities using the U.S. Commercial Service International Company profile (ICP) service. Please contact the U.S. Commercial Service, Islamabad, Pakistan for more information on this service.

LOCAL PROFESSIONAL SERVICES

The U.S. Commercial Service offices located in Islamabad, Karachi and Lahore maintain contact with reputable companies that offer various services and may be of assistance to U.S. businesses in completing a specific task in this market. Contact information for these service providers may be obtained directly from the individual offices. Pakistan has a fairly sophisticated services industry offering high level of professional lawyers, accountants, business and management consultants, IT experts, and advertising professionals.

Various professional services are listed on the following website, which is Pakistan's largest online Yellow Pages:

www.jamals.com

WEB RESOURCES

http://www.export.gov

LEADING SECTORS FOR U.S. EXPORT AND INVESTMENT

OIL & GAS FIELD EQUIPMENT AND SERVICES

Crude Oil:

Recoverable reserves of crude oil in Pakistan as of December 31, 2014 were estimated at 362 million barrels. The average crude oil production during July 2012-2014 was 76,277 barrels per day (bpd) as against 66,032 bpd during the same period last year. Recently there have been new oil discoveries and the daily production of crude oil reached an all-time high of 100,000 bpd in May 2014. Demand for petroleum stands at approximately 450,000 bpd. The state-owned Oil and Gas Development Company Limited (OGDCL) is the largest producer of crude oil in Pakistan, followed by the United Energy Group of Hong Kong, Pakistan Petroleum Limited, Pakistan Oilfields Limited, BHP, ENI and OMV, which recently acquired Petronas' assets in Pakistan.

The Government of Pakistan (GOP) continues to attach very high importance to this sector as it wants to reduce its dependency on imported oil.

Natural Gas:

As of June 30, 2014, Pakistan's recoverable natural gas reserves were estimated at 24.7 trillion cubic feet. The average production of natural gas during July 2012 – March 2014 was 4,259 million cubic feet per day (mmcfd) as against 4,236 mmcfd during the corresponding period in the year 2011-2012. The estimated unrestrained demand for natural gas is approximately 8,000 mmcfd. Presently Pakistan does not import any natural gas and has a massive shortage that worsens in the winter when domestic heating and cooking demand increases. The shortage reduces the supply of electricity from gas-fired power plants by approximately 2000 megawatts and requires dual-fired plants to switch to fuel oil. Pakistan's fertilizer and cement industry is heavily dependent on natural gas as is the transportation sector.. More than 2 million vehicles in Pakistan use Compressed Natural Gas (CNG) as their primary fuel. A government-imposed rationing scheme gives priority to household consumers, then power plants, fertilizer, cement other industry and lastly, CNG distributors. Most CNG stations are open only two or three days a week.

In April 2014, the Government of Pakistan contracted for construction of a Liquefied Natural Gas (LNG) import facility. The government projects that imports of LNG equivalent to 200 mmcfd will begin in the first quarter of 2015 and will increase to 400 mmcfd in the second quarter of 2015. The Government of Pakistan has also signed an agreement with Iran for the construction of a gas pipeline connecting the two countries, though the project has stalled due to financing constraints and the impact of sanctions. Due to the prevailing sanctions against Iran, U.S. firms are barred from participating in this pipeline project, and if construction begins, there could be wider negative implications for doing business with firms or entities involved in the project.

The Government of Pakistan approved a new Petroleum Exploration & Production Policy in August 2012. The policy provides higher gas prices for new finds. An auction for 50 concession blocks was conducted in December 2014. Thirty-seven of the blocks were

awarded to the state-owned companies. The Government of Pakistan is developing a policy for production of shale gas and other unconventional resources in the country.

SUB-SECTOR BEST PROSPECTS

Drilling Equipment: Oil & Gas
Chemicals
Instrumentation
Pipes
Compressors
Petrochemical Equipment
Mud chemicals
Oil & Gas Field Services

OPPORTUNITIES

The Government of Pakistan is actively seeking investment in onshore and offshore exploration activities, development of explored wells and construction of gas pipelines. Pakistan's current petroleum policy is available on the following web site: http://www.mpnr.gov.pk

WEB RESOURCES

Ministry of Petroleum & Natural Gas Resources of Pakistan: http://www.mpnr.gov.pk
Oil & Gas Development Company Limited: http://www.ogdcl.com
Hydrocarbon Development Institute of Pakistan: http://www.hdip.com.pk/

TELECOMMUNICATION EQUIPMENT & SERVICES

The liberalization in the telecom sector during the previous years has made telecommunications one of the most promising sectors in Pakistan. Today, five cellular companies are operating in the country with a customer base approaching 130 million subscribers. The private sector is now actively involved in the expansion and development of telecommunication services. It provides cellular telephone services, card payphone, internet/ broadband services, and, with the privatization of Pakistan Telecommunication Company Limited (PTCL), it also provides fixed line telephone services.

Competition for U.S. equipment manufacturers during the next several years will remain strong, particularly with the European telecommunication firms because Nokia-Siemens and Alcatel–Lucent have established most of the software protocols in Pakistan (which are now fully integrated with the PTCL network). In the cellular sector, Mobilink, the largest operator, which had initially installed a Motorola network, has now switched to Ericsson for its network expansion and 3G rollout program, whereas the other four networks have opted for the Chinese ZTE equipment. A few years back, Warid contracted with Motorola to plan, design and deploy a nationwide wireless broadband voice and data network using WIMAX technology. Pakistan's total import of telecommunication equipment during the year 2012-2014 was $918.4 million out of which $467.1 million constituted import of cellular handsets and batteries. During the year 2011-2012, Pakistan's import of telecommunication equipment totaled $ 954.05 million, showing a decline of 3.7 percent over the one-year period. This decrease is mainly attributed to the fact that much of the infrastructure in the cellular telecommunication is already in place and the pace of growth in the overall telecommunication sector has slowed down considerably. However, with the introduction of 3G and 4G technologies in the local market, cellular operators will likely need to make additional investment in their respective networks and at the same time raise tariff rates to cover these additional costs. It may be noted that all the cellular networks in Pakistan are foreign-owned or managed by a foreign business entity.

FOREIGN DIRECT INVESTMENT IN TELECOM SECTOR

Overall, foreign direct investment is up slightly in Pakistan during fiscal year 2014-14. The total FDI in Pakistan stood at $1.36 billion through May 2014. The net inflows of FDI in the telecommunication sector showed an increase of $556 million due to the payment of license fees. A major development in the telecom sector was the auction of 3G/4G license by the Government of Pakistan. With the exception of Warid, the remaining four cellular operators participated in the auction and 3G licenses were awarded to Mobilink, Ufone, and Telenor and 3G/4G license was awarded to Zong. Warid did not bid for these licenses as the company had already acquired a "technology neutral" license and has plans to launch its 4G LTE (Long Term Evolution) service; however, the Pakistan Telecommunication Authority (PTA) has challenged this decision and may prevent Warid from launching this network unless it also acquires a 3G license.

Teledensity:

At the end of FY2014, Pakistan's total teledensity increased to 71.7 percent, showing a growth of 4.7 percent over the previous year. Telecom operators achieved this growth despite continued slow economic growth in the country. Cellular mobile, being the most vibrant segment of the telecom sector in Pakistan, contributed solely towards this increase in teledensity.

Year	Fixed landline (%)	Cellular (%)	Wireless local Loop (%)	Total Teledensity (%)
2007-08	1.10	40.90	3.0	54.70
2008-09	1.40	54.70	2.7	58.22
2009-10	1.60	58.20	2.2	60.40
20109-11	1.60	60.40	2.1	64.76
2011-12	1.60	64.80	1.9	68.54
2012-13	1.64	68.39	1.7	71.73

Cellular Telephone Sector: The growth in this sector has been phenomenal, and as of November I 2014 there were approximately 129.6 million cellular subscribers in Pakistan. The growth pattern in this sector has been as follows:

YEAR	SUBSCRIBERS (Million)
2001 - 02	1.6
2002 - 03	2.4
2003 - 04	5.0
2004 - 05	12.7
2005 - 06	33.93

2006 - 07	63.16
2007 - 08	88.05
2008 - 09	94.34
2009 - 10	99.19
2010 - 11	108.89
2011 - 12	120.15
2012 - 13	129.6

Pakistan's five cellular operators are Pakistan Mobile Communication Ltd. (Mobilink), Telenor Pakistan Ltd. (Telenor), Pakistan Telecom Mobile Ltd. (Ufone), Warid Telecom Ltd. (Warid) and China Mobile Pakistan Ltd. (Zong). All these cellular companies are owned by foreign principals: VimpelCom (Netherland-based), Etisalat (UAE), China Mobile (PRC), Telenor Group (Norway) and Abu Dhabi Group (UAE), respectively. The fixed line operator, Pakistan Telecommunication Company Ltd. is also partly owned and managed by Etisalat of UAE.

Market share of cellular companies:

Cellular Companies	Market share (%)
Mobilink	28.9
Telenor	26.1
Ufone	18.7
Zong	16.4
Warid	9.9

Telecom Equipment & Services:

The present market size for the import of telecommunication equipment (including handsets) is estimated at $920 million.

The world's leading telecom infrastructure providers like Ericsson, Alcatel-Lucent, ZTE and Huawei have established their branches in Pakistan and are engaged in design, development, installation, configuration and maintenance of telecom installations.

Other vendors of telecom equipment and services in Pakistan include Advance Digital, Inc.; GD Satcom; iDirect; Comtech EF Data Corp.; NEC Corporation; Conexant Systems; Agere Systems; Al-Futtaim; Cambridge Silicon; Panasonic; Catecom; Quanta; Ruckus; Computational Systems; Tellabs, Symbol Technologies and Emerson Process, etc.

SUB-SECTOR BEST PROSPECTS

Telecom switches

Radio communication links

Fiber optic cables

Towers, poles, ducts and pits used in conjunction with other infrastructure facilities.

Broadband services

Back-up power for telecommunication towers

Opportunities

Based on industry estimates, the telecom sector is now going into the consolidation phase. This is demonstrated by the fact that the Average Revenue Per User (ARPU) has been sliding for the last couple of years. An unstable Pak Rupee has also played a role in pushing ARPU downwards and it stood at an average of $ 2.11 in the last quarter of 2014- 2014.

The telecommunication sector in Pakistan experienced very rapid growth from 2001 to 2008; however, since most of the infrastructure is already in place, investment in this sector has declined. With the recent auctioning of 3G/4G licenses, further investment in this sector is expected, although it may be noted that the cellular operators had already imported and installed much of the needed equipment before obtaining their licenses.

Web Resources

Pakistan Telecommunication Authority – http://www.pta.gov.pk

Pakistan Telecommunication Company Limited – www.ptcl.com.pk

ELECTRICAL POWER SYSTEMS

Unit: USD Thousands

	2011	2012	2014	2014 (estimated)
Total Market Size	1,777.2	1,812.7	1,903.3	2,093.6
Total Local Production	182.2	182.2	182.2	182.2
Total Exports	10.5	10.5	10.5	10.5
Total Imports	1,605.5	1,637.6	1,719.4	1,819.3
Imports from the U.S.	963.3	982.6	1,012.0	1,113.2
Exchange Rate (Pak Rupees/US)	90.45	99.45	103.45	99.40

Pakistan is suffering from an acute power deficit of approximately 4,700 MW (demand and supply gap). The government of Pakistan is making a concerted effort to close this gap by boosting generation and offering attractive returns on power sector projects, but efficiencies and theft remains a serious problem. Currently, it is estimated that the present power shortage has reduced Pakistan's GDP growth by up to 3-4% on a year-on-year basis.

Below is the breakdown of Pakistan's total installed capacity.

Hydroelectric 6,773 MW
Thermal Public 4,829 MW
Thermal Private 8,835 MW
Nuclear 750 MW
KESC 2,216 MW
Total Installed 23,403-MW

Circular Debt Situation and Steps Taken

The inter-corporate circular debt problem plaguing the power sector stems from a disparity between the cost of generation and the selling price to consumers. The government sets power prices lower than the cost of generation which creates a substantial cost tariff differential. According to industry experts, various suppliers in the energy sector had Rupees 300 billion (about $3 billion) in circular debt through April 2014. This situation was further complicated by the depreciation of the rupee and the price of oil, a major input in the generation of electricity. As the subsidy element (difference between cost and tariff) grew, large amounts of circular debt were created whereby power producing companies were unable to receive payments from distribution companies and in turn the power producers could not make payments to the fuel suppliers. While the GOP raised the price of electricity in late 2014, , theft and line losses continue to plague the system and impair recovery. y.

PPIB (Private Power and Infrastructure Board)

The Private Power and Infrastructure Board (PPIB) was created in 1994 to facilitate private sector in the participation of power generation in Pakistan. PPIB provides a One-Window facility to private sector investors in matters concerning power projects and related infrastructure including the negotiation of the required Implementation Agreement (IA). PPIB also provides support to the power purchaser and fuel supplier while negotiating the Power Purchase Agreement (PPA), Fuel Supply Agreement (FSA)/Gas Supply Agreement (GSA), other related agreements, and liaise with the concerned local and international agencies for facilitating and expediting progress of private sector power projects. PPIB is working to attract and facilitate FDI in Pakistan's power sector. A number of foreign investors have expressed interest in setting up power generation projects that would develop Pakistan's indigenous resources including hydroelectric, wind, natural gas, and coal. Their proposals have been evaluated and the prospective investors encouraged development of power projects focusing on maximum utilization of available local resources.

Growth in Consumers

The number of consumers has been increasing due to expansion of the electric network to villages and other areas. The growth in number of consumers increased by 21.05 million during calendar year 2012-13 against 20.85 million in same period the previous year.

NUCLEAR ENERGY

The Pakistan Atomic Energy Commission (PAEC) is responsible for planning, construction and operation of nuclear power plants in the country. Presently, five nuclear power plants; Karachi Nuclear Power Plant (K-1) and Chashma Nuclear Power Plant unit-1, 2,3 4, and 5 (C-1, C-2, C-3, C-4, and C-5) are in operation. Pakistan Atomic Energy has been assigned the task of installing an 8,800-MW nuclear power by the year 2030.

SUB-SECTOR BEST PROSPECTS

The most promising sub-sectors within this sector for FY2014 are:

Power Generation Equipment: $70 million
Power Transmission Equipment: $235 million
Power Distribution Equipment, including equipment for Rural Electrification: $160 million

Web Resources

http://www.ppib.gov.pk (Private Power & Infrastructure Board)

http://www.statistics.gov.pk (Federal Bureau of Statistics)
http://www.pakwapda.com (Water and Power Development Authority)

RENEWABLE ENERGY

Pakistan's total energy consumption through renewable energy (RE) sources stood at approximately 450-MW during the fiscal year 2012-13. The available resources - solar, biogas, biomass, micro-hydel, and wind, offer substantial business opportunities for U.S. suppliers. The GOP through its 2006 Renewable Energy Policy heavily emphasizes the development of renewable and clean energy.. The GOP has decided to strengthen the current resource infrastructure through the Alternate Energy Development Board (AEDB) in order to reach a target of 10 percent share of overall energy requirements by 2020.

Alternate Energy Development Board

In its bid to diversify the local energy mix, the GOP has focused great emphasis on the development of Alternative/Renewable Energy (ARE) resources. In 2010 the GOP granted the AEDB the mandate to implement ARE commercial projects unilaterally or through joint ventures with public or private sector entities. Along with the AEDB, the Pakistan Council of Renewable Energy Technologies (PCRET) has also acquired and updated know-how for the promotion and mass propagation of Renewable Energy Technologies. PCRET's main function is to develop, acquire, adapt, promote and disseminate renewable energy technologies in the country.

Mega Wind Power Projects

AEDB has issued Letters of Intent (LOI) to 50 independent power producers pursuing development of wind power projects. Land was allocated to 19 IPPs for 50 MW wind power projects each in Gharo-Keti Bander Wind Corridor. Projects with a cumulative capacity of approx. 950 MW are at various stages of development on these lands. The National Electric Power Regulatory Authority (NEPRA) has recently approved a new feed-in tariff of US$0.135 per Kilowatt Hour that, despite some shortcomings, is considered commercially viable by local market players and will result in additional investments in the sector. At present, two 50-MW wind power projects are operational in the country.

Biogas

Pakistan generates an enormous amount of municipal waste (up to 50,000 tons/day) and agricultural waste in the form of biogas, cotton sticks, and rice husks. Converting this waste into energy can generate up to 5,000-MW of power. Pakistan offers lucrative opportunities in this sector in which a number of projects are already being implemented.

So far PCRET has installed 4,015 biogas plants (with net generation capacity of 17980 million cubic meters per day) on a cost sharing basis throughout the country. During the period in reference, 234 biogas plants have been installed. PCRET has installed 1000 biogas plants of 5 cubic meters each with annual production of 1.941 Million cubic meters of gas, 1.567 Million kg of manure and 4.7 Million kg of carbon dioxide abatement. In addition the Council has installed 30 commercial-size biogas plants ranging from 50-250 million cubic meters by providing technological support for irrigation and power generation.

A World Bank-funded project to conduct a detailed study for Biomass/Waste-to-Energy projects in 20 cities of Pakistan has been initiated. Another Waste to Energy Study, funded by U.S Trade and Development Agency (USTDA) is being carried out for Karachi to generate 5-10 MW power.

AEDB has issued a Letter of Intent (LOI) to set up a 12-MW Biomass to Energy power project in Sindh, based exclusively on Biogas/Agricultural Waste. The project is jointly sponsored by investors from US and local entrepreneur (the SSJD Bio Energy). Another LOI has been issued to Lumen Energia (Pvt.) Ltd., to set up a 12-MW power plant at Jhang based on agricultural waste including cotton sticks, rice husks, sugarcane trash, biogas, wheat chaff and other crops as multi-fuel sources. AEDB has issued an LOI to Pak Ethanol (Pvt.) Ltd., to set up a 9-MW biogas power project at Matli in Sindh province.

Small/Mini/Micro Hydroelectric

The GOP-sponsored Productive Use of Renewable Energy (PURE) project is being implemented to install 103 hydro power plants in Khyber Pakhtunkhwa (KPK) and Gilgit Baltistan (GB), with atotal cost of US$ 19.5 million. Another project for 250 plants is under preparation for the same areas. Eight small hydro projects have been initiated under the Renewable Energy Development Sector Investment Program (REDSIP) with the support of the Asian Development Bank (ADB). These projects are being implemented in KPK and Punjab with an estimated cost of $290 million. Another two small hydro power projects have been initiated under REDSIP. The Government of Punjab has issued LOIs to private investors for establishment of 10 small hydro projects with a cumulative capacity of 142-MW at different locations in Punjab. AEDB has initiated a program with the assistance of Deutsche Gesellschaft für Internationale Zusammenarbeit (GIZ) to assist the provinces to solicit private investments in the small hydro sector. Under this program prefeasibility studies have been completed for 25 hydro sites in AJK, Sindh, Punjab and KPK with a cumulative capacity of 284.14-MW. Public sector Hydro power projects have been initiated in (a) KPK (valued at U$ 150.99 Million; 17-MW, 36.6-MW and 2.6-MW); (b) Punjab (valued at U$ 138.74Million; 5.38-MW, 4.04-MW, 2.82-MW, 4.16-MW and 7.64-MW) and (c) Gilgit Baltistan (valued at U$ 71.12 Million; of 26-MW and 4-MW).

Solar

For solar energy, 6 LOIs for a cumulative capacity of 148-MW on-Grid Solar PV power plants have been issued by the AEDB. Additionally 3 LOIs of 70-MW capacities have been issued by the Punjab Power Development Board (PPDB). The sponsors are currently preparing feasibility studies. The Solar Village Electrification Program was initiated under the former Prime Minister's directive and Three thousand solar home systems have been installed in 49 villages in Tharparkar, Sindh. Another 51 villages in Sindh and 300 villages in Balochistan have been approved for electrification using solar energy and will be implemented shortly. AEDB is also conducting the Parliamentarian Sponsored Village Electrification Program and has so far prepared and submitted 27 feasibilities for approval. Funds for three schemes have so far been released under People Work Programs-II (PWP-II) and the work is underway.. NEPRA is working on a feed-in tariff for solar power plants. The rapid approvals of the tariff will be likely lead to increased interest in the sector.

In April 2014, Prime Minister Nawaz Sharif inaugurated a 1,000-MW mega solar generation park in the Bhawalpur district, which is expected to commence operation by December 2016.

Bagasse

Studies are underway to assess the generation of biomass-based electric power, primarily from thermal combustion and from biogas digesters. It is believed that bagasse (sugar cane waste) available from sugar mills can be used to generate up to 2,000-MW of electricity. NEPRA has approved feed-in tariffs for bagasse co-generation plants allowing sugar mills to sell electricity directly to the grid at US cents 10.6 per Kilowatt Hour. Sugar mills that opt for the tariff will have two years to reach commercial operations.

SUB-SECTOR BEST PROSPECTS

U.S. companies are competitive in the local market along with European and Chinese suppliers. Roughly 50 percent of demand is being met through domestic indigenous capacity. The AEDB and PCRET are playing major roles in establishing the current infrastructure of resources in Pakistan.

OPPORTUNITIES

The most promising sub-sectors within this sector for FY-2015 are:

Solar Panels / Photovoltaic Panels

Dry Batteries

Wind Farm Equipment (especially turbines)

Biomass Boilers

Transmission Equipment

Distribution Equipment

Biogas Equipment

Technical Consultancy

WEB RESOURCES

Alternate Energy Development Board: http://www.aedb.org
Pakistan Council for Renewable Energy Technologies: http://www.pcret.gov.pk
Renewable & Alternative Energy Association of Pakistan (REAP): http://www.reap.org.pk/

CONSTRUCTION EQUIPMENT & SERVICES

Unit: $ Thousands

	2011	2012	2014	2014 (estimated)
Total Market Size	2,020.0	2,183.3	2,270.6	2,338.7
Total Local Production	785.0	846.7	855.2	860.2
Total Exports	35.0	35.0	35.0	35.0
Total Imports	1,270.0	1,371.6	1,426.5	1,469.3
Imports from the U.S.	930.0	930.0	930.0	910.0
Exchange Rate (Pak Rupees/US)	90.45	99.45	103.45	99.40

. The local construction market can be segregated in to three major categories: (1) earthmoving and construction machinery, (2) real estate and housing development, and (3) construction contractor services.

Earthmoving and Construction Machinery: Due to the ongoing economic slowdown, the local earthmoving and construction machinery sector has seen declining growth. According to industry sources, the construction machinery sector holds an approximate market share of 45 percent of the overall construction market. During FY 2012-13, the construction machinery sector, with a market totaling of $2.5 billion, declined by approximately 20 percent compared to the previous fiscal year. The construction machinery market is almost entirely dependent on imports. Major international brands from the United States, Germany, the United Kingdom, Japan, and South Korea, China have established a strong presence in the local market, either through agent/distributorship arrangements or through opening their own offices in the country.

Real Estate and Housing Development: The real estate and housing development sector is showing healthy signs of growth in Pakistan. According to industry experts, during the past year, the real estate sector grew approx. 3.0 percent and represents a total market size of $ 1.75 billion. The GOP through its housing sector reforms program has launched several initiatives including the policy re-structuring of the real estate sector, distribution of free houses to low-income families, attractive incentives for foreign investors in both civil and commercial construction projects, and the initiation of a modern-village concept in the rural areas of Pakistan.

The housing sector in Pakistan is in need of massive investment. According to the Ministry of Housing and Urban Development, out of a population of 190 million people, 33 percent live in urban areas versus 67 percent in rural communities.. According to available statistics, there are 21 million single-family dwellings currently in existence in Pakistan, and the demand for new single-family dwellings is approx. 6.50 million per annum. This demand has continuously increased at the rate of .60 million housing units per annum. The real estate and housing sector holds an approximate 35 percent share of the overall construction market and in light of future demand projections, this market share is expected to reach 30 percent by the end of 2014.

Construction Contractor Services: This sector has seen a rapid growth trend over the last 5-6 years, which is mainly attributable to the initiation of significant construction projects including high-rise commercial/residential towers, roads and civil infrastructure, and real estate development in both the public and private sectors. The total market share of this sector is approximately 20 percent, which is expected to grow 1.2 percent by the end of current year.

BEST PROSPECTS/SERVICES

The most promising sub-sectors within the local construction market for FY-2015 are:
Construction Machinery (Product Description)
Aerial Devices/work platforms
Asphalt Production and Paving
Backhoe Loaders
Cable Placers
Concrete Preparation & Finishing
Cranes
Drilling Equipment
Dumpers
Excavators
Graders
Scrapers
Trucks/Trailers
Wheel Loaders

Real Estate Development & Housing
Design/Architectural Engineering
Project Management
Project Construction
Advanced Building Materials
Management and Maintenance
Turkey Solutions
Roofing and Insulation materials
Construction Contractor Services
Civil Construction
Mechanical Erection
Electrical Services
Instrument Services

ENGINEERING DESIGNS OPPORTUNITIES

The local construction market has shown moderate growth in terms of its volume and FDI contribution during the past year. Both the public and private sectors have initiated projects including high-rise commercial/residential building, small dams and hydropower generation projects, infrastructure, and real estate development. According to industry experts, the local market continues to offer sizeable business opportunities to the local and foreign companies for the coming several years.

WEB RESOURCES

Association of Builders and Developers (ABAD): http://www.abad.com.pk/
Institute of Architects Pakistan (IAP): http://www.iap.com.pk/
Pakistan Council of Architects & Town Planners: http://www.pcatp.org.pk/
Ministry of Housing & Works – http://www.housing.gov.pk
National Housing Authority – http://www.pakistan.gov.pk

COMPUTERS & PERIPHERALS

($ millions)

	2011	2012	2014	2014 (estimated)
Total Market Size	300.4	315.4	326.4	342.7
Total Local Production	1.55	1.55	1.55	1.55
Total Exports	0.0	0.0	0.0	0.0
Total Imports	298.8	313.8	324.8	341.0
Imports from the U.S.	44.0	46.0	47.0	45.0
Exchange Rate (Pak Rupees/US)	90.45	99.45	103.45	99.40

Pakistan's market for computers and peripherals has seen moderate growth during the past several years, and is expected to continue this trend in coming years. With virtually no domestic production, the local computer and equipment market relies heavily on imports. The local market is receptive to U.S. brands which are regarded for their quality and reliability, despite having strong competition from China, Japan, South Korea, Malaysia, and Taiwan. Major U.S. brands including Dell, Hewlett Packard, Intel, and Cisco have established a strong presence in Pakistan.

The expansion of the information technology industry in Pakistan has seen steady growth during FY 2012-13, with computers and peripherals emerging as a major industry sector. Both the GOP and private businesses place high priority on the availability of computers and other information technology (IT) equipment in regular workflows, research and development, and educational activities. The GOP introduced its new IT Policy in FY 2000, with major emphasis on computer availability, usage, connectivity, and manpower training. The GOP encourages the use of computer technology in both public and private institutions/organizations and has introduced several incentives for both local and foreign firms including 100 percent equity ownership, and 100 percent remittance of profits from Pakistan. In addition, the GOP, in collaboration with the private sector, has launched several projects to ensure the widespread availability of computers to the masses. Some initiatives include development of software technology parks, the provision of demand-based training, internet accessibility including broadband, wireless broadband, and fiber optic connectivity to public utilities, research and development, federal and provincial government web portals, distribution of free laptops to deserving college students, and digitization of government records.

The primary users for computers and peripherals in Pakistan are private businesses, IT and IT-enabled services companies, call centers, business process outsourcers (BPOs), Internet Service Providers, government authorities, educational institutions, and domestic users. At present, there are 900 IT and IT-enabled companies, employing over 70,000 qualified IT professionals in Pakistan. The BPO sector, particularly call center businesses, has emerged as a major sub-sector during the last several years. There are presently 50 call centers operating in all major cities of the country. According to the latest industrial statistics approximately 2,500 to 3,000 qualified professionals are associated with this sector and this number is expected to grow at an annual rate of 3.0 percent in the coming years.

The majority of the international call centers operating in Pakistan are from the U.S. and the United Kingdom. In FY 2014, the cumulative outsourcing business in the country totaled approximately $4.0 million. According to industry statistics, the BPO sector is expected to grow by at least 2.5 percent in the next five years. Local demand for internet and wireless broadband services and its associated equipment has been very strong, as, at present, there are 85 ISPs operating countrywide, with approximately 30 million total subscribers. Under the GOP's broadband policy, the bandwidth tariff has been drastically reduced for high-speed Internet services, including DSL, ADSL, WiFi, VPN, ISDN, fiber optic, and wireless connections.

BEST PROSPECTS

The most promising sub-sectors within Computers and Peripherals for FY 2015 are:

Data Processing Machines/Main Frames
I/O Units – Tapes/Disks/Printers
Computer Networking Equipment
Personal Computers (Used/New)
Servers/Gateways
Modems
Wireless and Broadband Modems
Multiplexes
Power Supplies/Battery Chargers
Wires, Cables, and connecting equipment
Computer Leads
Cathode Ray Tube (CRT) Monitors
Liquid Crystal Display (LCD) / Light Emitting Diode (LED) Monitors

COMPUTER LAPTOPS AND TABLETS

OPPORTUNITIES

Despite slow economic growth, the past year has seen a growing trend of computer users, especially at home using used/refurbished computers and laptops. This has resulted in a large influx of used computers, both branded and unbranded, into local market. This trend has had only a minor impact on available international brands; however, as corporations still prefer new and branded equipment, and these corporations traditionally make up the bulk of the market.

WEB RESOURCES

Ministry of Information Technology: http://www.moit.gov.pk
Ministry of Economic Affairs & Statistics: http://www.statistics.gov.pk
Pakistan Software Export Board: http://www.pseb.org.pk
Punjab Information Technology Board: http://www.pitb.gov.pk
Ministry of Science and Technology: http://www.most.gov.pk
Pakistan Software Houses Association: http://pasha.org.pk/
Pakistan Computer Association: http://www.pakcomputerassociation.com

AGRICULTURAL MACHINERY AND IMPLANTS

Agriculture is the mainstay of Pakistan's economy and a primary source of livelihood for its citizens.. During FY 2012-13, the agriculture sector contributed 21.0 percent of the country's GDP and employed 43.7 percent of the total labor force. During this period the sector grew 2.1 percent versus 2.9 percent the previous year.

The agriculture machinery and implants sector has seen a moderate growth pattern over the last several years, mainly attributed to easy credit facilities, awareness and training programs, and higher purchase prices from the government. According to the Pakistan Agriculture Machinery Census 2012, the total area under cultivation in the country is 42.6 million acres, which has grown 4.2 percent as compared to the previous year.

According to the Pakistan Economic Survey, the total size of the agricultural machinery sector is approximately US$180 million, and mainly consists of tractors, harvesters, and other small-scale agricultural machinery. In Pakistan, tractors play a seminal role in farm mechanization. During 2012-13 the manufacturing of tractor units declined due to energy shortages and only 25,185 tractor units were manufactured versus 30,855 during the previous year. The majority of tractor-owning farmers possess cultivators as the only accessory for their tractors. The pace of farm mechanization is constricted mainly because of small farm size, affordability and lack of information.. Tractors are produced locally under license arrangements with the foreign companies including Messy Ferguson Belarus, and Shifeng China. In addition to tractors, other large-scale agricultural machinery including harvesters are imported used from the U.S. and the EU.

SUB-SECTOR BEST PROSPECTS

The most promising sub-sectors within this sector for FY2015 are:

Tractors
Combine Harvesters
Cultivators
Culti-packer
Harrow
Subsoiler

Rotator
Broadcast seeder
Planter
Seed Driller
Fertilizer Spreader
Transplanter
Drip Irrigation Systems
Weight Sorter
Round Baler
Sprayers

Opportunities

The local agricultural machinery and implants sector has shown moderate growth in terms of volume and investment during the past year. Both the public and private sectors have or are in the process of initiating small and large-scale projects to boost the development of this sector. According to industry experts, the local market will continue to offer sizeable business opportunities for local and foreign suppliers for coming years.

Web Resources

http://www.finance.gov.pk (Ministry of Finance)

http://www.pbs.gov.pk (Pakistan Bureau of Statistics)

http://www.pc.gov.pk (Ministry of Planning, Development and Reforms)

AVIATION - AIRPORT AND GROUND SUPPORT EQUIPMENT

Despite the slow economy, Pakistan's three established air carriers -- Pakistan International Airlines (PIA), Air Blue, and Shaheen Air -- continue to expand their fleets by acquiring newer aircraft on dry and wet lease. Additionally, Air Indus (Pvt.) Ltd. commenced domestic operations within the last year. Their fleet consists of narrow body aircraft and they intend to add a turboprop aircraft to the fleet. Three more business groups have applied for airline licenses to commence operations in the country.

State-owned PIA posted operating revenue amounting to $960 million (approx.)in year 2014 with passenger revenue of $785 million (approx.). PIA has remained in the red for the past several years and relies heavily on government subsidies and government-backed loans to remain afloat.

The U.S. has a major market share in the following product categories: wide–body aircraft, aircraft ground support equipment, communication and navigation equipment, air-conditioning, electrical and fuelling equipment, passenger loading bridges, etc. American companies like Boeing, FMC, Nordco, Hobart, Wilcox, AS&E, Airplane, Garsite, S&S, Stearns, GE, Pratt & Whitney, Trilectron and Westinghouse are familiar names locally.

Local production is extremely limited, as are exports. PIA's Precision Engineering

Complex provides custom-made parts, engineering and overhaul support for Boeing aircraft. Estimates for the U.S. share of the import market are between 62-65 percent for aircraft, engines and parts. Other suppliers include those from the U.K., France, Germany, and Netherlands.

SUB-SECTOR BEST PROSPECTS

Air Traffic Control
8526.10 Radars
8529.90 Aeronautical Communication System
8526.91/9014.10 Navigational Aids: Calibration Equipment, Voice Recorders
8535.40 Runway Lighting System
9015.10-80 Meteorological Equipment
Ground Support Equipment
9022.19 X-ray Scanners
8428.40/9403.70 Airport Terminal Equipment: Satellites, Walkways, Counters, etc.
7610.10 Passenger loading bridges
8709.00 Aircraft Tow Tractors
8503.00 Ground Power Units
8705.00 Runway Sweepers/Rubber Deposit Remover Machines
8471.92 Flight Information Display System and Parts
8413.19 Fuelling Equipment
8705.00 Fire Fighting Equipment
8511.50 Pneumatic Engine Starters
8428.40 Passenger Stairways
9022.19 Airport Security Equipment
8709.00 Aircraft Loaders
4010.10 Conveyor Belts
4010.10 Passenger Transport Vehicles
9026.10 Avionics Equipment
9014.20 Electrical Equipment
8703-Motor Cars and Vehicles for transporting persons
8703330010-Ambulances
8519938000- Tape players, Cassette Type
8517301500-Central Office Telephone switching Systems
8525203040-Radio transceiver

OPPORTUNITIES

New Islamabad International Airport/Benazir Bhutto International Airport at Islamabad: Construction is underway at the new Islamabad International Airport. The project was initially estimated at a cost of $300 million and now is estimated at $900 million, of which approximately 40 percent will be earmarked for the purchase of airport ground support equipment. The project completion date has been delayed several times and is now expected in 2016.

New Gwadar International Airport: The airport was expected to be completed by the end of 2014, but only 27% of the work is completed and further delays are expected.

A new National Aviation Policy is expected to be finalized in this year. According to the existing National Aviation Policy, available on the Civil Aviation Pakistan website (see below), a uniform duty of 10% is levied on the import of aircraft, engines and spare parts. The airline may pay 5% as a down payment and the remaining 5% within two years in installments. Used aircraft engines/parts are allowed to be imported with a 10 percent. The ramp area at airports is a duty free area/zone. Government taxes and duties are subject to review by the Federal Board of Revenue through Special Regulatory Orders (SROs). Current SROs may be viewed at website www.fbr.gov.pk .

WEB RESOURCES

Pakistan International Airline (PIA): http://www.piac.com.pk
Air Blue: http://www.airblue.com
Shaheen Air International: http://www.shaheenair.com
Air Indus: http://www.airindus.com.pk/introduction-and-scope.html
Pakistan Civil Aviation Authority: http://www.caapakistan.com.pk
United States Trade & Development Agency:
http://www.ustda.gov/news/pressreleases/2010/SouthAsia/Pakistan/PakistanPIAMRO_082510.asp

FRANCHISING

The concept of franchising has gained wide acceptance in Pakistan. Major U.S. franchise operations in Pakistan include Pizza Hut, KFC, Dunkin Donuts, Domino's Pizza, Papa John's Pizza, Hardees, McDonald's, TGI Friday's, Subway, Taco Maker, Nacho Nana's, Sheraton, Day's Inn, Best Western, Nike Retail, UPS, FedEx, Princeton Review, Berlitz, Gymboree, Gloria Jean's Coffee, Hertz and Avis. KFC already operates 64 outlets in Pakistan and several more are planned. McDonald's has 27 restaurants. Recent franchise entrants include Johnny Rockets, Nine West and Fatburger. U.S. Franchisors either find franchisees directly or through Gulf-based master franchisees.

U.S. companies dominate the franchise market in Pakistan in large part due to the fact that U.S. firms were the pioneers in this sector and have the strongest marketing to support their brands. Many U.S. brands such as McDonald's and KFC were well-known and recognized in urban areas of Pakistan before commencing local operations. U.S. brands are favored by Pakistanis for their superior quality control and customer service standards.

A key consideration in establishing a franchise operation in Pakistan is quality control, particularly if the enterprise proposes to use locally produced items. In Pakistan, all imported food items -- particularly meat items -- must be certified "Halal" (slaughtered in accordance with Islamic law).

U.S. firms are advised to identify and evaluate franchisee candidates carefully. Prior to entering into an agreement with a local company, U.S. firms may perform due diligence by using the International Company Profile offered by the Commercial Service.

The franchise agreement must be carefully drafted to protect the interests of the parties. The franchisor must be able to retain some direct control over operations, even after transfer of business and technical know-how. Crucial elements of the franchise agreement include territorial coverage, duration, franchise rate, and protection of trade secrets, quality control and minimum performance clauses. The U.S. firm should ensure that its patents and trademarks will be registered in its own name rather than that of the franchisee.

The Government of Pakistan does not impose any restrictions on investors, but foreign investors are required to inform the Board of Investment and the State Bank of Pakistan, primarily for the purpose of repatriation of franchise fee or any profits accrued.

SUB-SECTOR BEST PROSPECTS

Food outlets
Hospitality
Education
Retail

MOVIE THEATERS/ENTERTAINMENT COMPLEXES

The advent of shopping malls in the larger urban areas of Pakistan will offer further growth opportunities for food outlets, fashion retail and cinema theaters.

For the last 3 years, the Pakistani retail market has been rapidly evolving with the rapid emergence of local and international brands.. Many international brands have captured Pakistan's market and have done well, including Next, Splash, Debenhams, Mango, Monsoon, Giordano, Timberland, Levis, Dockers, Mother care, Baby shop, Accessorize, Body Shop, Crabtree & Evelyn, Nike, Adidas, Puma, Crocs, Nine West, Pedro, Charles & Keith, Clarks and Sketchers.

WEB RESOURCES

International Franchise Association: www.franchise.org

World Franchise Associates Pakistan: http://www.worldfranchiseassociates.com/pakistan/

Francorp Pakistan: http://www.francorp-pakistan.com/francorpfranchising.html

AGRICULTURAL SECTORS OPPORTUNITIES

AGRICULTURE IN THE ECONOMY

Agriculture is central to economic growth and development in Pakistan. Being the dominant sector it contributed 21.4 percent to GDP in 2014, employs 45 percent of the country's labor force and contributes in the growth of other sectors of the economy. Nearly 62 percent of the country's population resides in rural areas, and is directly or indirectly linked to agriculture for their livelihood. Unlike India, land reform has been limited in Pakistan. There are a large number of landless sharecroppers and agricultural laborers.

Important crops, such as wheat, rice, maize, cotton and sugarcane account for 25.2 percent of the value added in overall agriculture and 5.4 percent to GDP. The other crops account for 12.3 percent of the value added in overall agriculture. Livestock contributes 55.4 percent to agricultural value added much more than the combined contribution of important and other crops (37.6 percent). Pakistan exports rice, fish, fruits, and vegetables and imports vegetable oil, wheat, cotton (net importer), pulses, and consumer foods. Agriculture contributes to economic growth as a supplier of raw materials to industry, as a market for industrial products, and is Pakistan's largest source of foreign exchange earnings -- when textiles are included. The nation's dominant export industry is textiles and garments, and therefore raw cotton is of particular importance.

The majority of Pakistan's population lives in the Indus River valley, in an arc formed by the cities of Faisalabad, Lahore, Rawalpindi/Islamabad, and Peshawar. As the result of increasing urbanization the average farm size has declined from 13.1 acres in the early 1970's to 7.7 acres in 2000. The agricultural sector consists of crops, livestock, fishing and forestry. The crop sector has gradually declined from 65 percent of agricultural activity in 1990-91 to 38 percent in 2012-13. By contrast, the share of livestock in agriculture has increased from 35 percent to 56 percent over the same period.

During 2012-13, the agriculture sector exhibited a growth of 3.3 percent on the back of positive growth in agriculture related sub sectors, Crops grew at 3.2 percent, Livestock 3.7 percent, Forestry 0.1 percent and Fishing 0.7 percent. Cotton, rice, and sugarcane are grown during the "kharif" season, (May-November) and wheat and oilseeds are grown during the "rabi" season (November-May). The majority of Pakistan's crop production is irrigated making water availability a critical issue for future agricultural growth. Years of neglecting repairs of irrigation canals, dams and levees has made Pakistan susceptible to flooding with less water each year.

DOMESTIC AGRICULTURAL POLICY

Pakistan does not have a formalized agricultural policy. At best agricultural policy can be characterized as strategic intervention for political reasons, not for sustainable growth. About two-thirds of Pakistan's 180 million people live in rural areas and depend on agriculture for their livelihood. A majority of Pakistani politicians and legislators are from rural backgrounds. These political leaders, along with powerful industry groups, including the All Pakistan Textile Mills Association and the Pakistan Sugar Mills Association, heavily influence agricultural policy. Traditionally, these interest groups consider their own particular needs over those of famers and consumers at large.

In June 2011, the GOP eliminated the Ministry of Food and Agriculture (MinFA) as mandated by Parliament due to a constitutional amendment to devolve responsibilities of select services to the provincial governments. Unfortunately, the transition of authorities under Amendment 18 has been difficult as the provinces found they were not adequately funded and their personnel were not trained to handle the new responsibilities.

In October 2011, the GOP created the Ministry of National Food Security and Research (MNFSR) to deal with some of the Provinces' shortcomings and ensure that Pakistan has ample food for its population and is accessible by the most food insecure. The new ministry, while sanctioned by the Prime Minister and approved by Parliament, is struggling in defining its role to implement its mandate. The Ministry's main focus is ensuring food availability through boosting domestic food production in coordination with the provincial agriculture, food and livestock departments. In the face of higher food prices, it has been emphasized that additional efforts would be required for supporting the marginalized and vulnerable segments of society. There is also a greater appreciation that integrated efforts should be taken to improve nutrition and the quality of food and to ensure better food utilization. The Ministry of National Food Security and Research plans to focus more on improving productivity of food crops and enhancing food access. MNFSR is also drafting a policy "National Food & Nutritional Security Policy" (2014-15) in line with the recommendations of Task Force on Food Security.

AGRICULTURAL TRADE ENVIRONMENT

Pakistan is a founding member of the World Trade Association (WTO) and an active member of various trade blocs and alliances. Pakistan, as a G-20 member, is supportive of the G-20's collective position of improving market access to western markets by eliminating their export subsidies and reducing their tariffs, and subsidies.

Pakistan has free trade agreements (FTA) with China, Malaysia and Sri Lanka, and a transit trade agreement with Afghanistan. Pakistan also has a preferential trade agreement with Iran and is party to two regional trade agreements: the Economic Cooperation Organization (ECO) and the South Asian Association for Regional Cooperation (SAARC). Pakistan is working to grant India Most Favored Nation (MFN) status, however, due to mounting opposition from several trade blocs, final approval is moving ahead slowly.

On December 05, 2014 the European Union (EU) Parliament approved the Generalized Scheme of Preferences (GSP) Plus status to Pakistan. Access to GSP Plus status means duty-free or lower duty access for almost all Pakistani products with almost 20% of exports entering the 27 European countries at zero tariff and 70% at preferential rates. The effort to establish GSP Plus for Pakistan began as part of the EU's efforts to help Pakistan's economy recover from losses from devastating floods in 2010. The GSP plus Act comes into force on January 1, 2014 and will be effective through 2017. Trade sources anticipate a growth of $1 billion in textile exports per year over the next several years.

In Pakistan, much of the food items are imported through Dubai where products are consolidated and shipped in approximately four days. A number of U.S. food items are imported this way, allowing importers to better control inventory and reduce the need for expensive storage costs. Pakistan lacks an adequate cold chain system that limits the import and movement of produce, meat, fish and dairy products throughout the country.

During FY 2012/13, Pakistan's imports of all products totaled $40.22 billion and total exports were valued at $24.79 billion. Textiles dominated exports, accounting for 48 percent of total export value. Other major exports included rice, seafood and products, sporting goods, leather products and carpets. Major imports included petroleum, machinery, edible oil, cotton, chemicals and transport equipment. The GOP has had limited success in bridging the trade deficit.

In FY 2012/13, Pakistan's imports of agricultural commodities and products were valued at over $3.91 billion. Major imports included vegetable oil ($1.95 billion), cotton ($969.74 million), pulses ($329.66 million), tea ($372.66 million), dry fruits ($81.83 million), spices ($65.77 million), and sugar ($6.16 million). Pakistan's exports of agricultural commodities and products were valued at over $4.14 billion in FY 2012/13. Major exports included rice ($1.87 billion), raw cotton ($167.44 million), fruits and vegetables ($423.73 million), fish and fish preparations ($336.15 million), meat and meat products ($224.43 million), spices ($41.07 million), oilseeds /nuts/kernels ($49.75 million), Tobacco ($27.84 million), and sugar ($431.16 million).

AGRICULTURAL TRADE WITH THE UNITED STATES

U.S. exports of agricultural and related goods to Pakistan increased 24.6 percent in the last five years from $293 million in 2009 to $388.6 million in 2014. The value of agricultural trade between the United States and Pakistan during FY 2012/13 totaled $388.6 million. Agricultural exports from the United States to Pakistan totaled $360.7 million, a 10 percent increase from FY 2011/12 due mostly to large young population, rapid urbanization, and a fast growing middle class. Exports were led by cotton ($199.2 million), consumer oriented products ($67.1 million), vegetable oils ($9.4 million), and planting seeds ($27.2 million), while agricultural exports from Pakistan to the United States totaled $121.8 million, led by exports of rice ($28.4 million), consumer oriented products ($24.7 million), and sugar/sweeteners ($22 million).

Pakistan is a major market for various bulk commodities, especially cotton, vegetable oil, and inputs for traditional food products. However, the increase in demand for consumer oriented products and forestry products are impressive. A record $67 million of consumer oriented food and beverage products were exported from the United States to Pakistan in 2014. Driven by the growing middle class demand for western products, sales were strong for dairy products, peas and lentils, tree nuts, and processed products and we expect additional growth in the demand for organic products, snack foods, and high quality ingredients. Pakistan is now the second largest importer of U.S. hard wood products as a result of a thriving construction boom.

Post has identified dairy cattle, animal genetics, wood, pulses, planting seeds, pima cotton, and consumer ready products as best prospect exports to Pakistan due to overall need and U.S. competitiveness in these products. However, a current lack of regulatory controls in intellectual property rights has limited the ability of U.S. biotech seed to be sold in Pakistan and the current ban on live cattle imports has denied the United States access to a growing dairy sector. Current political instability continues to deter U.S. exporters from visiting Pakistan to develop potential markets and build business relationships. Nevertheless, the Office of Agricultural Affairs/Islamabad (OAA) believes that there is a growing interest in U.S. agricultural and food products in Pakistan. As the United States begins to draw down its forces in Afghanistan and U.S. Pakistani relations strengthen, there will be increased opportunities for U.S. agricultural exports. The OAA has begun an outreach program to familiarize Pakistani food processors, farmers, dairy producers and agro-industry representatives of the services USDA provides.

DUTIES ON AGRICULTURAL PRODUCTS

Pakistan tariffs range from zero to 35 percent. The GOP also levies additional surcharges on imports of most items. Revenue collection remains problematic due to a narrow tax base and a culture of tax evasion. As a result, the GOP collects a 17 percent sales tax on imports upon arrival.

LEADING SECTORS FOR U.S. EXPORTS

Cotton

Pakistan imports a significant quantity of better grade, cleaner cotton for producing quality fabrics for export market. Post expects a significant increase in imports of U.S. ELS/Pima and upland cotton in MY 2014/15 in response to the growing exports. Pakistan's cotton consumption for MY 2014/15 is forecast at 12 million (480 lbs.) bales, one of the highest in the past six years and is marginally higher than MY 2014/14 revised estimate of 11.88 million bales, up 7 percent compared with the last ten years average of 11.2 million bales.

Pakistan is a net importer of cotton, primarily because of strong demand for better grades of cotton for blending and for producing export oriented quality textile products. MY 2014/15 imports are projected at 2.6 million bales, 23 percent lower than MY 2014/14 estimates. With offtake outstripping local production, Post's estimate of MY 2014/14 cotton imports were increased 25 percent to 3.37 million bales, up 53 percent over the previous year. Significant increase in imports estimate is also the result of enhanced demand by the industrial sector after the grant of GSP plus by the EU. So far, exporters from India have taken maximum advantage from Pakistani market by arranging export of more than two million bales of raw cotton and the yarn through land route. Pakistani importers are benefiting from this opportunity from India due to lower transaction cost(less than 2 percent) compared with more than 5 percent cost on cotton imports from the North.

Dairy Products

In spite of being one of largest producer of milk in the world, Pakistan is a growing market for dairy products due to country's rapidly industrializing dairy sector, as consumer preferences shift from traditional to hypermarkets which require processed dairy products in their shelves. This trend will continue as large number of population still relies on traditional markets to meet their needs. In 2014, Pakistan imported $165 million worth of dairy products with the United States as the lead country-of-origin at $31 million, followed by India with $29 million, and New Zealand with $26 million. Most of the imports are dry milk, which constitute 70 percent of total imports, as it's being reconstituted and mixed with fresh milk to meet local demand. Whey consists of 20 percent of dairy imports which is mostly used as a food ingredient in the bakery sector. This trend will continue as urban consumer still relies on specialty products.

Wood Products

Pakistan is emerging as a leading destination for American wood products. During the last five years U.S. wood product exports to Pakistan increased 400% ($7 million in 2008 versus $28 million in 2014) with 2014 trade expected to surpass $30 million (U.S. wood product exports saw a 23% increase in Jan-Nov 2014). In 2012, the United States was the largest exporter of wood products to Pakistan, accounting for $28 million out of total of $93 million in imports. The imported wood species from the U.S. are mainly hardwood and softwood logs, lumber, veneer, red oak, maple, walnut, eastern white pine, and ponderosa pine etc.

The wood market continues to enjoy high rates of growth because of the shift from local wood products to high quality imported products due to an increasing demand by Pakistani consumers for higher quality imported products. Increasing awareness among Pakistani buyers of the availability and quality of U.S. wood products are important factors driving increased U.S. wood product exports to Pakistan. Given its strong domestic demand for construction, furniture, panel products, and paper industry and the lack of modern forestry production and management techniques, Pakistan will remain dependent on wood products imports for the foreseeable future.

Peas and Lentils

Pulses have been a staple in the Pakistani diet for decades. They are often referred to as the "common man's meat" and an important source of protein for the poor. In 2014, Pakistan imported $375 million worth of peas and lentils, with India as the lead origin with $220 million, followed by Canada with $38 million and the United States ranked sixth, with sales of $9 million. The market demand for US yellow peas, chickpeas, and lentils is increasing in Pakistan; therefore US should capitalize in this sector by increasing its market share.

Dried Nuts

U.S. dried nuts have been able to attain considerable market penetration as demand, mostly for almonds and pistachios, increased 100 fold to 40,000 metric tons in the last ten years. However, Iran, the U.S.'s closest competitor, has a preferential tariff rate due to its trade agreement with Pakistan, and it has a zero percent tariff rate versus an applied 10 percent tariff rate for U.S. almonds. Exports of dried nuts will remain strong as bakeries and supermarkets proliferate throughout Pakistan. We expect U.S. dried nut exports to Pakistan grow between seven to ten percent annually for the next 5 years.

Food Ingredients and Processed Products

The market demand for food ingredients in Pakistan is steadily increasing in the high-end hotels, restaurants, and bakeries. In 2012, Pakistan imported $195 million worth of food ingredients and processed products with China as the top exporter at $24 million, followed by the Netherlands with $23 million, and the US ranked fifth with sales of $12 million.

The U.S. has gained considerable market share as demand for processed food products has increased in Pakistan due to increasing urbanization, large young population, and growing middle class. The U.S. should capitalize in this market due to increasing popularity of imported products vs shortage of quality domestic products in the market.

Planting Seeds

In 2014, Pakistan imported $94 million worth of planting seeds, with the United States as the lead suppliers with $37 million, followed by India with $19 million, and Egypt with $16 million. The key sector is the hybrid corn market which accounts for 75 percent of all U.S. planting seeds.

According to Pakistani trade sources, the seed industry in Pakistan at present is providing less than 20 percent of the potential seed demand through both local production and import. Therefore, there is potential for the U.S. in the ever-growing agrarian sector of Pakistan, however in order to see significant increases in trade, improvements need to be made with the current seed legislation in order to make sure that the seed company's intellectual property rights are protected.

TRADE REGULATIONS, CUSTOMS AND STANDARDS

IMPORT TARIFFS

Pakistan uses the Harmonized System to classify goods. Customs duties are levied on ad-valorem basis. Pakistan's overall average applied tariff in 2014 was 14.4 percent. In the 2014 budget, the government reduced the maximum general tariff rate from 30 percent to 25 percent (except for vehicles) and simplified the tariff structure by reducing the number of duty brackets 7 to 6. Other than customs duty, the government charges sales tax (17.0 percent) on the duty paid value of a variety of goods produced in or imported into the country. Customs duty and other charges are payable in rupees.

Export subsidies - Pakistan seeks to encourage exports through rebates of import duties, sales taxes, and income taxes, as well as through subsidized export financing.

TRADE BARRIERS

Pakistan's 2014 Import Policy Order bans the import of 44 categories of products, mostly on religious, environmental, security, and health grounds. Pakistan also bans the import of live animals i.e. cattle, buffalo, sheep and goats, meat and bone meal, tallow containing protein and feed ingredients from any BSE affected countries; however, the ban on the import of live animals from the United States has now been lifted. Any dispute or clarifications regarding import status of any product which cannot be resolved by the Customs Authorities are referred to Ministry of Commerce for a final decision. The government reserves the power to grant sector-specific duty exemptions, concessions, and protections under Statutory Regulatory Orders (SROs). In recent years, the use of SROs has decreased. SROs and other trade policy and regulatory documents are published on the Federal Board of Revenue's website, www.fbr.gov.pk .

In January 2000, Pakistan implemented the WTO Customs Valuation agreement and modified its system for valuation of goods. Since then, a number of traders in the food and consumer products sectors have expressed concerns regarding a lack of uniformity

in customs valuation. Similarly, a few major U.S. companies in the machinery and materials sector have reported specific concerns that customs officials have erroneously assessed goods based on a set of minimum values rather than the declared transactional value.

IMPORT REQUIREMENTS AND DOCUMENTATION

The following documents are required for imports and exports:

Bills of lading; invoices; packing lists; certificates of origin; copies of letters of credit; and insurance certificates.

U.S. EXPORT CONTROLS

Certain government and business entities in Pakistan are barred from receiving high-end U.S. technology. Information on these organizations is available on the following web site:

www.bis.doc.gov

TEMPORARY ENTRY

GOP import regulations permit temporary import of legally importable items by foreign companies (e.g., commercial samples), and goods imported by oil and gas companies, oil exploration and production companies, their contractors and sub-contractors, refineries, mining companies, foreign airlines and shipping companies, construction companies and contracting firms provided that a bank guarantee or indemnity bond is provided to Customs to ensure that the items will be re-exported. Similarly, domestic industrial firms may import items for test, trial, and re-export, subject to submission of indemnity bond or bank guarantee. The chief executives of companies have to certify that their contractors, sub-contractors and services companies are importing products for tests, trials and re-export.

Export of imported goods in their original form is not allowed except for parts obtained from ship breaking, scrapped battery cells, waste dental amalgam, waste exposed x-ray films, old machinery, items imported against back to back letters of credit and items. Re-export of old and second hand machinery is allowed, subject to the condition that no refund of import levies and duty drawback shall be made.

Re-export is made against sight letters of credit or advance payment and payment of full duties if re-exported through land routes.

Customs permits Pakistani exporters to replace exported goods that are found defective during the warranty period subject to furnishing of a copy of contract and a communication from a buyer giving the details of the goods that have been found defective.

Export-Cum-Import: The Ministry of Commerce allows export-cum-imports in case of repairs and replacement of imported items, subject to the conditions that the applicant will submit an indemnity bond assuring that the goods will be re-imported after repair and replacement.

LABELING AND MARKING REQUIREMENTS

Pakistan has no uniform or universal system of imposing labeling and marking requirements on products. However, individual industries or sectors are subject to the regulations of specific bodies. For example, the Ministry of National Health Services, Regulation & Coordination sets requirements for the pharmaceutical industry. The Ministry of Agriculture sets requirements for pesticides and edible products.

PROHIBITED AND RESTRICTED IMPORTS

The Government of Pakistan has banned the import of the following items: arms and ammunition, high explosives, radioactive substances, security printing, currency and mint, alcoholic beverages.

CUSTOMS REGULATIONS AND CONTACT INFORMATION

Customs regulations and contact information may be obtained from the following website: www.fbr.gov.pk

The Pakistan Customs has its head office in Karachi, located at the following address:

Pakistan Customs
Custom House, Near KPT
Karachi, Pakistan
Tel: 92-21-99214170, Fax: 92-21-99214234
Contact: Collector of Customs (Preventive or Appraisals)

Pakistan Customs has a presence at all other major points of entry into the country and also has several inland dry ports.

TRADE AND CUSTOMS STANDARDS

The technology department of the Ministry of Science and Technology sponsors and encourages public and private organizations in the standardization of products and services according to ISO standards. In this regard, the Ministry of Science and Technology and the Ministry of Commerce have jointly launched an incentive program for entrepreneurs to facilitate their ISO certification. This program provides an incentive grant for achieving ISO 9000/14000 certification.

Further information is available on: www.pakistan.gov.pk

STANDARDS ORGANIZATIONS

The Pakistan Standards and Quality Control Authority (PSQCA) is the national standards body. The functions of PSQCA include the establishment and enforcement of national standards, registration of inspection agencies, and assessment of industrial raw materials and finished products for compliance with international standards.

PSQCA has been designated as the WTO-TBT National Enquiry Point on Technical Barriers to Trade (TBT) of Pakistan under the TBT Agreement (Article 10.1, 10.2 and 10.3) to facilitate the exporters/traders/ manufacturers in the country and also importers from WTO member countries. This enquiry point is responsible to disseminate information on TBT notifications, deals with queries regarding standards, technical regulations, and conformity assessment procedures.

NIST Notify U.S. Service

Member countries of the World Trade Organization (WTO) are required under the Agreement on Technical Barriers to Trade (TBT Agreement) to report to the WTO all proposed technical regulations that could affect trade with other Member countries. Notify U.S. is a free, web-based e-mail subscription service that offers an opportunity to review and comment on proposed foreign technical regulations that can affect your access to international markets. Register online at Internet URL: http://www.nist.gov/notifyus/

CONFORMITY ASSESSMENT

The Pakistan Standards & Quality Control Authority is responsible for the conformity assessment. This organization may be reached as follows:

Pakistan Standards & Quality Control Authority
Ministry of Science and Technology
Block 77, Pak Secretariat
Karachi, Pakistan
Tel: 92-21-99206260
Fax: 92-21-99206263

PRODUCT CERTIFICATION

The Pakistan Standards & Quality Control Authority is responsible for product certification. This organization may be reached as follows:

Pakistan Standards & Quality Control Authority
Ministry of Science and Technology
Block 77, Pak Secretariat
Karachi, Pakistan
Tel: 92-21-99206260
Fax: 92-21-99206263

ACCREDITATION

The Pakistan National Accreditation Council (PNAC), Ministry of Science and Technology, Islamabad handles accreditation matters. Pakistan National Accreditation Council signed the Mutual Recognition Arrangement with International Laboratory Accreditation Cooperation (ILAC) and Asia Pacific Laboratory Accreditation Cooperation (APLAC), which has put Pakistan at par with the members of these organizations including U.S.A and E.U in terms of accreditation of testing and calibration laboratories. The contact for PNAC is as follows:

Pakistan National Accreditation Council
Evacuee Property Complex
Aga Khan Road, F-5/1
Islamabad, Pakistan
Tel: 92-51-9209509
Fax: 92-51-9209510
E-mail: pnac@isb.paknet.com

PUBLICATION OF TECHNICAL REGULATIONS

The Pakistan Council of Scientific and Industrial Research (PCSIR) and the Ministry of Science and Technology regularly publish technical regulations governing industry standards.

LABELING AND MARKING

Pakistan has no uniform or universal system of imposing labeling and marking requirements on products. However, individual industries or sectors are subject to the regulations of specific bodies. For example, the Ministry of Health sets requirements for the pharmaceutical industry, whereas the Ministry of Agriculture sets requirements for pesticides and edible products.

CONTACTS

All government ministries and departments may be accessed through the following website: www.pakistan.gov.pk

TRADE AGREEMENTS

Pakistan and the United States began negotiating a Bilateral Investment Treaty (BIT) in 2004. Negotiations have proceeded intermittently since. Pakistan has bilateral investment agreements with Australia, Azerbaijan, Mauritius, Bahrain, Bangladesh, Morocco, Belarus, Netherlands, Belgo-Luxemburg Economic Union, Oman, Philippines, Bosnia, Portugal, Bulgaria, Qatar, Cambodia, Romania, China, Singapore, Czech Republic, South Korea, Denmark, Spain, Egypt, Sri Lanka, France, Sweden, Germany, Switzerland, Indonesia, Syria, Iran, Tajikistan, Italy, Tunisia, Japan, Turkey, Kazakhstan, Turkmenistan, Kuwait, U.A.E, Kyrgyz Republic, United Kingdom, Lebanon, Uzbekistan, Laos and Yemen.

These investment treaties generally include dispute settlement provisions.

If a dispute cannot be settled through mutual consultation, investors can generally take cases to arbitration under rules of the U.N Commission on International Trade Law, the World Bank's International Center for Settlement of Investment Disputes, or to the Court of Arbitration of the International Chamber of Commerce. Pakistan is a member of the Multilateral Investment Guarantee Agency (MIGA), an arm of the World Bank.

Pakistan has free trade agreements with Sri Lanka, China, and Malaysia. Pakistan is also a part of South Asian Association for Regional Cooperation (SAARC) and has preferential trade agreements with Iran and Mauritius.

The United States and Pakistan have had a bilateral tax treaty in force since 1959. Pakistan also has double taxation agreements with Austria, Canada, Germany, Indonesia, Italy, Lebanon, Mauritius, Poland, Switzerland, Turkmenistan, Kazakhstan, the United Arab Emirates, Belgium, China, France, Greece, Iran, Japan, Libya, Saudi Arabia, Romania, Sweden, Belarus, Hungary, Jordan, Kenya, Kuwait, Malaysia, Netherlands, Nigeria, Norway, Oman, Philippines, Qatar, South Africa, Syria, Tunisia, Uzbekistan, the United Kingdom, Bangladesh, Denmark, Finland, India, Ireland, South Korea, Malta, Singapore, Sri Lanka, Thailand, Azerbaijan, and Turkey.

WEB RESOURCES

Pakistan government portal: www.pakistan.gov.pk

Trade Development Agency of Pakistan: www.tdap.gov.pk

Pakistan Ministry of Commerce: www.commerce.gov.pk

INVESTMENT AND BUSINE CLIMATE

Pakistan is located in South-Central Asia. Despite a relatively open foreign investment regime, Pakistan remains a difficult environment for foreign investors. An unpredictable security situation, chronic energy shortages and a challenging business climate – lengthy settlement of disputes faced by investors, poor intellectual property rights enforcement, and inconsistent taxation policies – have led to a significant drop in Foreign Direct Investment (FDI) in recent years. Currently Pakistan is ranked 128 out of 189 countries in the World Bank's 2015 Report in the category of Ease of Doing Business.

The Pakistan Muslim League-Nawaz (PML-N) government was elected in May 2013 on pledges to turn around Pakistan's economy, enhance trade and investment, and bridge the energy shortage. In September 2013, the Government of Pakistan (GoP) and the International Monetary Fund (IMF) entered a three-year USD 6.8 billion Extended Fund Facility (EFF) arrangement, which includes a series of reform benchmarks. The government has implemented some macroeconomic and energy reforms, resumed dormant privatization efforts, and committed to sell government stakes in 31 companies identified by the IMF. In 2014, the government completed and auctioned a long-awaited 3G/4G wireless spectrum. Nonetheless, progress towards privatization has been slow overall.

The United States has consistently been one of the largest sources of foreign direct investment (FDI) in Pakistan and one of its most significant trading partners. The Karachi-based American Business Council (ABC), an affiliate of the U.S. Chamber of Commerce, has a membership of 64 U.S. companies, most of which are Fortune 500 companies, operating in Pakistan across a range of industries. The Lahore-based American Business Forum (ABF) also provides assistance to U.S. investors. American companies have profitable investments across a range of sectors, specifically in fast-moving consumer goods and financial services.

In 2003, the United States and Pakistan signed a Trade and Investment Framework Agreement (TIFA). TIFA Council meetings are held annually and the most recent one was in March 2015, in the city of Islamabad.

1. OPENNESS TO, AND RESTRICTIONS UPON, FOREIGN INVESTMENT

Attitude toward Foreign Direct Investment

The GoP welcomes foreign investments and offers incentives to attract new capital inflows. These incentives include tax exemptions, tariffs reductions, infrastructure, and investor facilitation services in designated special economic zones. Since 1997, Pakistan has established and maintained a largely open investment regime. The PML-N government introduced the Investment Policy 2013 that further liberalizes investment policies in most sectors. In addition to expressing concern about the deteriorating law and order situation, foreign investors continue to advocate for the Government of Pakistan to improve legal protections for foreign investments, protect intellectual property rights, and establish a clear and consistent policy of upholding contractual obligations and settlement of tax disputes.

Net inflows of FDI peaked at USD 5.4 billion in fiscal year 2008, before dropping by 73 percent over the following five years. Since the PML-N government took office in June 2013, the numbers have marginally improved. In FY2014, net FDI was USD 2.8 billion, up 5.4 percent from FY2013. (Note: Throughout the document, "fiscal year" or FY refers to the Pakistani fiscal year measured from July of the previous calendar year to June of the fiscal year marker. End Note.) The majority of FDI – USD 928 million – was in the information, communication and telecom sector (ICT) followed by USD 792 million in the upstream oil and gas sector. Analysts identified the deteriorating security environment, a chronic energy crisis, and macroeconomic instability as the biggest drivers of the overall decline in FDI. Pakistan remains a profitable market for the fast-moving consumer goods sector in which multinational corporations have a robust presence. In other sectors, such as pharmaceuticals, challenging pricing policies are said to be squeezing profit margins.

The current administration has been moderately successful in reversing the decline in FDI by attracting international investors through the Board of Investment (BOI). In the first nine months of FY 2015, net FDI inflows were USD 615.4 million, up four percent from the same period in FY 2014. Pakistan's Overseas Chamber of Commerce and Industry (OICCI), which represents 196 foreign investors in Pakistan, released a "Perception and Investment Survey" in January 2014 showing that more than 80 percent of its members were optimistic that the new government would improve the business climate.

Foreign investors in Pakistan report that the wide array of federal and provincial taxes and tax regulations are difficult to navigate. For example, as detailed in the 2015 World Bank "Ease of Doing Business" Report, obtaining construction permits in Karachi requires 11 procedures, takes an average of 222 days, and costs 190.4 percent of per capita income (over USD 2500 based on 2013 World Bank Gross National Income per capita). Tax assessment procedures often lack transparency, resulting in discrimination among taxpayers, inefficiency, and corruption. Attempts to reform the tax system date back to the 1980s but have failed to deliver significant results, except for an increase in indirect (i.e. sales) taxes. Pakistan has one of the lowest tax-to-Gross Domestic Product (GDP) ratios in the world, approximately 10.4 percent in 2013. The tax regime is discriminatory and poorly organized. Multinational corporations shoulder the largest portion of the tax burden. The Board of Investment (BOI) is no longer required to register investors, but investors must still register with the Securities and Exchange Commission of Pakistan (SECP) and the State Bank of Pakistan (SBP). Complicated procedures required by various government departments/agencies for setting up a business in Pakistan were simplified in 2007. This is a step in a right direction that may help Pakistan improve its ease of business.

Pakistan permits most-favored-nation (MFN) exemptions in the financial and telecommunication sectors. MFN serves as a tool for promoting joint ventures and reciprocity among ECO countries (Azerbaijan, Kazakhstan, Kyrgyzstan, Tajikistan, Turkmenistan, Uzbekistan, Afghanistan, Iran, Turkey and Pakistan). Islamic banks in Pakistan are subject to the same regulatory requirements as conventional banks.

Other Investment Policy Reviews

Pakistan improved its financial services commitments after signing the World Trade Organization (WTO) Financial Services Agreement in December 1997. Foreign entities have the right to establish banks. Foreign banks and financial brokerage houses take over the rights and obligations of the companies they acquire. Foreign banks are permitted to establish locally incorporated subsidiaries, provided they have the minimum global tier-one paid up capital of USD 5 billion or they belong to member countries that participate in the same regional organizations and associations as Pakistan (e.g., the Economic Cooperation Organization – ECO – and the South Asian Association for Regional Cooperation). Absent these requirements, foreign banks are limited to a maximum 49-percent equity stake in locally incorporated subsidiaries. Foreign and local banks must submit an annual branch expansion plan to the SBP for approval. The SBP approves branch openings depending on the bank's net worth, adequacy of capital structure, future earnings prospects, credit discipline, and the need of the local population. All banks are required to open 20 percent of their new branches in small cities, towns, and villages.

In 1989, the financial sector in Pakistan opened up to private investments (local and foreign) as a part of the GoP's policy of deregulation and privatization. SBP forbids 100 percent local ownership of new commercial banks, requiring foreign financial institution partner.

Laws/Regulations of Foreign Direct Investment

The GoP provides the same treatment and legal protection to foreign and domestic investments in all sectors except defense and broadcasting. The 1976 Foreign Private Investment Promotion and Protection Act, Economic Reforms Act, and Investment Plan deal with the rights of foreign investors. The Foreign Private Investment Promotion and Protection Act provides that foreign investments will not be subject to higher income tax levels than similar investments made by Pakistani citizens. While Pakistan's law and economic policy does not discriminate against foreign investments, execution of contracts can be problematic because of the inefficiency and lack of transparency in domestic courts.

Industrial Promotion

In FY2007, Pakistan eliminated some tariff exemptions for various manufacturing sub-sectors, specifically the value-added, priority, and high-tech industries. Currently, the manufacturing sector pays up to five percent customs duty on imported plants and machinery. In its FY2007 budget, the government eliminated sales tax on all types of plants and machinery. Export industries are entitled to duty-free import of raw materials. There is no minimum equity investment or national ownership requirement for investments in the manufacturing sector and the GoP allows 25 percent first-year depreciation for all fixed assets in this sector. The GoP also allows 25 percent of the cost of a plant and machinery to be counted as the first-year depreciation in infrastructure and social sectors.

The Companies Ordinance from 1984 regulates mergers and acquisitions. Mergers are allowed between international companies as well as between international and local companies.

Limits on Foreign Control

In the 2013 Investment Policy, the GoP eliminated minimum initial capital investment requirements for all sectors. There is no minimum requirement for the amount of foreign equity investment or upper limit on the share of foreign equity allowed, except in the airline, banking, agriculture and media sectors. Foreign investors in the services sector may retain 100 percent equity "for the life of the investment." Pakistan allows foreign companies in the services sector to repatriate 100 percent of profits. To start a cellular operation network, investors need to obtain licenses from the Pakistan Telecommunication Authority. In the social and infrastructure sectors, 100 percent foreign ownership is allowed. In the agricultural sector, 60 percent foreign ownership is allowed. Corporate farming is permitted, though only companies incorporated in Pakistan can own farmland. There are no limits on the size of corporate farmland holdings, which foreign companies can lease for up to 50 years, with renewal options. The raw materials, plants, and machinery for agricultural and agro-based industries can be imported without customs duty. The tourism, housing, construction, and information technology sectors have been granted "industry status," which makes them eligible for lower tax and utility rates than businesses categorized as "commercial sector" such as banks and insurance companies. Only Pakistanis can invest in small-scale mining valued at less than Rs. 300 million (about USD 3 million).

As mentioned in Section 1.3 above, the GoP provides the same treatment and legal protection to foreign and domestic investments in all sectors except defense and broadcasting. The 1976 Foreign Private Investment Promotion and Protection Act, Economic Reforms Act, and

Investment Plan deal with the rights of foreign investors. The Foreign Private Investment Promotion and Protection Act provides that foreign investments will not be subject to higher income tax levels than similar investments made by Pakistani citizens. While Pakistan's law and economic policy does not discriminate against foreign investments, execution of contracts can be problematic because of the inefficiency and lack of transparency in domestic courts.

Privatization Program

From 2002-2007, Pakistan attracted significant foreign investment through the privatization of state-owned enterprises (SOEs) in the financial services and telecommunications sectors, though privatization stalled from 2008- 2013. Pakistan's EFF agreement with the IMF identifies 31 SOEs for entire or partial privatization beginning with the sale of government stakes in high-performing, publicly-traded firms via capital markets transactions. Privatization of the largest and most money-losing state-owned firms, such as Pakistan Railways, Pakistan International Airlines (PIA), and Pakistan Steel, will require significant restructuring prior to privatization and is likely to face substantial political resistance. Foreign and local investors are permitted to bid on SOEs and financial institutions on equal terms. The government can only investigate a privatization deal up to one year after it is finalized.

Screening of FDI

Since 1997, the GOP no longer screens industrial sector foreign investment unless investors apply for special incentive packages or government tariff protection and price guarantees. The same year, the GOP also eliminated requirements that foreign investors seek provincial government clearance for project location.

Competition Law

The Competition Commission of Pakistan (CCP) is responsible for regulating the anti-competitive and monopolistic practices of both private and public sector organizations. In June 2007, the Pakistani Cabinet approved competition ordinances, drafted with technical assistance from the World Bank. These ordinances resulted in the creation of the CCP. Previously, competition law in Pakistan was under the jurisdiction of the Monopoly Control Authority, an independent regulatory authority that lacked enforcement capacity.

The 2010 Competition Commission Act codified the mandate of the CCP into law and revised the appeals process to include an appellate tribunal in Islamabad tasked with issuing decisions within six months. The law also reduced the fine for offenders from 15 percent to 10 percent of turnover and authorized the CCP to collect three percent of the earnings of other major regulatory agencies to supplement their budget. CCP issued 65 orders against monopolistic and anti-competitive practices from April 2008 to November 2013.

Investment Trends

A majority of the incoming FDI was directed towards the ICT sector, specifically with the auction of 3G/4G spectrum earlier in 2104. This was followed by FDI in the energy, oil & gas exploration, financial services and food industries respectively.

Table 1

Measure	Year	Index or Rank	Website Address

TI Corruption Perceptions index	**2014**	**126 of 177**	**transparency.org/cpi2014/results**
World Bank's Doing Business Report "Ease of Doing Business"	2015	128 of 142	**doingbusiness.org/rankings**
Global Innovation Index	2014	129 of 142	**globalinnovationindex.org/content.aspx?page=data-analysis**
World Bank GNI per capita	2013	USD 1,360	**data.worldbank.org/indicator/NY.GNP.PCAP.CD**

2. CONVERSION AND TRANSFER POLICIES

Foreign Exchange

SBP maintains strict controls over the exchange rate and monitors foreign exchange transactions in the open market. However, banks are required to report and justify outflows of foreign currency. Travelers leaving or entering Pakistan are allowed to physically carry a maximum of USD 10,000 in cash. There are no restrictions on payments of royalties and technical fees for the manufacturing sector. However, there are restrictions on other sectors, including a USD 100,000 limit on initial franchise investments and a cap on subsequent royalty payments to five percent of net sales for five years. Royalties and technical payments are subject to a 15-percent income tax.

To facilitate commercial banks, in 2002 SBP allowed cross-border payments of interests, profits, dividends, and royalties, without submitting prior notification. However, banks still have to report loan information, which allows the SBP to verify remittances against repayment schedules.

In 2004, the SBP made it mandatory for all foreign currency exchange businesses to register, making them subject to SBP audits. This subjected the foreign exchange market to more stringent regulations, including higher minimum capital requirements and closer monitoring. Exchange companies are permitted to buy and sell foreign currencies for individuals, banks, and other exchange companies. Additionally, they can sell foreign currencies to incorporated companies to facilitate the remittance of royalty, franchise, and technical fees. In recent years, there has been an increase in overseas worker remittances sent through these companies.

Remittance Policies

The GoP reports that it allows remittance of full capital, profits, and dividends, though for transactions over USD 5 million, though Economic Coordination Committee approval is often required. Dividends are tax-exempt.

There are no limits on dividends, remittance of profits, debt service, capital, capital gains, returns on intellectual property, or payment for imported equipment in Pakistani law, though for selected transactions that could impact Pakistan's Foreign Exchange reserves prior Economic Coordination Committee approval is required. However, banks are required to report and justify outflows of foreign currency and investor remittances can only be made against a valid contract or agreement registered with the SBP within 30 days of execution.

In recent years, there has been an increase in overseas worker remittances sent through these companies. SBP, the Ministry of Overseas Pakistanis, and the Ministry of Finance created the Pakistan Remittance Initiative in 2009 to facilitate faster, cheaper, and more efficient flow of remittances. Per Section 114.4 of the 2001 Income Tax Ordinance of Pakistan, the GoP exempted taxes on any amount of foreign currency remitted from outside Pakistan through normal banking channels and converted into rupees.

The 1976 Foreign Private Investment Promotion and Protection Act guarantees remittance of profits earned through sale and appreciation in value of property.

3. EXPROPRIATION AND COMPENSATION

The 1992 Furtherance and Protection of Economic Reforms Act protect FDI in Pakistan from expropriation by the 1976 Foreign Private Investment Promotion and Protection Act. The Investment Policy 2013 reinforces GoP commitment regarding the security and safety of FDI.

4. DISPUTE SETTLEMENT

Legal System, Specialized Courts, Judicial Independence, Judgments of Foreign Courts

Pakistan's legal system is based on British common law and is strongly influenced by Islamic Sharia Law. The application of Islamic Sharia Law remains primarily confined to the areas of domestic or personal matters. There are two classes of courts; the superior or high courts and the lower or subordinate courts. The superior judiciary is composed of the Supreme Court, the Federal Shariat Court and five High Courts. The Supreme Court holds the highest jurisdiction. Neither the Supreme Court not a High Court may exercise jurisdiction in relation to Tribal Areas, except in the cases where this is clearly stipulated. The lower courts are composed of civil and criminal district courts, and various specialized courts specifically covering areas such as; banking, customs & excise, smuggling, drug trafficking, terrorism, tax law, environmental law, consumer protection, insurance and corruption. The government also has the authority to set up administrative courts, over which they exercise exclusive jurisdiction. Each province has a high court, which hears appeals from district courts in civil cases and session courts in criminal cases. It is common for the one judge to preside over the district and session courts. The Supreme Court has jurisdiction over the provincial high courts, referrals from the federal government, and cases involving disputes among provinces or between a province and the federal government. Special courts and tribunals deal with taxation, banking, and labor.

Bankruptcy

Pakistan does not have a bankruptcy law, and court-appointed liquidators who auction the property of a bankrupt company organize the bankruptcy process. This process can take years to complete.

With regards to companies, winding up of the companies takes place under Companies Ordinance 1984 and banking companies exit takes place under Banking Companies Ordinance 1962. SECP and SBP have further streamlined the process for filing for bankruptcy and liquidation.

Investment Disputes

One of the main reasons for a decline in the foreign direct investment (FDI) is the difficulties faced by investors related to timely settlement of their investment disputes. Pakistan is a member of the International Center for the Settlement of Investment Disputes (ICSID). However, foreign investors are still concerned about how the arbitration cases are resolved in Pakistan.

Several high profile foreign investment disputes in the mining and energy sectors remain active cases in Pakistani courts.

International Arbitration

Even though, the Pakistan Arbitration Act of 1940 provides guidance for arbitration in commercial disputes; Commercial cases in the courts typically take years to resolve, and most foreign investors typically write into their contracts the right to international arbitration.

For example, in1998 a U.S. multinational filed a lawsuit against its Pakistani partner. Despite a favorable ruling by the International Chamber of Commerce (ICC) Arbitral Panel in 2000 and subsequent rulings by the Lahore Civil and High Courts upholding the ICC verdict, the local partner dragged the case on in Pakistani courts until finally withdrawing its appeal in 2009.

ICSID Convention and New York Convention

Pakistan is a member state to the International Centre for the Settlement of Investment Disputes (ICSID Convention). In 2005, Pakistan ratified the convention on the Recognition and Enforcement of Foreign Arbitral Awards (1958 New York Convention).

Duration of Dispute Resolution

There is no specific duration for dispute resolutions. Dispute resolutions can take decades to resolve.

5. PERFORMANCE REQUIREMENTS AND INVESTMENT INCENTIVES

WTO/TRIMS

Pakistan has been a World Trade Organization (WTO) member since 1 January 1995 and a GATT member since 1948. Pakistan provides most favored nation (MFN) treatment to all member states with the exception of India and Israel. Since 2012, imports from India are conducted on the basis of a negative list. There are about 1,200 products that cannot be imported from India. Pakistan does not conduct any trade with Israel.

During the period under review, Pakistan has been a respondent in one dispute settlement case initiated by Indonesia, concerning anti-dumping and countervailing duties imposed by Pakistan on certain paper products from Indonesia. In 2014, Pakistan also notified the WTO of a request for consultations with the European Union regarding the imposition of countervailing measures by the EU on imports of certain polyethylene terephthalate (PET) from Pakistan.

Pakistan considers the multilateral trading system to be the cornerstone of its trade policy. It also believes that preferential trade agreements (PTAs) are complementary to the multilateral trading system. Pakistan is a signatory to the South Asia Free Trade Agreement. It also has bilateral free-trade agreements with China, Indonesia, Iran, Malaysia, Mauritius and Sri Lanka.

Investment Incentives

The GoP investment policy provides domestic and foreign investors with the same incentives, concessions, and facilities for industrial development. Though some incentives are included in the federal budget, Special Regulatory Order (SRO) issued by the Federal Board of Revenue (FBR) promulgates most tax incentives. For example, the sales taxes on industrial machinery and customs duties on imported agricultural machinery have been abolished. Additionally, export-oriented industries have been granted customs duty exemptions on the import and purchase of raw materials. Custom duties for machinery imported by the manufacturing and social service sectors are under five percent.

The FY 2014 budget retained all these incentives. In 2011, the GoP imposed sales taxes ranging from four to six percent on unregistered companies working in the supply chain of export-oriented sectors, including textiles, surgical, sports, leather, and carpets. Registered companies within the supply chain of these sectors remain exempt from sales tax. Retailers in the same export-oriented sectors are subject to a four percent sales tax irrespective of registration.

Separately, in 2014 FBR issued a new SRO imposing a 17 percent sales tax on imported finished textile and leather goods while keeping the sales tax on similar locally produced products at five percent. FBR has stated that they intend to equalize the tax rates but have not provided a timeline. The vast majority of import tariffs (nearly 94 percent) are under 30 percent of the value of the good. Vehicle imports attract the highest duties. The GoP reduced customs duties on 88 raw materials for the pharmaceutical industry from 10 percent to 5 percent. As part of the IMF program, Pakistan has pledged to further reduce the number of tariff slabs (previously reduced from eight to seven) for the pharmaceutical industry.

Petroleum companies receive royalties at the rate of 12.5 percent of the value of petroleum at the field gate.

Research and Development

In Pakistan, there are no provisions for research and development initiatives. However, hi-tech industries, which include power tools, information technology and solar energy utilization, benefit from a wide range of fiscal incentives that are mentioned above.

Performance Requirements

Pakistan does not have a mandate for performance requirements of foreign entities operating in the country. There is no requirement to hire locals at any grade or their representation on the company's board of directors in the country.

U.S. businesspeople are granted multiple entry visas valid for five years with a 90-day stay. To obtain a visa, the US citizen is required to present a recommendation letter from a US chamber of commerce coupled with an invitation letter from a business endorsed by a Pakistani chamber of commerce, or a recommendation letter from a Pakistani foreign commercial attaché. Technical and managerial personnel working in sectors that are open to foreign investments are not required to obtain special work permits. Sectors that are open to foreign investments include the manufacturing, infrastructure, agricultural, services, health, and education sectors. Work visas for technical and managerial personnel are granted for one year and can be extended on a yearly basis.

Data Storage

Foreign investors are allowed to sign technical agreements with local investors without disclosing proprietary information. According to the 2013 Investment Policy, industrial units (manufacturers) that are bringing new technology to Pakistan receive the same incentives available in Special Economic Zones (SEZs). The 2007-2008 Trade Policy provides the same incentives as the export-processing zone (EPZ). Existing enterprises that export at least 80 percent of their production are eligible for incentives under this program, but enterprises formed after the passage of the policy are required to export 100 percent of their product in order to be eligible. In 2013, the GoP issued a Strategic Trade Policy Framework 2012-15, which also retains these measures. For new investments, a 25 percent first-year depreciation allowance for industrial plant machinery and equipment can be used to offset taxable income, and unused allowances can be carried forward. An investment tax credit of up to 25 percent of the cost of plant machinery and equipment is available to encourage expansion and modernization.

6. RIGHT TO PRIVATE OWNERSHIP AND ESTABLISHMENT

Foreign and domestic investors are free to establish and own businesses in all sectors except the following: arms and munitions manufacturing, high explosives manufacturing, currency/mint operations, non-industrial alcohol manufacturing, and radioactive substance manufacturing. In retail food sales, the GoP influences pricing of essential foodstuffs (such as flour, rice, and lentils) through its several hundred Utility Stores (state-owned grocery stores that provide subsidized essential food items). Market leaders in the cement and sugar industries allegedly operate cartels. Investments in the energy sector, particularly conventional gas, are obstructed by a policy that sets unrealistically low prices for resources.

Additionally, there is continuous disagreement between the federal and provincial governments regarding the ownership of natural resources. Though the 2012 Petroleum Policy increased the wellhead price for natural gas to USD 6 per million British thermal units in order to increase exploration and attract new investors, it has not been fully implemented.

7. PROTECTION OF PROPERTY RIGHTS

Real Property

Pakistan's legal system offers incomplete protection for the acquisition and disposition of property rights. The 1979 Industrial Property Order safeguards industrial property in Pakistan against government use of eminent domain without sufficient compensation, even in the public interest, in accordance with provisions of the law. The order protects both local and foreign investments. The 1976 Foreign Private Investment Promotion and Protection Act guarantees remittance of profits earned through the sale or appreciation in value of property.

Intellectual Property Rights

Pakistan remained on the US Trade Representative's Priority Watch List in the 2014 Special 301 review, and will likely remain on the list in 2015. The report cites weak protection and enforcement of intellectual property rights (IPR), particularly with respect to copyrights, pharmaceutical data, and media piracy. Pakistan did not take any significant steps to improve copyright enforcement, particularly involving the pirating of books and optical discs in 2014. A very small proportion of piracy-related arrests resulted in prosecutions that carried minor sentences. To address this, Pakistan should take steps to fully implement the 2012 Intellectual Property Organization of Pakistan Act (IPO Act), particularly by establishing specialized IP Tribunals and an operational Policy Board, which met for the first time in February 2015. The GOP has identified intellectual property protection as a key area for its "second generation" economic reforms, though it has taken few concrete steps to address it.

Pakistan has enacted five major laws relating to patents, copyrights, trademarks, industrial designs, and layout designs for integrated circuits, but inherent flaws in the legislation along with weak enforcement have limited the impact of these laws. Each of these laws would benefit from revision.

In April 2005, in an effort to improve the protection of intellectual property within Pakistan, the Government of Pakistan transferred inter-agency responsibility for the enforcement of intellectual property laws to the Federal Investigation Agency (FIA). FIA staff received specialized training in intellectual property enforcement and technologies, which enabled the agency to expand enforcement operations to target manufacturers of pirated goods. Expanding manpower and training at the FIA remains a key challenge. The Federal Board of Revenue (FBR), which manages customs authority in Pakistan, faces numerous challenges in properly identifying and interdicting counterfeit material at Pakistan's borders. However, in a promising sign, the FBR recently established an IPR Directorate to improve enforcement capacity.

Also in 2005, in response to longstanding domestic and international criticism of Pakistan's lack of a functioning central IPR regulatory and enforcement authority, as well as the need to implement its WTO TRIPS obligations, the Pakistani President created the Intellectual Property Organization (IPO). The IPO, a semi-autonomous body under the administrative control of the Pakistani Cabinet, consolidates into one government agency the authority over trademarks, patents, and copyrights – areas that were previously handled by offices in three separate ministries. IPO's mission is to initiate and monitor the enforcement and protection of intellectual property rights through law enforcement agencies, in addition to dealing with other IPR-related issues. While IPO's establishment represented an important milestone, it has not led to consistently measurable results in terms of increased public awareness of intellectual property rights, stepped up enforcement, or prompt action to address specific legislative and policy weaknesses. IPO has conducted training courses for IP professionals in accordance with WIPO standards. The 2012 Intellectual Property Organization law provides for specialized IPR tribunals to adjudicate cases and a policy board with private sector representation to assess policy decisions. The GoP has made little progress in implementing the provisions of the law. Though the GoP recently approved and publicized the establishment of IPR tribunals, the government has not appointed judges to make the tribunals operational. Pakistan has made some progress in combating large-scale illegal optical disc production and retail sales of pirated and counterfeit products. Further action is required to combat book piracy, aggressively prosecute IPR crime, and ensure that courts issue deterrent-level sentences for IPR infringers.

Pakistan's existing regulatory structure provides virtually no IPR for seeds or plant biotechnology. Pakistan produces biotech cotton, but the technology was smuggled into the country in 2002 and spread through informal multiplication. The government officially approved a number of biotech varieties in 2010, but given the absence of patent protection, the technology, while dated, has been in the public domain for over a decade. Most major US and international seed companies have operations in Pakistan that import and sell traditional hybrids. However, none have plans to introduce biotechnology or large-scale seed production until the regulatory structure improves. Pakistan's biotechnology regulatory system has been in disarray since the devolution of key federal powers to the provinces in 2010. Currently, the Lahore High Court is reviewing a case that considers whether the federal or provincial governments are in charge of plant biotechnology regulation. Meanwhile, the federal government's draft Biosafety Ordinance, which would formally reestablish the federal regulatory structure, is currently under review at the Law Ministry. Two other key pieces of legislation have been in various stages of the approval process for years. Amendments to the 1976 Act would broaden private sector participation in the industry and strengthen enforcement without conferring IPR. The National Assembly recently approved the draft legislation and sent it to the Senate for a vote. Pakistan's 2000 Patents Ordinance excludes plants. Among current legislation, the Plant Breeders' Rights Act has been the most thorough in establishing IPR in the short-term by enabling firms to register their varieties with the IPO, though enforcement will likely be a persistent concern.

Pakistan is a party to the Berne Convention for the Protection of Literary and Artistic Works, and is a member of the World Intellectual Property Organization (WIPO). On July 2004, Pakistan acceded to the Paris Convention for the Protection of Industrial Property. Pakistan has not yet ratified the WIPO Copyright Treaty or the WIPO Performance and Phonograms Treaty.

Patents

Pakistan enacted the Patent Law in 2000 in accordance with its WTO obligations. Under this law, the owners of patent and licensees can file suit against violators. However, a Patent Ordinance passed in 2002 weakened the 2000 Patent Law by eliminating use patents, restricting patent filings to single chemical entities, limiting protection for derivatives, and introducing barriers to patenting biotechnology-based inventions. The ordinance generated great concern among US pharmaceutical firms seeking to sell their products in Pakistan. In addition, the GoP has not implemented patent linkages, effectively authorizing the sale of pharmaceuticals without requiring checks to confirm that another firm does not hold an active patent on the compound. Pakistan has failed to make progress in providing effective protection against unfair commercial use of undisclosed tests and other data generated to obtain marketing approval for pharmaceutical products. Although draft data protection regulations were formulated in 2009, the regulations remain under GOP review and have not been promulgated. Pakistan currently does not have an effective system to prevent the issuance of marketing approvals for unauthorized copies of patented pharmaceutical products. In 2009, Pakistan's President issued an ordinance that removed an 18-month patent application-processing deadline, slowing the processing of pending patent applications. This ordinance further frustrated the pharmaceutical industry, as many companies had already been waiting for years for approval of their product patents. The GoP maintains that other countries do not adhere to an 18-month application-processing period. While the former Health Ministry claimed that this change was made to avoid litigation in view of capacity constraints, the ordinance has effectively created an environment where the potential for discriminatory treatment exists.

Trademarks

Pakistan announced its Trademarks Ordinance in 2000, which provides for the registration and better protection of trademarks, and restricts the use of fraudulent trademarks. The ordinance has been enforced since April 2004. The GOP has eliminated the requirement that pharmaceutical firms label the generic name with equal prominence to that of the brand name on all products. Trademark infringements remain widespread. The Competition Commission of Pakistan (CCP) has authority under Section 10 of the Competition Act to take action against companies for "deceptive marketing practices" for using other companies' trademarks in advertising. The CCP is working on a memorandum of understanding with the IPO regarding authority over such cases.

Copyrights

Pakistan's market for printed reading materials remains dominated by pirated products, although print piracy is increasingly giving way to pirate photocopying. Informal markets in Karachi and Lahore, once major sources of pirated printed materials, were raided in 2013, although book piracy has continued to spread. Pirates now make illegal photocopies from one master copy legitimately purchased online or overseas. The illegal photocopying of title covers has taken on a new dimension: pirates now obscure the author's names, publisher's names, logos, ISBN numbers, etc, to prevent tracking. Print piracy also consists of smuggled books from Iran and Afghanistan by land, Saudi Arabia by air, and overruns by legitimate printers in Pakistan. Unauthorized India-only reprints are also being imported into Pakistan. A wide range of books are pirated, from English language novels to fiction and non-fiction. Sellers of pirated print materials are highly organized and well-connected. They often succeed in convincing authorities to drop cases immediately after any enforcement action or avoid enforcement action altogether. In some cases, they have even resorted to threats of violence and intimidation to avoid prosecution. Some pirate enterprises are now able to produce fairly high-quality counterfeit copies that are difficult to differentiate from legitimate versions. Additionally, the National Book Foundation continues to use compulsory licenses to copy books, and this is contrary to Pakistan's international obligations under the Berne Convention. According to the International Property Alliance, publishers operating in Pakistan reported an increase in enforcement activity and claimed that piracy levels were proportionately similar to Bangladesh, Iran, and Sri Lanka. Pakistani authorities, especially the Federal Investigations Agency (FIA) in Islamabad, have taken some actions against sellers of pirated printed materials throughout Pakistan.

Despite significant public awareness and enforcement drives by the Business Software Alliance over the past several years, enterprise end-user software piracy remains a serious problem. The GoP did not take any significant steps to improve copyright enforcement in 2014, especially with respect to optical disc piracy. The vast majority of software piracy-related arrests failed to result in prosecution, and the few that were prosecuted were given insignificant sentences. Optical media piracy remains a major concern in Pakistan. The import and export of pirated media was banned under the 1969 Customs Act. However, the easy import of pirated movies and music CDs and DVDs continues in large quantities from China.

The Pakistan Federal Investigation Agency (FIA) continues to conduct occasional raids. However, most of the time, a higher court postpones hearings until the FIA investigation team provides sufficient evidence. Media reports indicate that Pakistan is a transit route for counterfeit products originating in Russia, Malaysia, Singapore, China, Bangladesh, and Sri Lanka for onward distribution to other countries. Since 2008, vendors have shifted production of pirated optical software to residential locations, making it difficult for authorities to investigate. Weak enforcement has allowed the sale of pirated CDs, books, movies, and software to grow in most local markets in Pakistan.

Internet use continues to rise in Pakistan, and, with it, online piracy. Publishers report that reference books, online journals, and trade books are being illegally digitized and provided by schools. Thus far, no steps have been taken to address increasing online piracy or illegal digitization. Pakistan has thousands of local small-scale cable television operators nationwide. Even though the Pakistan Electronic Media Regulation Authority (PEMRA) has prohibited pirated content on television, cable operators frequently broadcast pirated content, because of weak enforcement from FIA.

The Industrial Designs Law allows the registration of designs for a period of ten years, with extension for up to twenty years. The Law for Layout Designs of Integrated Circuits provides protection of layout designs for ten years starting from its first commercial exploitation anywhere in the world. Penalties and legal remedies are also available in case of infringement on industrial designs, layout designs, and trademarks. Implementing rules to enforce these ordinances remain incomplete. In 2009, the Cabinet approved a draft Plant Breeder's Rights Law and an amendment to the Seed Act of 1976, both of which are pending approval in Parliament and passage from the provincial assemblies.

For additional information about treaty obligations and points of contact at local IP offices, please see WIPO's country profiles at http://www.wipo.int/directory/en/."

Resources for Rights Holders
Contact at Mission:
Mark Miller
Economic Officer
+92-51-208-0000
MillerGM@state.gov

8. TRANSPARENCY OF THE REGULATORY SYSTEM

A number of government agencies, including SECP, BOI, and SBP, oversee the commercial and financial regulatory system. Under the 1984 Companies Ordinance, all companies are required to register with SECP. Additionally, the SECP regulates the securities market through its Securities Market Division. The SECP and the national stock exchanges collaborate to streamline procedures to register and list securities. The 1971 Securities and Exchange Rules regulate by the 1969 Securities and Exchange Ordinance and equity markets. The Companies Ordinance provides a guideline for the closure of a company, while the Banking 1962 Companies Ordinance provides the procedure for closing of a bank. SECP and SBP have simplified the process for filing for bankruptcy and liquidation.

The SBP, in its role as bank regulatory authority, has established a formal process of consultations with banks on draft regulations. Under Section 40 of the 1997 SECP Act, the SECP also publishes draft regulations to seek public comment prior to finalization. The FBR issues SROs, which are used to reduce or enhance duties, in order to give special relief to certain sectors. The FBR does not solicit public input on SROs.

As mentioned earlier, the Competition Commission of Pakistan (CCP) is responsible for regulating the anti-competitive and monopolistic practices of both private and public sector organizations. The Pakistani Cabinet approved a competition ordinance, drafted with technical assistance from the World Bank, in June 2007. This ordinance resulted in the creation of the CCP. Previously, competition law in Pakistan was under the jurisdiction of the Monopoly Control Authority, an independent regulatory authority that lacked enforcement capacity.

The 2010 Competition Commission Act codified the mandate of the CCP into law and revised the appeals process to include an appellate tribunal in Islamabad tasked with issuing decisions within six months. The law also reduced the fine for offenders from 15 percent to 10 percent of turnover and authorized the CCP to collect three percent of the earnings of other major regulatory agencies to supplement their budget. CCP issued 65 orders against monopolistic and anti-competitive practices from April 2008 to November 2013.

With the end of licensing regimes, the rationalization of bureaucratic controls, and broad-based market liberalizations, market entry barriers have been reduced but not fully eliminated.

9. EFFICIENT CAPITAL MARKETS AND PORTFOLIO INVESTMENT

Pakistan's financial sector policies support the free flow of resources for domestic and foreign investors. The SBP and SECP continue to expand their regulation and oversight of financial and capital markets. The top five banks (of which only one is state owned) control 52.6 percent of all banking sector assets. In 2014, banking sector assets totaled USD 180 billion. As of December 2014, net non-performing bank loans (NPLs) totaled approximately USD 1.2 billion, almost three percent of net total loans.

Interest rates are dependent on the reverse repo rate (the policy rate). The SBP consistently lowered the policy interest rate from a high of 10 percent at the last quarter of 2014 to eight percent at the close of the first quarter of 2015 and expects to continue lowering the rate. Foreign entities are allowed to borrow from the domestic banks without limits. Banks are required to ensure that total debt exposure to any domestic or foreign entity does not exceed 25 percent of the bank's equity. The private sector predominantly accesses credit from commercial banks, which are rebalancing their assets to include more government securities holdings. Pakistan's domestic corporate bonds, commercial papers, and derivative markets remain in the early stages of development. According to the 2013 Investment Policy, foreign investors in all sectors are allowed domestic credit lines subject to prevailing the rules and regulations of the SECP and SBP, and observance of the required debt-to-equity ratio. The policy extends the use of loans, previously limited to import of industrial plant machinery, to any purpose.

The Karachi Stock Exchange (KSE) is a member of the Federation of Euro-Asian Stock Exchanges (FEAS) and the South Asian Federation of Exchanges (SAFE). The KSE is also an affiliated member of the World Federation of Exchanges and the International Organization of Securities Commissions. In FY2014, Pakistan's stock markets outperformed global stock markets including those of India, China, Hong Kong, Tokyo, the U.S. and UK. The stock market performance was driven by portfolio investment inflows in addition to the better rates of return on Pakistani stocks. The KSE currently has 581 listed firms with a market capitalization of USD 7.5 billion.

In 2010, the GoP implemented a capital gains tax of 10 percent on stocks held for less than six months and almost 8 percent on stocks held for more than six months but less than a year. No capital gains tax is applied on holdings that exceed 12 months. The 2012 Capital Gains Tax Ordinance appointed the National Clearing Company of Pakistan Limited to compute, determine, collect, and deposit the capital gains tax. Portfolio investments, capital gains, and dividends can be fully repatriated.

Recent capital market reforms include the introduction of minimum capital requirements for brokers, linking of exposure limits to net capital, strengthening of brokers' margin requirements, introduction of system audit regulations (mandating audit of 60 percent of brokers), introduction of over the-counter (OTC) markets to facilitate registration of new companies with less paid-up capital, and introduction of a National Clearing and Settlement system. The SECP implemented a number of other regulations, including on clearing houses, margin trading, proprietary trading, and abolition of the group account facility. Capital market legal, regulatory, and accounting systems are consistent with international norms.

Pakistan has adopted international accounting standards, with comprehensive disclosure requirements for companies and financial sector entities, and Pakistan adheres to the majority of international accounting and financial reporting standards.

Money and Banking System, Hostile Takeovers

The size of the banking sector has grown steadily with better financial health. To further enhance the assessment of the health and soundness of the financial sector, the SBP continues to work on developing a preliminary "encouraged" set of financial soundness indicators (FSIs). The legislative and regulatory framework is largely compliant with Basel core principles of banking supervision, international standards of Anti-Money-Laundering and Combating the Financing of Terrorism (AML/CFT) and Basel III for capital adequacy.

Pakistan's monetary policy has undergone significant changes in tandem with the changing economic landscape. During 2013-2014, monetary expansion decreased to 12.5 percent from 15.9 percent in 2012-2013. This decrease was principally due to lower government borrowings from the banking system.

The SECP regulates the insurance industry, and while the SBP oversees the banking sector. The GOP opened the insurance industry for foreign investors as a part of its financial sector reforms i. In 2007.Under these reforms, the GOP government allowed 100 percent percent foreign equity in the insurance business. Foreign investors in the insurance sector are required to subject to the condition that foreign investors are required to bring a minimum paid up capital of USD 5.3 million in life insurance and USD 3.1 million in non-life/general insurance.

SBP requires that foreign banks have at least USD 300 million in capital reserves at their flagship location in Pakistan and a minimum of 8 percent capital adequacy ratio in order to operate in Pakistan and to open branches. In addition, foreign banks are required to maintain the following minimum capital requirements which vary based on the number of branches they are operating:

1 to 5 branches - Required to maintain USD 28 million in assigned capital,

6 to 50 branches - Required to maintain USD 56 million in assigned capital,

Over 50 branches - Required to maintain USD 94 million in assigned capital.

The GoP enacted legislation providing a legal framework for friendly and hostile takeovers in 2002. The law provides that companies have to disclose any concentration of share ownership over 25 percent. There are no laws or regulations that authorize private firms to adopt articles of incorporation that discriminate against foreign investment.

Per the Foreign Exchange Regulations, any foreign investor can invest in shares and securities listed on Stock Exchanges in Pakistan, and can repatriate profits, dividends, or disinvestment proceeds. The investor has to open a Special Convertible Rupee Account with any bank in Pakistan in order to make portfolio investments.

10. COMPETITION FROM STATE-OWNED ENTERPRISES

The GoP's 16-year privatization campaign came to a halt in 2006 when the Supreme Court reversed the privatization of Pakistan Steel Mills, setting a precedent for future offerings. Large and inefficient SOEs have retained a monopoly in a few key sectors, and the GoP provides annual subsidies to cover SOEs' losses. Three of the largest SOEs are Pakistan Railways, Pakistan International Airlines, and Pakistan Steel Mills. Since the Sharif Administration took office in June 2013, it has restarted privatization efforts, pledged to privatize 31 state-owned companies, and hired transaction advisors for the first several transactions that are expected before the end of 2015.

Pakistan Railways (PR): PR is the only provider of rail services in Pakistan and the largest public sector employer with close to 90,000 employees. Decades of corruption and mismanagement have caused PR's market share in freight traffic to fall by over 76 percent since 1970. Of PR's 500 locomotives, only 206 were operational in 2014. The company relies on government bailouts of USD 2.8 million a month to pay salaries and pensions. In the FY2014 budget, total government grant payments to PR are budgeted at USD 395 million. In 2014, Pakistan initiated the public-private partnership policy (which was deferred since 2012), the private sector would be offered commercial management and passenger facilitation of 14 express, four passenger, one rail car each for mail, mixed, and shuttle trains.

Pakistan International Airlines (PIA): PIA continues to struggle and is criticized for poor management, excessive staffing, inefficient operations, and a non-competitive market strategy. PIA's aging and fuel-inefficient fleet is suffering in the current competitive global environment. In contrast to PR, PIA is technically not operating as a monopoly. It faces domestic private sector competition from Air Blue and Shaheen Air and very strong competition from Gulf carriers and other regional airlines on international routes. In a February 2013 meeting, the Cabinet Economic Coordination Committee approved a financing plan for PIA including guarantees for the repayment of USD 104 million in loans in 2013 alone, extension of GoP guarantees measuring USD 482 million and new guarantees against loans of USD 127 million, additional funding of USD 113 million and provision of USD 46 million for the acquisition of narrow-body aircrafts on dry lease. PIA's current debt is USD 28.8 billion. The first quarter results of FY 2015 show that PIA has attained an operating profit of USD 17 million, versus a loss of USD 57.4 million in the same period last year. One of the conditions of the IMF EFF arrangement is to privatize up to 26 percent of PIA. The Privatization Commission has begun this process by hiring a financial advisory firm that has decided to sell PIA shareholdings in the petroleum and banking sectors; however, political resistance is strong, and the effort has stalled.

Pakistan Steel Mills (PSM): Established by the GoP as a cheaper option than importing steel, PSM has deteriorated into a money-losing enterprise that relies on a ban on steel imports to remain afloat. In 2006, the Supreme Court halted the proposed USD 360 million sale of a 75 percent stake in PSM after facing opposition from a strong workers' union and the general public. There was also concern that the transaction undervalued PSM. At present, as a result of a government-backed financial restructuring package worth USD 185 million in the first quarter of 2014, the mill is operating at 30 percent of its capacity as compared to three percent during the same period last year. PSM's current debts and liabilities are worth USD 710 million.

OECD Guidelines on Corporate Governance of SOEs

State-owned enterprises (SOEs) continue to have an important role in Pakistan's economy.

State involvement occurs mainly in manufacturing (e.g. fertilizers, steel and engineering goods), energy (oil, gas, and electricity) and key services (e.g. banking, insurance and transportation). In Pakistan, SOEs represent one third of the total stock market capitalization. However, Pakistani SOEs do not follow OECD guidelines for their corporate governance. In 2010, Pakistan initiated the process of issuing an SOE Code, however with the change of government in 2013 and the conditionalities – including the privatization of key SOEs – of the IMF program, there has been no progress since then.

Even though SOEs operate with their own budget they are still governed by various ministries. For examples, Pakistan Steel Mills is governed by the Ministry of Industries and Production, whereas the Ministry of Railways governs Pakistan Railways.

In March 2007 the Government of Pakistan clarified the Powers of the Governing Boards of Companies Established under the Companies Ordinance 1984 as follows:

Government established/owned companies under the Companies Ordinance may use full powers to the extent given in the Companies Ordinance provided their decisions do not impact the Federal Budget in any way.

In case of organizations, established under specific enactments (other than Companies Ordinance) the BOD will act according to their respective laws. However, in such cases, the agenda for the meeting of BOD may be circulated well ahead of time so that finance division representatives on the boards may consult and get orders of the appropriate authorities and act accordingly in the meeting of BOD.

Separation of Chairman and CEO functions/officers – some SOEs have separated the offices/functions of Chairman of the Board and the CEO (e.g. Pakistan State Oil, Pakistan International Airlines, Oil & Gas Development Corporation, Pakistan Petroleum Limited etc).

The role of Independent Non-Executive Directors – Some SOEs have sufficient number of Independent Non-executive Directors on their Boards and Board committees' e.g. State Life Insurance Corporation, Civil Aviation Authority, Employees Old Age Benefit Institution.

However, the above initiatives are proposed to be reinforced through the issuance of the SOE Regulations i.e. the SECP, the premier regulator of corporate bodies, framed the Draft Public Sector Companies (Corporate Governance) Regulation in November 2007. The Pakistan Institute of Corporate Governance vetted the draft in December 2007 and proposed appropriate amendments. The proposals were also peer reviewed by the International Finance Corporation. The final proposals/comments were sent to the Commission in December 2007.

Sovereign Wealth Funds

In Pakistan, there is no specific exemption for foreign sovereign wealth funds (SWFs) under the current domestic tax law. Foreign SWFs are taxed like any other non-resident person under domestic tax law unless specific concessions have been granted under an applicable tax treaty to which Pakistan is a signatory.

Under domestic tax law, the taxation of non-residents with respect to Pakistan source income depends on the nature of the income. Dividends are subject to Withholding Tax (WHT) at 10 percent of the gross amount. The final tax cannot exceed 10 percent WHT on dividends declared or distributed by companies engaged in power generation or purchasers of power projects is 7.5 percent and the final tax cannot exceed 7.5 percent.

Interest income is subject to WHT at the following rates:

0 percent on interest paid to foreign corporations, if the security, arrangement, loan is approved by the Federal Government depending on the nature of exemption sought (see below); and,

10 percent in all other cases if the lender has no permanent establishment (PE) in Pakistan.

The following interest payments are tax exempt:

Interest received by a non-resident person on security approved by the FBR and issued by a resident person, if both persons (resident and non-resident) are not associates; the security was widely issued outside Pakistan by the resident person for use in business carried on by the resident person in Pakistan; and profit is paid outside Pakistan.

Interest on Government securities is exempt from tax under certain income tax treaties.

Interest payable to a non-resident on a private loan utilized on a project in Pakistan. The approval of the Federal Government is required in this case as regards the loan amount, nature of loan, rate of profit, terms of repayment and nature of the project.

Interest on moneys borrowed under a loan agreement or in respect of foreign currency instrument approved by Federal Government.

Any profit on debt derived from foreign currency accounts held with authorized banks or certificate of investment issued by investment banks in accordance with Foreign Currency Accounts Scheme introduced by SBP, by a foreign association of persons, companies registered and operating abroad and foreign nationals residing in Pakistan.

Foreign SWFs may also be exempt from Pakistan taxation on interest income under some income tax treaties to which Pakistan is a party.

11. CORPORATE SOCIAL RESPONSIBILITY

There is an increase in awareness of corporate social responsibility among producers and consumers in Pakistan. Foreign and some local enterprises follow the accepted CSR principles and promote their messages through various media platforms. However, one major consequence is that CSR is frequently equated with corporate philanthropy/charity, especially in the case of local corporations. Some consider CSR to be simple compliance with the law. This creates a difficulty because top management in many cases is still uncertain about the true meaning of CSR. The state of CSR in Pakistan is, therefore still in its infancy. Some indigenous companies have also developed written CSR policies, but the majority, unfortunately, are 'either unaware of the benefits brought by CSR or they feel that even if they do not adopt such policies, there are not in any state of danger.

Proctor and Gamble-Pakistan was the 2011 recipient of the Secretary of State's Award for Corporate Excellence (ACE) for demonstrating CSR in flood relief, support of education and orphans, implementation of science and technology standards, reduction of carbon dioxide emission at its facilities, and collaboration with universities to develop young business leaders.

OECD Guidelines for Multinational Enterprises

There are no specific OECD guidelines that the Pakistani government encourages foreign and local enterprises to follow.

However, in March 2014 the European Parliament, through a resolution on Pakistan's regional role and political relations with the EU, invited the Pakistani authorities to sign up to the ILO/IFC-led Better Work Programme and called on all those responsible for the 2012 factory fire that killed over 250 workers at the Ali Enterprises garment factory to finally pay compensation to the survivors of the fire.

12. POLITICAL VIOLENCE

The presence of several foreign and local terrorist groups throughout Pakistan poses a serious danger to U.S. citizens. There are frequent terrorist attacks across the country against civilians, government, and foreign personnel and organizations. There have also been frequent attacks on Pakistani military establishments across the country. Major Pakistani cities are frequently on high-security alert with paramilitary and police patrolling the streets. Terrorist groups in Pakistan pose a threat to U.S. citizens and other westerners. There is potential for anti-U.S protests, which can turn violent. Embassies of most western countries, including the United States, United Kingdom, Canada, Australia, and New Zealand, have issued travel advisories against non-essential travel to Pakistan. Consequently, western businesses operating in Pakistan require costly security measures.

The Board of Investment, in collaboration with Provincial Investment Promotion Agencies, coordinates airport-to-airport security for foreign investors. To avail of this service, registered foreign investors or potential investors should make a request to the BOI with adequate notice and details of their itinerary. The service includes a police escort and guidance on making secure lodging and transportation arrangements.

13. CORRUPTION

Corruption remains widespread in Pakistan at the federal level, especially in government procurement, international contracts, and taxation. There are anecdotal reports that corruption has increased at the provincial level following the 2010 Constitutional Amendment that devolved responsibility for many service-delivery oriented issues, such as health, education, and environmental regulations, from the federal to the provincial governments. Offering and accepting bribes are criminal acts punishable by law and could result in confiscation of property, imprisonment, recovery of dishonest gains, and dismissal from government service or a penalization in governmental grade. In 2014, Pakistan ranked 126 out of 177 countries on the Transparency International Corruption Perceptions Index.

Government officials frequently engage in corrupt practices without any consequences. Constituted under the 1999 National Accountability Ordinance, the National Accountability Bureau (NAB) is the country's anti-corruption organization, with a mandate to expose and prevent corrupt activities, and to enforce anti-corruption laws. Initially, NAB was used as a tool to target political opponents. However, after receiving criticism from the public, the NAB refocused its strategy in 2002. NAB struggles with insufficient funding and staffing.

The CCP targets corrupt activities, such as collusive practices, abuse of market dominance, and deceptive marketing. Despite dynamic leadership, active community engagement, and triumphs in lower level courts, the CCP is hindered by insufficient government funding and slow progress of cases in the court of appeals. Corruption is pervasive in politics and government, and various politicians and government officials have faced allegations of corruption, including bribery, extortion, cronyism, nepotism, patronage, graft, and embezzlement.

The 2007 National Reconciliation Ordinance (NRO), promulgated under former President Pervez Musharraf, allowed the government to grant amnesty to public officials accused of corruption, embezzlement, money laundering, murder, and terrorism between January 1, 1986, and October 12, 1999. In December 2009, the Supreme Court declared the NRO null and void, and reopened all 8,000 cases against those who had received amnesty, including President Musharraf and sitting ministers and parliamentarians. Supreme Court decisions about the beneficiaries of NRO are still pending implementation.

Corruption within the lower levels of the police and customs officials is common, even considered normal by the general public. Transparency International notes that the major root cause of corruption is the lack of accountability and enforcement of penalties, followed by the lack of merit-based promotion and earnings, as well as overall low salaries. According to a survey, some police officers even charge fees to report complaints. Using bribes to avoid criminal prosecution is common practice. The appointment of station house officers – a powerful rank in the Pakistani police force – is politicized.

The previous government was voted out of office based on widespread corruption cases that emerged during their term. Some cases made it up to the Supreme Court, such as the rental power plant projects, ephedrine import, and the Hajj corruption case. Since 2013, PML-N has made progress towards introducing anti-corruption policies and prosecuting high officials accused of being involved in corruption.

There are reported cases of bribery and nepotism in the district and lower courts. Judges in lower courts lack independence and are sometimes pressured by higher court judges. Lower courts remain corrupt, inefficient, and subject to pressure from prominent wealthy, religious, and political figures. Political involvement in judicial appointments increases the government's hold over the court system.

The 2002 Freedom of Information Ordinance allows public access to federal government records. The ordinance does not apply to government-owned corporations or provincial governments. The government must respond to requests for access to information within 21 days of the request being submitted. Classified documents that could be harmful to pending cases or that would cause grave and significant damage to the economy and the interests of the nation if released are restricted from public access. NGOs criticized the ordinance for exempting broad swaths of information and for failing to encourage government departments to disclose information proactively.

UN Anticorruption Convention, OECD Convention on Combatting Bribery

Pakistan is not a signatory to the Organization of Economic Cooperation and Development (OECD) Convention on Combating Bribery, but is a signatory to the Asian Development Bank/OECD Anti-Corruption Initiative. Pakistan has also ratified the UN Convention against Corruption.

Resources to Report Corruption
Contact at government agency or agencies are responsible for combating corruption:
Major (Retd) Qamar Zaman Chaudhary
Chairman
National Accountability Bureau
ATTATURK AVENUE G-5/2, Islamabad
+92-51-111-622-622
chairman@nab.gov.pk

Contact at "watchdog" organization (international, regional, local or nongovernmental organization operating in the country/economy that monitors corruption, such as Transparency International):

Sohail Muzaffar
Chairman
Transparency International

5-C, 2nd Floor, Kahayan-e-Ittehad, Phase VII, D.H.A., Karachi
0092-21-35390408-9
ti.pakistan@gmail.com

14. BILATERAL INVESTMENT AGREEMENTS

Pakistan and the United States began negotiating a Bilateral Investment Treaty (BIT) in 2004. Negotiations have been held intermittently since then and are currently stalled. Pakistan has bilateral investment agreements with Australia, Azerbaijan, Mauritius, Bahrain, Bangladesh, Morocco, Belarus, the Netherlands, the Belgo-Luxemburg Economic Union, Oman, Philippines, Bosnia, Portugal, Bulgaria, Qatar, Cambodia, Romania, China, Singapore, Czech Republic, South Korea, Denmark, Spain, Egypt, Sri Lanka, France, Sweden, Germany, Switzerland, Indonesia, Syria, Iran, Tajikistan, Italy, Tunisia, Japan, Turkey, Kazakhstan, Turkmenistan, Kuwait, the United Arab Emirates, Kyrgyz Republic, United Kingdom, Lebanon, Uzbekistan, Laos, and Yemen.

Bilateral Taxation Treaties

The United States and Pakistan have had a bilateral tax treaty in force since 1959. Pakistan also has double taxation agreements with Austria, Canada, Germany, Indonesia, Italy, Lebanon, Mauritius, Poland, Switzerland, Turkmenistan, Kazakhstan, the United Arab Emirates, Belgium, China, France, Greece, Iran, Japan, Libya, Saudi Arabia, Romania, Sweden, Belarus, Hungary, Jordan, Kenya, Kuwait, Malaysia, Netherlands, Nigeria, Norway, Oman, Philippines, Qatar, South Africa, Syria, Tunisia, Uzbekistan, the United Kingdom, Bangladesh, Denmark, Finland, India, Ireland, South Korea, Malta, Singapore, Sri Lanka, Thailand, Azerbaijan, and Turkey.

15. OPIC and Other Investment Insurance Programs

The Overseas Private Investment Corporation (OPIC) maintains an active portfolio of projects in Pakistan, including new investments in renewable energy. Projects must meet OPIC eligibility guidelines both for investment insurance and co-investment.

16. LABOR

Pakistan's civilian workforce consists of approximately 60.5 million workers, but this estimate does not include the informal sector or child workers. The majority of the labor force works in the agricultural sector (45 percent), followed by the services sector (34.2 percent), and manufacturing (13.8 percent). Officially, the unemployment rate hovers at around 6 percent, but this figure is widely believed to be significantly understated. Additionally, a large number of the employed are underemployed. Pakistan is also an extensive exporter of labor, particularly to the Middle East.

The18th Constitutional Amendment gives jurisdiction over matters related to labor to the provinces. In Punjab, Khyber Pakhtunkhwa, and Islamabad, the minimum wage is PKR 12,000 per month (USD 120). In Sindh, it is PKR 11,000 per month (USD 110), and in Baluchistan is PKR 9,000 per month (USD 90). Labor law enforcement is weak at both the federal and provincial levels. Required labor inspections by and large do not take place, and low-level labor courts are generally considered corrupt and strongly biased in favor of employers. Furthermore, labor protection does not extend to a majority of the labor force, most notably agricultural workers. Pakistan does not comply with International Labor Organization (ILO) conventions, despite having ratified 34 conventions relating to human rights, workers' rights, and working conditions. International employers and exporters often have international certifications demonstrating that they meet labor obligations, while local businesses often do not. The only significant area of U.S.

investment in which workers' rights are legally restricted is the petroleum sector, which is subject to the Essential Services Maintenance Act (ESMA). The ESMA bans strikes, limits workers' rights to change employment, and presents limited options to a fired employee. While ESMA provides collective bargaining rights, it is almost never applied.

Widespread criticism of Pakistan's confusing labor laws led to the creation of a government commission in 2000 with the mandate to revise and consolidate Pakistan's labor legislation. The President enacted the Industrial Relations Ordinance on July 18, 2011. All the provinces have enacted the Industrial Relations Acts. According to government estimates, approximately five percent of the industrial labor force and two percent of the overall workforce are unionized. The GoP announced labor welfare measures in 2010 including the extension of social security eligibility to workers earning up to PKR 10,000 (USD 100) a month, creation of a Complaint Cell to address workers complaints, guaranteed payment of full wages to suspended workers, expansion of the government retirement benefits plan to establishments employing five or more workers, an increase in marriage and death grants, and increase in workers' eligibility for company profit-sharing awards. The provinces are responsible for implementing these measures. As part of its commitments to the EU under the Generalized System of Preferences (GSP) Plus preferential trade scheme, Pakistan has agreed to ratify and implement 27 international conventions on human and labor rights, sustainable development, and good governance.

17. FOREIGN TRADE ZONES/FREE PORTS/TRADE FACILITATION

The GoP established the first Export Processing Zone (EPZ) in Karachi in 1989, providing special fiscal and institutional incentives to export-oriented industries. The GoP subsequently established seven other EPZs in Risalpur, Gujranwala, Sialkot, Saindak, Gwadar, Reko Dek and Duddar. Only the zones in Karachi, Risalpur, Sialkot, and Saindak are operational. The main incentives for EPZ investors are exemptions from taxes and duties on equipment, machinery, and materials (including components, spare parts, and packing material); indefinite loss carry-forward; and access to EPZ Authority "One Window" that facilitates the issuance of import permits and export authorizations. The EPZA collects between 0.5 and 1.25 percent in taxes for exported goods, in addition to a 0.5 percent development surcharge. Otherwise, there is an exemption from all federal, provincial, and municipal taxes for production dedicated to exports and full repatriation of capital and profits for foreign investors is allowed. There are no minimum or maximum limits on investment in EPZs.

Despite offering substantial financial, investor service, and infrastructural incentives to reduce the cost of doing business, most of these zones have failed to attract any significant investment due to their inability to offer reliable gas, electricity, and water supplies. The 2012 Special Economic Zones (SEZ) Act represented an effort to create industrial clusters with liberal incentives. Regulations allow private parties to establish companies as well as public-private partnerships within SEZs.

The GOP offers incentives for other categories of export manufacturing. An Export-Oriented Unit (EOU) is a stand-alone industrial entity that exports 100 percent of its production. EOUs are allowed to operate anywhere in the country. EOU incentives include duty and tax exemptions for imported machinery and raw materials in addition to duty-free import of two vehicles per project.

18. FOREIGN DIRECT INVESTMENT AND FOREIGN PORTFOLIO INVESTMENT STATISTICS

Table 2: Key Macroeconomic Data, U.S. FDI in Host Country/Economy

	Host Country	USG or	USG or International Source of Data: BEA; IMF; Eurostat;

	Statistical source*		international statistical source		UNCTAD, Other
Economic Data	Year	Amount	Year	Amount	
Host Country Gross Domestic Product (GDP) ($M USD)	2014	254,002	2014	224,891	www.worldbank.org/en/country
Foreign Direct Investment	Host Country Statistical source*		USG or international statistical source		USG or international Source of data: BEA; IMF; Eurostat; UNCTAD, Other
U.S. FDI in partner country ($M USD, stock positions)	2014	319.1	2012	218	http://bea.gov/international/factsheet/factsheet.cfm?Area=622
Host country's FDI in the United States ($M USD, stock positions)	2013	92	2012	66	http://bea.gov/international/factsheet/factsheet.cfm?Area=622
Total inbound stock of FDI as % host GDP	2013	0.13%	2012	0.10 %	

*State Bank of Pakistan http://sbp.org.pk/ecodata/index2.asp

Table 3: Sources and Destination of FDI

Direct Investment from/in Counterpart Economy Data					
From Top Five Sources/To Top Five Destinations (US Dollars, Millions)					
Inward Direct Investment			Outward Direct Investment		
Total Inward	10,586	100%	Total Outward	829	100%
United Kingdom	1,905	18%	United Arab Emirates	165	20%
United Arab Emirates	1,638	15%	Kingdom of Bahrein	73	9%
United States	1,204	11%	United States	60	7%
China	589	6%	Sri Lanka	56	7%

Netherlands	533	5%	Oman	51	6%

"0" reflects amounts rounded to +/- USD 500,000.

Source: IMF Coordinated Direct Investment Survey

Table 4: Sources of Portfolio Investment

Portfolio Investment Assets								
Top Five Partners (Millions, US Dollars)								
Total			Equity Securities			Total Debt Securities		
All Countries	483	100%	All Countries	236	100%	All Countries	247	100%
Saudi Arabia	216	45%	Saudi Arabia	194	82%	United Arab Emirates	46	19%
United Arab Emirates	50	10%	Virgin Islands, British	12	5%	Qatar	31	13%
Qatar	31	6%	United Kingdom	8	4%	Saudi Arabia	22	9%
Cayman Islands	25	5%	Switzerland	6	2%	Cayman Islands	22	9%
Japan	22	4%	United States	5	2%	Turkey	20	8%

Source: IMF Coordinated Portfolio Investment Survey

IMPORTANT CONTACTS

ATTORNEYS.

Muhammad Mahboob Alam
Address: # No. 4, 1st Floor, Arshad Sharif Plaza, Sector G-11 Markaz, Islamabad
Mobile: 0300-9567-148
E-mail: advocatemahboob@hotmail.com

Bilal Law Associates
Office: 217 Masco Plaza, 64-WS, Block 'H' Blue Area 44000 Pakistan
Office: 051-2271000-1 Residence: 051-2293923
Fax: 051-2271002 Email: tariq@bilal-law.com
Webpage: www.bilal-law.com

Anees Jillani Address: No. 13, Fourth floor 109-West Blue Area, Sardar Begum Plaza Islamabad
Office: 051-227-9255, 051-287-5884
Mobile: 0300-856-1958 , 333-526-1961
Fax: 051-2279-256
E-mail: sparc@comsats.net.pk , jillani@jillani.org
Website: http://jillani.org

Choudhry Ghazanfar Ali
Address: District Courts Sector F-8 Markaz, Islamabad
and
661 Suhrawardy Road Aabpara Market, Islamabad Mobile: 0333-5176-645
(0333-517-5935 for emergency only)

BJ Law Associates
Address: House 2-B, Main Nazimuddin Road Sector F-6/1, Islamabad
Office: 051-2814190-91, 051-282-9772
Fax: 051-2872376
Mobile: 0333-520-9511
E-Mail: bjlawassociate@gmail.com

Khan & Piracha
(Saleem Zulfiqar Khan and Amna Piracha)
Address: No. 1, Second Floor, 6-B Super Market, Islamabad
Office: 051-287-5542, 051-282-652, 051-282-6933
Fax: 051-282-5196, 051-282-9764

Mobile: 0321-517-9399
E-mail: kp@comsats.net.pk

Fahad Ullah Khan & Adil Jamal
Address: House 17, Street 28, F-8/1
Islamabad
Office: 051-222 2951, 051-282 1654
E-mail: info@khanandjamal.com
Website: www.khanandjamal.com

Abdul Hafiz Pirzada
Address: Senior Advocate House No. 6-A, St. 90-A
Sector G-6/3, Islamabad
Office: 051-282-7305
Residence: 051-227-3252
Fax: 051-282-7813

M. Amjad Iqbal Qureshi
Advocate Supreme Court (former Judge Islamabad High Court)
Address: Office # 6, 1st Floor Chaudhary plaza Sector F-10 Markaz, Islamabad
Office: 051-211-2485
Mobile: 0333-511-1079
E-mail: mswn2009@hotmail.com

Hafiz S. A. Rehman
Advocate
Address: 338-F Satellite Town
Rawalpindi
Office: 051-441-2906
Residence: 051-229-3261
Mobile: 0333-515-4139
E-mail: hafizsar@yahoo.com

Akram Sheikh
Senior Advocate
Address: House No. 1-A, St. 26
Sector F-6/2, Islamabad
Office: 051-2274-386/7
Mobile: 0333-5135199
0333-5134630
0300-8086666
Fax: 051-2823972
E-mail: makram.sheikh786@gmail.com
Website: http://asla.com.pk/

Syed Zafar Zaidi
Advocate Supreme Court
Address: No. 8, Shah Residency, Lane 7
Gulistan colony, Rawalpindi, Pakistan
Phone: 051-515 0356, 0333- 911 5051

Sardar Muhammad Ishaq Khan (Criminal)
Address: 55-B Rashid Minhas Road
Rawalpindi Office: 051-556-4346, 051-556-5346
Mobile: 0300-854-2142

Farrukh Karim Qureshi Address: 32-A St.38, Main Nazimuddin Rd
Sector F-10/4, Islamabad Office: 051-211-1595-8 Mobile: 0300-855-5260
E-mail: fqureshi@samdaniqureshi.com
Website: http://samdaniqureshi.com

Yousaf M. Qureshi
Address: Plot 18, Street 60,
Sector F-11/4, Islamabad
Phone: 051-227 9191-2, 0314 510 0550
Fax: 051-227 9193
E-mail: yousafqureshi@lawyer.com

RIAALAW
Islamabad Office: Nazimuddin Road Sector F-8/4, Islamabad
Office: +92 51 111529937 Fax number: +92 21 35870014, 35865107 Email: islamabad@riaalaw.com
Website: www.riaalaw.com
**** Other offices: Karachi/Lahore/Peshawar**

Syed Mohammad Tayyab
Address: 13-Lower Ground Floor, Shalimar Center
Sector F-8 Markaz, Islamabad
Office: 051-226 2742
Fax: 051- 226 2742
E-mail: tayyabisb@gmail.com

E-mail: szaz65@yahoo.com

TRADE AND PROJECT FINANCING

METHODS OF PAYMENT

Imports of goods into Pakistan generally require a Compulsory Letter of Credit (L/C), unless a special exemption is obtained in advance. Revolving, transferable, and packing letters of credit are not permissible. Letters of credit should provide for negotiation of documents within a period not exceeding 30 days from the date of shipment.

Payment to the beneficiary (stipulated in the L/C) may be made either in the country of origin or in the country of shipment of goods. Other payment terms are subject to approval by the State Bank of Pakistan (SBP). Remittances may be made soon after goods have been cleared by Customs.

Pakistan Customs authorities require a commercial invoice and a bill of lading (or airway bill). Exporters should forward documents separately if shipment is by sea, but should include them with air shipments. Until recently, "Certificates of origin" were not legally required but recently there have been cases where the Customs authorities have asked for it. Also, a statement of country of origin should appear on the invoice. Consular invoices are not required.

The exporter should also be sure to ascertain from the importer the precise number of copies of each document that will be required. Importers, depending on the specific circumstances as insurance certificates and packing lists, also may request other documents. Customs authorities require special certificates for imports of plants and plant products and used clothing (e.g., a U.S. Food and Drug Administration certificate for foods and pharmaceuticals). In order to expedite the process and to avoid potential delays and penalties, exporters should request detailed instructions from the Pakistani importer prior to shipping.

BANKING SYSTEM

The banks have increased their loans to the government and the private sector credit has decreased in last two years. Though the banks' investments in government securities are not as productive as lending to businesses and households, it has provided an avenue for banks for risk-free earnings and enabled them to post profits even in weak economic environment. The banking sector earnings continued to accumulate on the back of healthy returns on growing stocks of risk free government securities. In addition, the lower provisions also contributed towards buildup of profits. The financial sector in Pakistan is going through a major transition period. New groups are buying out Pakistan operations of foreign banks and the number of listed banks is also increasing. While the income from core banking activity is increasing due to higher business volume, earnings are also expected to further improve due to greater trends toward consumer finance, housing finance and enhanced lending to the agriculture sector.

Pakistan's banking sector consists of commercial banks, foreign banks, Islamic banks, development finance institutions (DFI's), and micro-finance banks. Presently there are 24 commercial banks, eight DFI's, and nine micro-finance banks operating in the country.

Further details about banking in Pakistan are available at: www.sbp.org.pk

FOREIGN-EXCHANGE CONTROLS

Pakistan has a very liberal foreign exchange regime and allows 100 percent repatriation of profits and dividends. Pakistan has a floating exchange rate, although the Pakistani rupee is freely convertible on the current account. During the past four years, the rupee has depreciated.

U.S. BANKS AND LOCAL CORRESPONDENT BANKS

Citibank is the only U.S. bank with operations in Pakistan, although, recently Citibank closed its consumer banking in Pakistan. A number of Pakistani banks either have branches in the U.S. or correspond with certain American banks to cater to the needs of their local and international clientele.

International Banks Operating in Pakistan:
Al Baraka Bank (Pakistan) Limited
Barclays Bank PLC
Citibank N.A. - Pakistan Operations
Deutsche Bank AG
Dubai Islamic Bank (Pakistan) Limited
HSBC Bank Middle East Limited
Industrial and Commercial Bank of China Limited
Oman International Bank SAOG
Standard Chartered Bank Limited
The Bank of Tokyo-Mitsubishi UFJ Limited

PROJECT FINANCING

Credit is allocated on market terms. Credit is allocated on market terms, and domestic interest rates have declined following interest-rate cuts by the central bank; the policy rate has fallen from 12% in June 2012 to 10% in November 2012. Foreign-controlled manufacturing, semi-manufacturing (i.e. goods that require additional processing before marketing), and non-manufacturing concerns are allowed to borrow from the domestic banking system without regulated limits.

The banks are required to ensure that total exposure to any domestic or foreign entity should not exceed 25% of banks' equity with effect from December 2014. Foreign-controlled manufacturing concerns are allowed to borrow from the domestic banking system without regulated limits. Foreign-controlled (minimum 51 percent equity stake) semi-manufacturing concerns (i.e., those producing goods that require additional processing for consumer marketing) are permitted to borrow up to 75 percent of paid-up capital, including reserves.

For non-manufacturing concerns, local borrowing caps are set at 50 percent of paid-up capital. While there are no restrictions on private sector access to credit instruments, few alternative instruments are available beyond commercial bank lending. Pakistan's domestic corporate bond, commercial paper and derivative markets remain in early stages of development.

WEB RESOURCES

Export-Import Bank of the United States: http://www.exim.gov
Country Limitation Schedule: http://www.exim.gov/tools/country/country_limits.html
OPIC: http://www.opic.gov
Trade and Development Agency: http://www.tda.gov/
SBA's Office of International Trade: http://www.sba.gov/oit/
USDA Commodity Credit Corporation: http://www.fsa.usda.gov/ccc/default.htm
U.S. Agency for International Development: http://www.usaid.gov

BUSINESS TRAVEL

BUSINESS CUSTOMS

In the major cities of Pakistan, men and women work together in offices. Most executives working for international corporations wear business attire (business suits in winter and shirt and tie in summer), and women dress conservatively and modestly. Western women traveling to Pakistan for business should dress conservatively, in pants suits or below the knee skirt suits or dresses with sleeves. Pakistan is a male dominated society; however, women are increasingly entering the job market and in most multinational offices men and women work together. In factories and other similar facilities it is not uncommon for men and women to work in segregated premises.

In most parts of the country meetings generally run late and last minute changes are not unusual. It is important to promptly respond to all communications.

During a meeting it is customary for the host to offer tea to business visitors. Most meetings will start with an exchange of pleasantries and very often the host will engage the U.S. visitor in small talk for several minutes; personal connections and relationships are important in Pakistan's business environment. Business cards are usually exchanged during the meetings.

TRAVEL ADVISORY

The travel advisory for Pakistan is available on the following website under the U.S. Citizen Services caption:

http://islamabad.usembassy.gov/

http://travel.state.gov/travelandbusiness

http://travel.state.gov/travel/cis_pa_tw/cis/cis_992.html

VISA REQUIREMENTS

U.S. citizens are required to obtain a visa for Pakistan before arrival in the country and are advised to apply for their visas well ahead of their anticipated travel. Further information on obtaining a Pakistani visa in the U.S. may be obtained from the following website:

http://www.embassyofpakistanusa.org

U.S. companies that require travel of foreign businesspersons to the United States should familiarize themselves with the visa process by going to the following links:

State Department Visa Website: http://travel.state.gov/visa/index.html

http://travel.state.gov/travel/cis_pa_tw/cis/cis_992.html#safety

United States Visas.gov: http://www.unitedstatesvisas.gov

U.S. Embassy, Islamabad: www.islamabad.usembassy.gov

U.S. Companies that require travel of foreign businesspersons to the United States should be advised that security evaluations are handled via an interagency process. Visa applicants should go to the following links.

State Department Visa Website: http://travel.state.gov/visa/

TELECOMMUNICATIONS

During the past five years, the telecommunication sector in Pakistan has grown tremendously. The privatized Pakistan Telecommunication Company Limited (PTCL) is the sole provider of landline service; however, there are now five cellular companies (Mobilink, Telenor, Ufone, Warid and Zong) operating in the market. In addition, there are four firms offering Wireless Local Loop (WLL) service. In addition to these services, there are several card payphone services, which offer highly competitive international calling rates, especially to the United States and United Kingdom.

Pakistan offers one of the lowest telecom rate structures in the region. The average tariff for the United States, using a pre-paid calling card, is currently Rs. 2.5 per minute (approximately 2.5cents per minute). Internet is widely available throughout the country, and there are several companies that offer fairly good DSL and Broadband connections. Most upscale hotels have business centers that offer a complete range of telecommunication facilities; most hotels now offer Wi-Fi networks for their guests.

TRANSPORTATION

In all large Pakistani cities, taxis are readily available and the fares are quite reasonable, although in most case the fare has to be negotiated in advance. Due to security reasons, U.S. travelers are advised not to use taxis. Instead, it is recommended that travelers rent a car, preferably from the hotel or guesthouse where they are staying or make use of the radio cab services, which is available in Karachi, Lahore and Islamabad. Most hotels and guesthouses in Pakistan provide complimentary airport pick-up service if they are informed in advance. When renting a car, either from the hotel or a rental agency, it is recommended that services of a chauffeur are also acquired along with the car. All the major airports in Pakistan offer radio cab service at a fixed, non-negotiable rate.

Air Transport:

No U.S. air carriers fly to Pakistan; however, there are several connecting flights from Dubai, Abu Dhabi, Doha and European and Asian cities to Karachi, Lahore, Islamabad and Peshawar. Pakistan International Airlines (PIA) has regular flights to New York (with one stopover in Europe). Other than PIA, Etihad, Emirates and Qatar Airways provide convenient connections to New York, Chicago, Houston and Washington, DC via Abu Dhabi, Dubai and Doha. The Pakistan International Airlines offers the largest network of domestic and international destinations. In addition to PIA, there are three other private airlines - namely Airblue, Shaheen Air International and the recently introduced Air Indus. There are also private air charter services, one of which is Princely Jets.

Shaheen Air International (SAI):

SAI was previously managed by Shaheen Foundation (a subsidiary of Pakistan Air Force). In July 2004 it was taken over by the Canadian group TAWA International.

Shaheen Air got its start as Pakistan's second national carrier. Shaheen Air International has twelve self-owned Boeing 737-200's in its fleet, and there are plans to acquire more in the near future. Shaheen Air International operates to a total of 14 destinations of which 5 are domestic and 9 international, and plans to operate new flights to the UK and Canada. The airline carries around 652,000 passengers annually.

Airblue:

This private airline commenced operations in June 2004; its fleet comprises three Airbus A320s and two A321s on dry lease, and one A321 on wet lease. Airblue operates domestic flights between Karachi, Lahore, Islamabad, Peshawar, Quetta, Faisalabad, and Gawadar. Airblue also operates daily international flights to Dubai from Karachi and Lahore, four flights a week to Dubai from Islamabad, and three flights a week to Dubai from Peshawar. Airblue commenced flights on the Lahore-Islamabad route in January 2007; in addition, Airblue introduced direct flights to Manchester from Pakistan in June 2007. Airblue has a 30 percent share of the domestic market and its revenue base is over $150 million. It employs cutting-edge IT systems and is the first airline in the region to operate 100 percent on e-tickets.

Air Indus:

Air Indus is another private airline with its headquarters based out of Karachi. Air Indus operates 3 Boeing 737-300 aircraft and started operations since 28 July 2014. With a very small fleet, airline links all major cities in Pakistan.

Princely Jets:

Akbar Group of Pakistan launched Princely Jets, another charter service, in 2006. Currently their fleet consists of a Bombardier- Challenger and Citation Bravo.

PIA, Airblue, and Shaheen offer online reservation services. Travelers on these three carriers can now make reservations and obtain e-tickets through the Internet. The relevant websites are as follows:

Pakistan International Airlines: www.piac.com.pk

Air Blue: www.airblue.com

Shaheen Airlines: www.shaheenair.com

JS Air: www.jsair.com.pk

Princely Jets: www.princelyjets.com

LANGUAGE

Urdu is the national language of Pakistan, but English remains an official language and is widely spoken and understood in most of the cities and urban areas. In the rural areas, the services of an interpreter may be required. All business correspondence is in English.

HEALTH

U.S. visitors seeking medical care in Pakistan will be expected to pay in cash at the time of service or on discharge from a hospital. Travelers to Pakistan are strongly recommended to verify that that their insurance company will honor overseas claims. Also, business travelers are advised that the U.S. Government will not arrange or pay for medical evacuations of unofficial U.S. citizens (private American citizens) overseas.

Polio Vaccination: Effective from June 1, 2014, passengers traveling outside of Pakistan will be required to provide proof of polio vaccination at the time of departing the country. This requirement has been mandated by the World Health Organization (WHO).

Food- and water-borne illnesses: Tap water and drinks with ice in Pakistan are generally not considered safe. Travelers should drink only bottled water or other bottled beverages. If thoroughly cooked hot foods are eaten, most food-borne infections can be avoided. Raw fruits should only be eaten if they have unbroken skin and can be peeled, or if they have been soaked in bleach. Travelers should avoid foods that may have been un-refrigerated for over two hours, particularly those containing poultry, eggs, meat and dairy products.

Healthcare facilities: Most of the major cities in Pakistan have fairly good hospitals and healthcare facilities. The Aga Khan Hospital in Karachi, Doctor's Hospital in Lahore and the Shifa International Hospital in Islamabad have several foreign trained doctors.

LOCAL TIME, BUSINESS HOURS, AND HOLIDAYS

Most private offices in Pakistan work from 9:00 a.m. to 6:00 p.m., with the week starting on Mondays and ending on Fridays. Some private sector offices observe a 6-day week and are open on Saturdays, but banks are generally closed on Saturdays. Government offices are usually open from 8:00 a.m. to 3:00 p.m. between Mondays and Thursdays. On Fridays, most government offices close at 12:30 p.m. for weekly Friday prayers. Business visitors planning a trip to Pakistan should take into account the following local holidays before finalizing their travel itinerary:

Pakistani Holidays:

- Pakistan Independence: Day August 14
- *Eid-ul-Fitr: July 29, 30, & 31
- *Eid ul Azha: Oct. 5, 6 & 7
- Iqbal Day: Nov. 9
- *9th & 10th of Muharram Nov. 3 & 4
- Birthday of Quaid-i-Azam: December 25

* (Based on the Islamic lunar calendar and may differ by one or two days from the expected dates – please check before travel or making appointments)

During the Islamic month of Ramadan, observant Muslims do not eat, drink, or smoke between sunrise and sunset. During this month, travel is more difficult, the pace of business activity slows (many offices close by mid-day), and it is therefore more difficult to accomplish business objectives. Ramadan begins 29 or 30 days before the festival of Eid-ul-Fitr. The month of Ramadan will commence on or about June 29 and end on July 28, 2014.

TEMPORARY ENTRY OF MATERIALS AND PERSONAL BELONGINGS

Temporary Entry of Materials and Personal Belongings: Current information regarding temporary entry of materials and personal belongings is available on the following website: http://www.fbr.gov.pk/tpef/customs/Brochures/Brochure-014.pdf

WEB RESOURCES

Pakistan Embassy, Washington, DC: http://www.embassyofpakistanusa.org/
Pakistan International Airlines: www.piac.com.pk
Air Blue: www.airblue.com
Shaheen Airlines: www.shaheenair.com
Air Indus: www.airindus.com.pk
JS Air: www.jsair.com.pk
Princely Jets: www.princelyjets.com

IMPORTANT GOVERNMENT AND BUSINESS CONTACTS

U.S. GOVERNMENT TRADE RELATED CONTACTS IN PAKISTAN

Commercial Counselor: David McNeill
U.S. Commercial Service
United States Embassy
Diplomatic Enclave, Ramna 5
Islamabad, Pakistan
Tel: 92-51-208-2449
Fax: 92-52-282-3981
E-mail: David.McNeill@trade.gov
E-mail: Cheryl.Dukelow@trade.gov (effective October 1, 2014)

Senior Commercial Specialist: Tariq Sayeed
U.S. Commercial Service
United States Embassy
Diplomatic Enclave, Ramna 5
Islamabad, Pakistan
Tel: 92-51-208-2064
Fax: 92-52-282-3981
E-mail: Tariq.Sayeed@trade.gov

Commercial Specialist: Ayan Ali Khan
U.S. Commercial Service
United States Embassy
Diplomatic Enclave, Ramna 5
Islamabad, Pakistan
Tel: 92-51-208-2963
Fax: 92-52-282-3981
E-mail: Ayanali.Khan@trade.gov

Commercial Specialist – Karachi: Malik Attiq
US Commercial Service
American Consulate General

Plot No. 3.4.5. New TPX Area
Mai Kolachi Road
Karachi- Pakistan
Tel: 92-21-3527-5017
Fax: 92-21-3561-2413\
E-mail: Malik.Attiq@trade.gov

Commercial Specialist – Lahore: Aftab Qamar
U.S. Commercial Service
U.S. Consulate General
50 Empress Road
Lahore, Pakistan
Tel: 92-42-3603-4082
Fax: 92-42-3603-4229
E-mail: Aftab.Qamar@trade.gov

Commercial Assistant – Lahore: Hassan Raza
U.S. Commercial Service
U.S. Consulate General
50 Empress Road
Lahore, Pakistan
Tel: 92-42-3603-4271
Fax: 92-42-3603-4229
E-mail: Hassan.Raza@trade.gov

USDA Agriculture Counselor for Pakistan: Clay Hamilton
U.S. Foreign and Agriculture Service
United States Embassy
Diplomatic Enclave, Ramna 5
Islamabad, Pakistan
Tel: 92-51-208-2274
Fax: 92-51-227-8142
Email: HamiltonCM@state.gov
Email: Clay.Hamilton@fas.usda.gov

AMERICAN CONSULATE
11-HOSPITAL ROAD
PESHAWAR CANTT
Peshawar, Pakistan
Tel: 92-91-526-8800
Fax: 92-91-527-6712 & 528-4171

U.S. Government Trade Related Contacts in Washington, D.C.
International Trade Administration
Africa, Near East, and South Asia
U.S. Department of Commerce
St, 14th Constitution Avenue, N.W.
Washington, D.C. 20230-0001
Tel: 240-755-4782
Fax: 202-482-5179 & 954-730-2117

Trade Information Center (TIC)
U.S. and Foreign Commercial Service
International Trade Administration

U.S. Department of Commerce
E-mail: tic@trade.gov
Website: www.export.gov

Foreign Agricultural Service (FAS)
U.S. Department of Agriculture
Box 1052
1400 Independence Ave., S.W.
Washington, D.C. 20250-1052
Tel: 202-720-7420
Fax: 202-690-4374
Website: www.fas.usda.gov

PAKISTAN MISSION IN THE UNITED STATES

Minister (Trade)
Embassy of Pakistan
3517 International Court, N.W.
Washington, D.C.
Tel: 202-243-6500
Fax: 202-686-6373
Email: commercialsection@embassyofpakistanusa.org
Website: http://www.embassyofpakistanusa.org

Commercial Counselor
Commercial Section
Consulate General of Pakistan
12 East, 65th Street
New York, NY 10065
Tel: 212-879-5800
Fax: 212-517-6987
E-mail: info@pakistanconsulateny.org
Website: http://www.pakistanconsulateny.org

Trade & Industry Associations (U.S. and Pakistan)
American Business Council of Pakistan
F-30, Block-7
K.D.A. Scheme No. 5
Kehkashan, Clifton
Karachi, Pakistan
Tel: 92-21-3587-7351 and 52; 3587-7390
Fax: 92-21-3587-7391
Email: abcpak@cyber.net.pk
Website: www.abcpk.org.pk

American Business Forum
NetSol IT Village, Main Ghazi Road
Lahore, Pakistan
Tel: 92-42-111-448-800; 3570-1061 (ext: 413)
Fax: 92-42-3570-1063
Website: http://www.abf.com.pk

Federation of Pakistan Chambers of Commerce and Industry
Federation House, Main Clifton Road

Karachi, Pakistan
Tel: 92-21-3587-3691, 93, 94;
(President's Office Direct Tel: 92-21-3587-3640)
Fax: 92-21-3587-4332;
(President's Office Direct Fax: 92-21-35873131)
Email: info@spcci.com.pk
Website: www.fpcci.com.pk

Overseas Investors Chamber of Commerce and Industry
Chamber of Commerce Building
Talpur Road, P.O. Box 4833
Karachi-74000, Pakistan
Tel: 92-21-3241-0814 and 15
Fax: 92-21-3242-7315
Email: Janet @oicci.org
Website: www.oicci.org

Karachi Chamber of Commerce and Industry
Aiwan-e-Tijarat Road, Off Shahrah-e-Liaquat
P.O. Box 4158
Karachi, Pakistan
Tel: 92-21-9921-8020; 9921-8030
Fax: 92-21-9921-8040
Email: president@kcci.com.pk
Website: www.kcci.com.pk

Islamabad Chamber of Commerce and Industry
Chamber House
Aiwan-e-Sanat-o-Tijarat Road
Sector G-8/1
Islamabad, Pakistan
Tel: 92-51-225-0526; 225-3145
Fax: 92-51-225-2950
Email: icci@brain.net.pk
Website: www.icci.com.pk

Rawalpindi Chamber of Commerce and Industry
39 Mayo Road, Civil Lines
Rawalpindi, Pakistan
Tel: 92-51-511-1051-54
Fax: 92-51-511-1055
Email: rcci@rcci.org.pk
Website: www.rcci.org.pk

Lahore Chamber of Commerce and Industry
11 Shahrah-e-Aiwan-e-Tijarat
Lahore, Pakistan
Tel: 92-42-111-222-499
Fax: 92-42-3636-8854
Website: www.lcci.com.pk

Sarhad Chamber of Commerce and Industry
G.T. Road
Peshawar, Pakistan

Tel: 92-91-921-3313 up to 15
Fax: 92-91-921-3316
Email: sccip.psh@gmail.com
Website: www.kpcci.org.pk

Quetta Chamber of Commerce and Industry
Zarghoon Road, P.O. Box 117
Quetta Cantt.
Tel: 92-81-282-1943; 283-5717
Fax: 92-81-282-1948
Email: qcci1@hotmail.com
Website: www.qcci.com.pk

Executive Director: Esperanza Gomez Jelalian
U.S. - Pakistan Business Council
U.S. Chamber of Commerce
1615 H Street, N.W.
Washington, D.C. 20062-2000
Fax: (202) 822-2491
E-Mail: uspbc@uschamber.com
Website: http://www.uspakistan.org

Government of Pakistan Offices
Secretary
Ministry of Commerce
Room 402, 4th Floor
Block-A, Pakistan Secretariat
Islamabad, Pakistan
Tel: 92-51-921-0277 and 910-3949
Fax: 92-51-920-3104
Email: secy@commerce.gov.pk
Website: www.commerce.gov.pk

Secretary
Ministry of Industries, Production & Special Initiatives
Room 110, 1st Floor
Block-A, Pakistan Secretariat
Islamabad, Pakistan
Tel: 92-51-921-1709 and 921-0192
Fax: 92-51-920-7748
Email: secretary@moip.gov.pk
Website: www.moip.gov.pk

Secretary
Ministry of National Food Security & Research
Room 311, 3rd Floor
Block-B, Pakistan Secretariat
Islamabad, Pakistan
Tel: 92-51-920-3307 and 921-0351
Fax: 92-51-920-6689
Email: secretarynfsr@Yahoo.com

Secretary
Ministry of Finance & Revenue

Room 213, 2nd Floor, Q-Block, Pakistan Secretariat
Islamabad, Pakistan
Tel: 92-51-920-2373; 920-3424
Fax: 92-51-920-1857
Email: secretary@finance.gov.pk
Website: www.finance.gov.pk

Punjab Board of Investment and Trade
23-Aikman Road, GOR-1
Lahore, Pakistan
Tel: 92-42-9920-5201 Ext 102; 92-42- 9920-4114
Fax: 92-42-9920-5171
Website: http://www.pbit.gop.pk

Sindh Board of Investment
Government of Sindh
1st Floor, Tower B
Finance & Trade Center
Shahra-e-Faisal, Karachi
Tel: 92-21-9920-7512 up to 4
Fax: 92-21-9920-7515
Email: info@sbi.gos.pk
Website: http://www.sbi.gos.pk

Director General, Americas
Ministry of Foreign Affairs
Constitution Avenue
Islamabad, Pakistan
Tel: 92-51-920-6206; 905-6634
Fax: 92-51-920-6206
Website: www.mofa.gov.pk

Director General
Civil Aviation Authority Headquarters
Terminal 1 Building
Quaid-e-Azam International Airport
Karachi
Phone: 92-21-9924-2002-3; 9907-1111; Ext 2001
Fax: 92-21- 9924-2004
Email: dgcaa@caapakistan.com.pk
Website: www.caapakistan.com.pk

Chairman
Securities and Exchange Commission of Pakistan
Ministry of Finance
NIC Building, Jinnah Avenue
Islamabad-44000, Pakistan
Tel: 92-51-920-3609 4; Ext 203 /920-7598
Fax: 92-51-920-4915
Website: www.secp.gov.pk

Directorate General Defense Purchase (DGDP)
Ministry of Defense Purchase
Pakistan Secretariat No. II

Adam Jee Road
Saddar, Rawalpindi
Pakistan
Tel: 92-51-927-0967
Fax: 92-51-927-0964

Chief Executive
Trade Development Authority of Pakistan (TDAP)
Government of Pakistan
5th Floor, Block A, Finance & Trade Centre
P.O. Box No. 1293, Shahrah-e-Faisal,
Karachi 75200, Pakistan.
Tel: 92-21-9920-6806
UAN: 92-21-111-444-111
Fax: 92-21-9920-2718
Email: tdap@tdap.gov.pk
Website: http://www.tdap.gov.pk

Chairman
Board of Investment (BOI)
Attaturk Avenue, G-5/1
Islamabad
Ph: 92-51-920-8717; 92-51-921-1999
Fax: 92-51-921-8323
Email: Chairman@boi.gov.pk
Website: www.pakboi.gov.pk

Federal Board of Revenue
FBR House
Constitution Avenue, Sector G-5
Islamabad, Pakistan
Ph: 92-51-920-1938; 920-8827
Fax: 92-51-920-5307; 920-5308
Website: www.fbr.gov.pk

Chairman
Karachi Port Trust
KPT Head Office
2nd Floor, Karachi
Ph: 92-21-9921-4310; 92-21-9921-4315
Fax: 92-21-9921-4330
Email: Chairman@kpt.gov.pk
Website: www.kpt.gov.pk

Chairman
Port Mohammad Bin Qasim Authority
Bin Qasim
Karachi – 75020, Pakistan
Ph: 92-21-9927-2147; 92-21-3473-0110
Fax: 92-21-3473-0109
Email: secretary@pqa.gov.pk
Website: www.pqa.gov.pk

Chief Collector Customs

Pakistan Customs
Customs House
Karachi
Ph: 92-21-9921-4170; 92-21-9921-4166: 21-9921-4980
Fax: 92-21-9921-4134; 92-21-9921-4172
Website: www.fbr.gov.pk

Managing Director
Pakistan International Airlines (PIA)
PIA Head Office
Jinnah International Airport
Karachi-75200, Pakistan
Ph: 92-21-3457-5900; 111-786-786
Fax: 92-21-3457-2225
Email: info@piac.aero
Email: mdpiac@piac.aero
Website: www.piac.com.pk

Governor
State Bank of Pakistan
3rd Floor, Central Directorate
State Bank Building
I.I. Chundrigar Road
Karachi, Pakistan
Ph: 92-21-9921-2447 and 448
Fax: 92-21-9921-2446.
Email: Governor.office@sbp.org.pk
Website: www.sbp.org.pk

Managing Director
Pakistan Tourism Development Corporation (PTDC)
Flashman's Hotel, The Mall
Rawalpindi - Pakistan
Ph: 92-51-9272017-18,
Fax: 92-51-9272020
Email: Paktourslimited@gmail.com
Website: www.tourism.gov.pk

Federal Secretary
Privatization Commission
Ministry of Privatization
5-A, Expert Advisory Cell (EDB) Building
Constitution Avenue
Islamabad, Pakistan
Ph: 92-51-920-5146 to 9
Fax: 92-51-920-3076 and 9211692
Website: www.privatisation.gov.pk

Chairman
Water & Power Development Authority
Room 701, WAPDA House
Shahrah-e-Quaid-e-Azam
Lahore
Ph: 92-42-9920-2222 and 23

Fax: 92-42-9920-2505
Email: chairman@wapda.gov.pk
Website: www.wapda.gov.pk

Multilateral Development Bank Offices
The World Bank
20-A, Shahrah-e-Jamhuriat
Ramna 5, P.O. Box 1025, G-5/1
Islamabad< Pakistan
Ph: 92-51-227-9641 up to 46
Fax: 92-51-227-9648 and 49
Website: www.worldbank.org/pk

Country Director
Asian Development Bank
Pakistan Resident Mission
Level 8, North Wing
Serena Office Complex
Khayaban-e-Suharwardy
Sector G-5, P.O. Box 1863
Islamabad, Pakistan
Ph: 92-51-260-0351-69; 208-7300
Fax: 92-51-260-0365 and 66
Email: adbprm@adb.org
Website: www.adb.org/PRM

SETTING UP A BUSINESS IN PAKISTAN

INCORPORATION OF COMPANIES

In accordance with the recommendation of Corporate Law Commission, Section: 4(a) of Monopolies and Restrictive Trade Practices (Control & Prevention) Ordinance, 1970 shall be deleted/repealed. There will be no ceiling of total value of assets of an undertaking/company for retaining 100% ownership by the investors.

1. METHODS OF CONDUCTING BUSINESS

There are three main forms of business:

a) Sole Proprietorship

b) Partnership

C) Company

SOLE PROPRIETORSHIIP

In sole proprietorship, a business or a profession is carried out by an individual on his own account. No formal procedure or formality is required to be followed for setting up a sole proprietary concern.

PARTNERSHIP

A partnership is a business relationship entered into by a formal agreement between two or more persons or corporations carrying on a business in common. The capital for a partnership is provided by the partners who are liable for the total debts of the firms and share profit and loss of a business concern according to the terms of the partnership agreement.

Partnerships (other than banking companies) are generally limited in size to twenty partners. The interest of a partner is transferable only with the prior consent of the other partner(s). However, a partner's right to a share of the partnership income may be received on trust for another person.

For taxation purposes, partnerships are classified into:

(I) Registered and

(ii) Unregistered Firms

The income of the registered firm is subject to Super Tax, before distribution to the partners. Also the individual income of the partners is subject to income tax at the usual rates.

For unregistered firms, income tax is levied on the income and the partners are not liable to pay tax on the share of profit received from the unregistered firm(s).

COMPANY

A company is legal entity be formed under the Companies Ordinance, 1984, it can have share capital or can be formed without share capital. A company having share capital may be formed as:

(i) Company limited by share.

(ii) Company limited by guarantee.

(iii) Unlimited company.

I) Company Limited by Share

Liability of its members is limited upto the extent of their share to paid upto capital of the company. These companies may further be classified as public limited and private limited companies.

Public Limited Companies can be formed by at least seven persons by subscribing their names to the 'Memorandum & Articles of Association' of the company. The word 'Limited' must be used as the last word of its name.

Private Limited Companies may be formed by at least two persons by subscribing their names to the 'Memorandum and Articles of Association' of the company. A private limited company, by its Article of Association' is restricted to:-

(i) The right to transfer shares

(ii) The number of its members is limited to fifty

(iii) Any invitation to the public to subscribe for share is prohibited. Private Limited Company is required to use the words "(Private) Limited" as the last words of its name.

II) Company Limited by Guarantee

Means a company having the liability of its members limited by memorandum to such amount as the members may respectively undertake to contribute to the share capital of the company in the event to its winding up. The company limited by guarantee is usually formed on a 'no profit basis'. Guarantee limited companies must use the words "(Guarantee) Limited" as the last words of their name.

III) Unlimited Company

Means a company having the liability of its members unlimited.

INDUSTRIAL SUB-CONTRACTING

Incentives/Concessions

The following incentives/concessions will be admissible to the proposed zones in addition to those which are being enjoyed by Export Processing Zones.

1. Local DFIs/Banks are allowed for project financing in Zone.
2. Sale upto 20% of exports are allowed to Domestic Tariff Area subject to payment of duties and taxes.
3. Export of waste and defective items allowed to tariff area as also to bonded manufacturing units.
4. Exporters of zone will be treated at par with tariff area counterparts for freight subsidy on certain item.
5. Sub-contracting by Export Processing Zone units in tariff area is permitted. It has been allowed the other way round, so that the investors could easily utilize idle capacity.
6. Inter-unit transfer of finished goods among exporting units may be allowed.
7. "Deemed export" benefits be allowed to supplies from DTA.

Criteria For Export Oriented Units (EOU)

The criteria for establishment of Export-Oriented Units will be as under:

i) The EOU shall undertake the entire production of goods for export, except sales permitted in the domestic tariff area (DTA) - (20%).

ii) The unit shall achieve the Minimum Value Addition (MVA) value addition as to be prescribed by the National Industrial Zone Authority.

iii)) The unit shall execute a bond/legal undertaking in prescribed form with the National Industrial Zone Authority or the agency designated by Authority.

iv) The National unit shall have marketing/buy-back arrangement and track record of the promoters.

v) Raising of funds through external commercial borrowing shall be preferred where outflow capital goods tie etc., involved.

Framework of operation

The above criteria for approval of a scheme would be subject to the basic condition that the unit shall undertake to manufacture the goods in bonded warehouse under Customs control and to export its entire production for a period of 10 years ordinarily and 5 years in the case of products having high degree of technological change. The Customs Authorities are to provide bond facilities to such units wherever located which is got to be revalidated on yearly basis depending on export performance of the unit and the place is declared as ware housing station. The fiscal concessions and facilities of Export Processing and Free Trade Zone will be admissible to Export Oriented Units (EOU).

FREE EXPORT ZONES

PROFILE OF EXPORT PROCESSING ZONES AUTHORITY

ORGANIZATION:
Export Processing Zones Authority (EPZA)

ADMINISTRATIVE MINISTRY:
Ministry of Industries & Production

ESTABLISHMENT:
The Export Processing Zones Authority (EPZA) was established in 1980 [vide Ordinance-IV of 1980]

CHARTER OF EXPORT PROCESSING ZONES AUTHORITY:

- To Plan the establishment of the Export Processing Zones
- Master Programming for the development of the Export Processing Zones
- Preparation of Scheme for infrastructure and its implementation
- Sanctioning of Industrial and Commercial Units.
- Managing the Zones.

MANAGEMENT:

Export Processing Zones Authority is headed by a Chairman and its affairs are managed by the Board of Directors consisting of 9 members. The members are the Board are appointed from those organizations which are concerned with Imports & Exports of Pakistan.

PROJECTS OF EXPORT PROCESSING ZONES AUTHORITY:

The 1st Project of EPZA was Karachi Processing Zone. It is planned on 500 acres of land, out of which 200 acres have been developed. Additional 100 acres is being developed on B.O.T. basis as a Phase-II program and the balance of 200 acres are to be acquired for which the Government of Sindh has been approached.

The 200 acres of land developed for industrialization has a very good infrastructure providing all necessary utility services like electricity, gas, water and telephone etc. Initially 330 industrial plots and 70 plots for Commercial Sector (Warehousing & Trading) and 33 plots for Financial Sector were planned. Presently the industrial sector has become saturated and very few plots are now available. This situation has encouraged EPZA to establish more zones in the country.

BASIC DATE OF KARACHI EXPORT PROCESSING ZONE (Current):
No. of Industrial Units Sanction = 162
Units in Production = 107
Units in various stage of implementation = 55

TOTAL EMPLOYMENT GENERATED: About 6000 workers are presently working in the Zone out of which 50% are men and 50% women. Thus, we are also meeting the I.L.O. requirement of equal opportunity to both sexes.

EXPORT PROCESSING ZONES AUTHORITY
Landhi Industrial Area Ext. Mehran Highway, Karachi-75150 P.O.Box No.2022
UAN: 111-777-222 Fax: 773 8188 E-mail: epza@jamal.com

Direct: Chairman: Tel. No: 773 8995 - 773 8022
Director (Investment Promotion) 773 9983
G.M. (Investment Promotion) 773 9980
Manager (Investment Promotion) 773 8273
Manager (Liaison Officer) 773 9981

NEW ZONES ESTABLISHED:

- SIALKOT EXPORT PROCESSING ZONE
- RAWALPINDI EXPORT PROCESSING ZONE
- PESHAWAR EXPORT PROCESSING ZONE

NEW ZONES IN THE OFFING:

- LAHORE EXPORT PROCESSING ZONE
- QUETTA/GWADAR EXPORT PROCESSING ZONE
- MULTAN EXPORT PROCESSING ZONE
- KARACHI EXPORT PROCESSING ZONE-(PHASE-II)
- KARACHI EXPORT PROCESSING ZONE-(PHASE-III)
- HUB (BALUCHISTAN) (GAWADAR/GADANI)
- MIRPUR (AZAD KASHMIR)
- D.G. KHAN
- NOORIABAD (HYDERABAD)

FACILITIES AND INCENTIVES:

Facilities

- One window service and simplified procedure. The investor has only to fill in a simple application form, and submit the same to EPZA processes the application expeditiously and the investor is kept informed about its progress. A special feature of the Zone is that investor have to deal with only one agency, namely EPZA, during pre-investment, construction and production stages of their industries.

- All infrastructural facilities like water, electricity, gas, telex, telephone are provided in the Zone by EPZA.
- Import permits and export authorizations are issued within 24 hours by EPZA. Export authorization is issued on payment of a development surcharge of 1% on the FOB value of exports.
- Production Oriented labour Laws framed by EPZA are applicable in the Zone. EPZA is vested with responsibility to administer labour matters for all enterprises in the Zone.
- Inexpensive and hard working both skilled and unskilled labour force available in abundance.
- Sub-contracting with Tariff area industries allowed.
- The garment manufacturing units, located in Export Processing Zone shall be eligible to participate in auction of quotas.
- GSP Concessions given by various countries to imports from Pakistan are available the manufacturers in the Zone.
- Off-Shore banking & insurance facilities are available in the Zone.
- Peaceful, secure and environmentally protected work area.

INCENTIVES

- 100% ownership rights.
- 100% Repatriation of capital.
- Income chargeable under the head "Capital Gains" is exempted from Tax.
- Income accruing outside Pakistan is exempted Tax.
- Exemption of income tax for 5 years on salaries of foreigners employed in the Zone.
- 100% Repatriation of profit.
- No minimum or maximum limit for investment.
- Duty & Tax Free Imports.
- Freedom from national imports restrictions.
- Duty & Tax free export of finished products.
- All goods imported in the zone from Pakistan tariff area entitle to all concessions as allowed for exports to other countries.
- Relief from double taxation subject to bilateral agreement.
- Selling of raw materials in the tariff areas allowed after payment of duties and taxes under the law.
- Supply of goods to a customs manufacturing bond in the tariff area is allowed.

PAKISTAN'S COMPETITIVE INVESTMENT PACKAGE

	Manufacturing Sector				Non-Manufacturing Sectors		
	Priority Industries						
	V.A + Export Cat (A)	Hi-Tech & IT Cat(B)	Engg+ Chem, Agri business, housing & construction, tourism Cat(C&D)	Other Industries	Agriculture	Infrastructure & Social	Services including IT & Telecom Services
Govt. Permission	Not required except 4 specified industries *				Not required except specific licenses from concerned agencies.		
Remittance of capital, profits, dividends, etc.	Allowed				Allowed		
Upper Limit of foreign equity allowed	100%				60%	100%	Initially 100% but to be diluted to 60% within five years.
Minimum Investment Amount (M $)	No				0.3	0.3	0.3
Customs duty on import of PME	5% **	5%**	10%**	5-25%	0% ***	10%***	0-10%***
Tax relief (IDA, % of PME cost)	50%				50%		
Royalty & Technical Fee	No restriction for payment of royalty & technical fee.				Allowed as per guidelines - Initial lump-sum upto $100,000 - Max Rate 5% of net sales - Initial period 5 years		

* Specified Industries:
-Arms and ammunitions -High Explosives. -Radioactive substances -Security Printing, Currency and Mint.
No new unit for the manufacturing of alcohol, except, industrial alcohol
PME= Plant, Machinery and Equipment IDA= Initial Depreciation Allowance V.A= Value Added
** SRO: 439(I)/2005 dated 18-6-2005 ***SRO:358(I)/2002 dated 15-6-2002

INVESTMENT POLICIES & OPPORTUNITIES FOR OPs

Small Industries

The primary objective of the Small & Medium Enterprise Development Authority (SMEDA) is to provide and facilitate with support services to small & medium enterprises. SMEDA has created a network of support institutions, experts and consultants through which SMEs are helped. The limit of bank financing for SMEs has been raised by the Government from Rs. 1.5 million to Rs. 30 million. Sectoral briefs, project profiles, pre-feasibilities and data base in different fields including the following are available with them and the Overseas Pakistanis can contact SMEDA for specific details and feasibility of the project of their choice with the help of their web-site www.smeda.org.

SECTORAL BRIEFS	**PRE FEASIBILITIES**
Fisheries	Animal dairy farm
DATABASE	**IDBP PROJECT PROFILES (Available with SMEDA)**

DATABASE	IDBP PROJECT PROFILES (Available with SMEDA)
Leather	Household appliances
Surgical instruments	Agricultural implements
IT	Foundry
Agriculture	Battery Cells
Marble	Chalk manufacturing
Fans	Electronics (Capacitor)
Gems and Wooden Furnitur	Electric Appliances
	DI processing unit
	Electronics Household Appliances (A/C adapters)

CIRC Projects (Units)

Corporate and Industrial Restructuring Corporation (CIRC) has offered the following units for sale on "Where is, As is" basis. These units offer attractive investment opportunities to the Overseas Pakistanis, Infrastructure facilities like factory building, machinery and power connections are already in place in most of the units, thus requiring lesser time and effort to begin with the production process.

Summit Knitwear Private Limited

Product Knitwear
Location Old Defence Road, Near Kana Kacha at Nala Ruhi,
Capacity 3,000 Kgs of Knitted Cloth / day
Year of 1993

Central Cotton Mills Limited

Spinning Mill
Plot No. 13-14, SITE Kotri, Distt. Dadu
10,560 spindles
1980

Current Garments Industries Private Limited

Product Textile Madeups
Location Plot No. 54-B, Sector 28, Korangi Industrial Area,
Year of 1983

Delta Tyres & Rubber Company Private Ltd.

Product Tyres & Tubes Manufacturing Unit
Location Main Hattar Taxila Road, Near Telephone Exchange,
Capacity 200,000 Sets of Tyres & Tubes per annum

Capacity 200,000 Sets of Tyres & Tubes per annum

Year of Installation 1984

Dress Leather Limited

Product Leather Tannery

Location 4,000 skins per shift (8 hours)

Capacity B-73 to B-80 Hub Industrial Trading Estate, Hub

Year of Installation 1987

Farooq Paper and Board Industries

Product Paper and Board

Location 30 Kms from Lahore on Sheikhupura Road

Capacity 20 Tones/day paper and/or board

Year of Installation 1992

Goreja Steel Private Limited

Product Steel Re-Rolling

Location 18 Kms Multan Road, Lahore

Capacity 8-10 Tones of Bars/Hr (1"-1.5" dia)

Year of Installation 1991

Haji Fazal Karim Weaving Mills Private Ltd

Product Grey Cloth

Location Kanga-Raiwind Road (7 Kms from Multan Road, Lahore)

Year of Installation 1993

Hussain Holding Ghee Mills

Product Ghee & Cooking Oil

Location Aimanabad More, GT Road, Gujranwala

Capacity 60 Metric Tones of Oil and Ghee/day

Year of Installation 1990

Imtiaz Steel Private Limited

Product Steel Billets

Location Bund Road, Shadi Pura, Lahore

Capacity 5 Tones/Charge

Year of Installation 1991

Malik Food Industries Private Limited

Product Fruit Juice of Oranges, Apples, Mangoes etc. in Bottles or Tetrapack

Location	Kot Lakhpat Industrial Area, Lahore
Capacity	6,000 tones/year of Fruit Juice on 3 shifts basis from Apples, Oranges, Mangoes and Guava in up to 54 million bottles
Year of Installation	1986

Paras Textile Mills Limited

Product	Textile Spinning
Location	14 Kms Bahawalpur-Karachi highway
Capacity	24,960 spindles of East German Origin
Year of Installation	1976

Punjab Cables Limited

Product	Telephone & Telecommunication Cables, ACSR&AAC Cables (range 70 sqm to 300 sqm)
Location	33 Kms Lahore-Sheikhupura Road, Distt. Sheikhupura
Capacity	5,766 million metres of various types of cables/ single shift/300 days per annum
Year of Installation	1991

Rex-Barren Batteries Limited

Product	Automotive Batteries
Location	60,000 batteries of different sizes per annum
Capacity	49 Kms off Multan Road near Phool Nagar, Distt. Kasur
Year of Installation	1990

Shahjehan Textiles Private Limited

Product	Grey Cloth
Location	Dipalpur-Haveli Lakha Roads (24 Kms From Dipalpur, Wasavewala, Distt Okara
Year of Installation	1992

Sulfi Ghee Mills Limited

Product	Ghee & Cooking Oil
Location	Jauharabad-Muzaffargarh Road, 7 Kms from Jauharabad, Distt. Khusab
Capacity	60 Metric Tones of Oil & Ghee/day
Year of Installation	1989

Taj Ghee & General Mills Private Limited

Product	Ghee & Cooking Oil

Location	Rashidpura road, Behind Pakistan Mint, GT Road, Lahore
Capacity	60 Tones/day
Year of Installation	1991

Tech Pak Extraction Limited

Product	Oil Extraction
Location	35 Kms on Sheikhupura Faisalabad Road, Mouza Budh Singh, Manawala, Distt. Sheikhupura
Year of Installation	1991

Ujala Match Factory Limited

Product	Matches
Location	Mouza Chah Saeedan Wala & Chah Bibi Budai Wala, Jhang Road, Chiniot, Distt. Jhang
Capacity	1500 gross per shifts (8 hours)
Year of Installation	1987

Zipper International Private Limited

Product	Plastic Zip Manufacturing
Location	Aminabad More, GT Road, Gujranwala
Capacity	7 plastic Zip making machines with Auxiliary equipment and machines (Taiwan Made)
Year of Installation	Not Available

Chaudhri Cables Private Limited

Product	Electric Cables
Location	2 Kms off GT Road, Near Mannooabad, Kala Shahkaku
Year of Installation	1977

Masud Sons Industries Limited

Product	PVC Pipes
Location	Plot No. 202-203, Sector I-9, Islamabad
Capacity	2160 Tones of different dia. pipes, Rnage 1/2" to 12" dia.
Year of Installation	1981

Ali Paper and Board Industries

Product	Paper & Paper Board
Location	27 Kms Lahore-Sheikhupura Road, (about 1 Km off the road)
Capacity	15-20 tones of paper (50 - 55 gms) per 24 hrs & 30

	tones of paperboard per 24 hours
Year of Installation	Late eighties

Modern Steel Re-Rolling Mills Private Ltd.

Product	Deformed/Twisted/Plain Rods/Girders/Mesh etc.
Location	Behind MBS steel mills, Opp. Badami Bagh, Railway Station, Badami Bagh, Lahore
Capacity	8 tones/hours of bar
Year of Installation	Not available

Tourism

Tourism has been declared an industry and as such holds great promise for prospective investors interested in exploring the true potential of a land as rich and diverse in its culture as it is in its geographical distribution.

From snowcapped mountains in the north, with vast fertile plains of the Punjab, rugged land of the south, deserts and a long seacoast, Pakistan has all the hall marks to become a major tourist attraction.

In Pakistan tourism has a huge growth potential with high returns and revenue for the investor. Hotels and other tourism projects hold great promise and rewards for the investor following the concessions extended by the Government to promote this industry and facilitate the growth of tourism in the country.

Marine complexes, beach resorts and mountain resorts can effectuate a huge revenue generation for Overseas Pakistanis interested in this sector.

Sale of Hotels / Lands of PTDC

The following hotels / motels and lands owned by Pakistan Tourism Development Corporation are available for sale through Privatization :

Sr. No.	PROPERTIES	LOCATIONS
1.	Motel at Astak	Skardu
2.	Motel at Birmoglasht	Chitral
3.	Motel at Bunni	Chitral
4.	Motel at Chaman	Pak-Afghan Border, Quetta,
5.	Motel at Chattar Plain	Mansehra
6.	Motel at Hawk's Bayt	Karachi
7.	Motel at Katas	District Chakwal
8.	Motel at Khuzdar	Quetta, Balochistan
9.	Motel at Mankial	Swat
10.	Motel at Moenjodaro	Sindh
11.	Motel at Satpara Lake	Skardu

11.	Motel at Satpara Lake	Skardu
12.	Motel at Torkham	Pak-Afghan Border, NWFP
13.	Daman-e-Koh Restaurant	Islamabad
14.	Jaltarang Restaurant	Rawal Dam, Islamabad
15.	Restaurant at Bahawalpur	Bahawalpur
16.	Restaurant at Chakdara	Malakand Division
17.	Land at Bambore	Thatta-Sindh
18.	Land at Benjosa	AJK
19.	Land at Gadani Beach	Sindh
20.	Land at Garam Chashma	Chitral
21.	Land at Hyderabad	Sindh
22.	Land at Ghazikot	Mansehra
23.	Land at Muzafarabad	AJK
24.	Land at Sukkur	Sindh
25.	Land at Thalechi	Gilgit
26.	Fletti's Hotel	Lahore
27.	Flashman's Hotel	Rawalpindi
28.	Malam Jabba Resort	Malam Jabba

Corporate Agriculture Farming (CAF)

<TD < TD>

- 0% customs duty on import of agricultural machinery, equipment and implements
- Exemption of duty on transfer of land for CAF
- Tax relief; Initial deprecation allowance @ 50% of machinery cost.
- Dividends from corporate agriculture farms not subject to tax
- Farm income given more favourable treatment

Projects/Investment Opportunities

<TD < TD>

- Land development/reclamation of barren, desert and hilly land for agriculture
- purpose and crops farming
- Reclamation of waterfront areas or creeks
- Crops, fruits, vegetables, flowers farming/integrated agriculture (cultivation and processing of crops)
- Modernization and development of irrigation facilities and water management
Plantations
- Forestry
- Horticulture
- Dairy farming
- Livestock farming and breeding
- Sheep and goat farming
- Production of quality seeds
- Fruits, vegetables and flowers, grading, processing, packaging, preservation
- Seafood (farming/fishing, processing preservation of fish, shrimps and other marine products)
- Agri-produce storage facilities
- Marketing/export of agri-produce
- Cool chains

IT Sector

Information Technology (IT) has assumed unprecedented importance in the global economic arena. In Pakistan, the Present Government is according a very high priority to this sector. The Government as the main facilitator, enabler, and promoter of the IT Sector, has evolved an effective national IT Policy and Action Plan that clearly caters to the needs of nurturing the industry and is responsive to the dynamic forces of change that can effect its future growth. The Private Sector is being brought into the mainstream as the main driver for growth. The following services in Telecommunication sector has been deregulated:

- E-mail / Internet / Electronic Information Services (IES)
- Data communication Network Services
- Trunk Radio Services
- Cellular Mobile Telephone Services
- Audiotex Services
- Voice Mail Services
- Card Pay Phone Services
- Close User Group for Banking Operations
- International Satellite Operators for Domestic Data Communications
- Paging Services
- Vehicle Tracking System (VTS)
- Burglar Alarm System (BAS)

- In order to deliver efficient IT infrastructure, PTCL would now provide international bandwidth and Internet connectivity to the ISPs and other corporate customers within 4 to 8 weeks
- As a first steps towards, Electronic commerce, the State Bank of Pakistan (SBP) has allowed banks to open Internet Merchant Accounts within Pakistan
- Internet delivery on Cable TV has been permitted which would result in substantial increase in the Internet usage
- The market is being opened up for the private sector participation in joint venture with PTCL in terms of tele-housing arrangement, voice over Internet, setting up international bandwidth gateways via satellite and cable
- Universal Access to the Internet even to non connected areas at the cost of a local using the unique '131' Universal Internet Numbers of ISPs has been extended
- Call Centres, which are important potential source of foreign exchange earnings and employment creation, have been allowed to establish in the private sector
- Computer networking and majority of IT equipment has been exempted from custom duties
- Income tax holiday for the IT Training Institutions has been extended by another five years
- Income of computer training institutions set upto 30-06-2005 is exempt form Income Tax
- For providing credit to software companies, banks are allowed to accept firm contracts with foreign principals as opposed to requiring opening of LCs
- Banks are allowed to invest in the form of equity in dedicated venture
- Export of IT Software, hardware and internet enabled services made eligible for concessionary export finance under the State Bank's export refinance scheme
- Software companies are allowed to retain 25% of their export earnings in foreign exchange to meet the expenditure on purchase of hardware/software, foreign travel, marketing and hiring of consultants

Technology Parks

- Information Technology Parks (ITPs) may develop both the hardware as well as the software
- Private sector may set up such parks on BOT/BOO basis and do the same for IT Incubation Centres

- To facilitate the private sector IT telecom industry and to enhance the investor's confidence in the Government, processing period for licence application in the deregulated sector has been reduced to 7 days
- In order to deliver efficient IT infrastructure, PTCL would now provide international bandwidth and Internet connectivity to the ISPs and other corporate customers within 4 to 8 weeks
- As a first steps towards, Electronic commerce, the State Bank of Pakistan (SBP) has allowed banks to open Internet Merchant Accounts within Pakistan
- Internet delivery on Cable TV has been permitted which would result in substantial increase in the Internet usage
- The market is being opened up for the private sector participation in joint venture with PTCL in terms of tele-housing arrangement, voice over Internet, setting up international bandwidth gateways via satellite and cable
- Universal Access to the Internet even to non connected areas at the cost of a local using the unique '131' Universal Internet Numbers of ISPs has been extended
- Call Centres, which are important potential source of foreign exchange earnings and employment creation, have been allowed to establish in the private sector
- Computer networking and majority of IT equipment has been exempted from custom duties
- Income tax holiday for the IT Training Institutions has been extended by another five years
- Income of computer training institutions set upto 30-06-2005 is exempt form Income Tax
- For providing credit to software companies, banks are allowed to accept firm contracts with foreign principals as opposed to requiring opening of LCs
- Banks are allowed to invest in the form of equity in dedicated venture
- Exports of IT software, hardware and inter-enable services will be eligible for concessionary export finance under the State Bank's export refinance scheme
- Software companies are allowed to retain 25% of their export earning in foreign exchange to meet the expenditure on purchase of hardware/software, foreign travel, marketing and hiring of consultants

Technology Parks

- Information Technology Parks (ITPs) may develop both the hardware as well as the software
- Private sector may set up such parks on BOT/BOO basis and do the same for IT Incubation Centres
- The facilities/incentives being offered by Export Processing Zone Authority (EPZA) and other Industrial zones in the country will be available to ITPs be fully utilized

- Lower utility and infrastructure rates for bulk consumers to ITP users
- Software exporting companies having a minimum export obligation verifiable through the State Bank of Pakistan in locations other than ITPs should be declared as EPUs (Export Processing Units) to avail the incentives equivalent to that of ITPs. IT hardware manufacturing units having a minimum import substitution capability, should be treated similarly
- The existing software companies shall be provided land on lease as commercial rates to build their campuses

Infrastructure

There are many investment opportunities for Overseas Pakistanis in developing the country's infrastructure which are highlighted below :

Water & Power Sector

In the Water and Power Sector following are the investment opportunities:

Jinnah Barrage Hydropower Project

TRAVELING TO THE COUNTRY

US STATE DEPARTMENT SUGGESTIONS

WARNING: The Department of State warns U.S. citizens to evaluate carefully the implications for their security and safety before deciding to travel to Pakistan.

Recent information received by the U.S. Government suggests a continued need for vigilance on the part of American citizens resident in, or traveling through, Pakistan.

The U.S. Government has received a growing body of information that suggests strongly that extremists based in Afghanistan are preparing to attack U.S. interests in Pakistan, in the near future.

Given the presence of international terrorist Usama Bin Ladin in neighboring Afghanistan and the public sympathy and support for him in Pakistan, the Department urges all American citizens resident in, or traveling through, Pakistan to take appropriate steps to increase their security awareness.

Further, due to recent threats against U.S. citizens in Pakistan, on August 6, the U.S. Embassy in Islamabad decided to defer all official travel to the tribal areas of Pakistan's northwest frontier province, areas which lie outside the normal jurisdiction of the Government of Pakistan. At the same time, the U.S. Embassy urges that private Americans defer planned travel through or to the tribal areas.

Additionally, while tension between India and Pakistan over the military situation in Kargil, Kashmir, has declined, certain extremist groups in Pakistan have voiced opposition to the Government of Pakistan's role in the de-escalation. In the past, such groups have also issued threats against Americans, the U.S. Government and U.S. facilities overseas. One such group, the Harakat-Ul-Mujahideen, recently issued "a ban" against "the travel of all American citizens, including diplomats," to Kashmir in India. This group, previously known as the Harakat-Ul-Ansar, has been active on both sides of the Line of Control between India and Pakistan.

U.S. citizens in Pakistan are strongly urged to register and obtain updated security information at the American Embassy in Islamabad, the U.S. Consulate General in Karachi, the U.S. Consulate in Lahore, or the Consulate in Peshawar at the addresses listed in the Registration/Embassy Location section below.

ENTRY REQUIREMENTS: A passport and visa are required. The visa must be obtained from a Pakistani embassy or consulate before arrival. Information on entry requirements can be obtained from the Embassy of Pakistan, 2315 Massachusetts Avenue, N.W., Washington, D.C., 20048, telephone (202)939-6200. Travelers may also contact one of the Consulates General of Pakistan located at 12 East 65th St., New York, NY 10021, telephone (212)879-5800, or 18050 Wilshire Blvd., Suite 1100, Los Angeles, CA 90010, (310)441-5114. If a traveler plans to stay longer than 30 days in Pakistan, he or she must register with the local police station and obtain a residence permit. This permit must be returned to the same office for an exit visa when the traveler is preparing to leave the country. Airlines may require travelers departing the U.S. to present multiple photographs and complete copies of passports and other travel documents.

SAFETY/SECURITY/AREAS OF INSTABILITY: Rallies, demonstrations and processions occur from time to time throughout Pakistan on very short notice and have occasionally taken on an anti-American or anti-Western character. Karachi and the southern parts of Punjab province have experienced protracted political or sectarian violence that, although not explicitly anti-American, poses a potential danger to American travelers. During the Islamic religious observances of Ramadan and Moharram, sectarian rivalry and violence often increase.

Northern Areas - Visitors wishing to trek in Gilgit, Hunza, Chitral and the upper Swat valley should use only licensed guides and tourist agencies. There have been occasional assaults and in 1998, a U.S. tourist who was not accompanied by a guide was murdered in Gilgit.

Northwest Frontier Province - Because of dangerous security conditions, the U.S. Embassy has decided to defer all official travel to the tribal areas. At the present time, the U.S. Embassy urges that private Americans also defer planned travel through or to the same areas, even if traveling overland to the Khyber Pass. Substantial areas within the Northwest Frontier Province are designated tribal areas and are outside the normal jurisdiction of government law enforcement authorities. Visitors risk being caught in armed clashes between feudal tribal factions or smugglers. Carjackings and the abduction of foreigners are occasionally reported from the tribal areas. If visitors must enter the tribal areas, a permit from the Home and Tribal Affairs Department is required. The permit may stipulate that an armed escort must accompany the visitor. Even in the settled areas of the Northwest Frontier Province, there is occasional ethnic, sectarian, and political violence as well as anti-foreign rhetoric; foreigners should steer clear of such demonstrations or known areas of conflict. However, the monthly steam train excursion for tourists through the Khyber Pass is well protected by local authorities.

Punjab Province - Sectarian violence decreased considerably during the first half of 1999, from the high 1998 levels of violence, which resulted in dozens of deaths. While Americans are not targets of this violence, the foreign community is not immune, as evidenced by the 1997 assassination of five Iranians in an attack widely believed to have had sectarian overtones. As a precaution against possible dangers resulting from sectarian violence, U.S. citizens are cautioned to avoid public transportation and crowded areas.

Sindh Province - In the areas of Karachi and Hyderabad there have been recurring outbreaks of ethnic and sectarian violence characterized by random bombings, shootings and mass demonstrations. These have resulted in deaths and the imposition of curfews. There have also been numerous incidents of kidnappings for ransom. In rural Sindh Province, the security situation is hazardous, especially in regard to overland travel. Foreigners have occasionally been kidnapped and, in a 1995 incident, the foreign kidnap victim was killed in a subsequent gunfight between police and bandits. The Government of Pakistan has recommended that travelers limit their movements in Sindh Province to the city of Karachi. If visitors must go into the interior of Sindh Province, the Government of Pakistan requests that travelers inform police authorities well in advance of the trip so that necessary police security arrangements can be made.

Baluchistan Province - The province of Baluchistan, which borders both Iran and Afghanistan, is notorious for cross-border smuggling. Armed battles between clans are frequent. Because provincial police presence is limited, travelers wishing to visit the interior of Baluchistan should consult with the province's Home Secretary. Advance permission from provincial authorities is required for travel into some areas. Local authorities have detained travelers who lack permission. Although Quetta, the provincial capital, is quieter than the interior, it has experienced serious ethnic violence that has led to gun battles in the streets and the imposition of curfews.

CRIME INFORMATION: Crime is a serious concern for foreigners throughout Pakistan, with violent crime increasing faster than any other category. Carjackings, armed robberies, house invasions and other violence against civilians have increased steadily in the major urban areas. Lahore and Karachi, in particular, experience high levels of crime. They are large cities beset by poverty, high unemployment, and underpaid, under-manned police forces. Travelers in Karachi are encouraged to use hotel shuttles from the airport rather than taxis, which are subject to police harassment, especially after dark. Petty crime, especially theft of personal property, is common throughout Pakistan.

The loss or theft of a U.S. passport abroad should be reported immediately to local police and to the nearest U.S. Embassy or Consulate. U.S. citizens can refer to the Department of State pamphlets *A Safe Trip Abroad* and *Tips for Travelers to South Asia* for ways to promote a more trouble-free journey. The pamphlets are available by mail from the Superintendent of Documents, U.S. Government Printing Office, Washington, D.C. 20402, via the Internet at http://www.access.gpo.gov/su_docs, or via the Bureau of Consular Affairs home page at http://travel.state.gov.

MEDICAL FACILITIES: Adequate medical care is available in major cities in Pakistan, but is limited in rural areas. Serious medical problems requiring hospitalization and/or medical evacuation to the United States can cost thousands of dollars or more. Doctors and hospitals often expect immediate cash payment for health services, and U.S. medical insurance is not always valid outside the United States. U.S. Medicare and Medicaid programs do not provide payment for medical services outside the United States.

MEDICAL INSURANCE: Uninsured travelers who require medical care overseas may face extreme difficulties. Check with your own insurance company to confirm whether your policy applies overseas, including provision for medical evacuation. Ascertain whether payment will be made to the overseas hospital or doctor or whether you will be reimbursed later for expenses you incur. Some insurance policies also include coverage for psychiatric treatment and for disposition of remains in the event of death. Useful information on medical emergencies abroad, including overseas insurance programs, is provided in the Department of State, Bureau of Consular Affairs brochure *Medical Information for Americans Traveling Abroad*, available via the Bureau of Consular Affairs Internet home page or by autofax at 202-647-3000.

OTHER HEALTH INFORMATION: Information on vaccinations and other health precautions may be obtained from the Centers for Disease Control and Prevention's hotline for international travelers at 1-877-FYI-TRIP (1-877-394-8747); fax: 1-888-CDC-FAXX (1-888-232-3299), or via their Internet site at http://www.cdc.gov.

TRAFFIC SAFETY AND ROAD CONDITIONS: Road travel in Pakistan is risky. Roads are crowded, drivers are aggressive and poorly trained, and many vehicles, particularly large trucks and buses, are badly maintained. Roads, including most major highways, also suffer from poor maintenance and often have numerous potholes, sharp drop-offs and barriers that are not sign-posted. Driving without experienced local drivers or guides is not recommended. For specific current information on road conditions along the Karakoram Highway, travelers may contact the Frontier Works Organization in Rawalpindi at telephone 92-51-566639.

The information below concerning traffic safety and road conditions in Pakistan is provided for general reference only, and may not be totally accurate in a particular location or circumstance.

Safety of Public Transportation: Poor
Urban Road Condition/Maintenance: Good to Poor
Rural Road condition/Maintenance: Poor
Availability of Roadside Assistance: Poor

AVIATION SAFETY OVERSIGHT: The U.S. Federal Aviation Administration (FAA) has assessed the Government of Pakistan's Civil Aviation Authority as Category 2 -- not in compliance with international aviation safety standards for oversight of Pakistan's air carrier operations. While consultations to correct the deficiencies are ongoing, Pakistan's air carriers are permitted to conduct limited operations to the U.S. subject to heightened FAA surveillance. For further information, travelers may contact the Department of Transportation within the U.S. at 1-800-322-7873, or visit the FAA's Internet website at http://www.faa.gov/avr/iasa/index.htm. The U.S. Department of Defense (DOD) does not permit its personnel to use air carriers from Category 2 countries for official business except for flights originating from or terminating in the U.S. For information regarding the DOD policy on specific carriers, travelers may contact DOD at 618-229-4801.

CUSTOMS REGULATIONS: Import of firearms, pornographic material and alcohol is restricted. An import permit and health certificate are required for animals. There are also restrictions on leaving Pakistan with antiquities or animals. Contact the Pakistani Embassy in Washington, DC or the nearest Pakistani consulate for specific information regarding customs.

CRIMINAL PENALTIES: While in a foreign country, a U.S. citizen is subject to that country's laws and regulations, which sometimes differ significantly from those in the United States and may not afford the protections available to the individual under U.S. law. Penalties for breaking the law can be more severe than in the United States for similar offenses. Persons violating Pakistani laws, even unknowingly, may be expelled, arrested or imprisoned. Penalties for possession of, use of, or trafficking in illegal drugs are strictly enforced. Long jail sentences are frequently imposed and large fines are assessed in some cases. Legislation passed in 1994 makes trafficking offenses punishable by death.

SPECIAL CIRCUMSTANCES: Pakistan is largely a cash economy. Personal checks are not commonly accepted. Most Pakistanis do not use checking accounts for routine transactions. Credit cards and traveler's checks are accepted by only a few establishments in the larger cities. There are bank branches as well as registered money changers in all international airports. ATMs are usually not found in airports. English is widely spoken by professional level airport staff. It is best to agree on taxi fares before hiring a driver. Currently, U.S. Embassy employees are restricted from using taxis for security reasons.

CHILDREN'S ISSUES: For information on international adoption of children, international parental child abduction, and international child support enforcement issues, please refer to our Internet site at http://travel.state.gov/children's_issues.html or telephone 202-736-7000.

REGISTRATION/EMBASSY AND CONSULATE LOCATIONS: American citizens living in or visiting Pakistan are encouraged to register at the Consular Section of the U.S. Embassy or Consulate in Pakistan and obtain updated information on travel and security within Pakistan. They are located at the following addresses:

-- The U.S. Embassy in Islamabad is located at Diplomatic Enclave, Ramna 5, telephone 92-51-2080-0000; consular section telephone (92-51) 2080-2700, fax (92-51) 822--632, web site http://usembassy.state.gov/posts/pk1/wwwhusis.html.

-- The U.S. Consulate General in Karachi is located at 8 Abdullah Haroon Road, telephone (92-21) 568-5170 (after hours: 92-21-568-1606), fax (92-21) 568-0496, web site http://usembassy.state.gov/posts/pk2/wwwhamcn.html.

-- In U.S. Consulate in Lahore is located on Sharah-E-Abdul Hamid Bin Badees, 50 Empress Road, New Simla Hills, telephone (92-42) 636-5530, fax (92-42) 636-5177, web site http://usconsulate-lahore.org.pk.

-- The U.S. Consulate in Peshawar is located at 11 Hospital Road, Peshawar Cantonment, telephone (92-91) 279-801, fax (92-91) 276-712, web site http://brain.net.pk/~consul/.

The normal work week in Pakistan is Monday through Saturday, with a half-day worked on Friday. However, the U.S. Embassy and consulates are open Monday through Friday.

GETTING THERE

Air

Pakistan's national airline is *Pakistan International Airlines (PK)*, linking Pakistan with 47 destinations around the world.

Approximate flight times

From Karachi to *Los Angeles* is 22 hours 30 minutes, to *New York* is 21 hours 40 minutes, to *Riyadh* is 3 hours 35 minutes, to *London* is 11 hours 50 minutes and to *Singapore* is 6 hours 55 minutes.

International airports

Karachi (KHI) (Quaid-e-Azam) is 15km (10 miles) northeast of the city (travel time - 25 minutes). Coaches to the city meet all arrivals. A bus runs from dusk to dawn every 30 minutes. Taxi services to the city are available. Good airport facilities exist, including duty-free shops, restaurant, post office, bank and shops.
Lahore (LHE), 18km (5 miles) southeast of the city (travel time - 20 minutes). Coaches leave every 20 minutes for the city. Buses go every 10 minutes. Taxi services to the city are also available. Airport facilities include car hire, bank, restaurant and shops. *Islamabad (ISB)* (Islamabad International) is 15km (9 miles) east of the city (travel time - 20 minutes). Coach and taxi services to the city are available. There are full duty-free facilities. *Peshawar (PEW)*, 4km (2.5 miles) from the city (travel time - 10 minutes). Full bus and taxi services to the city are available.

Departure tax

PRs800 for passengers travelling first class, PRs600 for club class and PRs400 for economy class. Transit passengers and children under two years of age are exempt.

Sea

The major port is Karachi (Kemari). It is both Pakistan's and Afghanistan's port for goods, together with Port Qasim. No passenger boats or ships for the general public sail to or from Pakistan at present.

Train

The Lahore-Delhi *Samjhota Express* leaves Lahore at 11 AM on Mondays and Thursdays. Check-in time at Lahore is 8 AM.
A rail link extends from Quetta (via the border crossing at Taftan) to Zahedan, Iran; the express train leaves Quetta every Friday at 10.50 AM (journey time - 27 hours); and the passenger train, which only travels as far as Taftan, leaves every Tuesday at 1045 from Quetta.

Road

From China: the Khunjerab Pass is open between May 1-October 31 for groups and until November 15 for individual tourists. Customs and Immigration posts are open daily from 8.30 AM-11 AM for outgoing tourists and until 4 PM for incoming tourists. Transport includes buses, vans and 4-wheel-drive vehicles.
From India: Wagha is the only land border open between Pakistan and India (Lahore-Amritsar route). The border post is open daily 8.30 AM-2.30 PM from April 16-October 15, and 9 AM-3 PM from October 16-April 15. A minibus leaves for Wagha from Lahore railway station every 15 minutes and there are also taxis available (travel time - 30 minutes).
From Iran: Travel is only possible via the Quetta-Taftan-Zahedan route. The border is open from 9 AM-5 PM. Several buses and coaches leave daily from Quetta to Taftan (journey time - 18 hours).
There is also a road from Kabul, Afghanistan to Peshawar.

Note: Visitors exiting Pakistan by land routes are subject to a road toll of PRs2.

GETTING AROUND

Air

Most domestic services are operated by *Pakistan International Airlines (PK)*. Other airlines are *Aero Asia* and *Shaheen*. There are many daily flights from Karachi to Lahore, Rawalpindi and other commercial centres. Air transport is the quickest and most efficient means of travel.

Departure tax

PRs40 for internal flights. Children under 2 years are exempt.

River

Traffic along the Indus River is almost exclusively commercial. Many goods are carried to Punjab and the north from the main port at Karachi.

Train

A legacy of British rule is Pakistan's extensive rail network. The main line, from Karachi to Lahore, Rawalpindi and Peshawar, has several daytime and overnight trains. Most other routes have several daily trains. Even first-class compartments can be hot and crowded. Travel in air-conditioned coaches is advised, as are reservations on long-distance journeys and overnight service. Children under 3 years of age travel free. Children aged 3-11 years pay half fare. *Pakistan Railways* offer concessions for tourists (on presentation of a certificate issued by PTDC), excluding Indian nationals travelling by rail. A discount of 25% is offered to individuals and groups, and 50% for students. Vehicles owned by foreign tourists or hired locally are also eligible for a 25% discount in freight charges when transported by rail. Details are available from railway offices in Pakistan.

Approximate travel times

Karachi to Lahore is 16 hours, to Rawalpindi is 28 hours and to Peshawar is 32 hours; and *Lahore* to Rawalpindi is 6 hours.

Road

Traffic drives on the left. The highway network between cities is well-maintained.

Bus

Regular services run between most towns and villages. Lahore-Rawalpindi-Peshawar has an hourly service. Air-conditioned coaches/buses are recommended for long distances. Advance booking is advised.

Car rental

Available in major cities, as well as at Karachi, Lahore and Rawalpindi airports. Most hotels can book cars for guests.

Documentation

An International Driving Permit is required.

Urban

Extensive bus and minibus services operate in Lahore, Karachi and other towns, although services can be crowded. **Taxi:** Reasonably priced and widely available, they are by far the most efficient means of urban travel. Note that they may not operate after sunset during Ramadan.

Auto-rickshaws are also available.

ACCOMMODATION

HOTELS

Pakistan offers a wide range of accommodation. Modern well-equipped hotels are to be found in most major towns and offer excellent facilities such as swimming pools and sports facilities. There are also cottages, Dak bungalows and rest houses in all principal hill stations and health resorts. A government room tax of 15% is added to the cost of accommodation. In all cases it is advisable to book well in advance and check reservations. For further information contact the Pakistan Hotels Association, PO Box 7448, Ground Floor, Shafi Court, Merewether Road, Civil Lines, Karachi 4 (tel: (21) 568 6407 *or* 568 5186; fax: (21) 568 3116).

PTDC HOTELS & MOTELS

The Pakistan Tourism Development Corporation (PTDC) operates 2 hotels, *Faletti's* at Lahore and *Flashman's* at Rawalpindi. PTDC also runs well-furnished and moderately priced motels at Ayubia, Balakot, Bahawalpur, Barseen (Karakoram Highway), Besham, Chitral, Gilgit, Hunza, Kalam, Khaplu, Malam Jabba Ski & Summer Resort,Miandam, Moenjodaro, Naran, Panah Kot (Dir), Saidu Sharif, Sost (Pakistan-China border), Skardu, Taftan (Pakistan-Iran border), Taxila, Torkham (Pakistan-Afghan border), Wagha (Pakistan-India border) and Ziarat.

Pakistan Tours Ltd (PVT): a subsidiary of PTDC, operates tours and provides ground handling facilities for domestic and foreign tourists throughout Pakistan. Its Head Office is located in 23-24 Flashman's Hotel, The Mall, Rawalpindi (tel: (51) 563 038 *or* 581 480; fax: (51) 513 054; e-mail: ptl@isb.comsats.net.pk).

YOUTH HOSTELS

The Pakistan Youth Hostel Association has nine hostels throughout the country, available to members of affiliated organisations. Details can be obtained from the Pakistan Youth Hostel Association, Shaheed-e Millat Road, Aabpara, Sector G-6/4, Islamabad (tel: (51) 826 899; fax: (51) 920 6417).

MONEY

CURRENCY

Pakistani Rupee (PRe, singular; PRs, plural) = 100 paisa. Notes are in denominations of PRs1000, 500, 100, 50, 10, 5, 2 and 1. Coins are in denominations of PRs2 and 1, and 50, 25 and 10 paisa.

COSTS

- Budget meal: US$2-3
- Moderate restaurant meal: US$3-8
- Top-end restaurant meal: US$5-10
- Budget room: US$4-5
- Moderate hotel: US$10-15
- Top-end hotel: US$22 and up

CREDIT CARDS

American Express is the most widely accepted card. MasterCard, Diners Club and Visa have more limited use. Check with your credit card company for details of merchant acceptability and other services which may be available.

TRAVELERS CHECKS

Generally accepted at most banks, 4- and 5-star hotels and major shops. To avoid additional exchange rate charges, travelers are advised to take travelers checks in US Dollars.

EXCHANGE RATE INDICATORS

The following figures are included as a guide to the movements of the Pakistani Rupee against and the US Dollar:

Date	Oct '99	Nov '99	May '00	Aug '00
$1.00=	51.79	51.89	51.89	53.35

CURRENCY RESTRICTIONS

The import and export of local currency is limited to PRs100 in denominations of PRs10 or less. The import and export of foreign currency are unlimited. Up to Prs500 may be reconverted into foreign currency, provided official exchange receipts are shown.

Banking hours: 9 AM-1.30 PM Monday to Saturday (9 AM-12 PM Friday).

BAKSHEESH

It isn't so much a bribe as a way of life in Pakistan. It can apply to any situation and is capable of opening all sorts of doors, both literal and metaphorical. Anything from a signature on a document to fixing a leaking tap can be acquired through the magic of *baksheesh*. Most top-end hotels will automatically add a 5-10% service charge to your bill, so any extra tipping is entirely up to you. Taxi drivers routinely expect 10% of the fare, and railway porters charge an officially-set Rs 7. The only time that a gratuity might not be welcome is in the rural areas where it runs counter to Islamic obligation to be hospitable.

If *baksheesh* is a way of life, bargaining is a matter of style, particularly in the many Pakistani bazaars. Unlike the western hesitancy for bargaining, shopkeepers in Pakistani love to bargain as long as it's done with style and panache. Bargaining usually begins with an invitation to step inside for a cup of tea followed by a little bit of small talk, a casually expressed interest by yourself in a particular item, a way-too-high price mentioned by the seller, a way-too-low counter offer by yourself and eventually, after much comic rolling of eyes, a handshake and mutual satisfaction for both parties. Bargaining should always be accompanied by smiles, good humor and an ability not to get fixated on driving the price into the ground.

SUPPLEMENT

OVERSEAS PAKISTANIS ASSOCIATIONS

Sr. No.	Association	Name & Designation	Address	Phone No.	Fax No.
1.	Pakistan International Chamber of Commerce	Mr. Ashraf Gohar President/ CEO	2495-A East Gate Place, Snellville, GA 30078, USA Email: Infor@pakchamber.com www.pakchamber.com	770-982-1340	770-982-0273
2.	Pakistan American Business Association (PABA)	M. siddique Sheikh Chairman/ Founder	9302 Old Keene Mill Road Suite B, Burke, VA 22015-4278 USA Email: Chairman@PABAusa.com www.PABAusa.com	703-440-1111	703-440-7777
3.	Pakistani American Business Executive Association	Mr. Pervaiz Lodhie Chairman	23105 Kashiwa Court, Torrance CA 90505 USA E-mail: info@pabe.org www.pabe.org	310-534	310-534-1424
4.	Association of Pakistani Physicians of North America (APPNA)	Mr. Mohammad Suleman, M.D. / President	6414 South Cass Avenue Westmont IL60559, USA	630-968-8585	630-968-8677
5.	Association of Pakistani Physicians Scientists and Engineers of N. America (APSENA)	Mr. Tahir A. Kazi President Tahir.Kazmi@nextel.com	Business Professionals 13300 claverdale PL Germen Town MD 20874 USA		
6.	Canadian Humantiarian Aid for Pakistan	Mrs. Sonia Ahmed President/ Editor	506-2055 Carling Ave, Ottawa Ontario K2a 1g6 Canada. E-mail: cahp_ottawa@yahoo.com	613-863-5811	
7.	Community Development Program, Pakistan (CDP)	Mrs. Nuzhat Islam President/ Editor/ Chairman	5831 quantrell Ave Suite # 509 Alexandria VA 22312 USA E-mail: info@mycdp.org	703-622-8679	
8.	Council of Pakistan American Affairs(COPAA)		895 Holly Glen Dr. Long Beach CA 90815 USA E-mail: mshahmd@aol.com www.copaa.org		
9.	DASTAK, Network of Pakistani Professionals, NA	Mr. Ahsan Naqvi President	67 Joni Avenue Hamilton, NJ 08690, USA Email: president@dastak.org Web: www.dastak.org	609-977-3170	443-785-0439

10.	Development in Literacy (DIL)	Mrs. Sara Abbasi Board Member	895 Holly Glen Drive Long Beach California 90815 USA www.4dil.org	862-894-6236	
11.	Lollywood Volunteers Associtiion	Mr. Maqbool Chaudhry President / Editor/ Chairman	87-42 Parsons Blvd Jamaica NY 11435 USA E-mail: lollywoodny@hotmail.com www.geocities.com/lollywoodny	718-206-0100	
12.	Old Ravians	Mr. Malik Nadeem Abid President	Mineola Ny 11501 USA E-mail: MNAbid@nycmail.com	1-516-74 2-9241	1-810-283-2503
13.	Organization of Pakistani Entrepreneurs of North America, (OPEN)	Mr. Imran Khan President	4 Maxwell Circle Hudson MA 01749 USA Email: info@open.us.org	781-2662141	781-266-2141
14.	Pakistani American Association of Tampa Bay	Mr. Arjumand Hashmi Managing Director	Pakistani American Association of Tempa Bay, P.O.Box. No. 270382 Tampa, FL-33688-0382 Email: paaoftb@yahoo.com	813-631-1443	
15.	Pakistani American Association of North Carolina	Mr. Nadeem Iqbal President	P.O.Box. No. 1995, Cary, NC 27512. E-mail: President@ncpaa.org www.ncppa.org		

PAKISTANI ASSOCIATIONS IN USA

US - Pakistan Business Council
United States Chamber of commerce, International Division, 1615 H Street, N.W. Washington, D.C. 20062-2004 USA Website : www.uspakistan.org
Association of Pakistani Physicians of North America (APPNA)
6414 S. Cass Avenue, Wastmont, IL 60559, Phone: 630-968-8585, 630-968-8606 Fax: 630-968-8606 E-mail: Appna@appna.org
Council of Pakistan American Affairs [COPAA]
Nature of Organization: Political, Social Work, Media Street Address: 895 Holly Glen Dr. City: Long Beach State/Province: CA Postal/Zip Code: 90815 Country: USA Phone: Fax: Email: mshahmd@aol.com Website: http://www.copaa.org Date Established:

Activities: No. of Members: Additional Info:
Association of Pakistani Scientists and Engineers Of North America [APSENA]
Nature of Organization: Business, Professionals Street Address: 13300 Cloverdale PL City: Germen Town State/Province: MD Postal/Zip Code: 20874 Country: USA Phone: Fax: Email: apsenagwcinfo@yahoo.com Website: www.apsenagwc.org Date Established: Activities: No. of Members: Additional Info:
Pakistan American Business Association [PABA]
Nature of Organization: Business, Professionals, Street Address: 9302 Old Keene Mill Road, Suite B City: Burke State/Province: VA Postal/Zip Code: 22015-4278 Country: USA Phone: (703) 440-1111 Fax: (703) 451-7777 Email: chairman@pabausa.com Website: www.pabausa.com Date Established: Activities: No. of Members: Additional Info:
Pakistan American Cultural Society [PACS]
Nature of Organization: Political, Media Street Address: 298 Tortoise Lane City: Franklin Lakes State/Province: NJ Postal/Zip Code: 07417 Country: USA Phone: Fax: Email: pacsmail@egroups.com Website: www.pakistanamericanculturalsociety.org Date Established: Activities: No. of Members: Additional Info:
Pakistan Association of Greater Boston [PAGB]
Nature of Organization: Social Work, Educational & Cultural Street Address: P.O.Box 412 City: Wayland State/Province: MA Postal/Zip Code: 01778 Country: USA Phone: Fax: Feedback Form http://www.serve.com/pagbweb/feedback.html Website: www.pagb.org Date Established:

Activities:
No. of Members:
Additional Info:

Pakistan Association of Greater Washington

Nature of Organization: Social Work, Educational & Cultural,
Street Address: P.O. Box 8466
City: State/Province: Gaithersburg
Postal/Zip Code: MD 20898-8466 Country: USA
Phone: Fax:
Email: pakistan_association@yahoo.com
Website: www.geocities.com/pakistan_association/
Date Established:
Activities: The Pakistan Association is unaffiliated with any government or political party, operates as a non-profit organization, and aims to serve the Pakistani-American community in the Greater Washington metropolitan.
No. of Members:
Additional Info:

Pakistan Development Alliance [PDA]

Nature of Organization: Relief, Social Work, Human Development,
Street Address: University of Texas at Austin
City: State/Province: Texas
Postal/Zip Code: Country: USA
Phone: (713) 933-0786 Fax:
Email: ozzy@cs.utexas.edu
Website: http://www.utexas.edu/students/pda
Date Established:
Activities:
No. of Members:
Additional Info:

Pakistan Education Fund (PEF)

Nature of Organization: Educational & Cultural,
Street Address: 101 W 23rd Street - #2295
City: New York State/Province: NY
Postal/Zip Code: 10011 Country: USA
Phone: 917.421.8712 Fax: 917.421.8712
Email: info@pakfund.org
Website: www.pakfund.org
Date Established: October 2004
Activities:
No. of Members:
Additional Info:

Pakistan International Chamber of Commerce

Nature of Organization: Business, Chamber of Commerce
Street Address: 2495A, East Gate Place
City: Snellville(Atlanta) State/Province: Ga
Postal/Zip Code: 30078 Country: USA
Phone: 770-982-0577 Fax:
Email: info@pakchamber.com

Website: www.pakchamber.com
Date Established: March 2004
Activities: Non profit business organization helping Pakistani throughout the world.
No. of Members: 55
Additional Info: Ashraf Gohar Goreja, President Please contact for free services.

Pakistan News Service

Nature of Organization: Business,
Street Address: 1111 W. El Camino Real, #109-218
City: Sunnyvale State/Province: CA
Postal/Zip Code: 94086 Country: USA
Phone: 510-475-0100 Fax: 510-475-0200
Email: editor@paknews.com
Website: www.paknews.com
Date Established: August 14, 1991
Activities: Wire Services, News and Information on Pakistan for overseas Pakistanis and International Audience and International Media
No. of Members: 218,000 subscribers
Additional Info: Pakistan's first and the BIGGEST online news service of Pakistan. Based in San Francisco, California with offices in Islamabad, Lahore, London, Washington DC and Toronto.

Pakistan Public Relations Council

Nature of Organization: Political, Educational & Cultural,
Street Address:
City: State/Province: California
Postal/Zip Code: Country: U.S.A.
Phone: Fax:
Email: pakpra@yahoo.com
Website: www.geocities.com/pakpra
Date Established: March 2002
Activities: Currently we are a web-based organization, we send out two weekly digests and a number of action alerts per month.
No. of Members: 4
Additional Info:

Pakistan Society of Southern California

Nature of Organization: Youth, Educational & Cultural,
Street Address: 1511 Columbia Street
City: Redlands State/Province: CA
Postal/Zip Code: 92374 Country: USA
Phone: 909.792.1282 Fax:
Email: shasan193@hotmail.com
Website:
Date Established: 1992
Activities: Non-political, social, cultural organization established to promote networking amongst Pakistanis. Pakistan Society of Southern California (PSSC) also awards cash prizes to member students who achieve GPAs 3.0 and above. prizes are also awarded to children who finsh the Holy Quran for the first time. It holds Eid dinners, fundraising programs,picnics, etc.
No. of Members: 35
Additional Info:

Pakistan Students Association

Nature of Organization: Social Work, Youth, Educational & Cultural,
Street Address:
City: State/Province:
Postal/Zip Code: Country:
Phone: Fax:
Email:
Website:
Date Established:
Activities:
No. of Members: 35
Additional Info: FOUNDER:Malik Mohsen

Pakistani American Association of Connecticut

Nature of Organization: Relief, Social Work, Youth, Human Development, Educational & Cultural,
Street Address: 93 Rockledge Drive
City: South Windsor State/Province: Ct
Postal/Zip Code: 06074 Country: USA
Phone: 860 841 5645 Fax: 801 881 1894
Email: Exec_paact@yahoogroups.com
Website: www.paact2004.org
Date Established: Feb 2004
Activities: By advocating peace, respect and tolerance of all other cultures, religions, races and people, promote a better understanding of all aspects of Pakistan. Assist Pakistanis in Pakistan in the areas of nutrition, medicine, education and infrastructure. Establish a directory of Pakistanis willing to assist other Pakistanis in the region. Amongst our American children create a greater awareness and pride of their Pakistani heritage. Network Pakistanis within the Connecticut region in order to create a united community. Hold various functions/social events throughout the year. These could include guest speakers, live entertainment, fund raisers, discussions, debates, picnics, sporting events, dinners, etc.
No. of Members: 300
Additional Info: Established in February 2004, the Pakistani American Association of Connecticut is a non-profit organization of Pakistanis, committed to preserving, supporting and enhancing the economic development of Pakistan and Pakistanis in Pakistan and in the United States. PAACT is devoted to remain politically unaffiliated and to deliver its program to promote economic development in Pakistan. VISION: By the year 2010 Pakistan and Pakistanis should develop the creditability, reputation and report to be one of the top 10 nations in the world for partnering with the United States government and corporate America. MISSION: To establish a partnership in Pakistani individuals and organizations of the same objectives and thoughts to maximize resources without duplicating efforts. Support Pakistanis and other non-political Pakistani organizations. Do an awareness campaign for Pakistan and Pakistanis as Positive, Creative, Hardworking and out-going Nation. OBJECTIVES: Promote education in Pakistan. Develop an awareness to have the best cultural and social responsibilities. Commence community development programs for Pakistanis in Pakistan and the United States for career opportunities. Support and recognize Pakistani entrepreneurs. Provide ideas and resources to those who want to open a business in, or out of Pakistan.

About the President/Editor/Chairman

First Name: M. Saud Last Name: Anwar
Street Address: 93 Rockledge Drive
City: South Windsor State/Province: CT
Postal/Zip Code: 06074 Country: USA
Phone: 860 841 5645 Fax: 801 881 1894

Email: sanwar@pol.net

Pakistani American Congress [PAC]
Nature of Organization: Political, Social Work,
Street Address: 29482 West Ten Mile Road
City: Troy State/Province: MI
Postal/Zip Code: 48336 Country: USA
Phone: (248) 474-3335 Fax: (248) 474-3280
Email: information@pakamrcongress.org
Website:
Date Established:
Activities:
No. of Members:
Additional Info:

FACILITIES FOR OVERSEAS PAKISTANIS

Pakistan Origin Card

Bank instructed for speedy delivery of home remittances:

- In recognition of the importance of the remittances by OPs to the economy of Pakistan, bonafide remittances made through the normal banking channel by
- No question will be asked for source of investment.
- The salary / income of Pakistani seafarers working on foreign vessels remitted to Pakistan through normal banking channels is being exempted from levy of income tax.
- OPs remitting US$ 2500 per annum will be entitled to avail facility of :

□ **Housing Scheme:**

<TD < TD> Special Immigration & Customs counters at all International Airports in Pakistan on arrival departure.

- OPs remitting minimum of US$ 10,000 per annum will be entitled to the following benefits :

<TD < TD> Reservation of special seats for OPs children in all the public sector professional colleges and universities on merit.

- Modalities for the above incentives will be put in place shortly through Pakistani Missions abroad.

□ **Pension Scheme:**

The Overseas Pakistanis Foundation (OPF) has introduced a self-contributory pension scheme to cover old age, death and disability. The salient features of the Pension scheme are as follows :

Scheme launched w.e.f. 01-07-2005.

- Pakistan Housing Authority (PHA) is planning to construct flats of various sizes at 18 locations in Karachi, Lahore, Islamabad and Peshawar, which are open for sale to Overseas Pakistanis. Details can be obtained from the PHA Web-site www.pha.gov.pk

Protection to Foreign Investment

- Foreign Private Investment (Promotion & Protection) Act 1976 provides protection to :
- Foreign capital / investment made by foreigner in an industrial undertaking.
- Imported machinery & equipment.
- Repatriation of Investment and profit allowed.
- Tax concessions on the basis of agreement for avoidance of double taxation.
- Equal treatment of industrial undertaking having local / foreign private investment.
- An Ordinance for protection of foreign currency accounts being promulgated to eliminate any future possibility of seizure / freezing of foreign currency accounts.

LIST OF POTENTIAL OVERSEAS PAKISTANIS IN U.S.A.

S.No.	Name	Address
1.	Mr. M. Safi Qureshi	7545 Irvene Centre Drive Suite 100, Irvene, CA 92618 Phone: 949 789 1111 Fax: 949 789 1120 Email: safiq@earthlink.net
2.	Mr. Masrur Javed Khan	Houston, 11201 Wilding Lane, Houston, Texas 77024, USA. Phone: 713-975-0786 Fax: 713-468-0786 E-mail: mjk786@asl.com
3.	Mr. Nadeem M. Sindhu	100 North Elmhurst Road, Prospect Heights, 1L 60070 USA. Phone: 847-342-1200/ 847-878-7500 Fax: 847-642-4202 Email: ssindhu@aol.com
4.	Mr. Shaukat Sindhu	CEO, Four Point Sheraton Hotel, 200 East Rand Road, Mount Prospect, 1L 60056 USA. Phone: 847-255-8822/ 847-878-7800 Fax: 847-255-8831 / 342-1202 E-mail: ssindhu@aol.com
5.	Mr. Shahid Khan	622 Broadway New York , NY 10012 Phone: 918-534-5214 Fax: 212-228-9919 E-mail: skhan@zefer.com
6.	Mr. Ayaz Khan	One Penn Plaza # 3600 New York, NY 10119. Phone: 212-849-6855 Fax: 509-356-5918 E-mail: akhan@ecredit.com
7.	Mr. Fasahat Mohiuddin	12375 Bissonnet St # 56, Houston, TX 77099 Tel: 281-568-9595-96 Fax: 281-568-9515

		Email: paktimes@hotmail.com
8.	Mr. Hamayun Qureshi	Capm Dresser & McKee Inc. One Glen Lakes, 8140 Walnut Hill Lane, Suite 1000 Dallas, Texas 75231 Tel: 214 346-2800 Fax: 214 987-2017 Email: qureshihs@cdm.com
9.	Mr. Abdul Qayyum	7322 W.W. Freeway Suite 1100 Houston, Texas 77074 Tel: 713-981-3238 Fax: 713-981-3234 Email: qayyum@alltel.net
10.	Mr. Mustafa Tyebbhoy	11200 Richmond Ave. Suite 552 Houston, TX 77082 (USA) Tel: (282) 558-5252 ext. 224 Fax:(281)558-5255 E-mail: mtyebbhoy@shipcomwireless.com
11.	Mr. Lutfi Hassan	10850 Richmond Ave., Suite 100 Houston, TX 77042 Tel: (713)789-3382 Fax: (713) 789-5535
12.	Mr. Mohammad Khan	P.O. Box 2852 Georgetown, TX 78627 Tel: 512 868 6767 Fax: 512 799 6055 Email: mkchevron@yahoo.com
13.	Mr. Shah Haqqi,	City of Houston, 901 Bagby, 3rd Floor, Houston, Texas 77002 Tel: (713)437-6171. Fax (713) 247-3010 Email: shah.haqaqi@cityofhouston.net
14.	Mr.Saeed B. Gaddi (Pres.)	P.O. Box No. 2554 Stafford. TX 77497 Tel: 832-277-6699 Fax: 281-265-3766 Email: sangeetradio@hotmail.com
15.	Syed Bukhari	14834 Redwood Bend Trail Houston, TX 77062 Tel: 281-486-5130 Mobile: 281-3521-3444 Fax: 281-218-0474 Sbukhari@aol.com
16.	Shamim Syed	Houston Bureau Chief 14258 Andreaway Ln. Houston, TX 77083 Tel: 281-748-6123 Fax: 281-495-6266 Email: shamimsyed12@hotmail.com
17.	Muhammad Mukhtar	1850 Richmond Ave. Suite 238 Houston, TX 77042- USA P.O. Box 37041 Tel: 713-784-3737

		Email: mmukhtarkk@cs.com Website: www.apsena.org
18.	Mohammed S. Huque, Ph.D.	Consolidated Trading Company 10065 Kemp Forest Drive Houston, Texas 77080 Phone: (713) 460-4265 Email: mhuque@hotmail.com
19.	Sajjad I. Burki	6776 Southwest Fwy Suite # 320 Houston, TX 77074 Tel: 713-781-9900 Fax: 713-781-9939 Mobile: 281-236-9492 Email: sidburki@hotmail.com
20.	Kamran Jilani	12375 Bissonnet St # 56 Houston TX 77099 Tel: 281-568-9595-96 Fax: 281-568-9515 Email: paktimes@hotmail.com
21.	Hamid A. Malik	1458 Manhattan Avenue Fullerton, CA 92831 Tel: (714) 630 2070, (800) 576 2070 Fax: (714) 635 9424 Email: hamid@amtrend.com Website: www.amtrend.com
22.	Farooq Vakil	611 Reyes Drive. Walnut, California 91789 Tel: (909) 594-7883, (800) 321-8100 Fax: (909) 594-6758 Email: fvakil@lightsofamerica.com Logic786@aol.com
23.	M. Riaz Ahmed	1630 E. St. Gertrude Place Santa Ana, CA 92705 Tel: (714) 557-3989 Fax : (714) 557-3585 Email: delknits@aol.com
24.	Sheikh Najam Ali,	12375 Bissonnet St # 56 Houston TX 77099 Tel: 281-568-9595-96 Fax: 281-568-9515 Email: paktimes@hotmail.com
25.	Wasif Siddiqui	Ramona Ave., Chino, CA 91710 Tel: (909) 591-5653 Fax: (909) 591-0643 Email: wasif@luminexlighting.com Website: www.luminexlighting.com
26.	Mr. M.E. Malik	728-Leanord Street, Brooklyn, New York, USA Phone: 718 609 5855-917 404 0454 Fax: 253 669 3337 Email: rightwaytrade@hotmail.com
27.	Mr. Mahmud Haq	7 Clyde Road, Suite 201 Somerset, NJ 08873 Tel: 732-873-5133

		Fax: 732-873-6858 Email: mhaq@mtbconline.com
28.	Ms. Zahra Jamshed	59 Maiden Lane, 30th Floor New York, NY 10038 Tel: 646-576-8847 Mobile: 201-446-8899 Email: zjamshed@netnumina.com
29.	Mr. Mohamed Cassam	7012 Raleigh Rd Annandale, VA 22003 Tel: (703) 658-1418 Mobile: (202) 255-0558 Fax: (703) 658-1669 Email: cassamm@aol.com
30.	Mr. Hussain Rokerya	Digital Technology Diamond Bar, CA Tel: 909-591-1852 Fax: 909-396-1524 Email: sales@antiquerugconnection.com
31.	Mr. Munir Hussain,	55 Webro Road Clifton, NJ 07012 Tel: (973) 574-1040 Fax: (973)574-1044 Email: munirefurniture@hotmail.com
32.	Mr. Sajjad “Saj” Chaudhry, President,	General Turbine Systems of Texas, Inc. 14102 Chrisman Road, Houston, TX 77039, Tel: 281-442-1681, Fax: 281-4421685 Email: sajjad@prodigy.net
33.	Mr. Ismail Mohammad, President,	Star Financial & Investment Group, 8313 S.W. Freeway, Suite 231, Houston, Texas 77074 Tel: 713-2700600, Fax: 713-2701168 Email: ismailmohd@aol.com
34.	Mr. Rafi M. Aziz, Reservoir Engineering Advisor & Project Coordinator	Halliburton Energy Services 10200 Bellaire Boulevard, 1SE34C Houston, TX 77072-5299, Tel: 281-5755022, Fax: 281-57554573, Email: rafi.aziz@halliburton.com
35.	Mr. Sammi Raza, PhD President, Petroleum Engineering Consultant	9354 Shady Lane Circle, Houston, Texas 77063 Tel: 8322513329, Fax: 8322513372, Mobile: 7134090487 Email: razash@yahoo.com
36.	Mr. Nasr Ullah Khan, Senior Vice President, United Central Bank,	8585 South Gessner Houston, Texas 77074 Main: 713-779-3388, Fax: 713-779-8833 Email: nasrkhan@hotmail.com

37.	Mr. Aamir Shah, Vice President, Special Assets Group Comerica Bank-Texas	One Shell Plaza 910 Louisiana, Ste.300 Houston, TX 77002 Tel: 713-220-5680, Fax: 713-2205552, Email: aamir_shah@comerica.com
38.	Mr. Masrur Javed Khan, President, Pakistan Association of Greater Houston	P.O.Box-721435, Houston, Texas 77272-1435, Cell: 713-3984829, Fax: 713/4680786, Email: mjk786@aol.com Res: 11201 Wilding Lane, Houston, Texas 77024-5308, 713/4680786
39	Mr. Arif Gafur, Business Advisor, Shell International Exploration & Production Inc.,	200 N. Dairy Ashford, Houston, Texas 77079 Tel: (281) 5442319, Fax: (281)5444602 P.O.Box 4741, Texas 77210, Email: agafur@shellus.com
40	Mr. Shahid S. Qadri General manager – Africa/ Middle East/Pakistan Black and Veatch International Company	11401 Lamar Avenue Over land park Kansas 66211 (USA) Tel: (913) 458-7848 Over Land park Fax (913) 485-2800 E-mail: qadriss@bv.com
41	Mr. Nadeem M. Zafar	Microtech International 47900 Warm Spring Bivd., Fremont, CA 94539 Tel: 510-2499100 Fax: 510-249-9292 E-mail: nadeem@mtionweb.com
42	Mr. Salan Khokhar	Koka Consulting 1793 riverside drive, Suite 5F New York, Ny 10028 917-767-5523 CELL E-mail: salkhokhar@kokaconsulting.com
43	Mr. Inaamul Haque Alternative Executive Director	The World Bank, 188 H Street, NW Washington, DC 20433, USA Tel # 202-458-1084 Fax # 202-477-9052 E-mail: ihaque@worldbank.org
44	Mr. Adeel A. Shah President	US-Pakistan Business Council 1747 Pennsylvania Avenue, NW, Suite 300 Washington, DC 20046-4604 Tel # (202) 293-8752 Fax # (202) 393-0363 E-mail: adeel_shah@telnia.com E-mail: uspakistan@aol.com
45	Mr. Pervaiz Lodhie President	LEDTRONICS, INC The future of Light 23105 Kashiwa Court Torrance, CA 90505

		Tel # 800-579-4875 / 310-534-1505 Fax # 310-534-1424 E-mail: plodhie@ledtronics.com
46.	Mr. Anwar Sindhu Continental Int. Inc.	Zane Investments LLC 2925 Lockport Dr, Suite 101 Falls Church VA-22042, Washington Tel # 703-237-2101 Fax # 507-295-8741 2291753/0300-8552554 E-mail: contex@zajil.net
47.	Mr. Omar G Naji, P.E. Senior Vice President	Automation Services Manager CDM Camp Dresser & McKee Inc. One Glen Lakes, 8140 Walnut Hill Lane, Suite 1000, Dallas, Texas 75231 Tel: 214 346-2800 Fax: 214 987-2017 E-mail: najilog@cdm.com
48.	Mr. Tariq Khan Founder Weekly Pakistan Chronicle	7400 Harwin Dr., # 216 Houston, Texas 77036 Tel: (Off) 713-914-0786 (Res) 281-875-0786 Fax: 713-914-0906 E-mail: editor@pakistanchronicle.com
49.	Mr. Waqar Khan President	International Satellite News 1503 McLean Ciorner Ln. McLean, VA 22101 115 E, 87th St., Ste. 8F, New York NY 10128 859 LeyLand Drive Diamond Bar, CA 91765 Tel: (909) 612-1138 Fax: (909) 612-1132 E-mail: worldreporter@yahoo.com
50.	Mr. Abbasi M. Ashraf Founding President	Pakistan Chamber of Commerce-USA P.O.Box-720335 Houston, TX-770272 9700 Club Creek, Suite # E. Houston Texas 77036 (USA) 713-669-0786. 713-669-0796 Fax E-mail: pkchamber@aol.com
51.	Mr. Waqar Ali Khan Editor in Chief The Pakistan Frontline	24439 E. Gold Point Place Diamond Bar, CA. 91765 Tel: (909) 612-1138 Fax; (909) 612-1132 E-mail: dildilpak@earthlink.net
52	Mr. Munir Hussain,	55 Webro Road Clifton, NJ 07012 Tel: (973) 574-1040 Fax: (973)574-1044 Email: munirefurniture@hotmail.com
53.	Mr. Tariq Malik	SPHINK, 155 Perry Street # 4-D,

		New York, NY 1004 Tel: 212-243-8826 Fax: 212-645-3030 E-mail: tmalik@sphinxsoftware.com
54.	Mr. Sohail Iqbal	Reliance Solutions, 1122 Coney Island Ave. Brooklyn, NY 11230 Tel: 718-434-0200 Fax: 718-434-7083 E-mail: iqbal@reliancesolutions.com
55.	Mr. Balall Yaqub	BRYJ Technologies Inc. 540 Madson Ave. on 55th Street, New York NY 10022 Tel: 212-754-9754 Fax: 212-754-9707 E-mail: Balallyaqub@bryjtech.com
56.	Mr. Anjum F. Akhtar	Donaldson Lufkin & Jenrette, 277 Park Ave. New York, NY 10172 Tel: 212-892-0644 Fax: 212-892-0135 E-mail: aakhtar@dlj.com
57.	Mr. Saqib Nisar Qureshi	Interim Technology 40 Broad Street, New York, NY 10004 Tel: 212-480-2613 Fax: 212-480-2625 E-mail: saqibqureshi@interim.com
58.	Mr. Shahid Khan	ZEFER, 622 Broadway, New York, NY 10012 Tel: 917-534-5014 Fax: 212-228-9919 E-mal: SKHAN@SEFER.COM
59.	Mr. Ayaz Khan	Credit.com One Penn Plaza # 3600 New York, NY 10119, Tel: 212-849-6855 Fax: 509-356-5918 E-mail: akhan@ecredit.com
60.	Mr. Fateh A. Tipu	Advisory Software Engineer IBM Thomas J. Watson Research Center, P.O.Box. 218 Yorktown Heighths, NY 10598 Tel: fateh@watson.obm.com
61.	Mr. Saud Ali Siddiqui Chief Editor	Azad Newspaper, New York P.O.Box. 2330 astoria New York 11102, USA. Tel: 718-358-2213 Mobile: 917-602-3245 E-mail: azadnewspaper@aol.com azadinpak@yahoo.com Web: www.azadnewpaper.com

IMPORTANT BUSINESS INFORMATION SOURCES

District Chakwal:- Beginning with a brief geographical introduction about Chakwal, the cultural section provides insight into the way of life of people living there, their dress; marriage customs; occupation; food and health. Superstitions and beliefs peculiar to the area, and customs and traditions also make for interesting reading. Details about the health units, education, agriculture, industry, district administration and important contact numbers are also available at this site. Tourists will find a guide to shrines in Chakwal, and historical information and beautiful images about Kallar Kahar, Katas Raj, and Malot Fort intriguing.
http://www.chakwal.sdnpk.org/
9/5/2005

Ministry of Labour, Manpower and Overseas Pakistanis:- The Ministry of Labour, Manpower and Overseas Pakistanis performs functions broadly related to policy formulation regarding labour administration, manpower planning, and employment promotion. The site begins with a brief introduction of its objectives and organizational structure. "The Future", the news magazine on child labour is also available here. There are links to government sites, attached departments, autonomous bodies, and subordinate offices. A news section, relevant contact information, and an online feedback form are also provided on this site.
http://www.labour.gov.pk/

FATA Development Statistics:- Development Statistics of FATA (1997 & 1998) website provides separate statistical document for FATA region. Statistics of almost all the development sectors has been given up to the year 1996-97. Besides, the latest data available for the year 1997-98 has also been provided in some sectors for the users. The contents are compiled and presented online under categories such as population, housing, public finance, agriculture, industries, education, health etc. Statistical abstracts and search engine facility is also available on the website.
www.fds.sdnpk.org
29/5/2005

Gwadar District:- This information rich website goes back to Gwadar's ancient history in its well-written introduction. It gives details of the hierarchial administrative setup, topography, and productive sources of economy. Intensive information about Gwadar's customs and beliefs, climate and environment, industries, social infrastructure, health, telecommunications, education, population, financial institutions, and NGOs' involvement make for enlightened reading.
http://www.gwadar.sdnpk.org

National Strategies for Sustainable Development:- Agenda 21, agreed at the Rio Earth Summit in 1992, called on all countries to introduce National Strategies for Sustainable Development (nssd). OECD's Development Action Committee (DAC), runs a project that involves a review of experience with nssds, and other strategies for environment and development, in a number of developing countries on the basis of consultations with a range of stakeholders. This site has been prepared as a web based planning tool to assist the process - providing necessary background and reference material in support of these dialogues. Pakistan figures prominently on the site which provides the latest information on its National Conservation Strategy (NCS), especially the details of NCS Mid Term Review. Links to other relevant sites are also given.
http://www.nssd.net/nssdpa01.htm

Dadu District:- The site is a database containing information on the district of Dadu, situated in the province of Sindh. Comprehensive information on the history, geography, culture and various other aspects of the district has been presented. Additionally, a special feature on the

environmental degradation Of Manchar Lake and a detailed drought report and links to other related information sites have also been provided on the website.
www.dadu.sdnpk.org

The Balochistan Conservation Strategy (BCS):- The Balochistan Conservation Strategy (BCS) was prepared by the government of Balochistan with the technical assistance of IUCN-The World Conservation Union. It is a strategic plan designed to define and address the issues affecting the socio-economic development of Balochistan, through the sustainable use of its natural resources. The BCS aims to devise ways and means to weave environment and natural resource conservation with development and to recommend an institutional framework that will bring ownership, sustainability and efficiency in management of these vital endowments. The BCS focuses on an action programme to be implemented over the next 10 years. The report has three parts and all the data has been provided with on the site.
www.bcs.sdnpk.org

KECH District:- The site is an extensive source of data on the Kech district of Balochistan. Kech is among the four largest districts within the province. In Makran it has a central position: geographically, politically and administratively. It is the most densely populated district in Makran division. The information has been classified under fifteen links containing sub-categories with further details. The site provides a downloadable report on 'District Consultative Meetings held at Kech' and links to other information channels.
www.kech.sdnpk.org

SBOS:- Bureau of Statistics has been releasing Development Statistics of Sindh since 1971. Development Statistics of Sindh 1998 contains statistical information on socio-economic sectors of the Sindh province and the present information is the latest in the series to the year 1998. The site covers available Statistics on almost all the socio-economic sectors of the province up to the year 1996-97. The data would serve as a useful reference material to planners, administrators, policy makers, research scholars and others interested in socio-economic development of the Province.
http://sbos.sdnpk.org

BDD:- Balochistan Districts Database (BDD) is a database containing information on the twenty-six districts in the Balochistan province. The data has been organized under various categories such as Administrative Division, Agricultural Statistics, Energy, Finance, Climate, Health, population etc. Hence the database is a descriptive catalog where one can find statistical index on miscellaneous aspects of the distinct districts of the province of Balochistan.
http://bdd.sdnpk.org

Asian Development Bank: Pakistan:- This section of ADB's website contains information about its operations in Pakistan in addition to some general development information about the country, details of the projects and latest news about them. List of publications, depository libraries and related links are also available. Some useful documents in the pdf format can be downloaded from the site.
http://www.adb.org/Pakistan/default.asp

Pakistan Board of Investment:- The Board of Investment was created in 1989 and has repeatedly proved its commitment to investors. The Board of Investment plays a key role in the formulation of investment policies. With the aim of streamlining the investment process, the Board of Investment is the focal point of contact between potential investors and all other Government departments handling investment projects. The Board provides all the necessary information to potential investors, both domestic and foreign. It assists investors in expeditious processing and implementation of their investment proposals and in coordinating with other government

departments. The Board also extends advisory facility on issues relating to direct investment in business and industry anywhere in the country. The site provides info on Pakistan, Doing Business in Pakistan, Investment Opportunities, Incentives, Facilities, Foreign Missions in Pakistan, Pakistani Embassies, BOI Offices and the what's new page gives all the latest activities of BOI.
http://www.pakboi.gov.pk/

International Monetary Fund - Pakistan:- The site contains different press releases, news briefs and publications (including staff country reports about Pakistan) related to IMF and Pakistan.
http://www.imf.org/external/country/pak/index.htm

Sales Tax:- This is an official web site of the Sales Tax department of Government of Pakistan. The federal taxes collected by the CBR are broadly classified as direct (Income Tax, Wealth Tax, Capital Value Tax, Corporate Assets Tax, and Worker's Welfare Fund) and indirect (Custom Duties, Sales Tax, Central Excise) taxes. The user can obtain the content regarding Sales Tax history, Organizational Chart, Modes of Tax Collection, SRO, Act 1990, its Gazette in the History, Organogram, Collectorates, SRO, The Sales Tax Act 1990 (in PDF format) and The Sales Tax Gazette links, respectively.
http://www.stax.gov.pk/

Securities and Exchange Commission of Pakistan:- Securities and Exchange Commission of Pakistan (SECP) having autonomous status has been established under the Securities and Exchange Commission of Pakistan Act, which was passed by the Parliament and promulgated in 1997. SECP regulates the securities market and related institutions like Mutual Funds, Central Depository Company and Credit Rating Institutions. Secondly, it administers Company Law. It also regulates some non-banking financial institutions like leasing companies and modarabas (funds operating on basis of Islamic economic principles). The visitor can find details about the organization, different guidelines, SECP Act 1997, Circulars/SROs, News related to SECP and amendments in corporate laws. The site encourages all sorts of feedback from the users.
http://www.secp.gov.pk/

Government of Sindh:- This is an official website of Government of Sindh, which gives the reader in-depth information about all the departments working in the province of Sindh. Different statistical graphs are given regarding the law and order in Sindh. This site contains details about - Historical / Cultural background & Geography of Sindh, Organizational structure & functioning of various Departments of Sindh, Business & Investment Opportunities, human rights, budget, important telephone numbers and related links. Hence you name the area of interest and you'll find it in this site.
http://www.sindh.gov.pk/index.shtml

STRATEGIC GOVERNMENT AND BUSINESS CONTACTS

U.S. EMBASSY TRADE RELATED CONTACTS

United States Embassy
Diplomatic Enclave, Ramna 5
Islamabad, Pakistan
Tel: 92-51-826161
Fax: 92-51-276427
William B. Milam, Ambassador
Amer M. Kayani, Senior Commercial Officer

U.S. Consulate-General - Karachi
8 Abdullah Haroon Road
Karachi, Sindh, Pakistan
Tel: 92-21-5685170
Fax: 92-21-5680496
Douglas B. Archard, Consul General

U.S. Consulate General - Lahore
50 Empress Road
Lahore, Pakistan
Tel: 92-42-6365530-9
Fax: 92-42-6365177
Geoffery R. Pyatt, Principal Officer

U.S. Consulate - Peshawar
11 Hospital Road
Saddar
Peshawar, Pakistan
Tel: 92-91-279801-3
Fax: 92-91-276712
Bradford E. Hanson, Principal Officer

In Washington

U.S. Foreign Commercial Service
U.S. Department of Commerce
Washington, D.C. 20230
Tel: (202) 482-4836; Fax: (202-482-5179)
Robert Marro, Regional Director
Christina Sharkey, Associate Director

Export-Import Bank of the United States
811 Vermont Avenue, N.W.
Washington, D.C. 20571
Tel: (202) 566-8885
Fax: (202) 566-7524
Vice President - Asia
(Note: No country coverage for Pakistan due to U.S. sanctions as a result of Pakistan's test of nuclear device)

U.S. Department of State

Pakistan Desk Officer
Pakistan, Afghanistan, Bangladesh Affairs
Office of South Asian
Affairs (SA/PAB)
2201 C Street, N.W.
Washington, D.C. 20520
Tel: (202) 647-7593
Fax: (202) 647-3001

Office of the U.S. Trade Representative
Winder Building
600 17th Street, N.W.
Washington, D.C. 20506
Tel: (202) 395-6813
Fax: (202) 395-3512
Director for Taiwan and South
Asian Affairs

U.S. Dept. of the Treasury
Office of Asian and Near East Nations
1500 Pennsylvania Ave. N.W.
Washington, D.C. 20220
Tel: (202) 622-0359

Overseas Private Investment Corporation
1100 New York Avenue, N.W.
Washington, D.C. 20527
Tel: (202) 336-8574
(N.B. No country coverage for Pakistan due to U.S. sanctions as a result of Pakistan's test of nuclear device)

U.S. Department of Agriculture
USDA/ERS/ATAD/APR
Room # 608d
1301 New York, Ave. N.W.
Washington, D.C. 20045-4789
Tel: (202) 219-0610
Fax: (202) 219-0942

Export Credits
Program Development Division
Ag. Box # 1034
Foreign Agricultural Service
Washington, D.C. 20250-1034
Tel: (202) 720-6301
Fax: (202) 690-3077

Pakistan Embassy

2315 Massachusetts Ave. N.W.
Washington, D.C. 20048
Tel: (202) 939-6200
Fax: (202) 387-0484

BILATERAL BUSINESS COUNCILS

American Business Council of Pakistan
NIC Building (6th Floor)
Abbasi Shaheed Road
G.P.O. Box 1322
Karachi 74400
Tel: 92-21-5676436
Fax: 92-21-5683935; 5660135

TRADE & INDUSTRY ASSOCIATIONS

In the United States

U.S. Feed Grains Council
Dr. T. J. Vorachek
Regional Director
P.O. Box 5285
Dubai, United Arab Emirates
Tel: (9714) 243880/243879
Fax: (9714) 243882

U.S. Wheat Associates
Mr. Mark Samson
Vice President for Asia
541 Orchard Road # 15-02
Liat Towers
Singapore 238881
Tel: (065) 7374409 - 7374311
Fax: (065) 733-9359

American Soybean Association
c/o Khungar's Business Center #5
3rd floor, Yashwant Place
Chanatya Puri
New Delhi-110021, India
Mr. Virgil D. Miedema
Regional Director
Asia Sub-continent
Tel: 91-11-687-0600; fax: 91-11-687-9300

American Soybean Association
Mr. Zahid Rasool
Representative
Room # 17, 2nd Floor
Taj Arcade, 73 Jail Road
Lahore, Pakistan
Tel: 92-42-7586570
Fax: 92-42-7586599

National Renderers Association
27e Kam Kin Mansion 123
Caine Road
Hong Kong
Tel: 5-490378
Fax: 852-895-5546
Mr. Phillip W. Laney
Asia Regional Director

U.S. Hide, Skin & Leather Association
President
1700 North Moore Street
Suite 1600
Arlington, Va. 22209
Tel: (703) 841-5485
Fax: (703) 841-9656

CONTACTS IN PAKISTAN

Federation of Pakistan Chambers of Commerce & Industry
Federation House, Main Clifton
P.O. Box 13875
Karachi
Tel: 92-21-5873691-94, 5873640-41
Fax: 92-21-5874332
President

Overseas Investors Chambers of Commerce and Industry
Chamber of Commerce Building
Talpur Road, P.O. Box 4833
Karachi 74000
Tel: 92-21-2426076, 222557-8
Fax: 92-21-2427315
President

Karachi Chamber of Commerce and Industry
Aiwan-e-Tijarat Road
Karachi
Tel: 92-21-2416091-94
Fax: 92-21-2416095
President

Sindh Industrial Trading Estate (SITE) Association

H-16 SITE
Karachi 75700
Tel: 92-21-2562884, 2560705
Fax: 92-21-2562884, 2563119
Chairman

Islamabad Chamber of Commerce and Industry
Aiwan-e-Sanat-o-Tijarat Road
Mauve Area, Sector G-8/1
Islamabad, Pakistan
Tel: 92-51-250526-253145
Fax: 92-51-252950
President

Rawalpindi Chamber of Commerce and Industry
Chamber House, 108-Adamjee Road
Rawalpindi, Pakistan
Tel: 92-51-584397,566238
Fax: 92-51-586849
President

Lahore Chamber of Commerce and Industry
P.O. Box 597, 11-Race Course Road
Lahore, Pakistan
Tel: 92-42-6305538, 6365737; Fax: 92-42-6304633
President

Sarhad Chamber of Commerce & Industry
Sarhad Chamber House
G.T. Road
Peshawar, Pakistan
Tel: 92-521-215459 and 216398
Fax: 92-521-217412
President

Quetta Chamber of Commerce & Industry
P. O. Box 117, Zarghoon Road
Quetta (Baluchistan), Pakistan
Tel: 92-81-821943
Fax: 92-81-821948
President

Pakistan Chemicals & Dyes Manufacturers Association
Chemical & Dyes House
Rambharti Street
Jodia Bazar
Karachi, Pakistan
Tel: 92-21-7732486

Pakistan Readymade Garments Manufacturers Association
53, Idrees Chambers, 4th Floor
Talpur Road
Karachi, Pakistan
Tel: 92-21-2416469
Fax: 92-21-4550699

Pakistan Sports Goods Manufacturers & Exporters Association
Abbot Road
Sialkot, Pakistan
Tel: 92-432-267962; 265080
Fax: 92-432-261774

Pakistan Sugar Mills Association
24-D, Rashid Plaza, Jinnah Avenue
Islamabad, Pakistan
Tel: 92-51-813722 and 812111
Fax: 92-51-217453

The Surgical Instruments Manufacturers Association of Pakistan
Kutchery Road
Sialkot, Pakistan
Tel: 92-432-266240; 263016
Fax: 92-432-265978

GOVERNMENT OF PAKISTAN OFFICES

Ministry of Foreign Affairs
Constitution Ave.
Islamabad, Pakistan
Ms. Rana Rahim
Director for the Americas
Tel: 92-51-9201757
Fax: 92-51-9202262

Ministry of Industries
Mr. Abu Shamim Arif
Secretary
Block A, Pakistan Secretariat
Islamabad, Pakistan
Tel: 92-51-9211709; 9210192
Fax: 92-51-9205130

Ministry of Commerce
Mian Iqbal Farid
Secretary
Block A, Pakistan Secretariat
Islamabad, Pakistan
Tel: 92-51-9201816; 9210277

Fax: 92-51-9203104

Ministry of Food, Agriculture
& Cooperatives
Pakistan Agricultural Research Council
Islamabad, Pakistan
Tel: 92-51-9210351; 824756
Fax: 92-51-9221246
Dr. Zafar Altaf, Secretary

Ministry of Finance
Mr. Moeen Afzal
Secretary
Q Block, Pakistan Secretariat
Islamabad, Pakistan
Tel: 92-51-9211518, 9202253
Fax: 92-21-9205166

Civil Aviation Authority
Headquarters
19 Liaquat Barracks
Karachi
Tel: 92-21-9201551
Fax: 92-21-9201514
Air Vice Marshal Aamir Ali Sharieff
Director General

Corporate Law Authority
Ministry of Finance
State Life Bldg, 7-Blue Area
Islamabad
Tel: 92-51-9207091
Fax: 92-51-9204915
Chairman

Directorate General Defense Purchase
(DGDP)
Ministry of Defense
Defense Production Division
Pak Secretariat No.II
Rawalpindi
Tel: 92-51-563324
Fax: 92-51-563631

Export Promotion Bureau
Government of Pakistan
Finance and Trade Center
Shara-e-Faisal
Karachi
Tel: 92-21-9206471; 9206487
Fax: 92-21-9206483

Board of Investment

Prime Minister's Secretariat
Attaturk Avenue, G-5/1
Islamabad
Tel: 92-51-9218439, 9217231
Fax: 92-51-9203281
Mr. M. Abdullah Yusuf
Secretary

Central Board of Revenue
CBR House (opposite Parliament House)
Islamabad
Pakistan
Tel: 92-51-9201938
Fax: 92-51-9205308
Mr. Moinuddin Khan, Chairman

Export Processing Zones Authority
8th Floor
Finance & Trade Center
Shara-e-Faisal
Karachi
Tel: 92-21-5673524
Fax: 92-21-5673882

Karachi Port Trust
Eduljee Dinshaw Road
Karachi
Tel: 92-21-2311534; 2310374
Fax: 92-21-2311567
Vice Admiral Khalid M. Mir
Chairman

Pakistan Customs
Custom House Karachi
Tel: 92-21-201155
Fax: 92-21-200492

Pakistan Steel
Bin Qasim
Karachi
Tel: 92-21-77694496; 4915764-67
Fax: 92-21-4913080
Chairman

Pakistan Int'l Airlines
PIA Building
Quaid-e-Azam Int'l Airport
Karachi
Tel: 92-21-4572011
Fax: 92-21-4575250; 4573778
Managing Director

Port Qasim Authority

Bin Qasim
Karachi
Tel: 92-21-7737640, 7737601-20
Fax: 92-21-7737639
Chairman

State Bank of Pakistan
Central Directorate
State Bank Building
I.I. Chundrigar Road
Karachi
Tel: 92-21-2417864, 2419036
Fax: 92-21-2417865, 2416608
Dr. Muhammad Yaqub
Governor

Pakistan Telecommunication
Company Limited (PTCL)
Head Quarters, Sector G-8/4
Islamabad
Tel: 92-51-282890, 844463
Fax: 92-51-843991
Mr. Naseem S. Mirza
Chairman

Pakistan Tourism Development
Corporation (PTDC)
House No. 170, Street 36, F-10/1
Islamabad
Tel: 92-51-9292682
Fax: 92-51-9292672
Hamid Ahmad Qureshi
Managing Director

Privatization Commission
Ministry of Finance & Economic
Affairs
5-A, Constitution Avenue
Expert Advisory Cell Building
Islamabad
Tel: 92-51-9208276, 9211285
Fax: 92-51-9203076
Khawaja M. Asif
Chairman

Pakistan Environmental Protection Agency
Kulsoom Plaza, 3rd Floor, Blue Area
Islamabad
Tel: 92-51-9209851;
Fax: 92-51-9202211
Mr. Asif Shuja Khan
Director General

Monopoly Control Authority
Ministry of Finance
P.O. Box 1227
Union Plaza, Blue Area
Islamabad, Pakistan
Tel: 92-51-9203768
Fax: 92-51-9219218
Director

Pakistan Railways
Headquarters
Allama Iqbal Road
Lahore
Tel: 92-42-6365460
Fax: 92-42-6367673
General Manager

Water & Power Development Authority
WAPDA House, The Mall
Lahore
Tel: 92-42-9202222
Fax: 92-42-6278836
Mr. Shamsul Mulk
Chairman

Market Research Firms

Aftab Associates (Pvt.) Ltd. (Head office)
5-E/1 Commercial, Gulberg-III
Lahore 54660
Tel: 92-42-5710987, 5754690, 5754693
Fax: 92-42-5711020

Business Research Bureau
A-4 Shaheen Chambers
Block 7 & 8 Commercial Area
K.C.H.S., Karachi
Tel:
Fax: 92-21-445423

EIP Investors Service
Al-Masiha Building
47 Abdullah Haroon Road
P.O. Box 7843, Karachi
Tel: 92-21-7728963, 7728434, 7728957
Fax: 92-21-7727582, 7736324

Market Research Link
403 Faiyaz Center
3-A S.M.C.H.S.
Shahrah-e-Faisal
Karachi 74400
Tel: 92-21-4540502

Fax: 92-21-4554120

Datamation
21/1, 28 Street
D.H.S., Phase V
Karachi, Pakistan
Tel: 92-21-577529; 570672
Fax: 92-21-5870004

COMMERCIAL BANKS

Allied Bank of Pakistan Ltd.
14th Floor, NIC Building
Abbasi Shaheed Road
Off Shahra-e-Faisal
Karachi
Tel: 92-21-5678071
Fax: 92-21-5682568
Chairman

First Women Bank
7th Floor, Mehdi Towers
S.M.C.H.S.
Shara-e-Faisal
Karachi
Tel: 92-21-4553110, 4556093, 4553149
Fax: 92-21-4556983
President

Habib Bank Limited
Habib Bank Plaza
I.I. Chundrigar Road
Karachi
Tel: 92-21-2418000; 5866591
Fax: 92-21-5866567
President

Muslim Commercial Bank
Adamjee House
I.I. Chundrigar Road
Karachi
Tel: 92-21-2414099, 2414090, 2415354
Fax: 92-21-2416982
President

National Bank of Pakistan
NBP Building
I.I. Chundrigar Road
P.O. Box 4937
Karachi
Tel: 92-21-2416789, 2416780, 2416612
Fax: 92-21-2410202
President

United Bank Limited
State Life Building No. 1
I.I. Chundrigar Road
Karachi
Tel: 92-21-2417021, 2147022
Fax: 92-21-2413492
President

American Express Bank Ltd.
Shaheen Commercial Complex
Dr. Ziauddin Ahmad Road
Karachi
Tel: 92-21-2630349, 2630343
Fax: 92-21-2631803

ANZ Grindlays Bank
Grindlays Bank Building
I.I. Chundrigar Road
Karachi 74000
Tel: 92-21-2412671
Fax: 92-21-2414914

Bank of America
Jubilee Insurance House
I.I. Chundrigar Road
Karachi
Tel: 92-21-2412528, 2412520
Fax: 92-21-2415371

Banque Indosuez
Mohammadi House
I.I. Chudrigar Road
Karachi 74000
Tel: 92-21-2417146, 2417155
Fax: 92-21-2417503

Chartered Bank
I.I. Chudrigar Road
P.O. Box 4896
Karachi
Tel: 92-21-2433545, 2428541

Citibank
State Life Building 1
I.I. Chudrigar Road
Karachi 74000
Tel: 92-21-2412882, 2412883
Fax: 92-21-2424474

Deutsche Bank AG
Unitowers
I.I. Chudrigar Road

Karachi
Tel: 92-21-2419619
Fax: 92-21-2416970

Hong Kong and Shanghai Bank
Shaheen Commercial Complex
M.R. Kayani Road
Karachi
Tel: 92-21-2630387, 2630386
Fax: 92-21-2635126

The Bank of Tokyo Ltd.
Shaheen Complex, 1st Floor
M.R. Kayani Road
Karachi 74200
Tel: 92-21-2630171, 2630175
Fax: 92-21-2631368

- Multilateral Development Bank Offices

The World Bank
20-A, Shara-e-Jamhuriat
Ramna 5, P.O. Box 1025
Islamabad
Tel: 92-51-819781; Fax: 92-51-279648

Asian Development Bank
Pakistan Resident Mission
OPF Building, Shara-e-Jamhuriat
G-5/2, Islamabad
Tel: 92-51-825011; Fax: 8233324

- TPCC Trade Center in Washington
1-800-USA-TRADE

U.S. Department of State Office for Business Affairs
Telephone: 202-746-1625; Facsimile: 202-647-3953

U.S. Department of Commerce Country Desk Officer
U.S. Foreign and Commercial Service
U.S. Department of Commerce
Washington, D.C. 20230
Tel: (202) 482-2955; Fax: 202-482-5330
Kent Stauffer
IEP/ANESA/OSA

Foreign Agricultural Service
U.S. Department of Agriculture
14th & Independence Ave. SW
Washington, D.C. 20250-1080
Tel: (202) 720-7053
Fax: (202) 720-6063
AME/FAA
U.S. DOA/FAS Trade Assistance and Promotion Office
Telephone: 202-720-7420

PREFERENTIAL TRADE AGREEMENT

Government of Pakistan have signed on agreement on the SAARC Preferential Trading Arrangement to promote and sustain mutual trade and economic co-operation between SAARC member countries.
It is informed all concerned that Government of Pakistan, have signed Agreement on the SAARC Preferential Trading Arrangement and Export Promotion Bureau is expected to start to issue certificate of origin under this Agreement (SAPTA).

By this Agreement the contracting states has established the SAARC Preferential Trading Arrangements. (SAPTA) to promote and sustain mutual trade and the economic cooperation among the contracting states through exchanging concessions.

The Government of the Peoples Republic of Bangladesh, the Kingdom of Bhutan, the Republic of India, Republic of Maldives, The Kingdom of Nepal, The Islamic Republic of Pakistan and Democratic Socialist Republic of Sri Lanka, are the contracting states to issue these certificate of origin.

The above states had committed this Agreement (SAPTA) to promote regional cooperation for the benefit of their people, expansion of trade, to accelerate the rate of economic growth to expand investment and production thus providing the greater opportunities of employment.

To liberalize the trade member states are convinced of the need to establish and promote regional preferential trading arrangements for strengthening infra regional economic cooperation.

SAPTA will be governed by the provisions of this agreements and also by the rules and regulations decisions, understandings and protocols to be agreed upon within its frame work by the contracting states.

The tariff concessions categorized:

Tariff (Customs duties mentioned in National tariff schedule).

Para tariff (border charges and fee, other than tariff on foreign trade transaction).

Non tariff (any measures, regulations or practice other than tariff and para tariff to restrict import negotiated and changed amongst contracting states incorporated in the National Schedules of concessions.

A list of more than three hundred products on which preferential tariff is granted is available in Export Promotion Bureau (Hqrs) and exporters are therefore advised in their own interest to avail this facility and to get SAARC Preferential Trading Arrangements (SAPTA) issued from EPB.

CONSOLIDATED NATIONAL SCHEDULE OF CONCESSIONS

Sr. No.	**HS Code**	**Description of Product**	**Tariff (%) as per Finance Act 1997-98**	**Extent of Tariff Concession under SAPTA (as a percentage of Tariff)**		**Any special NTBS with particular reference to Qrs**	**Concession to SAARC countries visa-vis such NTBs/Qrs**	**REMARKS**
				Far all member countries	for LDCs			
51	2007.10	Homogenized preparations (Jams, fruit, jellies, marmalades etc.)	45	-	15	- do -	-	-
52	2007.91	Citrus fruit (jams jellies)	45	-	15	- do -	-	-
53	2007.99	Other jams, jellies	45	-	15	- do -	-	-
54	2008.11	Ground-nuts	45	-	15	- do -	-	-
55	2008.19	Other nuts including mixtures	45	-	15	- do -	-	-
56	2008.20	Pineapples canned	45	-	15	- do -	-	-
57	2008.30	Citrus fruit	45	-	15	- do -	-	-

58	2008.40	Pears	45	-	15	- do -	-	-
59	2008.50	Apricots canned	45	-	15	- do -	-	-
60	2008.60	Cherries	45	-	15	- do -	-	-
61	2008.70	Peaches	45	-	15	- do -	-	-
62	2008.80	Strawberries	45	-	15	- do -	-	-
63	2008.91	Palm hearts	45	-	15	- do -	-	-
64	2008.92	Mixtures	45	-	15	- do -	-	-
65	2008.99	Other Fruit Pulp	45	-	15	- do -	-	-
66	2009.11	Frozen orange juice	45	-	15	- do -	-	-
67	2009.19	Other orange juice	45	-	15	- do -	-	-
68	2009.20	Grape fuit uice	45	-	15	- do -	-	-
69	2009.30	Juice of any other single citrus fruit	45	-	15	- do -	-	-
70	2009.40	Pineapple juice	45	-	15	- do -	-	-
71	2009.50	Tomato juice	45	-	15	- do -	-	-
72	2009.60	Grape juice (including grape must)	45	-	15	- do -	-	-
73	2009.70	Apple juice	45	-	15	- do -	-	-
74	2009.80	Juice of any other single fruit or vegetable	45	-	15	- do -	-	-
75	2009.90	Mixtures of juices	45	-	15	- do -	-	-
76	2101.12	Instant Coffee	45	10	-	-	-	-
77	2304.00	Meal of soyabean slvnt extrcts	10	10	-	-	-	-
78	2305.00	Oil cakes	25	10	15	-	-	-
79	2306.90	Oil cakes and oil cake meal of other oil seeds	25	10	-	-	-	-
80	2504.90	Natural Graphite - Others	15	10	-	-	-	-
81	2515.11	Marbles, (travertine/crude	45	-	15	-	-	-

		or roughly trimmed cut into blocks or slabs)						
82	2516.90	Other monumental stone	45	-	15	-	-	-
83	2517.10	Pebbles, gravel stone	45	-	15	-	-	-
84	2520.10	Gypsum any hdride	45	10	-	-	-	-
85	2525.10	Crude Mica and mica rified into sheet or splittings	35	10	-	-	-	-
86	2525.20	Mica powder	35	10	-	-	-	-
87	2525.30	Mica waste	35	10	-	-	-	-
88	2601.11	Iron ore fines or lumps	10	10	-	-	-	-
89	2614.00	Titanium ores and concentrates	10	10	-	-	-	-
90	2811.11	Hydrogen fluoride (hydroflouric acid)	15	10	-	-	-	-
91	2811.21	Carbon dioxide	15	10	-	-	-	-
92	2811.23	Sulphur dioxides	15	10	-	-	-	-
93	2816.10	Hydroxide and peroxide of magnesium	15	10	-	-	-	-
94	2816.30	Oxide, hydroxide and peroxide of barium	15	10	-	-	-	-
95	2818.10	Artificial corundum of aluminum oxide	10	10	-	-	-	-
96	2819.10	Ghromium trioxide	10	10	-	-	-	-
97	2820.10	Flectrolytic Maganese dioxide	10	10	-	-	-	-
98	2821.00	Hydroxide	10	10	-	-	-	-

99	2822.00	Cobalt oxides and hydroxides commercial cobalt oxides	10	10	-	-	-	-
100	2823.00	Titanium oxides	10	10	-	-	-	-

Sr. No.	HS Code	Description of Product	Tariff (%) as per Finance Act 1997-98	Extent of Tariff Concession under SAPTA (as a percentage of Tariff)		Any special NTBS with particular reference to Qrs	Concession to SAARC countries visa-vis such NTBs/Qrs	REMARKS
				Far all member countries	for LDCs			
151	2909.60	Alcohol peroxides, ketone peroxides and their derivatives	15	10	-	-	-	-
152	2910.10	Oxirane	10	10	-	-	-	-
153	2910.30	1-chloro-2.3-epoxypropane	15	10	-	-	-	-
154	2911.00	Acctals and hemiacetals and their derivatives	15	10	-	-	-	-
155	2916.11	Acrylic acid and its salts	15	10	-	-	-	-
156	2916.12	Esters of acrylic acid	15	10	-	-	-	-
157	2916.13	Methacrylic acid and its salts	15	10	-	-	-	-
158	2916.14	Esters of methacrylic acid	15	10	-	-	-	-
159	2916.15	Oleic, linoleic or linoenic acid, their salts and esters	15	10	-	-	-	-
160	2916.20	Cyclanic cyclenic and their derivatives	15	10	-	-	-	-
161	2917.12	Adipic acid its dalts and esters	15	10	-	-	-	-
162	2917.13	Azelaic acid, sebacic acid, their	15	10	-	-	-	-

		salts and esters						
163	2917.20	Cyclanic, cyclenic and their derivatives	15	10	-	-	-	-
164	2917.39	Other Dimethyl phthalate	15	10	-	-	-	-
165	2918.11	Lactic acid	15	10	-	-	-	-
166	2918.16	Gluconic acid	15	10	-	-	-	-
167	2918.17	Phenylglycolic acid (mandelic acid) its salts and esters	15	10	-	-	-	-
168	2918.21	Salicylie acid	15	10	-	-	-	-
169	2918.22	Accetyle salicylic acid	15-45	10	-	-	-	-
170	2918.23	Others esters of salicyclic acid	15	10	-	-	-	-
171	2923.10	Choline and its salts	15	10	-	-	-	-
172	2923.20	Lecithins and other phosphoaminolipids	15	10	-	-	-	-
173	2929.10	Lsocyanates	15	10	-	-	-	-
174	2930.10	Dithiocarbonates (xanthates)	15	10	-	-	-	-
175	2930.20	Thiocarbamates and dithiocarbamates	15	10	-	-	-	-
176	2930.40	Methionine	15	10	-	-	-	-
177	2937.10	Oxytocin Pituitary (anterior) similar harmones and other derivatives	15	10	-	-	-	-
178	2938.10	Rutoside (rutin) and its derivatives	15	10	-	-	-	-
179	3003.10	Medicaments containing penicillins	10	-	15	-	-	-
180	3003.20	Medicaments Other anliboitics	10	-	15	-	-	-
181	3003.31	Medicaments Insulin	10	-	15	-	-	-

182	3003.39	Meidcaments Others	10	-	15	-	-	-
183	3003.40	Medicaments Alkalocoids	10	-	15	-	-	-
184	3003.90	Ayurvedic Products	10	-	15	-	-	-
185	3004.10	Medicaments containing Penicillins in measured doses	10	-	15	-	-	-
186	3004.20	Medicaments containing other antiboitics	10	-	15	-	-	-
187	3004.31	Medicaments containing insulin	10	-	15	-	-	-
188	3004.32	Medicaments containing adrenal cortical hormones	10	-	15	-	-	-
189	3003.39	Other medicaments	10	-	15	-	-	-
190	3004.40	Medicaments containing alkaloids or derivatives thereof	10	-	15	-	-	-
191	3004.50	Cod liver oil-other medicaments	10-45	-	15	-	-	-
192	3004.90	Ayurvedic Products	10	-	15	-	-	-
193	3102.10	Urea	0	10	-	-	-	-
194	3103.10	Super Phosphates	0	10	-	-	-	-
195	3201.10	Qucbracho extract	25	10	-	-	-	-
196	3201.20	Waltie extract	25	10	-	-	-	-
197	3201.90	Other tanning extracts	25	10	-	-	-	-
198	3202.10	Synthetic organic tanning substances	25	10	-	-	-	-
199	3203.00	Other colouring materials	45	10	-	-	-	-
200	3204.11	Disperse dyes & preparations	25	10	-	Importable subject to the	-	-

						condition that the consignment shall not be released unless a certificate from the suppliers to the effect that the dyes sought to be imported are neither based on Benzidrine not contain any contents thereof is produced		

Sr. No.	HS Code	Description of Product	Tariff (%) as per Finance Act 1997-98	Extent of Tariff Concession under SAPTA (as a percentage of Tariff)		Any special NTBS with particular reference to Qrs	Concession to SAARC countries visa-vis such NTBs/Qrs	REMARKS
				Far all member countries	for LDCs			
251	4104.21	Bovine leather	15	-	15	-	-	-
252	4104.29	Other wet blue leather	10-15	-	15	-	-	-
253	4104.31	Bovine leather prepared after tanning	15	-	15	-	-	-
254	4105.11	Sheep or lambshin leather tanned	15	-	15	-	-	-
255	4105.19	Other wet blue leather	10-15	-	15	-	-	-
256	4105.20	Parchinent-dressed or prepared after tanning	15	-	15	-	-	-
257	4106.11	Goat or kid skin leather	15	-	15	-	-	-

		tanned or retanned						
258	4106.19	Other wet blue leather	10-15	-	15	-	-	-
259	4106.20	Parchment-dressed or prepared after tanning	15	-	15	-	-	-
260	4107.21	Leather of reptiles	15	-	15	-	-	-
261	4107.29	Other leather of reptiles	15	-	15	-	-	-
262	4107.90	Other animals leather	15	-	15	-	-	-
263	4204.00	Articles of leather or of composition leather, of a kind used in machinery	35	-	15	-	-	-
264	4206.10	Catgut	35	10		-	-	-
265	4206.10	Catgut	35	-	15	-	-	-
266	4206.90	Other aticles of gut, goldbeater's skin, of bladdrs or of tendons	35-45	-	15	-	-	-
267	4404.20	Other teak wood of non-coniferous	45	10	-	-	-	-
268	4405.00	Wood wool/flour	45	10	-	-	-	-
269	4406.00	Wooden sleepers for Railways	35	10	-	-	-	-
270	4410.19	Particle board of wood	45	-	15	-	-	-
271	4410.90	Other particle board of wood	45	-	15	-	-	-
272	4418.20	Doors and their frames and thresholds	35	10	-	-	-	-

273	4418.30	Wooden parquet panels	35	-	15	-	-	-
274	4420.00	Wood carving	45	-	15	-	-	-
275	4504.10	Cork Agglomerated in blocks, plates, sheets	45	10	-	-	-	-
276	4602.10	Bamboo goods of vegetable materials	45	-	15	-	-	-
277	4801.00	Newsprint paper	10	10	-	-	-	-
278	4802.10	Hand-made paper and paper board	25	10	-	-	-	-
279	4802.10	Hand-made papers	25	-	15	-	-	-
280	4806.10	Vegetable parchment	15	10	-	-	-	-
281	4806.20	Greaseproof papers	35	10	-	-	-	-
282	4806.30	Tracing papers	35	10	-	-	-	-
283	4813.00	Cigarettee paper	45	10	-	-	-	-
284	4901.91	Dictionaries and encyclopedias and serial installments thereof	0	-	15	-	-	-
285	4901.99	Other printed books brochures, leaflets and similar printed matters	0	-	15	-	-	-
286	4904.00	Music printed or in manuscript, whether or not bound and illustrated	45	10	15	-	-	-

287	4904.00	Music, printed or in manuscript, whether or not bound or illustrated	45	-	15	-	-	-	
288	5062.00	Raw silk (not thrown)	25	-	15	-	-	-	
289	5003.10	Silk-waste: Not carded or combed	45	-	15	-	-	-	
290	5003.90	Other Silk-waste	45	-	15	-	-	-	
291	5112.11	Combed fine animal hairs	45	-	15	-	-	-	
292	5308.10	Coin yearn baled and non baled	45	10	-	-	-	-	
293	6802.21	Marble blocks/tiles, polished	45	10	-	-	-	-	
294	6802.23	Granite blocks/tiles, polished	45	-	-	-	-	-	
295	6804.10	Millstones and grindstones for milling grinding or pulping	35	10	-	-	-	-	
296	6805.20	Natural or artificial abrasive powder or grain. On base of woven textile fabrics only	45	10	-	-	-	-	
297	6805.20	Natural or artificial abrasive powder or grain. On base of paper or paper board only	45	10	-	-	-	-	
298	6814.10	Plates, sheets and strips of	45	10	-	-	-	-	

		agglomerated or reconstituted mica						
299	6815.10	Non-electrical item of graphite or other carbon	15	10	-	-	-	-
300	6815.99	Alumina Balls	25	10	-	-	-	-

TOP 300 COMPANIES IN PAKISTAN BY ALPHABETICAL ORDER

Company Name	Rs. in Million Net Worth	Rs. in Million Net Income	Rs. in Million Net Profit
A.A. Textiles Ltd.	223.2	822.3	53.9
Abbott Laboratories Pakistan Ltd.	999.3	2542.5	179.5
Adamjee Insurance Company Ltd.	1255.4	3042.5	155.9
Agriauto Industries Limited	134.1	342.9	24
Ahmad Hassan Textile Mills Ltd.	209.8	659.4	101.8
Al-Abbas Sugar Mills Ltd.	377.9	819.7	46.7
Al-Abid Silk Mills Ltd.	352.3	2033.1	80.8
Al-Ghazi Tractoers Ltd.	1208.2	2188.4	289.7
Al-Hamad Textile Mills	96.3	380.2	28.2
Allawasaya Textile 7 Finishing Mills Ltd.	77.6	589.4	28.9
Allied Bank Limited	3012.5	3854.5	10.5
Al-Meezan Investment Investment Bank Ltd.	988.5	288	126.4
Al-Noor Sugar Mills Ltd.	349.6	1360.3	19.8
Al-Zamin Leasing Modaraba	155.5	59.3	2.4
American Life Insurance Comapny Ltd.	436.3	149.5	49
Apollo Textile Mills Ltd.	213.3	968.8	18.8
Arif Habib Securities Ltd.	494.7	180.1	132.6
Artistic Denim Mills Ltd.	231.2	917.2	55.4
Asian Leasing Corporation Ltd.	92.5	17.3	16.7
Askari General Insurance company Ltd.	84	111.9	13.1

Askari Leasing Ltd.	638.9	911	91.5
Atlas Batteries Ltd.	99.6	480.8	14.1
Atlas Investment Bank Ltd.	476.6	244.2	21.3
Atlas Lease Ltd.	316.9	244.2	21.3
Attock Refinery Ltd.	512.8	365.4	29.2
Aventis Pharma Pakistan Ltd.	345.6	1800.6	57.8
Ayesha Textile Mills Ltd.	152.8	1211.6	118.2
B.R.R International Modaraba	690.1	585.8	76.9
Baluchistan wheels Ltd.	237	336.9	50
Bank Al Habib Ltd.	1322.2	1090	246
Bank of Punjab	2179	1121.2	157.4
Bata Pakistan Ltd.	325.2	2188	46.5
Bengal Fibre Industries Ltd.	91.8	389.5	19.3
Bhanero Textile Mills Ltd.	325	1308.3	165.2
Blessed Textile Ltd.	215.8	693	116.4
BOC Pakistan Ltd.	1039.7	1143.2	262.4
Bolan Bank Ltd.	592	472.1	1.6
Bolan Castings Ltd.	114	457.3	52.8
Burewala Textile Mills Ltd.	337.9	431.1	60.5
Capital Asset Leasing Corporation Ltd.	98.9	29.6	2.5
Central Insurance Company Ltd.	367.5	9	43.3
Century Insurance Comapny Ltd.	94.7	44.1	20.6
Century Paper & Board Mills Ltd.	781.3	2143.5	144.5
Chakwal Cement Company Ltd	5839.4		
Chanab Fiber Ltd.	108.6	478.6	47.8
Cherat Cement Co. Ltd.	907	1341.5	75.3
Cherat Electrict Ltd.	140.8	200.2	1.2
Cherat Papersack Ltd.	227.8	534.4	16.1
Clariant Pakistan Ltd.	349.8	2968.1	112.5
Colgate Palmolive Pakistan Ltd.	282.2	1519.7	58.5
Colony Textile Mills Ltd	96.4	683.3	147.7
Commercial Union Life Assuances Ltd	302	219.1	70.1

Crescent Investment Bank Ltd	1407	1874	510
Crescent Leasing Corporation Ltd	338.4	173.9	30
Crescent Steel & Allied Products Ltd	693.1	121.2	90
Crescent Steel & Allied Products Ltd	278.5	1318.6	80.2
Crescent Sugar Mills & Distillery Ltd	1425.9	4632.5	246
Dadex Eternit Ltd	422.6	599	21.9
Dares Salaam Textile Mills Ltd	92.3	452.1	82.5
Dawood Cotton Mills Ltd	407.1	84.4	49.5
Dawood Hercules Chemical Ltd	3420	2886	764
Dawood Leasing Company Ltd	306.7	214.4	31.1
Dawood Farooq Motors Ltd	766.4	3389.4	31.2
Dewan Khalid Textile Mills Ltd	254.7	560.6	31.9
Dewan Mushtaq Textile Mills Ltd	124.8	761.7	38.5
Dewan Salman Fibre Ltd	458.4	6723.7	514.2
Dewan Sugar Mills Ltd	458.4	1782	37.3
Dewan Textile Mills Ltd	685.4	2282	121.6
D.G. Khan Cement Company Ltd.	3165.5	1094.4	444
Dilon Ltd	100.7	186.6	18.5
Dream World Ltd	323.8	88.3	9.1
Dynea Pakistan Ltd	190.2	485.8	31
East West Insurance Company Ltd	150	159	6.8
FFU General Insurance Ltd	269.1	1131	69
English Leasing Ltd	136.7	49.3	16.2
Engro Chemical Ltd	5218.6	8393.9	1126.3
Escorts Investment Bank Ltd	212.7	94.6	8.1
Essa Cement Industries Ltd	575	573.5	6.1
Exide Pakistan Ltd	241.9	857.2	16.2
Faisal Spinning Mills Ltd	387.9	714.3	127.9
Faran Sugar Mills Ltd	162.4	1417.1	41.1
Fateh Sports Wear Ltd	74	291.6	1.5
Fateh Textile Mills Limited	585.2	3636.2	21.9
Fauji Cement Company Ltd	799.1	2574.5	283

Faujio Fertilizer Company Ltd	8869.0	10201.3	2643.9
Faysal Bank Ltd	25241.1	1125.7	275.7
Fazal Cloth Mills Ltd	257.5	1553	107.2
Fecto Cement Ltd	565.7	1173.7	79.9
FFC Jordan Fertilizer Company Ltd	135.3	6068.8	3434.2
First Allied Bank Modaraba	422.5	73	5.1
First Al-Noor Modaraba	239	64	22.9
First Capital Securities Ltd	390.1	65	26.9
First Crescent Modaraba	306.2	482.2	18.5
First Equity Modarba	330.4	72.3	49.9
First Grindlays Modaraba	647.3	871.9	135.3
First Habib Bank Modaraba	495.8	273.2	104.4
First Habib Modaraba	357	366	68
First Ibrahim Modaraba	145.6	25.6	35.7
First International Investment Bank Ltd	361.3	382.7	45.9
First Islamaic Modaraba	105.9	20.1	5.7
First Leasing Corporation Ltd	297.4	190.2	27.1
First Professional Modaraba	89.9	41.1	5.9
First Punjab Modaraba	401.2	102.8	3.8
First Tri-Star Modaraba	163.7	1.6	0.6
Frontier Sugar Mills Ltd	168.5	160	18.5
Gadoon Textile Mills Ltd	1332.5	3438.6	485.4
Gatron Industries Ltd	1709.6	4924.9	349.9
General Tyres & Rubber Company Ltd	667.3	1967	189.2
Genertech Pakistan Ltd	481.2	561.9	11
Ghandara Leasing Company Ltd	91.8	36.8	17.6
Ghani Glass Ltd	345.6	487.1	214
Gillette Pakistan Ltd	214.7	538.3	71.8
Glaxo Wellcome Pakistan Ltd	2233.6	3221.8	501.9
Grays Leasing Ltd	134.9	58	24.8
Grays of Cambridge Pakistan Ltd	176.1	100.3	77.3
Gul Ahmed Textile Mills Ltd	1322	4516	558

Gulistan Spinning Mills Ltd	214.5	592.8	76.8
Gulistan Textile Mills Ltd	875.8	2323.6	120.2
Gulistan Spinning Mills Ltd	512.2	4373.4	99.8
Habib Arkady Ltd	294.4	521.2	83.8
Habib Bank Ltd	12534	14613	493
Habib Insurance Company Ltd	145.9	105.4	26.1
Habib Sugar Mills Ltd	588.1	1035.1	72.6
Haseeb Waqas Sugar Mill Ltd	799.7	1229.8	36.3
High Noon Laboratories Ltd	134.9	633	20
Honda Atlas Cars Ltd	1260.3	4485.4	204.5
Hub Power Company Ltd	27685.4	29086.3	10858.7
Huffaz Seamless Pipe Industries Ltd	88.3	230.8	11.9
Husein Sugar Mills Ltd	217	645	12
Hussein Industries Ltd	276.1	1188.6	35.7
Ibrahim Fires Ltd	5138.1	6944.2	474.8
Ibrahim Leasing Ltd	141.9	45.8	15.2
Ibrahim Textile Mills Ltd	239.9	1161.6	52.8
ICC Textiles Ltd	147	629	31.8
ICI Pakistan Ltd	2355.5	12815.4	566.6
Ideal Energy Ltd	231	264	42
Ideal Spinning Mills Ltd	137.2	536.5	22.8
Indus Dyeing & Manufacturing Co Ltd	281.2	2184.7	134.6
Indus Motors Company Ltd	1635.9	9054.7	203.4
Inter Asia Leasing Company Ltd	81.7	33.4	12.3
International General Insurance (Pak) Ltd	355.8	104	2.8
International Industries Ltd	381.2	2791.6	163
International Multi Leasing Corporation	86	23.9	4.5
Ishaq Textile Mills Ltd	218.7	742.8	10.8
Ismail Industries Ltd	76.8	527.6	11
Jahangir Siddiqui & Co Ltd	702.8	316	168.1
Jahangir Siddiqui Investment Bank Ltd	258.9	102.4	20

Japan Power Generation Ltd	1264.4	374.5	67.6
Javed Omer Vohra Ltd	147.3	3.8	27.6
Karam Ceramics Ltd	131.4	445.5	16.2
Khadim Ali Shah Bukhari & Co. Ltd	433.7	238	87.3
Khalid Siraj Textile Mills Ltd	144.6	367.4	46.5
Knoll Pharmaceuticals Ltd	454.9	810.4	116.8
Kohat Cement Company	475.0	1022	151
Kohat Textile Mills Ltd	96.2	532.3	27.7
Kohinoor Energy Ltd	2514.7	1693.3	393.6
Kohinoor Power Company Ltd	384.9	210.6	29.3
Kohinoor Raiwind Mills Ltd	525.4	1372.9	132
Kohinoor Sugar Mills Ltd	174.5	776.1	19.1
Kohinoor Textile Mills Ltd	502.8	2251.8	97.7
Kohinoor Weaving Mills Ltd	741.8	2140	308.7
KSB Pumps Company Ltd	236.4	531.8	0.2
Lakson Tobacco Company Ltd	1101.8	15466.2	394.7
Landmark Spinning Industries Ltd	121.2		
Lawrencepur Textile Mills Ltd	245.6	298.7	29.8
Lease Pak Ltd	101	58.8	4.9
Leather Up Ltd	75.6	232.3	4.7
Lever Brothers Pakistan Ltd	1258.6	20508	1339
Liberty Mills Ltd	193.3	1455.7	35.1
Lucky Cement Ltd	3648.4	2203.2	256.2
Mahmood Textile Mills Ltd	816.1	2936	421.3
Maple Leafg Cement Factory Ltd	2902.7	2351.3	284.4
Maple Leaf Electric Company Ltd	894.1	554.8	149.2
Maqbool Textile Mills Ltd	146.7	640.7	34
Mari Gas Company Ltd	1128.7	931.5	191.6
Mehran Sugar Mills Ltd	248.3	663.1	15.5
Metropolitan Bank Ltd	1452.7	923.5	225.7
Main Textile Industries Ltd	114.3	807.6	51.4
Millat Tractors Ltd	803.5	5679.2	262.4

Mirpurkhas Sugar Mills Ltd	156.5	558.1	9.1
Mitchells Fruit Farms Ltd	163	636.8	43
Muslim Commercial Bank Ltd	4483.7	9649	734.7
N.P. Spinning Mills Ltd	155.8	922.3	61
Nadeem Textile Mills Ltd	188.5	406.7	54.4
Nafees Cotton Mills Ltd	197.3	992.1	51.2
Nakshbandi Industries	262.6	1067.2	27.6
National Asset Leasing Corporation	74.4	36.5	27.4
National Bank of Pakistan	12242.2	29677.9	461.2
National Development Leasing Corporation	1250	643	47
National Refinery Ltd	2829.3	36124.2	775.7
Nayab Spinning & Weaving Mills Ltd	251.6	413.5	12.3
Nestle Milkpak Ltd	840.7	6575.2	272.4
Network Leasing Corporation Ltd	113.3	68.6	7.7
Nimir Industrial Chemical Ltd	904.6	44.8	105
Nina Industries Ltd	352.3	892.4	16.3
Nishat Chunian	595.5	2367	357.5
Nishat Mills Ltd	4569.6	10134	700.9
Noon sugar Mills Ltd	343.7	862.5	69.8
Oil & Gas Development Company Ltd	41499.4	25137.3	10555.9
Orix Leasing Pakistan Ltd	1030.2	1346.5	154.2
Otsuka Pakistan Ltd	132.8	320.5	30.6
Pacific Leasing Company Ltd	148	59.7	14.6
Packages Ltd	2285.6	2236	193
Pak Arab Refinery Ltd	13041.3	4404.7	2161.9
Pak Datacom Ltd	188.2	137.2	17
Pak Suzuki Motors Ltd	1807.8	7976.1	87
Pak Apex Leasing Company Ltd	120.2	39.6	44.6
Pak Gul Leasing Company Ltd	107.6	24.3	11.6
Pakistan Cables Ltd	120.4	721.3	6.7
Pakistan Hotel Developers Ltd	218.7	138.8	7.3

Pakistan Industrial & Commercial Leasing Ltd	229.9	167.5	15.6
Pakistan Industrial Credit and Investment Company Ltd	1011.8	1481.8	381.6
Pakistan Industrial Leasing Corporation Ltd	581.2	592.3	21.5
Pakistan Oil Fields Ltd	3560.4	4175.7	1097.8
Pakistan Paper Sack Ltd	310.9	731.8	20
Pakistan Petroleum Ltd	6536	4100	459
Pakistan Refinery Ltd	266.6	25323.5	75.6
Pakistan Services Ltd	678.2	1562	40.5
Pakistan State Oil Ltd	9808.2	169726.4	2251.4
Pakistan Synthetics Ltd	995.9	1624.2	97.2
Pakistan Telecommunication Corporation Ltd	68896.8	62040.7	18154.6
Pakistan Tobacco Company Ltd	2217.9	15907	18154.6
Paramount Leasing Ltd	294.9	15907	25.2
Paramount Spinning Mills Ltd	286.6	830.7	3
Parke Davis & Company Ltd	623.7	1006.4	65.1
PICIC Commercial Bank Ltd	804	316.2	111.6
Plastobag Ltd	78.3	126.8	0.5
Platinum Commercial Bank Ltd	774.4	700.2	55.6
Premier Insurance Company Ltd	205.7	143.4	37
Premier Sugar Mills & Distellery Co Ltd	777.7	630	175.9
Prime Commercial Bank Ltd	1127.9	1060.9	96.1
Prosperity Weaving Mills Ltd	244	1141.1	78.5
Quetta Textile Mills Ltd	245.9	1792.9	110.4
Rafhan Best Food Ltd	568.2	1484.6	140
Rafhan Maiz Products Ltd	1200.7	3126.4	347.4
Reckitt Benckiser Pakistan Ltd	514.7	2081	12.2
Reliance Cotton Spinning Mills Ltd	236.1	701.3	40.3
Reliance Insurance Company Ltd	106.2	77.6	8.5
Reliance Weaving Mills Ltd	313.4	1306.9	143.1

Rupali Polyster Limited	1374.1	2175.2	140.4
S.G. Fibre Ltd	417	808	66
S.G. Power Ltd	295.9	126.6	18.3
Saadi Cement Co Ltd	1850		
Saif Textile Mills Ltd	506.1	1066	28
Samin Textile Mills Ltd	256.5	1012.9	32.1
Sanghar Sugar Mills Ltd	171.5	523.1	11.2
Sapphire Energy Ltd	173.2	184.1	55.7
Sapphire Fibres Ltd	1305.7	2499.6	500.9
Sapphire Textile Mills Ltd	1108.3	4128.1	650.2
Saudi Pak Leasing Company Ltd	353	407.4	36.3
Searle Pakistan Ltd	336.9	1139.7	35.2
Security Leasing Corporation Ltd	121.5	97.9	12.6
Security Papers Ltd	684.5	519.4	293.5
Service Industries Ltd	451.3	2008.6	31.1
Shabbir Tiles & Ceramics Ltd	294.9	527.8	4935
Shadman Cotton Mills Ltd	296.6	1706.7	58.5
Shahmurad Sugar Mills Ltd	292.9	1216.7	20.4
Shahpur Textile Mills Ltd	161.2	416.6	24.6
Shahtaj Sugar Mills Ltd	246.1	1072.1	38.4
Shahtaj Textile Mills Ltd	146.8	474	39.6
Shakarganj Mills Ltd	456.3	1180.7	4.3
Shehzan International Ltd	159.6	695.2	31.4
Shell Gas LPG Pakistan Ltd	118.6	220.8	15.6
Shell Pakistan Ltd	5389.6	65725	1056
Siemens Pakistan Engineering Company Ltd	1469.9	4460.5	253.9
Sindh Abadgar Sugar Mills Ltd	147.8	662.9	4.1
Singer Pakistan Ltd	181.3	582.8	6.8
Sitara Chemical Industries Ltd	491.8	2611.8	246
Sitara Energy Ltd	831.1	1002.5	174.1
Soneri Bank Ltd	1272.6	1815.7	16.4

Southern Electric Power Company Ltd	1509.1	1687.5	295.9
Spencer & Co. (Pakistan) Ltd	240.9	0.9	29.1
Sui Northern Gas Pipelines Ltd	6264.4	26569.7	0.5
Sui Southern Gas Company Ltd	8425	22931.1	792.5
Sunrays Textiles Mills Ltd	91.9	861.6	87
Suraj Cotton Mills	418.4	1566.3	138.2
Suzuki Motorcycle Pakistan Ltd	135	407	20
Tandlianwala Sugar Mills Ltd	337.2	919	23.1
Tariq Glass Industries Ltd	114.5	568.6	62.4
Tata Textile Mills Ltd	223.5	793.3	120.7
Telecard Ltd	292.7	715.8	99.2
Thal Industries Corporal Ltd	133.3	481.5	17.4
Thal Jute Mills Ltd	331.2	1406.4	68.8
Toweller Ltd	384.2	1766.4	43.3
Treet Corporation Ltd	190.8	634.8	29.6
Tri Star Power Ltd	218.1	16.5	0
Tri Pack Films Ltd	464.3	420.4	74.3
Trust Leasing Corporation Ltd	367.5	95.7	4.1
Trust Modaraba	408	106.5	22.9
Umer Fabrics Ltd	539	1604	238
Union Bank Ltd	1077.6	175101	1.3
Union Leasing Ltd	288.3	59.9	13.2
United Bank Ltd	6726.6	7172.6	667.1
United Distributors Pakistan Ltd	104	59.6	11
Wah Nobel Chemicals Ltd	103.8	161.7	27.6
Worldcall Payphones Ltd	611.7	301.9	102.6
Yousaf Weaving Mills Ltd	225.9	1271.9	47.9
Yusuf Textiles Mills Ltd	122	603	89.1
Zainab Textiles Mills Ltd	261.1	991.5	61.1
Zaman Textile Mills Ltd	89.4	407.2	21.6

THE TOP 300 COMAPNIES (BY INCOME)

S #	Company Name	Income	Net Profit (in Millions)	Net Worth
1	Pakistan State Oil Ltd.	169726.4	2251.4	9808.2
2	Shell Pakistan Ltd	65725.0	1056.0	5389.6
3	Pakistan Telecommunication Corporation Ltd	62040.7	18154.6	68896.8
4	National Refinery Ltd	36124.2	775.7	2829.3
5	National Bank of Pakistan	29677.9	461.2	12242.2
6	Hub Power Company Ltd	29086.3	10858.7	27685.4
7	Sui Northern Gas Pipelines Ltd	26569.7	0.5	6264.4
8	Pakistan Refinery Ltd	25323.5	75.6	266.6
9	Oil & Gas Development Company Ltd	25137.3	10555.9	41499.4
10	Sui Southern Gas Company Ltd	22931.1	792.5	8425.0
11	Attock Refinery Ltd	22841.3	29.2	512.8
12	Lever Brothers Pakistan Ltd	20508.0	1339.0	1258.6
13	Pakistan Tobacco Company Ltd	15907.0	884.5	2217.9
14	Lakson Tobacco Company Ltd	15466.2	394.7	1101.8
15	Habib Bank Ltd	14613.0	493.0	12534.0
16	ICI Pakistan Ltd	12815.4	566.6	2355.5
17	Fauji Fertilizer Company Ltd	10201.3	2643.9	8869.0
18	Nishat Mills Ltd	10134.0	700.9	4569.6
19	Muslim Commercial Bank Ltd	9649.0	734.7	4483.7
20	Indus Motors Company Ltd	9054.7	203.4	1635.9
21	Engro Chemical Ltd	8393.9	1126.3	5218.6
22	Pak Suzuki Motors Ltd	7976.1	87.0	1807.8
23	United Bank Ltd	7172.6	667.1	6726.6
24	Ibrahim Fibres Ltd	6944.2	474.8	5138.1
25	Dewan Salman Fibres Ltd	6723.7	514.2	3779.6
26	Nestle Milk Pak Ltd	6575.2	272.4	840.7
27	FFC Jordan Fertilizer Company Ltd	6068.8	3434.2	135.3
28	Millat Tractors Ltd	5679.2	262.4	803.5
29	Gatron Industries Ltd	4924.9	349.9	1709.6
30	Crescent Textile Mills Ltd	4632.5	246.0	1425.9
31	Gul Ahmed Textile Mills Ltd	4516.0	5558.0	1322.0
32	Honda Atlas Cars Ltd	4485.4	204.5	1260.3
33	Siemens Pakistan Engineering Company Ltd	4460.5	253.9	1469.9
34	Pak Arab Refinery Ltd	4404.7	2161.9	13041.3
35	Pakistan Oil Fields Ltd	4175.7	1097.8	3560.4
36	Sapphire Textile Mills Ltd	4128.1	650.2	1108.3
37	Pakistan Petroleum Ltd	4100.0	459.0	6536.0
38	Allied Bank Limited	3854.5	10.5	3012.5
39	Fateh Textile Mills Limited	3636.2	21.9	585.2
40	Gadoon Textile Mills Ltd	3438.6	485.4	1332.5
41	Dewan Farooq Motors Ltd	3389.4	31.2	766.4
42	Glaxo Wellcome Pakistan Ltd	3221.8	501.9	2233.6

43	Rafhan Maize Products Ltd	3126.4	347.4	1200.7
44	Adamjee Insurnace Company	3042.5	155.9	1255.4
45	Clariant Pakistan Ltd	2968.1	112.5	349.8
46	Mahmood Textile Mills Ltd	2936.0	421.3	816.1
47	Dawood Hercules Chemical Ltd	2886.0	764.0	3420.0
48	International Industries Ltd	2791.6	163.0	381.2
49	Sitara Chemical Industries Ltd	2611.8	246.0	491.8
50	Fauji Cement Company Ltd	2574.5	283.0	799.1
51	Abbott Laboratories Pakistan Ltd	2542.5	179.5	999.3
52	Sapphire Fibres Ltd	2499.6	500.9	1305.7
53	Nishat Chunian Ltd	2367.0	357.5	595.5
54	Maple Leaf Cement Factory Ltd	2351.3	284.4	2902.7
55	Gulistan Textile Mills Ltd	2323.6	120.2	875.8
56	Dewan Textile Mills Ltd	2282.0	121.6	685.4
57	Kohinoor Textile Mills Ltd	2251.8	97.7	502.8
58	Packages Ltd	2236.0	193.0	2285.6
59	Lucky Cement Ltd	2203.2	256.2	3648.4
60	Al ghazi Tractors Ltd	2188.4	289.7	1208.2
61	Bata Pakistan Ltd	2188.0	46.5	325.2
62	Indus Dyeing & Manufacturing Co Ltd	2184.7	134.6	281.2
63	Rupali Polyster Limited	2175.2	140.4	1374.1
64	Century Paper & Board Mills Ltd	2143.5	144.5	781.3
65	Kohinoor Weaving Mills Ltd	2140.0	308.7	741.8
66	Reckitt Benckiser Pakistan Ltd	2081.0	12.2	514.7
67	Al Abid Silk Mills Ltd	2033.1	80.8	352.3
68	Service Industries Ltd	2008.6	31.1	451.3
69	General Tyres & Rubber Company Ltd	1967.0	189.2	667.3
70	Crescent Investment Bank Ltd	1874.0	510.0	1407.0
71	Soneri Bank Ltd	1815.7	164.4	1272.6
72	Aventis Pharma Pakistan Ltd	1800.6	57.8	345.6
73	Quetta Textile Mills Ltd	1792.9	110.4	245.9
74	Dewan Sugar Mills Ltd	1782.7	37.3	458.4
75	Toweller Ltd	1766.4	43.3	384.2
76	Union Bank Ltd	1751.1	1.3	1077.6
77	Shadman Cotton Mills Ltd	1706.7	58.5	296.6
78	Kohinoor Energy Ltd	1693.3	393.6	2514.7
79	Southern Electric Power Company Ltd	1687.5	295.9	1509.1
80	Pakistan Synthetics Ltd	1624.2	97.2	995.9
81	Umer Fabrics Ltd	1604.0	238.0	539.0
82	Suraj Cotton Mills Limited	1566.3	138.2	418.4
83	Pakistan Services Limited	1562.0	40.5	678.2
84	Fazal Cloth Mills Ltd	1553.0	107.2	257.5
85	Colgate Palmolive Pakistan Ltd	1519.7	58.5	282.2

86	Rafhan food Ltd	1484.6	140.0	568.2
87	Pakistan Industrial Credit and Investment Corp Ltd	1481.8	381.6	1011.8
88	Liberty Mills Ltd	1455.7	35.1	193.3
89	Faran Sugar Mills Ltd	1417.1	41.1	162.4
90	Thal Jute Mills Ltd	1406.4	68.8	331.2
91	Gulshan Spinning Mills Ltd	1373.4	99.8	512.2
92	Khinoor Raiwind Mills Ltd	1372.9	132.0	525.4
93	Al Noor Sugar Mills Ltd	1360.3	19.8	349.6
94	Orix Leasing Pakistan Ltd	1346.5	154.2	1030.2
95	Cherat Cement Co. Ltd	1341.5	75.3	907.0
96	Crescent Sugar Mills & Distillery Ltd	1318.6	80.2	278.5
97	Bhanero Textile Mills Ltd	1308.3	165.2	325.0
98	Reliance Weaving Mills Ltd	1306.9	143.1	313.4
99	Yousaf Weaving Mills Ltd	1271.9	47.9	225.9
100	Haseeb Waqas Sugar Mills Ltd	1229.8	36.3	799.7
101	Shahmurad Sugar Mills Ltd	1216.7	20.4	292.9
102	Ayesha Textile Mills Ltd	1211.8	118.2	152.8
103	Hussein Industries Ltd	1188.6	35.7	276.1
104	Shakarganj Mills Ltd	1180.7	4.3	456.3
105	Fecto Cement Ltd	1173.7	79.9	565.7
106	Ibrahim Textile Mills Ltd	1161.6	52.8	239.9
107	BOC Pakistan Ltd	1143.2	262.4	1039.7
108	Prosperity Weaving Mills Ltd	1141.1	78.5	244.0
109	Searle Pakistan Ltd	1139.7	35.2	336.9
110	EFU General Insurance Ltd	1131.0	69.0	269.1
111	Faysal Bank Ltd	1125.7	275.7	2524.1
112	Bank of Punjab	1121.2	157.4	2179.6
113	D.G. Khan Cement Company Ltd	1094.4	444.0	3165.5
114	Bank al Habib Ltd	1090.0	246.0	1322.2
115	Shahtaj Sugar Mills Ltd	1072.1	38.4	246.1
116	Nakshbandi Industries Ltd	1067.2	27.6	2626.6
117	Saif Textile Mills Ltd	1066.0	28.0	506.1
118	Prime Commercial Bank Ltd	1060.9	96.1	1127.9
119	Habib Sugar Mills Ltd	1035.1	72.6	588.1
120	Kohat Cement Company Ltd	1022.0	151.0	474.0
121	Samin Textile Mills Ltd	1012.9	32.1	256.5
122	Park Davis & Company Ltd	1006.4	65.1	623.7
123	Sitara Energy Ltd	1102.5	174.1	831.1
124	Nafees Cotton Mills Ltd	992.1	51.2	197.3
125	Zainab Textile Mills Ltd	991.5	61.1	261.1
126	Apollo Textile Mills Ltd	968.8	18.8	213.3
127	Mari Gas Company Ltd	931.5	191.6	1128.7
128	Metropolitan Bank Ltd	923.5	225.7	1452.7

129	N.P. Spinning Mills Ltd	922.3	61.0	155.8
130	Tandlianwala Sugar Mills Ltd	919.0	23.1	337.2
131	Artistic Enim Mills Ltd	917.2	55.4	321.2
132	Askari Leasing Ltd	911.0	91.5	638.9
133	Nina Industries Ltd	892.4	16.3	352.3
134	First Grindlays Modaraba	871.9	135.3	647.3
135	Noon Sugar Mills Ltd	862.5	69.8	343.7
136	Sunrays Textile Mills Ltd	861.6	87.0	91.9
137	Exide Pakistan Ltd	857.2	16.2	241.9
138	Paramount Spinning Mills Ltd	830.7	3.0	286.6
139	A.A. Textiles Ltd	822.3	53.9	223.2
140	Al Abbas Sugar Mills Ltd	819.7	46.7	377.9
141	Knoll Pharmaceuticals Ltd	810.4	116.8	454.9
142	S.G. Fibre Ltd	808.0	66.0	417.0
143	Main Textile Industries Ltd	807.6	51.4	114.3
144	Tata Textile Mills Ltd	793.3	120.7	223.3
145	Kohinoor Sugar Mills Ltd	776.1	19.1	174.5
146	Dewan Mushtaq Textile Mills Ltd	761.5	38.5	124.8
147	Ishaq Textile Mills Ltd	742.8	10.8	218.7
148	Pakistan Paper Sack Ltd	731.8	20.0	310.9
149	Pakistan Paper Sack Ltd	721.3	6.7	120.4
150	Telecard Ltd	715.8	99.2	292.7
151	Faisal Spinning Mills Ltd	714.3	127.9	387.9
152	Reliance Cotton Spinning Mills Ltd	701.3	40.3	236.1
153	Platinum Commercial Bank Ltd	700.2	55.6	774.4
154	Shehzan International Ltd	695.2	31.4	159.6
155	Blessed Textile Ltd	693.0	116.4	215.8
156	Colony Textile Mills Ltd	683.3	147.7	96.4
157	Mehran Sugar Mills Ltd	663.1	15.5	248.3
158	Sindh Abadgar Sugar Mills Ltd	662.9	4.1	147.8
159	Ahmad Hassan Textile Mills Ltd	659.4	101.8	209.8
160	Husein Sugar Mills Ltd	645.0	12.0	217.0
161	National Development Leasing Corporation	643.0	47.0	1250.0
162	Maqbool Textile Mills Ltd	640.7	34.0	146.7
163	Mitchelss Fruit Farms Ltd	636.8	43.0	163.0
164	Treet Corporation Ltd	634.8	29.6	190.8
165	High Noon Laboratories Ltd	663.0	20.0	134.9
166	Premier Sugar Mills & Distellery Co Ltd	630.0	175.9	777.7
167	ICC Textiles Ltd	629.0	31.8	147.0
168	Yusuf Textile Mills Ltd	603.0	89.1	122.0
169	Dadex Enternit Ltd	599.0	21.9	422.6
170	Gulistan Spinning Mills Ltd	592.8	76.8	214.5
171	Pakistan Industrial Leasing Corporation Ltd	592.3	21.5	581.2

172	Allawasaya Textile & Finishing Mills Ltd	589.4	28.9	77.6
173	B.R.R. International Modaraba	585.8	76.9	690.1
174	Singer Pakistan Ltd	582.8	6.8	181.3
175	Essa Cement Industries Ltd	573.5	6.1	575.0
176	Tariq Glass Industries Ltd	568.6	62.4	114.5
177	Genertech Pakistan Ltd	561.9	11.0	4581.2
178	Dewan Khalid Textile Mills Ltd	560.6	31.9	254.7
179	Mirpurkhas Sugar Mills Ltd	5558.1	9.1	156.5
180	Maple Leaf Electric Company Ltd	554.8	149.2	894.1
181	Gillette Pakistan Ltd	538.3	71.8	214.7
182	Ideal Spinning Mills Ltd	536.5	22.8	137.2
183	Gherat Papersack Lrtd	534.4	16.1	227.8
184	Kohat Textile Mills Ltd	532.3	27.7	96.2
185	KSB Pumps Company Ltd	531.8	0.2	236.4
186	Shabbir Tiles & Ceramics Ltd	527.8	49.5	294.9
187	Ismail Industries Ltd	527.6	11.0	76.8
188	Sanghar Sugar Mills Ltd	523.1	11.2	171.5
189	Habib Arkady Ltd	521.2	83.8	294.4
190	Security Papers Ltd	519.4	293.5	684.5
191	Ghani Glass Ltd	487.1	214.0	354.6
192	Dynea Pakistan Ltd	485.8	31.0	190.2
193	First Crescent Modaraba	482.2	18.5	306.2
194	Thal Industries Corporation	481.5	17.4	133.3
195	Atlas Batteries Ltd	480.8	14.1	99.6
196	Chenab Fibres Ltd	478.6	47.8	108.6
197	Shahtaj Textile Ltd	474.0	39.6	146.8
198	Bolan Bank Ltd	472.1	1.6	592.0
199	Bolan Castings Ltd	457.3	52.8	114.0
200	Dares Salaam Textile Mills Ltd	452.1	82.5	92.3
201	Karam Ceramics Ltd	445.5	16.2	131.5
202	Burewala Textile Mills Ltd	431.1	60.5	337.9
203	Tri Pack Films Ltd	420.4	74.3	464.3
204	Shahpur Textile Mills Ltd	416.6	24.6	161.2
205	Nayab Spinning & Weaving Mills Ltd	413.5	12.3	251.6
206	Saudi Pak Leasing Company Ltd	407.4	36.3	353.0
207	Zaman Textile Mills Ltd	407.2	21.6	89.4
208	Suzuki Motorcycle Pakistan Ltd	407.0	20.0	135.0
209	Nadeem Textile Mills Ltd	406.7	54.4	188.5
210	Bengal Fibre Industries Ltd	389.5	19.3	91.8
211	First International Investment Bank Ltd	382.7	45.9	361.3
212	Al Hamd Textile Mills Ltd	380.2	28.2	96.3
213	Japan Power Generation Ltd	374.5	67.6	1264.4
214	Khalid Siraj Textile Mills Ltd	367.4	46.5	144.6

215	First Habib Modaraba	366.0	68.0	357.0
216	Atlas Lease Ltd	365.4	21.3	316.9
217	Agiauto Industries Limited	342.9	24.0	134.1
218	Baluchistan wheels Ltd	336.9	50.0	237.0
219	Otsuka Pakistan Ltd	320.5	30.6	132.8
220	PCICI Commercial Bank Ltd	316.2	111.6	804.0
221	Jahangir Siddiqui & Co Ltd	316.0	168.1	702.8
222	Worldcall Payphones Ltd	301.9	102.6	611.7
223	Lawrencepur Textile Mills Ltd	298.7	29.8	245.6
224	Fateh Sports Wear Ltd	291.6	1.5	74.0
225	Al Meezan Investment Bank Ltd	288.0	126.4	877.5
226	First Habib Bank Modaraba	273.2	104.4	495.8
227	Ideal Energy Ltd	264.0	42.0	231.0
228	Atlas Investment Bank Ltd	244.2	21.3	176.6
229	Khadim Ali Shah Bukhari & Co. Ltd	238.0	87.3	433.7
230	Leather Up Ltd	232.3	4.7	75.6
231	Huffaz Seamless Pipe Industries Ltd	230.8	11.9	88.3
232	Shell Gas LPG Pakistan Ltd	220.8	15.6	118.6
233	Gommercial Union Life Assuances Ltd	219.1	70.1	302.0
234	Dawood Leasing Company Ltd	214.4	31.1	306.7
235	Kohinoor Power Company Ltd	210.6	29.3	384.9
236	Cherat Electric Ltd	200.2	1.2	140.8
237	First Leasing Corporation Ltd	190.2	27.1	297.5
238	Dilon Ltd	186.6	18.5	100.7
239	Sapphire Energy Ltd	184.1	55.7	173.2
240	Arif Habib Securities Ltd	180.1	132.6	494.7
241	Crescent Leasing Corporation Ltd	173.9	30.7	338.4
242	Pakistan Industrial & Commercial Leasing Ltd	167.5	15.6	229.9
243	Wah Nobel Chemicals Ltd	161.7	27.6	103.8
244	Frontier Sugar Mills Ltd	160.0	18.5	168.5
245	East West Insurance Company Ltd	159.0	6.8	150.0
246	Paramount Leasing Ltd	149.6	25.2	294.9
247	American Life Insurnace Company Ltd	149.5	49.0	436.3
248	Premier Insurance Company Ltd	143.4	37.0	205.7
249	Pakistan Hotel Developers Ltd	138.8	7.3	218.7
250	Pak Datacom Ltd	137.2	17.0	188.2
251	Plastobag Ltd	126.8	0.5	78.3
252	S.G. Power Ltd	126.6	18.3	295.9
253	Crescent Steel & Allied Products Ltd	121.2	90.0	693.1
254	Askari General Insurance Company Ltd	111.9	13.1	84.0
255	Trust Modaraba	106.5	22.9	408.0
256	Habib Isurance Company Ltd	105.4	226.1	145.9
257	International General Insurance (Pak) Ltd	104.0	2.8	355.8

258	First Punjab Modaraba	102.8	3.8	401.2
259	Jahngir Siddiqui Investment Bank Ltd	102.4	20.0	258.9
260	Grays of Cambridge Pakistan Ltd	100.3	77.3	176.1
261	Security Leasing Corporation Ltd	97.9	12.6	121.5
262	Trust Leasing Corporation Ltd	95.7	4.1	367.5
263	Escorts Investment Bank Ltd	94.6	8.1	212.7
264	Dream World Ltd	88.3	9.1	323.8
265	Dawood Cotton Mills Ltd	884.8	49.5	407.1
266	Reliance Insurance Company Ltd	77.6	8.5	106.2
267	First Allied Bank Modaraba	73.0	5.1	422.5
268	First Equity Modarba	72.3	49.9	330.4
269	Network Leasing Corporation Ltd	68.6	7.7	113.3
270	First Capital Securities Ltd	65.0	26.9	390.1
271	First Al Noor Modaraba	64.0	22.9	239.0
272	Union Leasing Ltd	59.9	13.2	288.3
273	Pacific Leasing Company Ltd	59.7	14.6	148.0
274	United Distributors Pakistan Ltd	59.6	11.0	104.0
275	Al Zamin Leasing Modaraba	59.3	2.4	155.5
276	Lease Pak Ltd	58.8	4.9	101.0
277	Grays Leasing Ltd	58.0	24.8	134.9
278	English Leasing Ltd	49.3	16.2	136.7
279	Ibrahim Leasing Ltd	45.8	15.2	141.9
280	Nimir Industrial Chemical Ltd	44.8	105.0	904.6
281	Century Insurance Company Ltd	44.1	20.6	94.7
282	First Professional Modaraba	41.1	5.9	89.9
283	Pak Apex Leasing Company Ltd	39.6	44.6	120.2
284	Ghandara Leasing Company Ltd	36.8	17.6	91.8
285	National Asset Leasing Corporation Ltd	36.5	27.4	74.4
286	Inter Asia Leasing Company Ltd	33.4	12.3	81.7
287	Capital Asset Leasing Corporation Ltd	29.6	2.5	98.6
288	First Ibrahim Modaraba	25.6	35.7	145.6
289	Pak Gulf Leasing Company Ltd	24.3	11.6	107.6
290	International Multi Leasing Corporation	23.9	4.5	86.0
291	First Islamic Modaraba	20.1	5.7	105.9
292	Asian Leasing Corporation Ltd	17.3	16.7	92.5
293	Tri Star Power Ltd	16.5	0.0	218.1
294	Central Insurance Company Ltd	9.0	43.3	367.5
295	First Tri Star Modaraba	1.6	0.6	163.7
296	Spencer & Co. (Pakistan) Ltd	-0.9	29.1	240.9
297	Javed Omer Vohra Ltd	-3.8	27.6	147.3
298	Chakwal Cement Company Limited	-	-	5839.4
299	Landmark Spinning Industries Ltd	-	-	121.2
300	Saadi Cement Co. Limited	-	-	1850.0

BASIC TITLE ON PAKISTAN

IMPORTANT!
All publications are updated annually!
Please contact IBP, Inc. at ibpusa3@gmail.com for the latest ISBNs and additional information

TITLE
Pakistan Air Force Handbook
Pakistan Air Force Handbook
Pakistan Army Weapon Systems Handbook
Pakistan Army, National Security and Defense Policy Handbook
Pakistan Army, National Security and Defense Policy Handbook
Pakistan Banking & Financial Market Handbook
Pakistan Banking & Financial Market Handbook
Pakistan Business and Investment Opportunities Yearbook
Pakistan Business and Investment Opportunities Yearbook
Pakistan Business and Investment Opportunities Yearbook Volume 1 Strategic Information and Opportunities
Pakistan Business and Investment Opportunities Yearbook Volume 2 Leading Export-Import, Business, Investment Opportunities and Projects
Pakistan Business Intelligence Report - Practical Information, Opportunities, Contacts
Pakistan Business Intelligence Report - Practical Information, Opportunities, Contacts
Pakistan Business Law Handbook - Strategic Information and Basic Laws
Pakistan Business Law Handbook - Strategic Information and Basic Laws
Pakistan Business Law Handbook - Strategic Information and Basic Laws
Pakistan Business Law Handbook - Strategic Information and Basic Laws
Pakistan Business Law Handbook Volume 1 Strategic Information and Basic Laws
Pakistan Business Success Guide - Basic Practical Information and Contacts
Pakistan Clothing & Textile Industry Handbook
Pakistan Clothing & Textile Industry Handbook
Pakistan Company Laws and Regulations Handbook
Pakistan Company Laws and Regulations Handbook - Strategic Information and Basic Laws
Pakistan Constitution and Citizenship Laws Handbook - Strategic Information and Basic Laws
Pakistan Country Study Guide - Strategic Information and Developments
Pakistan Country Study Guide - Strategic Information and Developments Volume 1 Strategic Information and Developments
Pakistan Country Study Guide Volume 1 Strategic Information and Developments
Pakistan Criminal Laws, Regulations and Procedures Handbook - Strategic Information, Regulations, Procedures
Pakistan Customs, Trade Regulations and Procedures Handbook
Pakistan Customs, Trade Regulations and Procedures Handbook
Pakistan Diplomatic Handbook - Strategic Information and Developments
Pakistan Diplomatic Handbook - Strategic Information and Developments
Pakistan Ecology & Nature Protection Handbook
Pakistan Ecology & Nature Protection Handbook
Pakistan Ecology & Nature Protection Laws and Regulation Handbook

TITLE
Pakistan Economic & Development Strategy Handbook
Pakistan Economic & Development Strategy Handbook
Pakistan Education System and Policy Handbook
Pakistan Electoral, Political Parties Laws and Regulations Handbook - Strategic Information, Regulations, Procedures
Pakistan Energy Policy, Laws and Regulation Handbook
Pakistan Energy Policy, Laws and Regulations Handbook
Pakistan Energy Policy, Laws and Regulations Handbook
Pakistan Export-Import and Business Directory
Pakistan Export-Import and Business Directory
Pakistan Export-Import Trade and Business Directory
Pakistan Export-Import Trade and Business Directory
Pakistan Fishing and Aquaculture Industry Handbook - Strategic Information, Regulations, Opportunities
Pakistan Foreign Policy and Government Guide
Pakistan Foreign Policy and Government Guide
Pakistan Free Economic Zones Handbook
Pakistan Free Economic Zones Handbook
Pakistan Government and Business Contacts Handbook
Pakistan Government and Business Contacts Handbook
Pakistan Healthcare Sector Organization, Management and Payment Systems Handbook - Strategic Information, Programs and Regulations
Pakistan Immigration Laws and Regulations Handbook - Strategic Information and Basic Laws
Pakistan Industrial and Business Directory
Pakistan Industrial and Business Directory
Pakistan Industrial Sectors Profiles Report
Pakistan Industrial Sectors Profiles Report
Pakistan Insolvency (Bankruptcy) Laws and Regulations Handbook - Strategic Information and Basic Laws
Pakistan Intelligence & Security Activities & Operations Handbook
Pakistan Intelligence & Security Activities & Operations Handbook
Pakistan Intelligence, Security Activities & Operations Handbook
Pakistan Intelligence, Security Activities & Operations Handbook
Pakistan Internet and E-Commerce Investment and Business Guide - Strategic and Practical Information: Regulations and Opportunities
Pakistan Internet and E-Commerce Investment and Business Guide - Strategic and Practical Information: Regulations and Opportunities
Pakistan Investment and Business Guide - Strategic and Practical Information
Pakistan Investment and Business Guide - Strategic and Practical Information
Pakistan Investment and Business Guide - Strategic and Practical Information
Pakistan Investment and Business Guide - Strategic and Practical Information
Pakistan Investment and Business Guide Volume 1 Strategic and Practical Information
Pakistan Investment and Business Guide Volume 2 Business, Investment Opportunities and Incentives
Pakistan Investment and Business Profile - Basic Information and Contacts for Succesful

TITLE
investment and Business Activity
Pakistan Investment and Trade Laws and Regulations Handbook
Pakistan Investment, Trade Strategy and Agreements Handbook - Strategic Information and Basic Agreements
Pakistan Justice System and National Police Handbook
Pakistan Justice System and National Police Handbook
Pakistan Labor Laws and Regulations Handbook - Strategic Information and Basic Laws
Pakistan Land Ownership and Agriculture Laws Handbook
Pakistan Medical & Pharmaceutical Industry Handbook
Pakistan Medical & Pharmaceutical Industry Handbook
Pakistan Mineral & Mining Sector Investment and Business Guide - Strategic and Practical Information
Pakistan Mineral & Mining Sector Investment and Business Guide - Strategic and Practical Information
Pakistan Mining Laws and Regulations Handbook
Pakistan National Development Strategy Handbook: Important Programs and Developments
Pakistan Nuclear Industry Laws and Regulations Handbook
Pakistan Nuclear Programs and Projects Handbook
Pakistan Nuclear Programs and Projects Handbook
Pakistan Oil & Gas Sector Business & Investment Opportunities Yearbook
Pakistan Oil & Gas Sector Business & Investment Opportunities Yearbook
Pakistan Oil and Gas Exploration Laws and Regulation Handbook
Pakistan President, Political System and Reforms Handbook
Pakistan Privatization Programs and Regulations Handbook
Pakistan Privatization Programs and Regulations Handbook
Pakistan Recent Economic and Political Developments Yearbook
Pakistan Research & Development Policy Handbook
Pakistan Research & Development Policy Handbook
Pakistan Research & Development Policy Handbook
Pakistan Scientific and Analytical Equipment Producers Directory
Pakistan Scientific and Analytical Equipment Producers Directory
Pakistan Starting Business (Incorporating) in Pakistan Guide
Pakistan Starting Business (Incorporating) in....Guide
Pakistan Tax Guide Volume 1 Strategic Information and Basic Regulations
Pakistan Taxation Laws and Regulations Handbook
Pakistan Telecom Laws and Regulations Handbook
Pakistan Telecommunication Industry Business Opportunities Handbook
Pakistan Telecommunication Industry Business Opportunities Handbook
Pakistan Transportation Policy and Regulations Handbook
Pakistan: Business in Pakistan for Everyone: Practical Information and Contacts for Success
Pakistan: Doing Business and Investing in Pakistan Guide
Pakistan: How to Invest, Start and Run Profitable Business in Pakistan Guide - Practical Information, Opportunities, Contacts

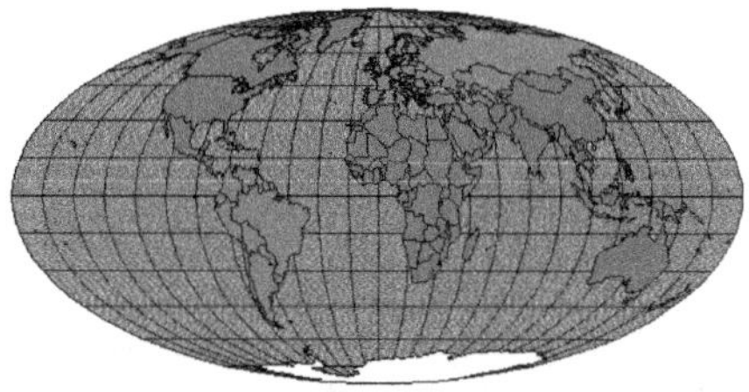

GLOBAL STARTING BUSINESS (INCORPORATING) IN LIBRARY

PRICE: $149.95 EACH

1. Albania Starting Business (Incorporating) in....Guide
2. Algeria Starting Business (Incorporating) in....Guide
3. Andorra Starting Business (Incorporating) in....Guide
4. Angola Starting Business (Incorporating) in....Guide
5. Antigua & Barbuda Starting Business (Incorporating) in....Guide
6. Antilles (Netherlands) Starting Business (Incorporating) in....Guide
7. Argentina Starting Business (Incorporating) in....Guide
8. Armenia Starting Business (Incorporating) in....Guide
9. Australia Starting Business (Incorporating) in....Guide
10. Austria Starting Business (Incorporating) in....Guide
11. Azerbaijan Starting Business (Incorporating) in....Guide
12. Bahamas Starting Business (Incorporating) in....Guide
13. Bangladesh Starting Business (Incorporating) in....Guide
14. Barbados Starting Business (Incorporating) in....Guide
15. Belarus Starting Business (Incorporating) in....Guide
16. Belgium Starting Business (Incorporating) in....Guide
17. Belize Starting Business (Incorporating) in....Guide
18. Bermuda Starting Business (Incorporating) in....Guide
19. Bolivia Starting Business (Incorporating) in....Guide
20. Bosnia and Herzegovina Starting Business (Incorporating) in....Guide
21. Botswana Starting Business (Incorporating) in....Guide
22. Brazil Starting Business (Incorporating) in....Guide
23. Brunei Starting Business (Incorporating) in....Guide
24. Bulgaria Starting Business (Incorporating) in....Guide
25. Cambodia Starting Business (Incorporating) in....Guide
26. Cameroon Starting Business (Incorporating) in....Guide
27. Canada Starting Business (Incorporating) in....Guide
28. Cayman Islands Starting Business (Incorporating) in....Guide
29. Chile Starting Business (Incorporating) in....Guide
30. China Starting Business (Incorporating) in....Guide
31. Colombia Starting Business (Incorporating) in....Guide
32. Comoros Starting Business (Incorporating) in....Guide
33. Cook Islands Starting Business (Incorporating) in....Guide

34.	Costa Rica Starting Business (Incorporating) in....Guide
35.	Croatia Starting Business (Incorporating) in....Guide
36.	Cuba Starting Business (Incorporating) in....Guide
37.	Cyprus Starting Business (Incorporating) in....Guide
38.	Czech Republic Starting Business (Incorporating) in....Guide
39.	Denmark Starting Business (Incorporating) in....Guide
40.	Dominica Starting Business (Incorporating) in....Guide
41.	Dominican Republic Starting Business (Incorporating) in....Guide
42.	Dubai Starting Business (Incorporating) in....Guide
43.	Ecuador Starting Business (Incorporating) in....Guide
44.	Egypt Starting Business (Incorporating) in....Guide
45.	El Salvador Starting Business (Incorporating) in....Guide
46.	Equatorial Guinea Starting Business (Incorporating) in....Guide
47.	Estonia Starting Business (Incorporating) in....Guide
48.	Falkland Islands Starting Business (Incorporating) in....Guide
49.	Fiji Starting Business (Incorporating) in....Guide
50.	Finland Starting Business (Incorporating) in....Guide
51.	France Starting Business (Incorporating) in....Guide
52.	Georgia Starting Business (Incorporating) in....Guide
53.	Germany Starting Business (Incorporating) in....Guide
54.	Gibraltar Starting Business (Incorporating) in....Guide
55.	Greece Starting Business (Incorporating) in....Guide
56.	Grenada Starting Business (Incorporating) in....Guide
57.	Guam Investment & Business Guide
58.	Guatemala Starting Business (Incorporating) in....Guide
59.	Guernsey Starting Business (Incorporating) in....Guide
60.	Guyana Starting Business (Incorporating) in....Guide
61.	Haiti Starting Business (Incorporating) in....Guide
62.	Honduras Starting Business (Incorporating) in....Guide
63.	Hungary Starting Business (Incorporating) in....Guide
64.	Iceland Starting Business (Incorporating) in....Guide
65.	India Starting Business (Incorporating) in....Guide
66.	Indonesia Starting Business (Incorporating) in....Guide
67.	Iran Starting Business (Incorporating) in....Guide
68.	Iraq Starting Business (Incorporating) in....Guide
69.	Ireland Starting Business (Incorporating) in....Guide
70.	Israel Starting Business (Incorporating) in....Guide
71.	Italy Starting Business (Incorporating) in....Guide
72.	Jamaica Starting Business (Incorporating) in....Guide
73.	Japan Starting Business (Incorporating) in....Guide
74.	Jersey Starting Business (Incorporating) in....Guide
75.	Jordan Starting Business (Incorporating) in....Guide
76.	Kazakhstan Starting Business (Incorporating) in....Guide

77. Kenya Starting Business (Incorporating) in....Guide
78. Kiribati Starting Business (Incorporating) in....Guide
79. Korea, North Starting Business (Incorporating) in....Guide
80. Korea, South Starting Business (Incorporating) in....Guide
81. Kuwait Starting Business (Incorporating) in....Guide
82. Kyrgyzstan Starting Business (Incorporating) in....Guide
83. Laos Starting Business (Incorporating) in....Guide
84. Latvia Starting Business (Incorporating) in....Guide
85. Lebanon Starting Business (Incorporating) in....Guide
86. Libya Starting Business (Incorporating) in....Guide
87. Liechtenstein Starting Business (Incorporating) in....Guide
88. Lithuania Starting Business (Incorporating) in....Guide
89. Luxemburg Starting Business (Incorporating) in....Guide
90. Macao Starting Business (Incorporating) in....Guide
91. Macedonia, Republic Starting Business (Incorporating) in....Guide
92. Madagascar Starting Business (Incorporating) in....Guide
93. Malaysia Starting Business (Incorporating) in....Guide
94. Malta Starting Business (Incorporating) in....Guide
95. Man Starting Business (Incorporating) in....Guide
96. Mauritius Starting Business (Incorporating) in....Guide
97. Mauritius Starting Business (Incorporating) in....Guide
98. Mexico Starting Business (Incorporating) in....Guide
99. Micronesia Starting Business (Incorporating) in....Guide
100. Moldova Starting Business (Incorporating) in....Guide
101. Monaco Starting Business (Incorporating) in....Guide
102. Mongolia Starting Business (Incorporating) in....Guide
103. Morocco Starting Business (Incorporating) in....Guide
104. Myanmar Starting Business (Incorporating) in....Guide
105. Namibia Starting Business (Incorporating) in....Guide
106. Netherlands Starting Business (Incorporating) in....Guide
107. New Caledonia Starting Business (Incorporating) in....Guide
108. New Zealand Starting Business (Incorporating) in....Guide
109. Nicaragua Starting Business (Incorporating) in....Guide
110. Nigeria Starting Business (Incorporating) in....Guide
111. Northern Mariana Islands Starting Business (Incorporating) in....Guide
112. Norway Starting Business (Incorporating) in....Guide
113. Pakistan Starting Business (Incorporating) in....Guide
114. Panama Starting Business (Incorporating) in....Guide
115. Peru Starting Business (Incorporating) in....Guide
116. Philippines Starting Business (Incorporating) in....Guide
117. Poland Starting Business (Incorporating) in....Guide
118. Portugal Starting Business (Incorporating) in....Guide
119. Romania Starting Business (Incorporating) in....Guide

120. Russia Starting Business (Incorporating) in....Guide
121. Samoa (American) Investment & Business Guide
122. Samoa (Western) Starting Business (Incorporating) in....Guide
123. Saudi Arabia Starting Business (Incorporating) in....Guide
124. Scotland Starting Business (Incorporating) in....Guide
125. Singapore Starting Business (Incorporating) in....Guide
126. Slovakia Starting Business (Incorporating) in....Guide
127. Slovenia Starting Business (Incorporating) in....Guide
128. South Africa Starting Business (Incorporating) in....Guide
129. Spain Starting Business (Incorporating) in....Guide
130. Sri Lanka Starting Business (Incorporating) in....Guide
131. St. Helena Starting Business (Incorporating) in....Guide
132. Sudan Starting Business (Incorporating) in....Guide
133. Suriname Starting Business (Incorporating) in....Guide
134. Sweden Starting Business (Incorporating) in....Guide
135. Switzerland Starting Business (Incorporating) in....Guide
136. Syria Export Import & Business Directory
137. Taiwan Starting Business (Incorporating) in....Guide
138. Tajikistan Starting Business (Incorporating) in....Guide
139. Thailand Starting Business (Incorporating) in....Guide
140. Tunisia Starting Business (Incorporating) in....Guide
141. Turkey Starting Business (Incorporating) in....Guide
142. Turkmenistan Starting Business (Incorporating) in....Guide
143. Uganda Starting Business (Incorporating) in....Guide
144. Ukraine Starting Business (Incorporating) in....Guide
145. United Arab Emirates Starting Business (Incorporating) in....Guide
146. United Kingdom Starting Business (Incorporating) in....Guide
147. United States Starting Business (Incorporating) in....Guide
148. Uruguay Starting Business (Incorporating) in....Guide
149. US Starting Business (Incorporating) in....Guide
150. Uzbekistan Starting Business (Incorporating) in....Guide
151. Venezuela Starting Business (Incorporating) in....Guide
152. Vietnam Starting Business (Incorporating) in....Guide
153. Serbia Starting Business (Incorporating) in....Guide

www.ingramcontent.com/pod-product-compliance
Lightning Source LLC
LaVergne TN
LVHW080033210926
848481LV00011B/3179